Architecture
of Spain

Architecture of Spain

ALEJANDRO LAPUNZINA

Reference Guides to National Architecture

David A. Hanser, Series Adviser

Greenwood Press

Westport, Connecticut • London

Library of Congress Cataloging-in-Publication Data

Lapunzina, Alejandro, 1960–
    Architecture of Spain / Alejandro Lapunzina.
        p.   cm.—(Reference guides to national architecture, ISSN 1550–8315)
    Includes bibliographical references and index.
    ISBN 0–313–31963–4 (alk. paper)
    1. Architecture—Spain.   I. Title.   II. Series.
    NA1301.L35   2005
    720'.946—dc22   2005017406

British Library Cataloguing in Publication Data is available.

Library of Congress Catalog Card Number: 2005017406
ISBN: 0–313–31963–4
ISSN: 1550–8315

First published in 2005

Greenwood Press, 88 Post Road West, Westport, CT 06881
An imprint of Greenwood Publishing Group, Inc.
www.greenwood.com

Printed in the United States of America

The paper used in this book complies with the
Permanent Paper Standard issued by the National
Information Standards Organization (Z39.48–1984).

10 9 8 7 6 5 4 3 2 1

Contents

Entries by Location

Entries are listed below by region and then by city or town within each region.

ANDALUCÍA

Córdoba

The Great Mosque of Córdoba

Granada

Palace of Carlos V at La Alhambra
Palace of La Alhambra and Gardens
   of El Generalife

Jaén

Cathedral of Jaén

Sevilla

Navigation Pavilion at Expo '92
   Sevilla
Roman Amphitheater at Itálica
   (near Sevilla)

ARAGON

Loarre (near Huesca)

Loarre: Castle and Fortified Walls

Teruel

Cathedral of Teruel

Zaragoza

Palace of La Aljafería

ASTURIAS

Oviedo

Monte Naranco: Palace of Ramiro I
   and San Miguel de Lillo

Pola de Lena (near Oviedo)

Santa Cristina de Lena

BALEARIC ISLANDS

Palma de Majorca

Ronda Promenade and Bastions

Park Güell
Plaza dels Països Catalans
Santa María del Mar

Igualada
New Cemetery-Park of Igualada

Ripoll
Santa María de Ripoll

St. Just Desvern
Walden-7 Apartment Building

Tarragona
Church of the Sacred Heart, Vistabella (near Tarragona)
Civil Government Building

Tarrasa
San Miguel, San Pedro, and Santa María Tarrasa

EXTREMADURA

Mérida
Augusta Emérita: Provincial Roman Capital
National Museum of Roman Art

GALICIA

Santiago de Compostela (Galicia)
Cathedral of Santiago de Compostela

Galician Center of Contemporary Art

MADRID (COMUNIDAD AUTÓNOMA)

Madrid
La Zarzuela Racetrack Grandstand
Museo del Prado
Plaza Mayor of Madrid
Sports Complex and Track and Field Stadium of Madrid
Torres Blancas Apartment Building
Valdemingómez Recycling Center

NAVARRA

Murazábal
Santa María de Eunate

VALENCIA (COMUNIDAD VALENCIANA)

Valencia
City of Arts and Sciences

Entries by Architectural Style and Period

Entries are listed chronologically within styles and periods.

Prehistoric Architecture

Prehistoric Caves (Paleolithic)

Ancient Architecture (Greek and Roman) (Third Century B.C.E. to Second Century C.E.)

Empúries: Greek-Hellenic and Roman Settlement (215 B.C.E.–25 C.E.)

Augusta Emérita: Provincial Roman Capital (25 B.C.E.–200 C.E.)

Roman Amphitheater at Itálica (circa 100s C.E.)

Roman Aqueduct at Segovia (circa 100s C.E.)

Early Christian, Pre-Romanesque, and Mozarabic Architecture (Third to Eleventh Centuries)

San Miguel, San Pedro, and Santa María Tarrasa (453–1110s)

San Juan de Baños (circa 661)

San Pedro de la Nave (680–711)

Monte Naranco: Palace of Ramiro I and San Miguel de Lillo (circa 848)

Santa Cristina de Lena (848–905)

San Miguel de Escalada (913–914)

Islamic Architecture (Sixth to Fourteenth Centuries)

The Great Mosque of Córdoba (786–990)

Mosque of Bāb-al-Mardūm (999)

Palace of La Aljafería (1031–1100s)

Palace of La Alhambra and Gardens of Generalife (1309–1354)

Romanesque Architecture (Eleventh and Twelfth Century)

Santa María de Ripoll (1020–1032)

San Martín Fromista (1060–1070s)

Loarre: Castle and Fortified Walls (1070–1200s)

Ávila City Walls (1090–1100s)

Santa María de Eunate (circa 1170)

Cathedral of Santiago de Compostela (1070–1140)

Preface

Architecture of Spain is part of Greenwood's reference series devoted to national architectures. This volume was conceived and written for those interested in learning about the most important monuments in the history of Spanish architecture, and especially for the curious who are not well versed in the history of architecture in general and that of Spain in particular. This book is intended to be informative and didactic, but also to help increase the knowledge of the English-speaking general public regarding architecture and architectural history; an effort was made to introduce historical knowledge and critical commentary about each of the buildings and sites presented here. Those who are knowledgeable in the architecture of Spain will also find useful reference information and critical notes that may serve as the initial step for a more profound study of the monuments discussed.

The core of the book consists of sixty-eight alphabetically organized short essays dedicated to individual discussion of relevant sites in the history of Spain's architecture. These essays are generally focused on one single building; however, some include a discussion of more than one architectural work. The selection of a limited number of sites was the first challenge in developing this volume because, in a country with so rich an architectural and cultural history, such as Spain, far more architecturally relevant sites exist than could be covered in one book. A significant effort was made to include the whole geographical and temporal extension of the country while making sure that no single masterpiece was left without the consideration that it deserved. In spite of this effort, the author is aware that, geographically, some areas may appear to be overrepresented—for example, the city of Barcelona—while other areas are not represented at all, notably the architecturally rich city of Valladolid, or the southeast region (Alicante and Murcia) and the Canary Islands, to name only the most obvious omissions. This was not intentional but the result of a difficult selection process.

Temporally, the reader will quickly observe that not all periods are treated equally. In this regard, I have intentionally emphasized periods in which the architecture of Spain made a more significant or innovative contribution to the history of architecture as a whole. For example, the vibrant pre-Romanesque and Romanesque architectural periods are represented by a large number of remarkable buildings when compared with, for instance, the Gothic or Renaissance periods, in which many more and much larger buildings were built but which were neither as innovative nor as interesting from the point of view of the history of world architecture. The most obvious unbalance concerns contemporary architecture (since 1975), which is, by far, the period most represented by individual essays. This was quite intentional, an appropriate homage to the unmatched richness, variety, vitality, and quality of Spain's architecture in the last quarter of the twentieth century.

Each individual essay is unique in structure and content; however, a general thread will become apparent to the reader. Each entry tries to determine the historical or architectural relevance of the building or site, incorporating a brief description of the geographical and historical context in which it was produced, and the importance of the architect(s) who designed and built it. The discussion of the architecturally relevant site incorporates a description as thorough and detailed as is considered appropriate in each case and, when possible, also includes historical and critical commentary. The images illustrate an important aspect of the building or site as discussed in the text; the reader is invited to consult more specialized publications for a better understanding of the buildings' descriptions, particularly—but not limited to—drawings of floor plans, sections, and elevations. A considerable effort was made to cross-reference the building or site discussed with those presented in other individual essays in this volume; thus, buildings shown in **boldface type** in the text of an entry refer to other related buildings or sites included in the list of sixty-eight individual essays. Expectedly, each entry often uses technical vocabulary that maybe unknown to the reader; therefore, a simple Glossary is included at the end of the volume to define terms that may be unfamiliar to the nonspecialist reader. These terms are identified in the text in *italic* type. Foreign words are also italicized at their first mention. Because the Glossary is not exhaustive, the reader should also consult a standard dictionary to look up unknown words, concepts, and expressions. Each essay ends with a short list of bibliographic sources (often cited in the text), which provide further and more detailed information on the entry subject. When available, I have referred to the English version of a work; however, many fundamental books dedicated to the history of Spain's architecture or to a single building have not been translated and are thus included in their original language version. Besides a detailed subject index, the volume also includes a bibliography of useful general works and two quick reference lists that categorize entries by location and architectural styles and time periods.

The sixty-eight individual essays are preceded by the Introduction. This introductory essay presents a succinct historical overview of Spain's architecture that places each of the individually discussed architectural sites within the historical, cultural, and political context in which they were built. Organized as a chronological narration of the country's architectural history, the Introduction also mentions numerous important architects and remarkable buildings and sites as well as singular building typologies (e.g., the Alcazars and the fifteenth-century Hospitals) that are not included in the individual building entries, thus trying to palliate, even if minimally, their absence from the core of the book. Likewise, the photographs included in the Introduction are of buildings and sites not discussed individually.

The renowned late historian of Spain's architecture, Fernando Chueca Goitía, who died recently at age ninety-three, said that "to study the architecture of a country is to study the country, an epoch, a society, an economic and political situation." Accordingly, this book studies the buildings through an attempt to understand the main aspects of the country's complex history and its multicultural constitution. Modern Spain is the result of millenary human occupation of the geographical area known as the Iberian Peninsula, or simply Iberia, which also includes modern Portugal. Through the centuries, as different cultures and political powers occupied this rich, vast, and accidented territory, the Iberian Peninsula received various names, from *Hispania* in the Roman period, and *al-Andalus* under the seven-centuries-long Muslim occupation, to a collection of regional denominations in the politically fragmented medieval period (Castilla, León, Aragon, Navarra, etc.), and finally to the Kingdom of Spain, or simply Spain, since the Catholic kings succeeded in unifying the territory under one crown in the last years of the fifteenth century. Therefore, the reader should understand that "Iberia," "Iberian Peninsula," "Hispania," "al-Andalus," and "Spain" all refer, basically, to the same geographical extension and place and that the distinctive use of one denomination or another is strictly related to the historical context of reference.

The critical attention and volume of publications dedicated to Spain's architecture has experienced a veritable "boom" in the last twenty-five years; appropriate editorial attention correlates to the vital architectural activity of the country in the same period. However, for reasons that would be too complex to discern and too long to explain, the contributions of Spain's architecture were often neglected or limitedly and partially considered by many historians and critics who turned their attention to the architecture of countries that seemed to have had a more gravitational role in the history of Western architecture (e.g., Italy, France, Germany, and the United Kingdom). This focus resulted in a partial coverage and limited understanding of Spain's architecture in many historical periods. While far from attempting to overturn this imbalance, this book attempts to contribute to a more comprehensive and objective knowledge of the role of Spain's architects, patrons, and builders as active participants in the evolution and development of Western architecture.

Acknowledgments

A published book is always a small reflection of how much effort and how many people are really involved in making what apparently seems very simple—to write about a theme and send it to print. From the seed of the project to its materialization, writing a book involves a multitude of events, situations, and people without whom it could not have been completed. The following paragraphs intend to recognize the roles of many individuals and organizations that, in one way or another, contributed to the publication of this book.

First, I want to thank David Hanser, a dear colleague and friend, who invited me to develop the volume devoted to Spain in Greenwood's series on national architectures. Very special thanks go to all the people at Greenwood Press who worked on this project, from Debbie Adams who established the first contact, to John Wagner, the project manager of the project. I especially appreciate his patience and understanding with the long delays in finishing the manuscript as well as his useful feedback at critical points of the project. Thanks also to Shelley Yeager for her work in the final stages of this book.

A substantial amount of traveling through Spain was necessary in order to visit and document the buildings, sites, and cities presented in this book (in fact, in most cases it was revisiting and photographing in black-and-white). Whereas a good part was done with personal and family means, it would have been impossible to undertake the long traveling periods without institutional support; I am especially indebted to the Research Board of the University of Illinois at Urbana-Champaign for the two grants for field research that I received for bringing this project to completion. I am also grateful to the institution to which I belong—the School of Architecture of the University of Illinois at Urbana-Champaign—for providing all the institutional support and encouragement I needed for developing this project. The support of colleagues from the School and the University—especially

Michael Andrejasich, Botond Bognar, Jordana Mendelson, and Henry Plummer—was vital at some crucial points of the project. Special thanks to Ricker Library—the University's Art and Architecture Library—and all its staff for providing me with the appropriate assistance every time I requested it, as well as to the library and staff of the *Ecole d'Architecture de Versailles* (France), the institution where, in my role as Director of Illinois' Architecture Study Abroad Program in Versailles, I have physically worked since 2002.

I would not have been able to satisfactorily complete many parts of this book without the assistance and contribution of many individuals, professionals, and institutions. I am extremely grateful to many contemporary architects whose work is included in this book—Abalos and Herreros, Ricardo Boffil, Cruz and Ortiz, Mansilla and Tuñón, Martinez Lapeña and Torres, Rafael Moneo, Luis Peña Ganchegui, Benedetta Tagliabue (from EMBT Architects), Guillermo Vazquez Consuegra, Albert Viaplana, and Helio Piñón—and various members who work at their offices, who responded to my letters, e-mails, and telephone calls requesting information, graphic materials, and verification of the texts written about their work. Likewise, I thank the many institutions and agencies of Spain that provided valuable information and materials. Very special thanks go to the Museo de Altamira for providing images and permission to include them in two portions of the book, to Josune Diez Extezarreta of San Sebastián's Kursaal for allowing me to have a special visit to the building, to Agar Ledo of the CGAC (Galician Center for Contemporary Art) for similar reasons, and to Celalba Ribera of the Tourism Office of Santiago de Compostela, who literally opened the doors that allowed me to visit many important buildings in that fabulous and historically rich city. Also in Santiago de Compostela, Angel Currás Fernández gave me a wonderful opportunity to visit the complex for the city's *Ciudad de la Cultura*, which is currently under construction. Finally, I extend a note of recognition to the administration of the Hotel Park, which is not only one of the buildings presented in this book but which also became my headquarters during one of many visits to Barcelona.

A very special acknowledgment goes to my colleagues and students at the Study Abroad Program in Versailles for their support, understanding, and patience during long days in which my attention was exclusively dedicated to finishing this project; and likewise to all members of my family for their enormous help, support, encouragement, and patience. Finally, books are customarily dedicated to one or more people whom the author considers important or influential for the completion of the work. I grew up in a home in which medicine and not architecture was the most usual "professional" theme of conversation; yet, beyond that, I learned from my parents to work seriously and to love the profession and discipline that one embraces. I will be always indebted to them for that as well as for the extraordinary education I received at home, and beyond. I dedicate this book to my mother and to the memory of my father.

Introduction

The Iberian Peninsula was inhabited by hominids from remote times, likely as far back as one million years ago, as the relatively recent discoveries at the archaeological site of *Atapuerca*, in the province of Burgos, convincingly suggest. Hundreds of thousands of years later two hominid species, the *Neanderthal* and *Cro-Magnon*, cohabited in a vast extension of the earth that included the Iberian Peninsula. More adaptable and creative, the latter prevailed, but the former was extinguished from the surface of the earth. Nomads, these early humans gathered in small groups and developed primitive but effective forms of communication; with time, they developed a language, and rituals, myths, codes, and other forms of social organization. Poorly equipped to confront extreme climatic conditions and more powerful animals, they found refuge in caves. Eventually, groups of humans began to occupy these caves for longer periods of time, one of the first signs of the transition from nomadic to sedentary life. Large caves offered multiple possibilities of use; likely intuitively, but possibly as an act of pure reflection, humans began to assign differentiated uses—eating, sleeping, creating—to different portions of the cave thus transforming it into a place more suitable to their needs.

Whereas it is true and obvious that these caves were neither built nor created by humans, in intentionally appropriating and using the readily available space for specific activities men transformed the emptiness of the cave into habitat. This transformation and taking possession of space that took place during the *Paleolithic* period, more than 15,000 years ago, constituted the transcendental moment in which humankind produced the first architectural act. Spain has a remarkable wealth of caves that were occupied by humans in remote times, especially on the Cantabrian coast. These **prehistoric caves** house abundant vestiges of human occupation as well as marvelous artistic representations. Undoubtedly, the *Cave of Altamira* (near

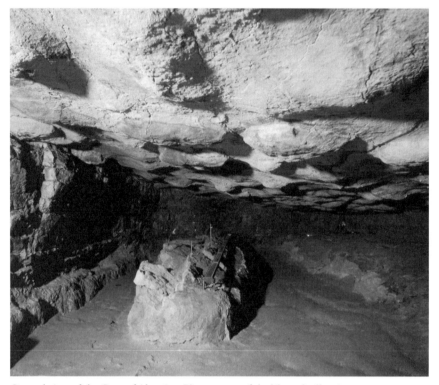

General view of the Cave of Altamira. *Photo courtesy of the Museo de Altamira.*

Santillana del Mar, Asturias) is, because of its splendid painted ceiling, the most famous and important known cave that was inhabited by prehistoric man worldwide.

The first constructions created and erected by men were surely related to their spiritual and ritualistic needs; they consisted of sacrificial altars and burial monuments such as dolmens and funerary chambers. The Mediterranean coast of Spain, the southern region of Andalucía, and the Balearic Islands house a large variety of burial sites, some of which are considered the most important of the respective period in the Western Hemisphere. Dolmens of various types exist in several parts of the Iberian Peninsula, while the caves of *Antequera, Viera, Menga,* and *del Romeral* in Málaga (Andalucía), and the *talayots* and *navetas* (funerary chambers made with stones) in the Balearic Islands are among the most sophisticated constructions made by our prehistoric ancestors.

Between the years 5000 and 3500 B.C.E., a major transformation took place: nomadic groups began to settle in some areas, developing agriculture, domesticating animals, and creating new and more advanced objects and utensils. This period coincided with the emergence of the first signs of urban

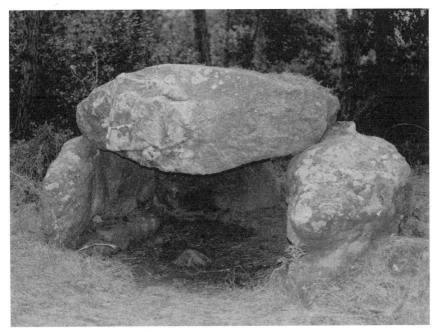

The Dolmen of Llafranc, Gerona, a prehistoric burial monument.

development, groups of small homes made with stones and adobe. It was the dawn of organized social and urban life; the settlements of *El Argar* (Almería), *Azaila* (Teruel), and the *Castro de Coaña* (Asturias) are among the oldest known indigenous settlements in the Iberian Peninsula.

By the year 2000 B.C.E., the coasts of Iberia were reached by the higher-developed cultures of the east and south of the Mediterranean basin. *Phoenicians* and later Greeks founded commercial trading posts and colonies along the peninsula's southern and eastern coasts, establishing the first contacts of the indigenous Iberian populations with the more advanced civilizations of the east. In the fifth or sixth century B.C.E., an expedition originated in the Greek-Hellenic colony of *Massilia* (modern Marseilles, France), landed in the northeastern corner of the peninsula, and founded *Emporion* at a short distance from a former *Phocean* village. Emporion was an independent commercial settlement built according to the principles of Greek-Hellenic urbanism; eventually, Emporion became an important trading post that controlled commerce in the northeastern region of the Mediterranean.

The Roman Period

The Romans arrived in the Iberian Peninsula as a result of their confrontation with Carthage for the control of the Mediterranean. After being defeated in the First Punic War, Carthage demonstrated expansionist ambitions in the Iberian Peninsula that led to the outbreak of the Second Punic War. The First Punic War had been for the control of Sicily, the second—largely fought in Iberia—determined the full control of the *Mare Nostrum*, as the victorious Romans called the Mediterranean Sea. Roman troops first arrived at Emporion in 218 B.C.E.; as a consequence of the peace treaty with Carthage after the First Punic War, the Greek-Hellenic commercial port was under Rome's protection. Initially, Rome respected the independent status of Emporion and established a military camp just outside the city walls but, within a few decades—after defeating Carthage in the Second Punic War—a new, entirely Roman city, *Emporiae*, began to emerge on the site of the former military camp, marking the beginning of a process of Romanization of the city that later extended to the rest of the peninsula. The new Roman town was built following the principles of Roman urbanism and it became a model for the development of other Roman cities, for example, *Tarraco* (modern Tarragona), that were founded along the Mediterranean coast during Rome's Republican period (510–31 B.C.E.). Progressively and forcefully, Romans occupied most of *Hispania* (as they called the peninsula), subduing and integrating the indigenous populations into Roman culture. At the beginning of the second century B.C.E., Hispania had been largely controlled by Rome and its vast territory was divided into two Roman provinces, *Ulterior* and *Citerior*.

The Romans proceeded with unforgiving methodology: they conquered territories by occupation, war, or invasion; they dominated by military force and civilized through their laws, their art, and their culture. This process of Romanization had a tremendous impact on the organization of conquered cities, aspects especially visible in the cities' urbanistic and architectural characteristics. The Romans, as great planners and innovative builders, saw both urbanism and architecture as prime vehicles for imposing Roman culture. The cities were equipped with a wide variety of urban structures—villa, *basilica*, bath, temple, theater, *forum*—model building types that were repeated in smaller or greater scale in all cities. These were laid out following an orthogonal grid of streets, called *cardines* and *decumani*, symbolical extensions of Rome, the capital and "mother" of all Roman towns.

The Romans were great innovators; they had inherited the constructive skill of the Etruscans (early occupants of central Italy, from whom they received the arch and the vault) and appropriated the *trabeated* system of the Greeks, creating a new synthesis that engendered a novel architectural language composed of arches, *vaults*, and domes integrated with the classical elements—columns, *architraves*, *pediments*—typical of Greek architecture. Key factors for developing this new system were the availability of materials—marble, granite, and other types of stone—and the invention of concrete, a mix of lime and *pozzolana* (a sandy material) that produced a strong, cohesive, and resistant building material.

Roman buildings were often derived from Greek classical types, but the Romans also excelled in adapting Greek typologies to their urban ideal as well as in creating new types. The forum, the temple, the basilica, and the market—that is, the sanctuaries and the spaces for civic activity—were the most important buildings and places of Roman cities during the Republican period. **Empúries**, the modern name of the originally Greek-Hellenic settlement of Emporion and its adjacent Roman town of Emporiae, was an important city in the early years of Roman occupation of Iberia. Eventually abandoned after a long period of decline, its ruins stand today as a valuable testimony of Roman urbanism during the Republican period; the logical grid layout of the streets and homes, organized around courtyards paved with beautiful mosaics, is still visible through the remnants of this once powerful commercial city.

Rome proceeded to control and expand through vast territorial extensions, thanks to the development of a great system of roads that facilitated the transportation of war legions and warfare. Topographical accidents presented problems that they resolved with constructive skill and ingenious engineering; thus, they created remarkable works of urban infrastructure, veritable feats for the time. Bridges, roads, and aqueducts are among some of the most wonderful and original contributions of the Romans to engineering and architecture, the vehicles that permitted them to conquer, dominate, and Romanize unprecedented territorial extensions. The standing Roman bridges of Alcántara and Mérida, and the **Roman Aqueduct** of Segovia, are among the most remarkable still-standing structures that testify to the Romans' engineering inventiveness and constructive creativity.

In spite of the incessant process of Romanization and territorial expansion, Roman legions had to constantly fight against indigenous revolts throughout Hispania. Ultimately, the full control and pacification of the peninsula was accomplished in the early years of Imperial rule in Rome (a series of civil wars and dictatorships brought the Republic to an end; Octavius became Emperor in 27 B.C.E.). Peaceful times triggered the development and growth of cities, which were equipped with great works of architecture and engineering in the image of Rome. As Frank Brown sharply stated, "the Empire was an empire of cities with a city at its head. Its order was an urban order. The architecture of the Empire, since it was Roman architecture, was an order of spaces shaped to constitute the environment of its moral order, matching its security and dignity with decorous spatial grandeur" (Brown 1961, 25–26).

The establishment of the Empire and the pacification of Hispania led to the foundation of cities for veteran legionaries as well as to an administrative reform that divided Hispania into three provinces: Citerior, along the eastern side of the peninsula with capital in the old city of Tarraco; *Baetica* in the south with capital in modern Córdoba; and, *Lusitania* (which comprised the west of modern Spain and modern Portugal) with capital in **Augusta Emérita** (modern Mérida), a newly founded city. The latter eventually became one of the most beautiful and important cities of the Empire; today, it houses a remarkable collection of standing Roman buildings. The

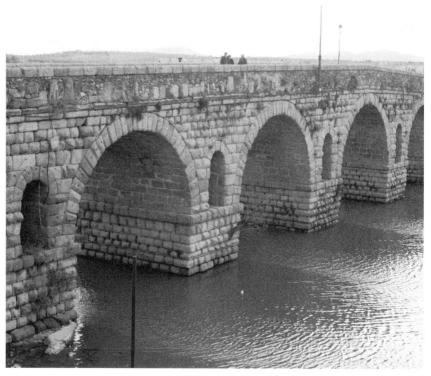

The Roman bridge over the Guadiana River at Mérida.

theater and amphitheater of Augusta Emérita, unusually constructed at approximately the same time and adjacent to each other, are the jewels of the ensemble; the theater in particular is one the most beautiful of the Empire and one of the best preserved Roman buildings worldwide. Typologically, the theater was directly derived from the Greek original model, but the amphitheater, while also inspired by the Greek theater, is an original Roman type conceived for entertainment—gladiatorial combats and other exhibitions and games—of the population. The **Roman Amphitheater at Itálica**, in southern Spain, was the largest outside the Italian peninsula, surpassed only by Rome's *Coliseum* and the amphitheaters of Capua and Pozzoli.

The beginning of the second century c.e. marked the peak of activity and embellishment of cities in Hispania, a period that coincided with the Imperial reigns of the Spanish Emperors Trajan (98–117 c.e.) and Hadrian (117–138 c.e.). However, later, and as a result of insufficient funding and poor maintenance, the urban areas of Hispania began to decline and the population abandoned the cities. At the same time, the Empire had grown too much and Rome could not support the armies needed to protect its enormous territory; the third century c.e. brought civil war and an unstable economy, a situation by which barbarian tribes that threatened the frontiers of the Em-

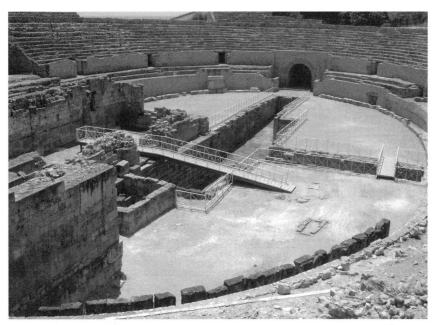

General view of the Roman amphitheater of Tarragona.

pire profited. In the early years of the fourth century, Constantine initiated a series of radical reforms that included religious conversion to Christianity (312–313 C.E.) and moving the central seat of power from Rome to Byzantium (c. 324)—in the more prosperous eastern side of the Mediterranean—where he founded New Rome, or *Constantinople* (modern Istanbul, in Turkey). Another radical reform took place in 364 C.E., with the partition of the Empire—the Eastern Empire with capital in Constantinople, and the Western Empire centered in Rome. Weakened and besieged by the rides of barbarian tribes, Rome finally collapsed in the fifth century, and with it, the Western Roman Empire of which Hispania was part disintegrated. Yet, more than six centuries of Roman rule had left an indelible cultural legacy in the Iberian population, which, despite the arrival of new rulers, remained attached to the heritage of Rome.

Early Christian and Visigothic Architecture

The Romans' adoption of Christianity as the Empire's official religion made necessary the creation of adequate buildings for the new faith of the State as well as for the clergy; the Roman control of the advanced cultures of the eastern Mediterranean had begun to generate a fruitful crossbreeding that had an impact on architecture and building techniques through the incorporation of typically Eastern motives. The ancient Greco-Roman classical language was relaxed and began to be freely intertwined with *Byzantine* influences.

Before being adopted by Rome as the official religion of the State, Christianity had had a clandestine existence in subterranean catacombs. The baptistery of *Gabia la Grande* (in Andalucía) and the church of *Santa Eulalia de Boveda* (in Galicia) are considered as two possible examples of Christian buildings before the Romans adopted it as the religion of the Empire. Once accepted as the official religion, the old Roman basilica served as a model for developing the churches of the new religion while the centralized-plan buildings of Eastern origin were often adopted as baptisteries. Christian temples based on basilican plans were erected in the most important cities of Hispania—Augusta Emérita, Tarraco, Córdoba—even if they were already in a process of urban decline. However, only some fragments of them remain and their function as religious buildings is still the subject of much controversy (Mérida's *Episcopio*, for example). The baptistery of the no longer extant Cathedral of Egara (modern Tarrasa), today known as **San Miguel Tarrasa** (part of a larger religious complex), is the most important *Early Christian* building still existing in Spain. Its *Greek-cross* centralized plan and the *groin vaults* of the interior suggest the influence of Byzantine buildings.

Rome's crisis of the early fifth century opened the doors of the Iberian Peninsula to Germanic and barbarian tribes that quickly devastated the frontiers of the Empire. After crossing the Pyrenees, armies of Alans, Sueves, and Vandals overran Hispania and occupied Galicia, Lusitania, and the Baetica, respectively. Toward the middle of the sixth century, one Germanic tribe, the *Visigoths*, prevailed over the others and, establishing their capital in *Toletum* (modern Toledo), inaugurated the *Visigothic* kingdom that ruled Iberia for two centuries. However, as Jerrylin Dodds sharply commented, Visigothic Spain consisted of a ruling class of 200,000 Visigoths that governed a population of eight million Hispano-Romans (Dodds 1989, 8). The first Visigothic rulers tried to keep separate the two populations—Goths and Hispano-Romans—by forbidding mixed marriages and applying differentiated codes of law. Thus, the two populations had a certain degree of independence: Hispano-Romans held administrative positions and were governed by Roman law, while Visigoths responded to Euric's Visigothic Code.

The religions of the two populations were also different; Hispano-Romans were Christian Catholics, while Visigoths ascribed to *Arianism*, a Christian heresy. The social, religious, and legal segregation of the native population provoked numerous problems between rulers and ruled. This tension began to be resolved during the reign of Leovigild (c. 568–586) through the promulgation of a new code of laws applicable to both Hispano-Romans and Goths, marking the first step in the integration of the two populations. The final step toward integration was made by his successor, Recared, who adopted Christian Catholicism as the kingdom's religion, ending the existence of two rival clergies. As Spanish historian Fernando García de Cortázar stated, it represented the definite submission of the victorious side to the culture of the defeated (García de Cortázar 2002, 45).

With a frank process of peaceful integration, the seventh century marked the peak of Toledo's Visigothic kingdom; new urban centers were developed and cultural activity revived. The "Etymologies" of Saint Isidoro (c. 630) is the most important written work of that period and a landmark of Western history. The absence of religious rivalry also prompted the construction of numerous churches, especially in the revitalized urban centers; however, no Visigothic churches remain in what were the most important cities of the kingdom (Toledo, Mérida, Córdoba), most likely because they were destroyed by the Muslim occupation that began in 711. Nevertheless, the most important extant buildings of the period—**San Juan de Baños**, **San Pedro de la Nave**, and *Santa Comba de Bande*—are faithful testimonies to the architectural characteristics of this first Visigothic architecture. All are based on the old Roman basilican model and incorporate aspects—decorative motifs and the *horse-shoe* arch—that denote the influence of Eastern architecture, but the first two are particularly significant as representatives of the two spatial variations of the basilican plan explored in Visigothic architecture. San Juan de Baños is the best extant example of the Visigoths' transformation of the Roman basilican plan, while San Pedro de la Nave has a cruciform plan inserted within a rectangular envelope; both shared a spatial fragmentation previously unknown, probably a consequence of the deterioration of building techniques and knowledge inherited from Rome. According to some critics and historians, this spatiality of seventh-century Visigothic architecture may represent the seed of a national style (neither Greek, nor Roman, nor Eastern), an original architecture that would eventually revive in the ninth century in northern Spain.

The successful pacification and reunification of the Iberian territory under Visigothic rule was short-lived; the internal struggles for the succession of the crown, the confrontation of nobles and monarchs, and the political ambition and interference of the clergy weakened the kingdom's incipient consolidation as initiated by Leovigild and Recared. In 711, Toledo's Visigothic kingdom collapsed; a new foreign army arrived from the opposite coast of the Mediterranean and easily conquered old Hispania, imposing new rules, customs, language, and religion, and a novel conception of architecture of unprecedented characteristics and sophistication in Western Europe.

Islamic Architecture in Spain

The year 711 marked a turning point in the history of Spain; an army composed of Arabs and Berbers led by Tariq crossed the Strait of Gibraltar and rapidly seized the most important cities of the Visigothic kingdom, including the capital Toledo. The amazing success and the virtually nonexistent resistance of the local population encouraged the Muslim army to expand across the entire peninsular territory and even beyond the Pyrenees until they were finally stopped in 732 by Charles Martel (grandfather of the future Charlemagne) in the famous battle of Poitiers (France). In 750, the Umayyad dynasty based in Damascus (at the Eastern extreme of the Mediterranean Sea, in modern Syria) that ruled over the old Arab Empire was overthrown by a rival faction; in 755, Abd-al-Rahman I—a Umayyad survivor—managed to escape and, after crossing into Iberia, was proclaimed ruler of the independent Emirate of *al-Andalus*, the new Arab name given to Hispania, which established the capital in Córdoba and inaugurated a more than seven-centuries-long Muslim political presence in Iberia.

The reign of Abd-al-Rahman I (756–788) was characterized by a tolerant domination of the native population who, in exchange for paying special tributes, were permitted to keep their Christian faith (they were named *Mozarabs*, that is, Christians living in Muslim-controlled territory); nevertheless, by the end of the eighth century the majority of the local Hispano-Roman and Visigothic population had converted to Islam. After gaining control of the numerous internal revolts and somehow pacifying the peninsula, Abd-al-Rahman launched an ambitious building campaign to erect mosques throughout al-Andalus, especially in the most important cities of the Emirate. Architecturally, the mosque was a new building type previously unknown in Europe. In general terms, it consists of a rectangular praying hall (the *haram*) punctuated by galleries (*riwaqs*) placed perpendicular to the *quibla* (a wall oriented toward Mecca and the most important component of a mosque); in most cases, the praying hall was preceded by a walled-in open courtyard (the *sahn*). Mosques were soon built in all the urban centers of the Emirate, often with unusual rapidity thanks to the reuse of readily available building elements pillaged from existing (or ruined) Roman buildings. Undoubtedly, **the Great Mosque of Córdoba**, initiated during the reign of Abd-al-Rahman I, is the greatest representative of Umayyad Islamic architecture in Spain, a universal masterpiece that testifies to the artistic splendor already reached in al-Andalus in the early years of the Emirate.

As the Muslim population of Córdoba increased, the city's Great Mosque was enlarged in successive stages to become a building of imposing scale and unusual beauty and elegance. In 929, Abd-al-Rahman III elevated the political and religious status of Córdoba by proclaiming the Caliphate, thus becoming both the political as well as religious authority of al-Andalus. His reign (912–961) marked the peak of Córdoba's Caliphate: culturally, al-Andalus was the most advanced civilization in Europe and attracted scientists, mathematicians, philosophers, poets, and artists from throughout the Mediterranean basin. In 936, Abd-al-Rahman III founded a new royal residential and administrative center—*Madinat-al-Zahara*—located outside of Córdoba. This vast building complex consisted of numerous residences, courtyards, gardens, and a mosque, as well as the facilities for the political administration of the Caliphate. The architectural characteristics are similar

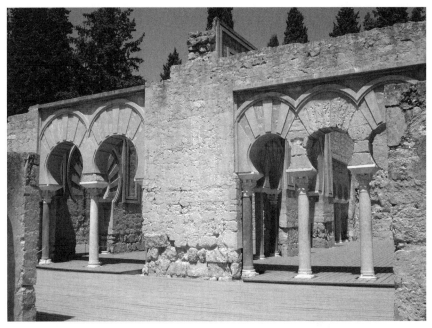

Fragment of the remains of Madinat-al-Zahara, a caliphal residence and administrative center of the Caliphate of Córdoba.

to those of the Great Mosque of Córdoba, but, built entirely from the ground up, the complex reveals the Muslims' predilection for designing spaces around open courtyards and gardens profusely ornamented with water features.

The prosperous cities of al-Andalus grew rapidly; therefore, new buildings, especially palaces and fortifications, but also mosques for less central quarters of the urban centers, were necessary. The small **Mosque of Bāb-al-Mardūm**, in Toledo, is a little masterpiece that clearly demonstrates the high level of technical, decorative, and spatial sophistication achieved during the caliphal period. The peak of territorial expansion was under the reign of Hisham II (r. 976–1009) and his *vizier* Al-Manzur, who raided the entire peninsula with his powerful militias, however, the focus on military domination and territorial expansion caused the decline of the intellectual and artistic splendor of the Caliphate, which finally disintegrated in 1031; the central political entity dissolved and a new political order comprised of small regional kingdoms—the *taifas*—governed by local princes of various ethnic origins emerged. The most important cities of al-Andalus became capitals of these smaller kingdoms. In spite of the territorial and political fragmentation, this period was, intellectually, almost as rich as the Caliphate's best years because some regional rulers revived artistic and scientific activity. Two of the most important taifas were based in Sevilla (in the south) and Zaragoza,

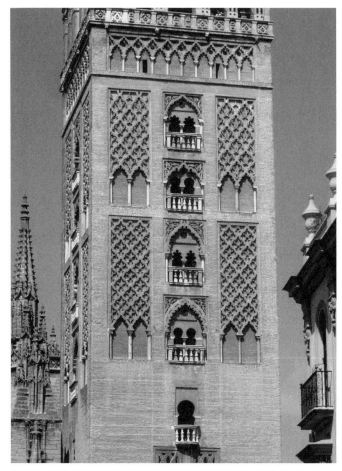

Details of La Giralda, the Almohad minaret of the no longer existant Mosque of Sevilla, which was replaced by the cathedral; the tower was appropriated as the cathedral's bell tower.

at the northern frontier with Christian kingdoms. The *Almohads*, who reigned in Sevilla, left a remarkable cultural legacy in a short time. The minaret of Sevilla's splendid mosque known as "La Giralda" (today used as the Cathedral's bell tower) is the most important remnant of the Almohads' architectural contribution. In the north, Zaragoza's **Palace of La Aljafería** is the most salient existing building of the taifas' period.

Divided and rivaling with each other, the taifas lacked political, social, and military cohesiveness; they soon succumbed to the advance of the Christian kingdoms that, after securing a stronghold behind the Cantabrian mountains, had decided to launch a slow but inexorable campaign to recover the possessions of the old Visigothic kingdom. One after the other, the most important cities of al-Andalus were recaptured by Christian armies by the end of the thirteenth century; the exception was Granada and its area of influence (the current provinces of Almería, Granada, and Málaga) where a *Nasrid* dynasty seized what remained of al-Andalus and during the next two centuries succeeded in restoring the intellectual and artistic splendor of the Caliphate by attracting Muslim artists, poets, mathematicians, and philosophers from other parts of the peninsula. The architectural and landscape complex of the **Palace of La Alhambra and Gardens of El Generalife** is the Nasrids' most salient creation. A universally recognized architectural masterpiece, La Alhambra is an enchanting place, the most important building complex that testifies to the long, fruitful, and extraordinarily sophisticated Islamic culture in Iberia.

While each of the different dynasties and periods introduced aspects that were unique to them, Islamic architecture as a whole made important contributions to the development of Spain's architecture. The insistence on the dematerialization of the plane through the application of sophisticated and intricate vegetal and geometric patterns (Islam prohibits the representation of human figures) is one of many aspects of Muslim architecture that had a lasting influence in Spanish architecture. The introduction of new building techniques and elements such as the multicentered horse-shoe arch, cusped arches and domes, fine plastering techniques, and the production of colored faience are other important aspects of the artistic and technical legacy left by Islam; however, the most important contributions are the new and generously open spatiality introduced by the mosque's large halls punctuated by rows of columns, and the intimate and sensual evocation of place in their secular and residential architecture.

In 1492, the Catholic Kings finally captured Granada and ended seven and one-half centuries of organized Muslim political presence in Iberia. However, their brilliant cultural and artistic moments had left an indelible legacy that marked the future of Spain, particularly its architecture; *Mozarabic*, *Mudéjar*, and *Plateresque* (and their respective influences in contemporaneous and future architectural developments) are unique architectural characteristics of a country that was impregnated with Islamic art and architecture, an aspect that differentiates Spanish architecture from contemporaneous developments in the rest of Europe.

Asturian-Visigothic and Mozarabic Architecture

After the fall of Toledo in 714, the Visigoths retreated north where—after defeating the expanding Muslim armies in the mythical battle of *Covadonga* (722)—they consolidated a stronghold behind the Cantabrian mountains and established a new Visigothic kingdom with capital in Oviedo (Asturias). Rather isolated, but protected from Muslim incursions by the natural topography, the new Christian kingdom of Asturias began to flourish in the ninth century and expanded to the northwest of the peninsula thanks to the arrival of refugees from the south. A notable building activity began during the reign of the second Visigothic king of Oviedo, Alfonso II (also known as Alfonso "the Chaste," r. 791–842) who was a contemporary of Charlemagne, with whom he had fluent relationships.

Primarily, the new buildings were churches that followed the old Visigothic canon of the basilican plan with three rectilinear eastern *apses* and *naves* separated by arcades supported on strong pillars. The small church of *San Julián de los Prados* (also known as *Santullano*) is the most important work of this period and the link between the old Visigothic buildings of the seventh century (for instance the already mentioned San Juan de Baños and San Pedro de la Nave) and the innovative Asturian-Visigothic architecture that evolved during the short reign of Alfonso II's successor, Ramiro I (r. 842–850). In effect, the masterpieces of Asturian-Visigothic architecture—the building complex at **Monte Naranco (Palace of Ramiro I and San Miguel de Lillo)**, in Oviedo, and the small church of **Santa Cristina de Lena**, twenty-five miles south of the kingdom's capital—were built at approximately the same time and are attributed to a same, yet unknown, architect. The architecture of these wonderful buildings has notable characteristics that anticipated some important features usually attributed as innovations of *Romanesque* and *Gothic* architecture. As Kenneth Conant commented, "the architecture of Asturias, Galicia and neighboring Portugal in the 9th and 10th centuries was like a laboratory experiment in Romanesque, performed in a remote region and not absorbed into the main current of architectural development" (Conant 1978, 87).

The salient characteristics of the Asturian architecture of Ramiro I's period included the development of the buildings' vertical dimension which created loftier and more slender structures. This was accompanied by notable constructive innovations such as the lightening of the exterior walls and the introduction of buttressing elements that—in the absence of thick walls—counter the lateral force of the vaults; *buttresses* were usually placed on the exterior in the form of massive rectangular pillars that punctuate the buildings' exterior façades at rhythmical intervals (for example at Santa Cristina de Lena), but also in the interior in the form of pilasters or clusters of cylindrical columns. The lightening of the walls was also possible by the construction of the wall as a sequence of blind arches that, structurally assisted by the buttresses, support the lofty stone vaults. While numerous historians suggest the influence of contemporaneous architectural developments from outside Spain—notably *Carolingian* architecture from central Europe and Eastern Byzantine architecture—the *Asturian-Visigothic* architecture of the ninth century is considered as the materialization of the first truly national architecture, a culmination of the process initiated in the Visigothic churches of the seventh century.

After consolidating its position around Oviedo, the new kingdom of Asturias began to expand southward, slowly recuperating the territory lost to

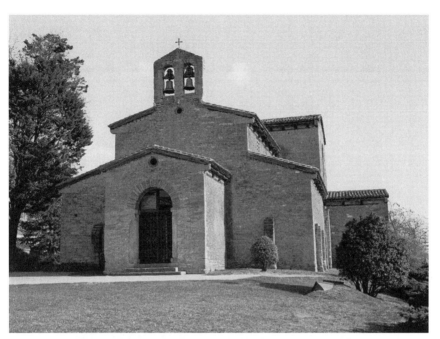

Exterior of San Julián de los Prados also known as "Santullano."

Muslims. In 914 the capital was moved to León, in recently conquered land. As the distinct architecture of the Asturian-Visigothic kingdom was developing, another Christian architecture of truly original characteristics had began to evolve in al-Andalus, especially during the periods in which the Caliphate of Córdoba was tolerant of the natives' Christian religion. However, despite their religious independence, the Christian population progressively assimilated the Arabic culture of the rulers; the term "Mozarabic," which means "arabized," refers to the people, life, and culture of Christians heavily dependent on or influenced by Arab culture. By nature, architecture is one of the areas in which the influence of Arabic culture is more visible; thus Mozarabic architecture refers to buildings—notably churches—that were built by Christians and reveal strong influences from Islamic architecture.

Numerous Christian churches of Mozarabic characteristics were surely built during religiously tolerant periods across al-Andalus; yet, most of them were destroyed or damaged in the years of confrontation and persecution. *Santa María de Melque*, in Toledo, and *San Cebrián de Mazote*, in Valladolid, are two important examples of Mozarabic architecture in Muslim-controlled territory; however, the most important Mozarabic churches are in the region of León, which, as the new Visigothic capital had begun to attract Christian clerics and laymen persecuted in al-Andalus. The most interesting and best preserved is **San Miguel de Escalada**, approximately twenty miles east of

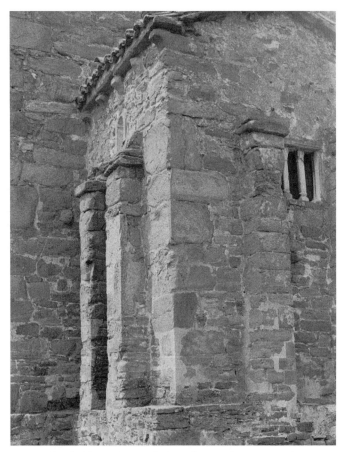

Exterior detail of Santa Cristina de Lena showing the innovative buttresses that project to the exterior of the building's envelope.

the kingdom's capital. Widespread and disconnected, Mozarabic architecture did not reach a synthesis to constitute a homogenous and consistent architectural system; rather, there is a wide variety of Mozarabic church typologies, variations of the basilican, *Greek-cross*, and *Latin-cross* plans. The unifying thread of Mozarabic architecture is the hybridization that resulted from the absorption and appropriation of elements more typical of Islamic architecture.

In 813, in the distant northwestern corner of Iberia (modern Galicia), a peasant discovered a shrine that was soon recognized as the tomb of the apostle St. James. This discovery had a transcendental importance for the history of Christian Spain as well as for Spain's architecture because, under the auspices of the *Benedictine* order of Cluny (based in central France), a massive pilgrimage to the sacred site developed with astonishing rapidity across Europe. One of the major consequences of this movement was the sudden increase of communication with trans-Pyrenean cultures, and the colossal penetration of clerics, artisans, and workers—especially from France—as well as enthusiastic volunteers who were ready to enlist in Christian armies to drive away Muslims from Western Europe. The influx of ideas and skilled artisans put an end to the development of distinctly national architectures—Asturian-Visigothic and Mozarabic—which were suppressed and replaced by the incorporation of architectural ideas and techniques that derived directly from the then-evolving French and Lombard Romanesque.

Romanesque Architecture

The High Middle Ages was a fascinating period that witnessed the development of a pan-European movement that generated unprecedented social, political, cultural, and religious transformations such as the emergence and consolidation of the feudal system, the establishment of the monarchy as the predominant political form of government, and Christianity as the common religion. This was a veritable pluri-cultural and pluri-ethnic movement, the genesis of the multinational conglomerate that constitutes modern Europe. In spite of the diverse social, cultural, and political evolution and the geographical differences of the various peoples, the architecture of the period exhibits an until then unusual uniformity. The rise of monasticism had a capital role, not only regarding religious but also all other aspects—social, cultural, economic—of medieval life; the energy and dynamism that emanated from the monasteries provided great impulse for architectural renewal and development. The whole period was largely marked by an extraordinary event—the discovery, in 813, of the (alleged) burial remains of the apostle Santiago (St. James) in Galicia, which, thanks to the propagandist exploitations of the Benedictines of Cluny (France), triggered a massive influx of people from all corners of Europe.

In the tenth century, the northern kingdoms of Spain had reaffirmed a strong position and begun to react against the presence of a Muslim state in the Iberian peninsula; King Sancho the Great of Navarra (r. 1000–1035) unified the Christian kingdoms under his rule and, with strong support from neighboring France, initiated the *Reconquista*, a long and relentless campaign to recapture the territory of Iberia that the old Visigothic kingdom had lost to Muslims in the eighth century. The Reconquista was driven by both the need for territorial expansion and the spiritual desire to reestablish Christianity throughout the peninsula. In the northeast, the *Marca Hispánica* (Hispanic Mark, modern Catalonia) marked the territorial border between Christian Europe and al-Andalus. The powerful Muslim taifa of Zaragoza—strategically placed as a wedge between the northern kingdoms and the Marca Hispánica—and the rugged landscape made difficult the communication between the two Christian-held kingdoms; consequently, while sharing the general transformations of the times, northern Spain and Catalonia followed, politically as well as culturally, parallel paths with distinct characteristics. The former had very strong links with France, upon which it became culturally dependent; the latter, on the Mediterranean, had closer relationships with Italy (particularly Lombardy), the Languedoc, and Provence.

Architecturally, it was a period of great transformations in which technical innovations and social changes demanded the conception of new building types—the monastery, burgs and castles, and massive fortifications—and engendered major changes in the design of churches, the predominant architectural manifestation. Briefly stated, as Christian Norberg-Schulz noted, the most significant characteristic of Romanesque (and Carolingian) architecture was the combination of massive enclosure with a strong vertical direction (Norbert-Schultz 1985, 78). An additional characteristic of singular importance was the volumetric identification of each of the buildings' components—nave, transept, apse, tower—and the manifestation of a hierarchical spatial relationship. The structural innovations of the times, which began to differentiate the buildings' structure of support—the skeleton—from the system of enclosure (an aspect that will achieve a higher degree of development in Gothic architecture), were of paramount importance for the formal and spatial evolution of Romanesque architecture. Spanish Romanesque, while strongly influenced by foreign developments, had some distinct characteristics; renown Spanish historian Vicente Lampérez y Romea pointed out that the more notable differences are "a higher roughness, a tendency to heavier proportions, the adoption of more elementary solutions and the simplicity of decorative elements" (Lampérez y Romea 1999, 346).

Toward the end of the ninth century, the Count of Barcelona Wilfred el Pilós (r. 874–898) succeeded in obtaining a certain level of independence for the Marca Hispánica that marked the beginning of a national Catalan sentiment. Wilfred founded the Benedictine abbey and church of **Santa María de Ripoll**, which eventually became the intellectual and religious center of Catalonia. In the early eleventh century, Ripoll's Abbot Oliva ordered the full-scale rebuilding of the church, which—with its fully stone-vaulted naves, seven parallel apses facing the transept, and prominent west front—became the paradigm of Catalonian Romanesque. The eleventh century was a fruitful period of religious expansion and architectural exploration in the region as the remarkable monastic complexes of *San Pere de Rodes* (c. 1022), *San Vicente de Cardona* (1020–1040), and *San Pere de Caserres* (1030s) perfectly reveal.

Whereas the Romanesque architecture of the northern kingdoms has different characteristics, it followed a similar path of formal and linguistic development. The discovery of the relics of St. James and the subsequent pilgrimages generated the rapid development of roads that led to Santiago de Compostela from all directions. In France, with the auspice of the Benedictine monks of Cluny, a new church typology—the pilgrimage church—had

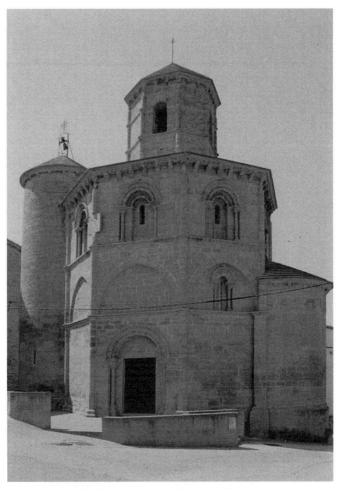

Exterior of the Romanesque chapel of Torres del Río.

originated, and was soon exported to the northern kingdoms of Spain, which, effectively, were under their influence in religious and other cultural aspects. **San Martin Fromista** (1060–1070s) is the most important and purest representative of the pilgrimage church in Spain, a clear and didactic demonstration of the principles of Romanesque architecture. Stimulated by the pilgrimage activity and the military victories of the Christian armies, the road of Santiago was quickly equipped with churches, hospitals, and monasteries that provided services to pilgrims across northern Spain. Deriving from Jerusalem's *Saint Sepulcre*, many small churches adopted a centralized octagonal plan instead of the typical basilican plan of the pilgrimage church; the most important among these are the *Chapel of Santo Sepulcro* in Torres del Río and **Santa María de Eunate**. The latter is particularly interesting be-

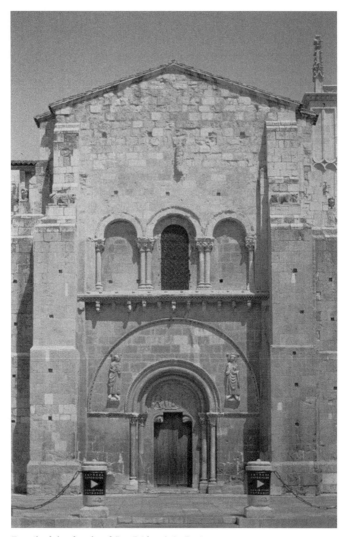

Detail of the façade of San Isidoro's in León.

cause of its unique surrounding exterior gallery, richly decorated portal, and beautiful relationship to the landscape. The church of *La Vera Cruz*, in Segovia, is another interesting example of a Castilian centralized church, while *San Isidoro de León* derived from the basilican plan.

The most important Spanish building of the period and one of the most significant representatives of Romanesque architecture worldwide is the **Cathedral of Santiago de Compostela**, a building of unusual scale and architectural splendor for the time. It is the paradigmatic example of the pilgrimage church, the high point of the technical, formal, and spatial search of the Romanesque, and a landmark in the evolution of Western architecture. While strongly indebted to French architecture, the Cathedral of Santiago de Compostela appears as the culmination of the search for massive formal presence and spatial height.

As the Christian kingdoms continued to advance over Muslim territory, towns and cities were strongly fortified to secure the recuperated land. The castle and fortified walls of **Loarre**, a small burg in northern Aragon, is one of the better-preserved examples of fortified burgs. Perched on a high promontory that operates as natural defense, it is further protected by fortifications that enclose the typical medieval burg beyond which there is a splendid castle and a magnificent chapel, veritable architectural jewels of the period. By the end of the eleventh century, the Reconquista had reached central Spain, including the recapture of many strategically important cities such as Toledo (1085), capital of the ancient Visigothic kingdom. However, the frontier between Christian and Muslim territory was constantly changing; thus, the repopulation and fortification of conquered cities became a priority for the Christian kings who wanted to secure their territorial progress. Consequently, the erection of military buildings—mostly castles and fortifications—became as important as the construction of religious buildings. The fortified **Ávila City Walls** offer the only extant full-scale original medieval enceinte of an entire city throughout Europe, prime reference of military Romanesque architecture.

Mudéjar and Gothic Architecture

Romanesque became the dominant architectural manifestation in Spain during the eleventh and twelfth centuries. Its severe and massive character seemed to mirror the nature of the Iberian people. The success and acceptance of Romanesque delayed the arrival of newer ideas and developments that originated in central Europe, especially in France. Moreover, in newly conquered territories, Christian Romanesque architecture experienced a crossbreeding with Islamic architecture that engendered a uniquely Spanish architectural development known as *Mudéjar*. Simultaneously, the novelty of *Gothic* architecture—which can be considered to have evolved from Romanesque architecture but also was a novel structural and spatial conception—was imported from France, not unlike Romanesque a century and a half earlier.

Throughout the thirteenth century Mudéjar and Gothic architecture coexisted and evolved rather independently, but sometimes they influenced each other in what had become a vast territorial extension controlled by Christian kingdoms. Mudéjar architecture is characterized by the use of building materials, techniques, and decorative patterns typically and generally used in Islamic architecture by Muslim builders applied to Christian buildings usually derived from medieval types, such as basilican churches, bell

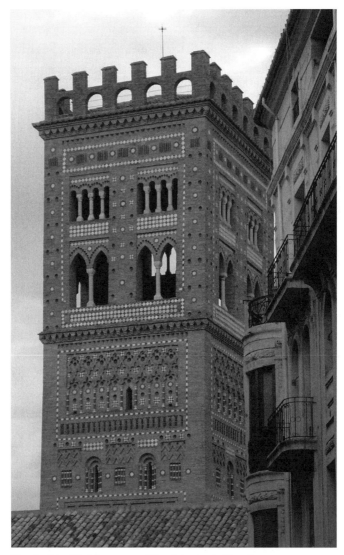

Detail of the Mudéjar tower of San Salvador in Teruel.

towers, palaces, and various types of military structures. The region of Aragon—previously controlled by the powerful taifa of Zaragoza—houses a wonderful wealth of a remarkable regional type of Mudéjar architecture. The city of Teruel—in the southern portion of the region—is dotted with bell towers and churches built in red brick and profusely covered by polychrome glazed ceramic tiles arranged in a wide variety of geometrical patterns. The towers of *San Salvador* and *San Martín*, the church of *San Pedro*, and the **Cathedral of Teruel** are the city's most important examples of Mudéjar architecture. In some periods, when Christian armies recaptured and controlled new cities they were rather tolerant of the population's religion and traditions; among many other positive things, this religious and cultural tolerance permitted the coexistence and crossbreeding of the different cultures. In central Spain, especially in Toledo—veritable crossroads of the peninsula—there was an important Jewish community; therefore, the crossbreeding reached a higher level of complexity and cultural exchange, a phenomenon known as "*las tres culturas*" (the three cultures: Christian, Muslim, and Jewish). The small church of **Santa María la Blanca**—originally a synagogue with characteristics evidently borrowed from Islamic architecture that was built after Christians recaptured Toledo—is the most relevant architectural example of this triple cultural crossbreeding.

The *chevet* of the Abbey of St. Denis (c. 1140), north of Paris, is considered as the first manifestation of Gothic architectural principles. In broad terms, these are characterized by the systematic implementation of the ribbed vault, the pointed arch, and the reduction of the building's structure to a minimal, skeletal expression; further, as major components of the building's structural system were pushed outside of the building's envelope, the interior space—enclosed by large surfaces of stained glass placed between structural members—became graceful and luminous as never before, vested with a vertical emphasis that had obvious spiritual associations. This brief description of Gothic architecture is evidently related to the construction of the soaring cathedrals built across Europe in that period which became inevitably associated with Gothic architecture.

The earliest Gothic buildings in Spain are the Cathedral of Ávila (c. 1180s), built adjacent to the majestic city walls, and the Cathedral of Tarragona (begun in the 1170s), located in Castilla and Catalonia, respectively. In fact, as it had happened in the preceding Romanesque period, Gothic architecture in Spain had two parallel lines of regional evolution—Castilian and Catalonian. Castilian Gothic was largely dependent on the influence of French architecture, which was the model of the **Cathedral of Burgos** and the **Cathedral of León**, the two most important Gothic buildings in Castilla. Both of them are heavily influenced by the Cathedral of Reims—a universally recognized masterpiece of the period—as well as by the cathedrals of Bourges and Amiens.

Catalonian Gothic was also heavily influenced by contemporaneous developments in French architecture; however, like the Romanesque period, it followed a parallel path of development and exhibited some clearly distinct features. The more important ones were the positioning of the buttresses inside the building's envelope, and the conception of the church's interior space as a large hall, that is, without making a major spatial distinction between the central and lateral naves. While still a hybrid between the two spatial conceptions, the Cathedral of Barcelona (early 1300s) is, because of its scale and architectural splendor, one of the landmarks of Catalan Gothic. However, Barcelona's much smaller church of **Santa María del Mar**, along with

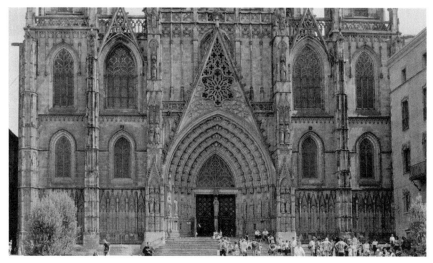

Lower portion of the west façade of Barcelona's cathedral.

the cathedrals of Gerona (begun c. 1270s) and Palma de Majorca (early 1300s), represent a more Catalonian version of Gothic architecture.

Gothic architecture continued to evolve through the thirteenth and fourteenth centuries, engendering a wide variety of stylistic and structural variations of the original. Not unlike in the rest of central Europe, cathedrals of Gothic characteristics continued to be erected in Spain throughout those two centuries (and even later). The Cathedrals of Seville, Oviedo, and Salamanca are but three good examples of this late Gothic architecture. A very interesting work, albeit of a much smaller scale, is the *Chapel of the Condestable* (see **Cathedral of Burgos**), a landmark of Gothic *Flamboyant* in Spain. In the late fifteenth century, a new national style that combined typical aspects originated in the dominant late Gothic and Mudéjar architectures with formal concepts and language from the emerging modernity of *Renaissance* ideas imported from Italy finally replaced Gothic architecture and provided a transition to the more purely Renaissance architecture of the second half of the sixteenth century.

The Transition to Renaissance: *Isabelline* and *Plateresque*

In the early decades of the fifteenth century, a social, political, artistic, and scientific humanistic revolution originated in the city-states of northern Italy. It brought to an end the epic Middle Ages, completing a historical cycle that had started with the disintegration of the Western Roman Empire and had encompassed almost ten centuries. The new period—commonly known as the Renaissance—was marked by radical transformations such as the consolidation of large national monarchies replacing the smaller feudal kingdoms, the rise of a powerful nobility allied but often confronted with the interests of the monarchy, the establishment of the city as an influential political entity and new center of political power, the slow emergence of an urban bourgeoisie, and great inventions and discoveries.

Naturally, this humanistic revolution had profound impact on the production of art and architecture. The more illuminated thinkers of the period launched a ferocious critique of the "barbaric" evolution that the arts and sciences had had in previous centuries and postulated a radical and immediate return to the canon of classical Greco-Roman culture. The emergent urban nobility eventually displaced the monastery as the primary center of power, knowledge, and artistic production. The figure of the *"mecenas"* (the art or scientific patron)—usually the powerful local sir—and the artist as a creating individual surged suddenly to definitively alter the system of commission, conception, production, and realization of works of art and architecture. The construction of the dome of *Santa María di Fiore* (Florence, Italy, c. 1420), designed by Filippo Brunelleschi, marked the beginning of the Renaissance in architecture, originally an Italian movement that eventually spread to the rest of Europe.

At that moment, the beginning of the fifteenth century, Spain was perhaps the most powerful European state. The Christian victory at the battle of *Las Navas de Tolosa* (1272) had sealed the fate of a Muslim state in Iberia, limiting its territorial extension to a small fragment of what once was the powerful Caliphate of Córdoba. In 1469, the marriage of Isabel of Castilla and Fernando of Aragon, the Catholic Kings, provided the long-sought unity of the Christian kingdoms of Spain and inaugurated one of the most fruitful periods in the history of the county. In one single year—1492—the Catholic Kings turned the history of Spain: on January 2, they conquered Granada expelling the last Muslim rulers of Iberia and thus completing the Reconquista of the entire peninsula that had been initiated six centuries earlier; ten months later, the vision of Queen Isabel had allowed Christopher Columbus to discover a new continent, an immensely rich and unexplored land unknown in Europe.

In spite of the consolidation of its geopolitical situation within Europe, Spain remained immersed in the modes of production and social organization of the Middle Ages. However, by the end of the fifteenth century the powerful nobility, which had strong relationships with northern Italy, began to absorb and import Renaissance ideas. Architecturally, the transition from Gothic to Italian Renaissance was very gradual, first engendering hybrid and uniquely Spanish types of architecture known as the *Isabelline* and *Plateresque*, also often referred to as Gothic Plateresque or Renaissance Plateresque, respectively.

The Isabelline encompasses the architectural production in the last decades of the fifteenth century, that is, a period coinciding with Isabel of Castilla's reign. It is regarded as a synthesis of late Gothic and Mudéjar architecture with aspects that reflect the slow arrival of Italian Renaissance. The salient characteristics of Isabelline architecture include the use of extravagant formal elements such as *helicoidal* columns and *mixtilinear arches* with complete disregard of their tectonic or constructive function in the building, and profuse display of high-relief ornamentation in stone, especially heraldic symbols. Plateresque had similar characteristics, but the planning of buildings, which in Isabelline remained deeply rooted in medieval practices, began to manifest a more visible influence of Renaissance principles and architectural language.

As in the rest of Europe, religious buildings in Spain continued to be built in Gothic style (the church of *San Juan de los Reyes*—Toledo, c. 1476—is a good example); however, the radical shift from religious to civil patronage (noble and aristocratic) was marked by the development of new building types and institutions such as the urban villa, the university, or the hospital. Having abandoned the rural castles and burgs to get established in the urbanized centers, particularly in Castilla where they built town palaces and urban villas, the new ruling class adopted Renaissance ideas to assert and demonstrate its dominant social and political position. The **Palace of El Infantado** in Guadalajara, designed by Juan Guas, one of the most important architects of the period, is a good example; built for the powerful Mendoza family, it is a landmark of Isabelline architecture. As it was typical of town palaces of the period, it is organized around a central courtyard surrounded by arcaded galleries around which the other dependencies of the palace are distributed. The *College of San Gregorio* (Valladolid, c. 1488) is another important representative of Isabelline architecture.

A similar organization to the Palace of El Infantado is found at **La Casa de las Conchas**, in Salamanca, another landmark of Isabelline-Plateresque architecture recently restored and converted into a public library. While similar in concept, the *Medinacelli Palace*, in Cogolludo, seems to have abandoned some "genetic" remnants of medieval architecture such as towers in the corners (as in La Casa de las Conchas) or the upper band of sentry boxes (as in El Infantado) to more closely resemble a typical Italian villa even if the openings and the articulation of the façade are definitely medieval.

In addition to palaces and urban villas for the nobility, Isabelline and Plateresque architecture was predominant in designing buildings for new institutions. The new front façade of the **Universidad de Alcalá de Henares**, masterpiece of Rodrigo Gil de Hontañón, is one the most representative institutional buildings of the Plateresque. The influence of Mudéjar architecture in all the buildings of this period is particularly notable in the *artesonados* (elaborated wooden ceiling structures) that used to cover the most important interior spaces; equally important are the "model" hospitals for the sick built by direct order of the Catholic Kings in Toledo, Santiago de Compostela, and Granada. Conceptually and stylistically similar to each other, these hospitals consisted of a series of differentiated wings organized around two-story

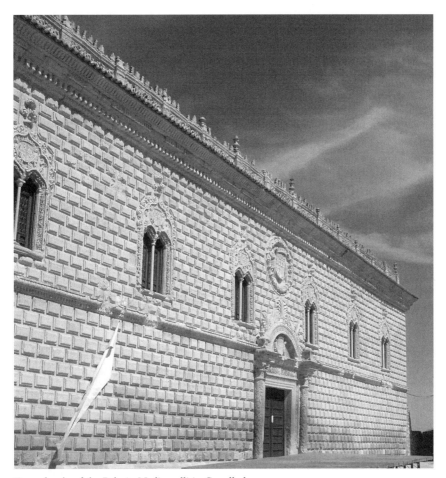

Front façade of the Palacio Medinacelli in Cogolludo.

square courtyards with arcaded galleries. The elegance and more restrained classical architectural language of the elements that enclose the courtyards of the Hospital of Santiago de Compostela denote the influence of Italian Renaissance, at least at a superficial level, in the evolution of late-fifteenth-century Spanish architecture.

Isabelline and Plateresque architecture operated as catalysts that prepared the arrival of full-fledged Renaissance architecture. In the sixteenth century, the architecture of Spain abandoned the unique path of evolution that represented the fusion of its pluralist demographic composition and culture and, as it had already happened in previous centuries, embraced the artistic and architectural principles that evolved in one of the neighboring countries, now Italy, with which it had strong political, social, and commercial connections.

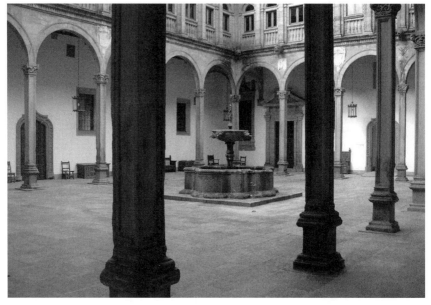

Courtyard of the Royal Hospital of Santiago de Compostela.

The Period of Spanish Renaissance and Baroque Architecture

The reign of the Catholic Kings marked a high point in the history Spain; the long-desired political and geographical unity was completed and thanks in part to the wealth generated by the conquest of American civilizations, it became a dominant European power. Moreover, the Catholic King Fernando II had devised an ambitious network of alliances with other European powers by marrying his three children to the descendants of other influential kingdoms. However, without a male successor (his only son, Philip I King of Castilla, had died in 1506), a crisis for his succession broke out when he died in 1516. With the support of the influential Cardinal Cisneros, the crown of Spain was inherited by Philip I's son, Carlos (grandson of the Catholic Kings as well as of Maximilian I, Emperor of the Holy Roman Empire based in Aachen, Germany), who had been raised in Ghent (modern Holland), did not know Spain's customs, and barely spoke the language. Years later, he inherited the crown of the Holy Roman Empire, becoming Carlos V, the head of an immense empire comprised of a conglomerate of states that included Spain and its colonies in the Americas and the Pacific and the possessions of the Holy Roman Empire. In spite of the tremendous authority and power that this vast extension represented, Carlos V had to confront numerous challenges. On the religious front Martin Luther launched the Reformation in 1521; the adherence to Luther's doctrines within a large portion of the Empire and Carlos V's resistance to accept them eventually provoked one of the most important schisms in the history of Christianity. On the military front, he faced pressure from Francis I of France and the expansionist ambitions of the Turkish-Ottoman Empire. The confrontation with France was focused on controlling the Italian Peninsula, the source of the most progressive developments in arts and science. Eventually, a temporary peace treaty with France granted control of northern Italy and Naples to Carlos V. Naturally, Italian Renaissance quickly expanded throughout Europe; Italian artists were attracted to work in the two powerful neighboring kingdoms—France and Spain—while Italy became the required destination for artists who wanted to master the principles of classical art and architecture.

Italian Renaissance ideas had already penetrated Spain in the last decades of the fifteenth century; however, their application was superficial and was "contaminated" with local architectural practices engendering the Plateresque. Yet, slowly, a more purely Italian Renaissance architecture began to emerge, thanks to the work of artists trained in Italy. The **Palace of Carlos V at La Alhambra**, designed by Pedro de Machuca (who had been trained in Italy), is considered to be the first building in Spain to exhibit a more purely Italian Renaissance architectural language; the palace's pure geometrical exterior form and interior courtyard (almost a perfect square and a perfect circle respectively), the careful attention to the proportional relationship of the different elements, its façades composed of a rusticated base and window openings framed by elements strictly derived from classical architectural language, and the trabeated system of construction are all typical characteristics of pure Italian Renaissance even if traces of the persistent Plateresque can be found in some decorative elements of the building's façades.

The propagation of Renaissance emanated from some of the most important urban centers of Spain such as Burgos, Salamanca, and Valladolid, veritable foci of Renaissance artistic activity in Spain. In Salamanca, the New Cathedral and various buildings for the famous University of Salamanca (also an important center of Plateresque architecture), and the *Cathedral* and the *Palacio de las Dueñas* in Valladolid, are just two among many significant representatives of Castilian Renaissance. The southern region of Andalucía, which through Sevilla's port had become the hub of transportation and commercial activity with the Americas, was another important center of Renaissance architecture, thanks to the work of some of the most talented Spanish architects of the time such as Pedro de Machuca, Enrique Egas, Diego de Siloé, and their disciples. The **Cathedral of Jaén**, designed by Andrés de Vandelvira (disciple of Siloé), is considered—along with those of Granada (designed by Egas and Siloé, c. 1520s) and Córdoba (conceived by Hernán Ruiz, 1523–1650)—to be one of the three great Renaissance cathedrals of Andalucía. The building's harmonic proportions, unusual east end, and spacious interior covered by an innovative vaulting system are clear manifestation of the creative audacity of Vandelvira.

There are many other relevant Renaissance buildings throughout Spain, especially in the regions that were more prosperous at that time; however, the building that epitomizes Spanish Renaissance architecture is the **Monastery of El Escorial**, an imposing and splendid complex commissioned by King Felipe II (son of Carlos V) and designed by Juan Bautista de Toledo and Juan de Herrera, two of the most important architects in the history of the country's architecture. The Escorial is not only a representative icon of Spain's architecture conceived and built at a high point of the country's history, but it is also one of the most important buildings of Europe's sixteenth-century High Renaissance architecture. The massive austerity and sobriety of the building complex that housed the King's Royal Palace, a Royal Pantheon, a college, a major church, and a *Hieronymite* monastery (a monastic order favored by his father, Carlos V) had enduring influence in Spain's architecture until the eighteenth century. Moreover, thanks to Felipe II's humanistic convictions and generous patronage El Escorial was profusely enriched with a wonderful collection of paintings made by some of the most important artists of the time—Titian, Ribera, Tibaldi—as well as with one of the most important libraries; in fact, the library of El Escorial is one of the most interesting spaces of the large building complex.

The crisis provoked by Luther's Reformation was confronted with a full-scale reaction from the Catholic Church known as the *Counter-Reform* in which the arts—especially painting, sculpture, and architecture—had an important role of communication and propaganda. *Baroque* art and architecture are the aesthetic and spatial expression of the Counter-Reform; not surprisingly, the artistic avant-garde was based in Italy, especially in Rome, where architects such as Maderno, Bernini, and Borromini produced brilliant works. However, Baroque was not limited to Rome and soon expanded throughout Italy—for example, in the work of Guarino Guarini in Turin—and the rest of Europe, especially in the countries that, allied with Rome, actively supported the Counter-Reform, even if eventually the unprecedented theatrical plasticity of Baroque space reached non-Catholic countries. The construction of churches and urban spaces were a priority of the architectural *programme* of the Counter-Reform.

The seventeenth century was a period of high building activity throughout Spain; Italian Baroque had a strong influence, even if the spatial plasticity and theatricality was, at least initially, substantially softened by the lasting influence of Herrera's austere architecture. During the reign of Felipe II, Spain was one of the dominant European powers; however, the vast kingdom where "the sun never set" did not have an officially designated capital and its royal court remained itinerant. Several Castilian cities—Toledo, Vaaladolid, Burgos—had claims to become the official royal capital of the kingdom. Yet in 1561, Felipe II designated Madrid, a rather underdeveloped city, as the official capital; the city then underwent an immediate and ambitious process of urban development and was soon equipped with palaces, churches, facilities, and public spaces appropriate to the caliber and reputation of the kingdom. The **Plaza Mayor of Madrid**, originally envisioned by Felipe II's architect Juan de Herrera and built by Juan Gómez de Mora (later restored by Juan de Villanueva), is one of the most important urban spaces created in that period, which also became a paradigm emulated in numerous Spanish cities. Juan Gómez de Mora, who succeeded Juan de Herrera as royal architect, was also the architect of the Jesuit church of **La Clerecía**, a masterpiece of early Spanish Baroque architecture partially modeled after Vignola's Jesuit church of *Il Gesú* in Rome. Considering that it took more than one century and the participation of two additional architects to complete it, this single building can be seen as synthesis of the evolution of seventeenth-century Spanish Baroque architecture.

The 1600s were politically conflictive for Spain, especially in the foreign front; yet, it was also a period of cultural production known as the *Siglo de Oro* (the Golden Century), a fabulous period represented by an extraordinary generation of writers such as Miguel de Cervantes (author of the universally praised *Don Quixote*), Lope de Vega, Tirso de Molina, and Calderón de la Barca; and painters like El Greco, Esteban Murillo, and Diego Velázquez. The architectural production echoed this remarkable activity, but did not attain the same level of universal innovation reached in literature and painting. In fact, in the seventeenth and eighteenth centuries there was great building activity throughout Spain; from Andalucía to Catalonia and from Galicia to Levante the whole country is dotted with noteworthy exponents of Baroque architecture, from exuberant manifestations to more restrained versions inspired by the French Classicism that emanated from Versailles. This febrile activity also extended to the American colonies where there are numerous significant Baroque buildings (the *Jesuit College in Tepotzotlán*, Mexico; the *Cathedral of Potosí* in Bolivia; and the *Palace Torres Tagle* in Lima, Peru, are just a few fine examples). Both in the Americas and in Spain, this astounding production of buildings was partially financed by the unprecedented richness produced by the exploitation of gold and silver mines in the colonies, especially in Mexico and Peru, the centers of the developed native Aztec and Inca civilizations.

In the eighteenth century Baroque architecture entered into a late phase, also known as *Rococo*, which is characterized by an exuberant plasticity, a multitude of curvilinear elements, and overwhelming decorative motifs. In Spain this period corresponded with the emergence of *Churrigueresque* architecture, a uniquely Spanish derivation of European late Baroque, typified by a lively and elaborated surface decoration of sculptural effects. The **Plaza Mayor of Salamanca**, designed by Alberto Churriguera, is a perfect exponent of Churrigueresque architecture in Castilla, while the *Obradoiro façade* of the **Cathedral of Santiago de Compostela**, designed by Fernando Casas y Novoa, is an excellent example of Churrigueresque in Galicia. In spite of the high productivity, Spanish Baroque remained a local and rather provincial phenomenon that, as renowned Baroque historian Christian Norberg-Schulz noted, had a rather negligible impact on the evolution of the Baroque conception of architectural space (Norberg-Schulz 1985, 174).

Neoclassical and Nineteenth-Century Architecture

The second half of the eighteenth century was a period of radical social, cultural, and political transformations. The Industrial Revolution, the French Revolution, and new developments in the area of knowledge—such as Diderot's *Encyclopedia*—were the catalysts for the collapse of an antiquated sociopolitical order that resisted the changes needed to meet the demands of the increasing urban populations. In architecture, a reaction to the extravagances and exuberance of the late Baroque as representative of the *Ancient Regime* (the old order) began to emerge in the form of a return to the basic principles of classical art, just as the Renaissance had reacted to the floridness of Flamboyant Gothic three centuries earlier. The new movement, known as *Neoclassicism*, appeared almost simultaneously across Europe, especially in France, Germany, Austria, and Russia.

The incipient emergence of a new epoch was also marked by the creation of new institutions and, as their architectural correlates, new building types and materials. The museum, the scientific academy, the theater, the assembly hall, and the house, and later the factory and the train station, slowly but assuredly began to replace the aristocratic palace and the church as the dominant architectural manifestations. Thus, the language of Neoclassical architecture was rather universally adopted for the emerging institutions of the time.

The eighteenth century marked the beginning of a long period of decline for Spain in which military defeats, an exhausting financial situation, the Napoleonic invasion and occupation, and the emancipation of numerous American colonies projected the once powerful European nation into a secondary position in Europe. Nevertheless, while limited by the weakening sit-

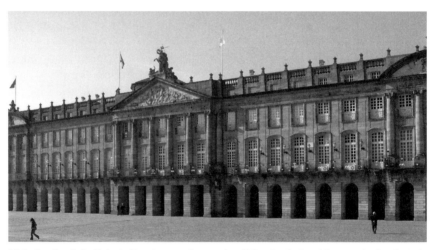

Main façade of the Palacio Raxoi, a good example of Neoclassical architecture in Santiago de Compostela.

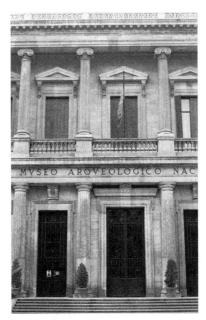

Detail of the main entrance to Madrid's Archeological Museum, a typical example of the institutional architectural language of Neoclassicim.

uation, culturally and artistically, Spain remained strongly related—even if sometimes dependent—to the evolution of arts, science, and culture in Europe. By the late eighteenth century the arts and architecture of Spain began to absorb the new Neoclassical postulates promoted, especially, in France and Germany.

Juan de Villanueva is Spain's most important Neoclassical architect. His masterpiece is the **Museo del Prado** (originally conceived as the Academy of Natural History), but he is also the creator of numerous other brilliant buildings such as the Astronomical Observatory of Madrid, the restoration of the **Plaza Mayor of Madrid**, and the *Casita del Príncipe del Pardo*, also in Madrid. His vast knowledge and sober understanding of the language of classical architecture was remarkable, elevating him to a high position among the most important representatives of Europe's Neoclassicism. Silvestre Pérez, who designed the *Hospital de Achurri* in Bilbao, and Josep Mas i Vila, author of the new façade of Barcelona's City Hall, are but two other important architects of the Neoclassicist period in Spain.

The radical transformations anticipated at the end of the eighteenth century finally detonated in the nineteenth century. Political power had shifted from the once powerful aristocracy to the emerging commercial and industrial bourgeoisie, while the development of industry—inevitably located in or near urban centers—provoked the rapid and uncontrolled growth of cities. Not surprisingly, the most illuminated thinkers of the time directed their attention to the new problems and challenges posed by this radical transformation. Throughout Europe, new ideas and theories related to the evolution of the city began to translate into projects for ideal cities or extension of existing ones. Ildefons Cerdá's *Eixample* of Barcelona (the extension of the city beyond the old medieval center) that began to be implemented in 1851, and the Linear City plan of Arturo Soria y Mata (1880s) are two important Spanish contributions to the growing discipline of urbanism.

Neoclassicism had been instrumental in restoring the classical language of architecture after the vagaries and extravagant grammar of the late Baroque. The impulse given to the proper study of classical language was partially a consequence of the development of archeological studies that brought to the surface an unprecedented volume of knowledge about the monuments of ancient architecture, particularly from Greece. In the mid-nineteenth century, the methodological study of monuments from the past extended to all historical periods. Consequently, the second part of the century witnessed a proliferation of artistic trends that—influenced by the ideas of thinkers from the *Enlightment*, *Romanticism*, and the *Arts and Crafts Movement*—presented a reaction against the language of Neoclassicism that tried to reconcile art (and of course architecture) with the radical social, political, and cultural changes of the times. The *Revivalism* of historical styles quickly spread throughout Europe; buildings began to be designed in a wide variety of "neo" styles often in relationship to their function. For example, many churches were built in "neo-Gothic" style. In Spain, "neo-Gothic," "neo-Mudéjar," and the combination of elements from various styles known as *Eclecticism* became widely accepted and often used in rather indiscriminate fashion.

Neo-Mudéjar buildings for religious, institutional, educational, and entertainment purposes abound throughout Spain; the old *Plaza de Toros* of Madrid (now demolished) and the *Aguirre Schools*, both designed by Emilio Rodríguez Ayuso, and the *Casa Vicens*—one of Gaudí's early works—are three important examples of neo-Mudéjar architecture. Neo-Gothic was particularly important in Catalonia where it became inevitably associated with a resurging national sentiment. The **Palace of Sobrellano**, located in Cantabria but designed by Catalan architect Joan Martorell i Montells for a Barcelonan client, is a significant example of neo-Gothic architecture in Spain, a building that also serves as a link between the Revivalist architecture of late nineteenth century and the turn of the century outbreak of *Modernismo* in Catalonia and its projection to other parts of Spain.

Modernismo and the Work of Antoni Gaudí

The nineteenth century proved to be a difficult political and social period for Spain; following the Napoleonic occupation and the subsequent War of

Independence the country became immersed in an internal conflict—the Carlist Wars—that for over three long decades involved two opposed groups supporting different heirs to the crown. Further, the penetration of liberal ideas and the surging of numerous political groups that advocated the institution of a constitutional system threatened the stability of the monarchy. The role of the military and its alliance with one or another political group often determined the immediate political destiny of the country and anticipated the military interventionism that marked Spain's twentieth-century history. After a short and unsuccessful Republican experiment, the monarchy was restored in 1875, leading to a period of almost fifty years of relative political stability. The more stable political situation allowed economic expansion and an auspicious prosperity; the construction of the railroad and industrial development, especially in the northern regions of the Basque Country and Catalonia (the two that historically had more direct contact with the rest of Europe), promoted a promising industrial and mercantile activity. In fact, one of the conflictive issues of the late nineteenth century was the claim for more economic and political autonomy of the more prosperous regions, which was systematically rejected by the central government.

In Catalonia, where the textile and naval industries were flourishing, the new and powerful industrial *bourgeoisie*, with the support of local artists and intellectuals, was heavily involved in advancing a Catalanist project known as the *Renaixença*. Catalonia's Modernismo is the artistic correlate of the Renaixença; architecturally as well as aesthetically, it is strongly related to contemporaneous movements in other European countries such as *Art Nouveau* in France and Belgium, *Jugendstil* in Germany and the *Secession Viennese* in Austria, to name only three of the most important. These movements, which emerged almost simultaneously toward the end of the nineteenth and the beginning of the twentieth centuries, shared a new repertoire of figurative and formal elements derived from recently developed techniques and materials (glass, wrought iron, industrial materials) as well as the renewal of building typologies—notably the apartment building. More importantly, they were the seed of a modern sensibility that anticipated the radical breakthrough of modern architecture in the second and third decades of the twentieth century.

The language of Modernismo, while related to peer European movements, had a unique evolution, profoundly imbued with Gothic Revivalism as a symbolic return to the glorious origins of Catalonia as a "nation." There were two intrinsically related parallel lines of exploration within Modernismo; one, more rational, was led by Lluís Domènech i Montaner and Josep Puig i Cadalfach; the other—more personal and expressive—was best represented by the work of Antoni Gaudí. The **Palau de la Música Catalana** is regarded as one of Domènech i Montaner's most important works as well as an emblem of the impulse given to the arts during the Renaixença. The **Casa Terradas**, a residential building complex located in Barcelona's then quickly developing Eixample is the most emblematic work of Puig i

Cadalfach and a perfect example of the neo-Gothicism that had permeated the language of Modernismo.

Undoubtedly, Antoni Gaudí is the salient figure of Barcelona's Modernismo, a remarkable and universally recognized architect whose extremely original work has become a permanent symbol of Barcelona's history and architectural legacy. As William Curtis noted, "the richness of Gaudí's art lies in the reconciliation of the fantastic and the practical, the subjective and scientific, the spiritual and the material. His forms were never arbitrary, but rooted in structural principles and in an elaborate private world of social and emblematic meanings" (Curtis 1996, 60). In effect, contrary to what it is usually believed, Gaudí was not a solitary, eccentric genius but a highly talented artist who faithfully represented the ideological conservative and nationalistic agenda of Catalonia's Renaixença; the "eccentricity" of his architecture should be then understood as an integral part of the sociopolitical and religious aspirations and objectives of Barcelona's powerful industrial and merchant class. In fact, the patronage of Eusebio Güell, one of the most prosperous and influential businessmen of Barcelona and—like Gaudí himself—key member of the Renaixença, was fundamental for the development and projection of Gaudí's architecture. The **Park Güell** is the most ambitious project undertaken by Güell and Gaudí; Güell's own *Palau Güell* in Barcelona and the *Colonia Güell*, a textile workers' community created by Güell, was planned by Gaudí, and where the architect had begun to build a church, are two other architectural testimonies to the fruitful collaboration between Eusebio Güell as patron and Antoni Gaudí as architect. While Güell was his most conspicuous patron, Gaudí also made buildings for many other members of Barcelona's elite such as the *Casa Batlló* and **Casa Milá**, two multifamily residential buildings located in the Eixample of Barcelona. One of

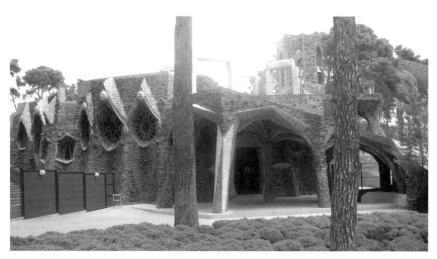

Exterior of Gaudí's Cripta Güell at Colonia Güell in Santa Coloma, Barcelona.

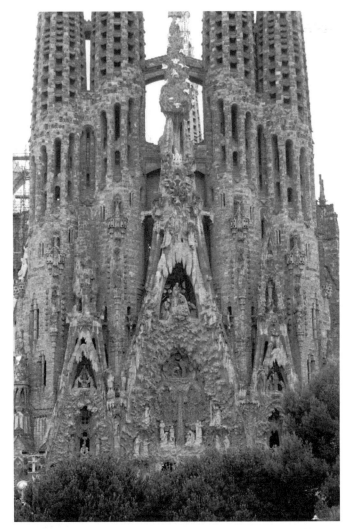

Detail of the façade of Sagrada Familia, one of Gaudí's most emblematic buildings.

his last and most famous works, the church of *Sagrada Familia*—under construction at his death and still unfinished today—is an emblem of the architect's work as well as a social and cultural symbol of Barcelona.

Gaudí's work was extremely influential for his disciples and followers; one of them, Josep María Jujol, is considered as the last representative of Modernismo. The Apartment Building on Barcelona's centric Diagonal Avenue and **Vistabella's Church of the Sacred Heart** are two among many remarkable buildings designed by Jujol in which, while the legacy of Gaudí's work is evident, the architect deployed his highly personal style. The architecture of Modernismo projected beyond Catalonia (there are interesting examples in Teruel, Comillas, and other cities); however, it was fundamentally a Catalan movement, the architectural and aesthetic expression of the nationalistic agenda of Barcelona's elite. Eventually, when the masters disappeared and the aspirations of the Catalan Renaixença got buried under Spain's internal conflicts and new centralist project incarnated by Primo de Rivera, the movement faded, leaving behind a wonderful artistic legacy, testimony of one of the most vibrant moments in the architectural history of Barcelona in particular, and Spain in general.

Modern Architecture in Spain

The social, political, cultural, technological, and aesthetic revolutions of the nineteenth century had provoked the emergence of various experimental movements that attempted to understand and respond to the radically changing situation; however, rather than engendering a uniform response, the multitude of explorations led to a certain, yet positive and stimulating, confusion. The outbreak of World War I exacerbated the confusing state of affairs; at the end of the war, the political map of central Europe changed, the economy was devastated, the population disillusioned, and cities had been severely damaged. The development of industry and the machine provided a much needed stimulus for quick recovery, but cities began to grow rapidly without being prepared to absorb the massive migration of the rural population seeking employment in the industrialized urban centers. The situation was ripe for the emergence of a new "total order"—social, political, cultural, and aesthetic—a modern world for the new machine age.

In the final years of the nineteenth century Spain was immersed in a difficult political situation and the restored monarchy confronted challenging situations on numerous fronts. The intellectuals of the Generation of '98 (such as Joaquín Costa and Miguel de Unamumo) called for the regeneration of the political system and the insitition of modern democratic Spain; workers' strikes and anarchy invaded the streets of some industrialized centers (notably Barcelona) and were severely repressed, while new claims for regional autonomy abounded in Catalonia and the Basque Country. In this context, with traditionalists and conservatives fearing anarchy and the disintegration of Spain, General Primo de Rivera staged a coup d'état and seized power in 1923, with the support of conservative classes and the military, without fully eliminating the monarchic system. A period of economic expansion fueled by exports helped to consolidate the dictatorship of Primo de Rivera; however, by 1929 a recession led to general discontent, and the opposition of students, workers, intellectuals, and the threat of Catalonia's secession and of civil war triggered the end of Primo de Rivera's regime. An alliance of representatives from an ample political and regional spectrum agreed to overthrow the monarchy; King Alfonso XIII left Spain in 1931 and the Second Republic was instituted.

The emerging generation of European architects believed that architecture and urbanism were called to have a vital role in the ensuing social transformations; further, they firmly believed that the human condition could be improved through architecture. The avant-garde artistic explorations—Cubism, Futurism, Dutch neo-plasticism—provided visual and conceptual materials for the emergence of a modern architectural language. Almost spontaneously and simultaneously a new uniform architectural vocabulary began to surface across Europe. The new movement was called *International Style*, a term coined after an exhibition organized in New York by Henry Russell-Hitchcock and Philip Johnson that presented European and American architects whose work exhibited a high degree of uniformity. As Christian Norberg-Schulz succinctly explained, "the 'modern' buildings of the period are distinguished by a few characteristic properties: they are usually derived from simple sterometric shapes; they appear as unitary volumes wrapped up in a thin, weightless skin of glass and plaster; and they show a puritan lack of material texture and articulating detail" (Norberg-Schulz 1980, 186). **The German Pavilion** (commonly known as the Barcelona Pavilion), designed by German architect Mies van der Rohe for Barcelona's World Fair of 1929, is a masterpiece of the period between the two world wars and one of the canonic works of twentieth-century architecture, a perfect synthesis of the new spatial postulates of modern architecture. However, while located in Spain, the German Pavilion is not representative of Spanish architecture of the period; rather, it represents the incipient internationalization of architecture at the beginning of the twentieth century.

In spite of the conservatism and traditionalism of Spanish architecture in that period, modern architectural ideas penetrated Spain through the work of notable architects such as Secundino Suazo and Fernando Mercadal who, in the 1920s, produced buildings with evident signs of the new architectural sprit. Suazo's Central Post Office Building in Bilbao (1926) and Mercadal's *Rincón de Goya*'s library in Zaragoza (1927) are two significant buildings of the 1920s. Also important are the Capitol Building (Madrid 1931) designed by Eced and Feduchi, and the work of Luis Gutierrez Soto and Rafael Bergamín. However, the most representative building of the International Style in Spain (in fact, the only one designed by Spanish architects that was included in New York's exhibition) is the **Club Náutico** of San Sebastián designed by Aizpurúa and Labayén, a building that exhibits the typical features of early modern architecture.

Stimulated by the institution of the Second Republic, young Josep Lluís Sert returned to Barcelona after collaborating with Le Corbusier in Paris for many years and quickly became one of the leading masters of Spain's modern architecture. In 1928 he had participated in the foundation of the CIAM (International Congress of Modern Architecture). Briefly stated, the CIAM sought to establish common architectural and urbanistic principles and a definition of the disciplines' principal tasks; social housing and a renewal of urban planning principles were at the center of its preoccupations. In Spain, Sert was co-founder of the *GATCPAC*, Catalonia's section of the GATEPAC, a group of Spanish architects, artists, and technicians who endorsed CIAM's general postulates. *Casa Bloc*, a workers' housing development in Barcelona (1931–1936) designed by Sert, Subirana, Torres, and the GATCPAC is the most representative building of CIAM's ideas in Spain. Sert's most interesting building, also designed in collaboration with Joan Subirana, Josep Torres, and the GATCPAC, is Barcelona's **Dispensario Antituberculoso**, a masterpiece of rationalist twentieth-century architecture. Sixto Illescas and German Rodriguez Arias are two other important representatives of Barcelona's Modern Architecture, while the works of Luis Soto and Rafael Bergamín and Agustin Aguirre stand out in Madrid.

The new possibilities offered by new building materials and techniques—reinforced concrete, steel, and glass—were an intrinsic part of the evolution of twentieth-century architecture. These were often advanced by engineers who, as building designers, incurred in a field traditionally reserved to architects; in fact, the role of engineering and the influence of engineers—Eiffel and Maillard, for example—had a tremendous influence in the development of modern architecture. Eduardo Torroja is considered a pioneer of reinforced concrete structures applied to architecture. His splendid and audacious structure for **La Zarzuela Racetrack Grandstand**, designed in collaboration with Carlos Arniches and Martin Domínguez, is a classic example of the aesthetic and new formal possibilities offered by new materials and techniques.

The outbreak of the Spanish Civil War (1936–1939) and the victory of the more conservative party led by Francisco Franco brought the Second Republic to an end; the new political situation suddenly interrupted the promising evolution of modern architecture in Spain because Franco's regime favored more traditional and conservative architecture. Consequently, many modern Spanish architects such as Sert, Antonio Bonet, and Felix Candela—to name only a few—continued their architectural careers exiled in the United States, Argentina, and Mexico, respectively, where they achieved importance and recognition. The return to a regressive architecture during Franco's regime is symbolized by Luis Gutierrez Soto's *Ministerio del Aire* in Madrid, a building with obvious resemblance to El Escorial that was taken as the emblem of a genuine Spanish architecture. Nevertheless, when the conditions permitted it, some architects continued developing an architecture rooted in modern principles; in this regard, the work of Miguel Fisac and Francisco Cabrero, as well as other buildings of Gutierrez Soto of the 1940s deserve special consideration.

In the late 1940s and 1950s, prompted by a recovering economy that stimulated construction, modern architecture was revived in Spain, particularly in Barcelona and Madrid. In 1952, a group of architects based in Barcelona founded the *Grup R*—an association of architects who organized lectures and other events with the participation of renowned international architects and critics such as Alvar Aalto, Gio Ponti, and Nikolaus Pevsner; these activities successfully reintroduced the debate and discourse of modern architecture in Spain. Moragas' **Hotel Park**, Josep A. Coderch's **La Marina Apartment Building** (among many of his remarkable buildings), and Xavier Busquets' **COAC Headquarters**, all of them in Barcelona, are—along with the work of other contemporaries such as Josep María Sostres, Mas Vidal, and Bassó and Gili—the built testimony to the reintroduction of an up-to-date modern architectural discourse in Catalonia. A similar reaction to the anti-modernism of the regime's official architecture began to take place in the work of Madrid-based architects, notably Alejandro de la Sota, Antonio Fernández Alba, and Francisco Saenz de Oíza. Curiously, de la Sota's reaction was often manifested in official buildings; the **Civil Government Building** in Tarragona and León's Central Post Office eloquently demonstrate it; together with the Gymnasium for the Maravillas School in Madrid, they constitute a triad of masterworks designed by the Galician architect. The *Convent of El Rollo* (1958–1962), near Salamanca, is one of the most interesting works of the period and the masterpiece of Fernandez Alba. A group of architects, artists, and critics affiliated to the architectural periodical entitled *Nueva Forma* was Madrid's correlate to Barcelona's Grup R; this group promoted a modern organic architecture inspired by the work of Frank Lloyd Wright and the critical writings of Bruno Zevi. Saenz de Oíza's **Torres Blancas Apartment Building** in Madrid became the emblem of *Nueva Forma*'s postulates, the masterpiece of Spanish organic modernism.

The ambitious programme of social and cultural renewal through architecture and urbanism postulated by the masters of modern architecture at the beginning of the twentieth century did not materialize except in some isolated and specific cases. In the second half of the century, the dogmatism of modern architecture's principles faced the first signs of strong opposition; in many cases criticism came from within, that is, from young architects who had been educated as "modern architects." One of the most interesting critiques of modern architecture originated in Italy, where architects, critics, and artists of the so-called *Neorealist* movement promoted a revision of the precepts and tenets of modern architecture. The **Pallars Housing Complex** in Barcelona—designed by Oriol Bohigas and Josep Martorell, the younger founding members of Barcelona's Grup R—is an excellent example of the penetration of Italian Neorealist ideas in Spain and was one of the first-built manifestations of the critique of modern architecture. Slowly but persistently the reaction against modern architecture proliferated across Europe and America. The CIAM, considered as the official organ that represented the ideas of the *Modern Movement* was dissolved in 1953; later, in the mid-1960s, Aldo Rossi and Robert Venturi, from Italy and the United States, respectively, published seminal books that, from two different vantage points, provided alternatives to the modern dogma. The new ideas propagated rapidly and were soon echoed by architects, writers, and critics worldwide. One of the most interesting and radical interpretations of the 1970s critique of the doctrines of modern architecture, and especially its conception of low-cost housing in Spain, was Ricardo Bofill's **Walden-7 Apartment Building**, located in an industrial suburb of Barcelona.

The new situation of architectural discourse comprised a wide range of formal, theoretical, pragmatic, and conceptual explorations. Virtually all variants of continuity of the modern language and *Postmodern* experimentations were represented in Spain's architecture of the 1970s through the work of the old national masters—for example, Saenz de Oíza—and professionals from emerging generations such as Luis Peña Ganchegui, Rafael Moneo, Tusquets and Clotet, and many others. Obviously well informed of the most recent aspects of the international debate, their work reflected a subtle and intelligent understanding of the specific conditions of Spain's architectural evolution and anticipated the veritable explosion of production—both built and written—of subsequent decades. The work of the masters who had effectively reinstated modern architecture in Spain—de la Sota, Coderch, Sostres, Saenz de Oíza—had had a decisive influence on the generation that began to develop their work in the late 1970s and 1980s. In the last years of Franco's regime, Spain's modern architecture had come to age and was ready to jump to the forefront of the international scene.

Contemporary Architecture (since 1975)

Francisco Franco died in 1975 and his long authoritarian regime ended; more than four decades after the departure of King Alfonso XIII, a new king—Juan Carlos I—was at the head of the State. The king had a decisive role in halting the attempts to establish the continuity of Franco's regime, and guaranteed the institution of a constitutional monarchy in Spain. After long decades of ostracism, Spain entered into a rather peaceful transition to democracy thanks to an ample agreement—known as the *Pacto de la Moncloa*—made by the ensemble of the country's political forces. Whereas numerous challenges lay ahead, the convincing return to a democratic system assured the full reinsertion of Spain in Europe and marked the beginning of an auspicious period of political and economic prosperity. However, the long years of isolation suffered by Spain during the dictatorship had left it ill equipped in comparison to its more developed European peers—France, England, Germany, and Italy.

In the 1980s, through initiatives launched by the central government and the newly created autonomic regions, Spain entered into a phase of febrile and ambitious building activity to construct a modern social structure and a rich architectural landscape. This activity was fundamentally oriented to create cultural facilities (museums, theaters, art centers); health centers and educational buildings; infrastructure facilities (modern railroads, highways, bridges, new train stations, and airports); regional and municipal sports facilities (stadiums, swimming pools, sports centers); social housing; and an astonishing number of public spaces (parks, plazas). The restoration and rehabilitation of the country's vast built historical heritage also occupied an important place in this ambitious process of constructing a contemporary social and urban landscape. As a renowned historian and critic of contemporary Spanish architecture stated, the 1980s was an "unusually energetic period in which several tenets of modern architecture have extended into new areas in response to massive social changes" (Curtis 1992, 6).

The task of designing the buildings for contemporary Spain was, expectedly, undertaken by or commissioned to Spanish architects who had been trained by modern masters. However, those responsible for orchestrating the construction of this new social space had the vision of promoting the participation of renowned international architects such as Tadao Ando, Gae Aulenti, Peter Eisenman, Norman Foster, Frank Gehry, John Hejduk, Herzog and de Meuron, Arata Isozaki, Jean Nouvel, Alvaro Siza, and many others, all of whom contributed raising Spain's architecture to a prominent position in contemporary architectural production. It is no coincidence that the most important critics of contemporary architecture turned their attention to Spain as one of the world's most interesting centers of architectural activity.

The **Plaza del Tenis and Peine del Viento**, an architectural, landscaping, and sculptural ensemble designed in collaboration between Luis Peña Ganchegui and the sculptor Eduardo Chillida, can be considered as conceptually bridging the pluralism of the 1970s and the evocative and abstract Spanish architecture of the final quarter of the twentieth century. Throughout this period, the work of Rafael Moneo is particularly relevant, especially (but not limited to) for the construction of buildings for culture and infrastructure. From one of his early masterpieces, the **National Museum of Roman Art** in Mérida, a building credited as having symbolically inaugurated this fruitful architectural period, to the more recently completed **Kursaal Auditorium and Congress Center** in San Sebastián, and key buildings such as *Logroño's City Hall*, *Atocha's Train Station*, and the extension to the **Museo del Prado** (currently in progress), Moneo's work synthesizes Spain's contemporary architecture.

Catalonia, and particularly Barcelona, had a significant participation in this process largely thanks to the vision and leadership of Oriol Bohigas who, from an administrative governmental role, made important decisions that had tremendous impact on the region's and the city's development. The **Plaça dels Països Catalans**, designed by Piñón and Viaplana, is representative of the initial success of Bohigas' indefatigable efforts to modernize Barcelona's social, architectural, and urban landscape. Bohigas also had a fundamental role in the development of the facilities for Barcelona's 1992 Summer Olympics games for which he involved internationally renowned architects (Gehry, Isozaki, Siza, SOM); well-established offices based in Barcelona (for example, Bach and Mora, Martinez Lapeña and Torres, Piñón and Viaplana, MBM); and young, emerging architects such as Eduard Bru, Miralles and Pinòs, and Ruisánchez and Vendrell, to name a few. Some of them were already involved in the final design phase or construction of important buildings of the period; Martinez Lapeña and Torres were rehabilitating and developing Palma de Majorca's **Ronda Promenade and Bastions**, and Miralles and Pinòs were working in the **New Cemetery-Park of Igualada**, two widely celebrated architectural and landscaping complexes completed in the early 1990s.

The year 1992 marked a peak of activity. Along with the celebration of the Olympic Games in Barcelona, Sevilla organized a World Fair known as *Sevilla Expo '92*, two events with which Spain celebrated the 500th anniversary of the country's reunification under the Catholic Kings and Columbus' discovery of America. Sevilla's Expo '92 became a showcase of international architecture in which Guillermo Vázquez Consuegra's **Navigation Pavilion** shone as the Expo's emblem. Throughout Spain, the building activity was immense; in the early 1990s virtually all cities were either developing plans or building major facilities; in Salamanca, the **Conference and Exhibition Hall** designed by Juan Navarro Baldeweg was completed in 1992; one year later Siza's **Galician Center of Galician Contemporary Art** in Santiago de Compostela was inaugurated; in Madrid, Cruz and Ortiz completed the region's **Sports Center and Track and Field Stadium** in 1994; and, construction of the **Guggenheim Museum** designed by American architect Frank Gehry—universally recognized as a masterpiece of late-twentieth-century architecture—had begun in Bilbao, while Valencia had started planning the development of what eventually became the **City of Arts and Sciences** designed by the city's native and internationally renowned architect Santiago Calatrava.

The febrile and unprecedented activity of building new facilities was accompanied by the ambitious preservation, restoration, and rehabilitation of the country's architectural heritage. Barcelona reconstructed **The German Pavilion** (dismantled in 1930) in exactly the same place of its original location. Martínez Lapeña and Torres rehabilitated the Romanesque monastery of *Sant Pere de Rodes*; Rafael Moneo adapted the nineteenth-century *Palacio de Villahermosa* to house the art collection of the *Museo Thyssen-Bornemisza*; López Cotelo and Puente converted **La Casa de las Conchas** into a public library; in Tarragona, Josep Llinàs rehabilitated works of Josep María Jujol and Alejandro de la Sota's **Civil Government Building**; and Tusquets restored and enlarged Barcelona's **Palau de la Musica Catalana**. These are, in fact, only a few relevant examples of this fantastic and unmatched initiative to preserve, recuperate, and modernize the country's monumental architectural legacy.

The rise of Spain's architecture was paralleled by the increasing reputation of its educational institutions and specialized journals, fundamental vehicles for the formation of younger generations. *El Croquis, Quaderns,*

Arquitectura Viva, and many other architectural periodicals contributed to elevating and promoting the knowledge, debate, and discourse of contemporary architecture; they deservedly became highly regarded publications worldwide. Academic institutions, especially in Madrid and Barcelona, became forums of active learning where the most important Spanish and international architects and critics educate the future generations of architects. The prestige of Spain's architecture also projected abroad, where numerous representatives of the country's contemporary architecture were called upon to design important buildings; Moneo's Cathedral of Our Lady of Los Angeles, in Los Angeles (United States); Miralles and Tagliabue's Scottish Parliament, in Edinburgh (Scotland); and Zaera and Moussavi's Yokohama Passenger Terminal (Japan) are just three among many.

At the turn of the millennium Spain had established a solid position of leadership in the international architectural scene. While the generation of "masters" of the period—Moneo, Viaplana, Torres—continues to have a relevant and active role in Spain's architectural production, the younger generations to whose development they contributed are taking the relay with major projects. Abalos and Herreros, Josep Llinàs, Mansilla plus Tuñón, Miralles and Tagliabue, Jose Luis Mateo, Piagem and Vialta, and Torres and Nadal are only some of a long list of architects and offices of this generational renewal who have already completed major works. The Archeological Museum of Zamora (1996) and the **Auditorium of León** are two brilliant buildings developed by the office of Mansilla plus Tuñón; Barcelona's **Diagonal Mar Parc** is one of

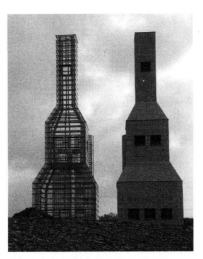

Towers designed for John Hejduk for another building that have been built as a posthumous homage to him as a symbolic gate to Peter Eisenman's Ciudad de la Cultura in Santiago de Compostela.

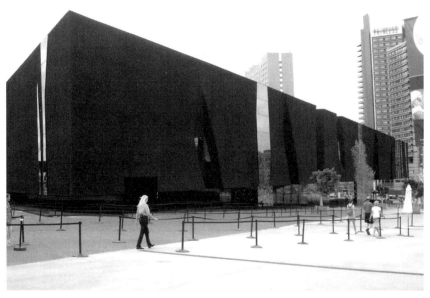

Partial exterior view of Herzog and de Meuron's building for the Barcelona Forum.

the most recently completed projects of Miralles and Tagliabue; and finally, the **Valdemingómez Recycling Center** is the most important building complex produced by Abalos and Herreros to date. All of them continue to work on ever more complex and more important commissions, in Spain as well as abroad, assuring the continuity of Spain's remarkable architectural production of the last thirty years, in terms of both quantity and quality.

International stellar architects also continue to have an important role. In Santiago de Compostela, American architect Peter Eisenman is building a major cultural and research complex—*La Ciudad de la Cultura*—that includes an already completed posthumous homage to John Hejduk. In 2004, wishing to reenact the energy that the 1992 Olympic Games had generated, Barcelona organized Forum 2004, a major event for which many remarkable works were built, notably the Forum Building commissioned to the Swiss architects Herzog and de Meuron. At the dawn of the twenty-first century, the production of a significant, critical, and progressive architecture is well established in Spain, promising a future for a country that—despite some periods of ostracism—offers to the world a rich, evocative, and vibrant architectural patrimony.

Further Reading

Brown, Frank E. *Roman Architecture*. New York: George Brazillier Publishers, 1961.
Conant, Kenneth John. *Carolingian and Romanesque Architecture 800–1200*. 2nd ed. Middlesex: Penguin Books, 1978.

Curtis, William J. R. "A Patient Search: The Art and Architecture of Juan Navarro Baldeweg." *El Croquis* 54 (1992): 4–22.

Curtis, William J. R. *Modern Architecture Since 1900.* 3rd ed. London: Phaidon Press Limited, 1996.

Dodds, Jerrilynn D. *Architecture and Ideology in Early Medieval Spain.* University Park, PA; London: The Pennsylvania State University Press, 1989.

García de Cortázar, Fernando. *Historia de España: de Atapuerca al euro.* Barcelona: Planeta, 2002.

Lampérez y Romea, Vicente. *Historia de la Arquitectura Cristiana Española en la Edad Media.* Vols. 1 and 2. 1908. Reprint. Valladolid: Ambito ediciones, 1999.

Norberg-Schulz, Christian. *Late Baroque and Rococo Architecture.* Milan; New York: Electa and Rizzoli, 1985.

Norberg-Schulz, Christian. *Meaning in Western Architecture.* New York: Rizzoli, 1980.

Architecture
of Spain

AUDITORIUM CITY OF LEÓN, LEÓN, CASTILLA Y LEÓN

Style: Contemporary Architecture
Dates: 1996–2002
Architects: Luis Moreno Mansilla and Emilio Tuñón Alvarez

The Auditorio Ciudad de León, the new auditorium of the city of León, is among the more significant buildings recently completed by the Madrid-based practice of Luis Moreno Mansilla and Emilio Tuñón Alvarez, a young team of architects who had already built celebrated works of recent Spanish architecture such as the Provincial Museum in Zamora (1992–1996) and the Swimming Center in San Fernando de Henares (1994–1998). Rafael Moneo—perhaps the most important Spanish architect since 1975 and with whom both Mansilla and Tuñón collaborated between 1982 and 1992—has praised their work for their "desire to make architecture intelligible, immediate" (2G 2003, 6).

The Auditorio Ciudad de León was commissioned to Mansilla and Tuñón as a result of a competition held in 1994 for which their project was awarded the first place. The site is located on Avenida de los Reyes Leoneses near the intersection with Avenida de Suero de Quiñones, in an area located less than one mile from the city's historic center and that is undergoing an interesting process of transformation. In fact, at a very short distance from the Auditorio, Mansilla and Tuñón are also building a major new center of contemporary art—the MUSAC—for the autonomous community of Castilla y León. However, the salient characteristic of the Auditorium's site is the neighboring presence of the Hostal de San Marcos, considered one of the masterpieces of *Plateresque* architecture.

The program consisted of designing a high-profile contemporary auditorium hall, with all the usual needs of this type of facility (seating hall, stage, practice rooms, locker rooms for performing artists, and storage), a small administrative wing, and an exhibition area. As already demonstrated in their previous projects, Mansilla and Tuñón's scheme was the result of a careful evaluation of the complex requirements imposed by both program and site at the same time that they developed a logical system of construction in which

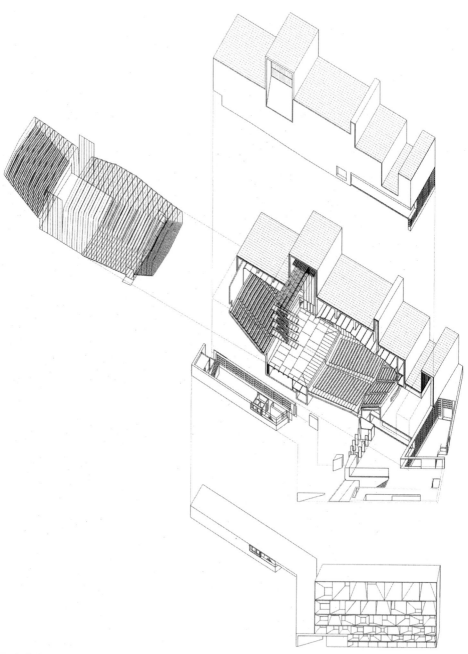

Exploded axonometric drawings of the Auditorio Ciudad de León showing the different volumetric components of the building complex. *Drawing courtesy of Mansilla + Tuñón Arquitectos.*

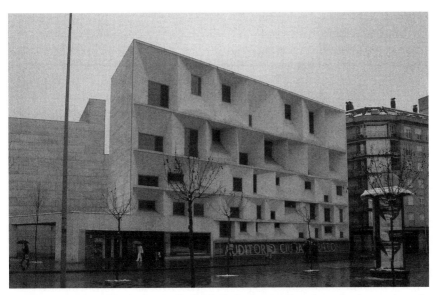

Partial exterior view of the Auditorio Ciudad de León showing the volume that houses the main entrance and exhibition wing.

materiality and the penetration of natural light have an important role in the production, perception, and definition of space. The distribution of the programmatic areas and the strategy of occupation of the site were intricately related; thus, the program was fragmented into three distinguishable but cleverly linked pieces of different size—auditorium, administration, and exhibition—each of which has a different role in the functional and volumetric organization of the building and its relationship to the site.

The largest and central piece is the virtually windowless volume of the auditorium, a marble-clad, predominantly rectangular box with protuberances that animate its silhouette; these protrusions respond to the auditorium's organization as a bifocal hall with a central stage and two opposed seating areas that can be used combined or separately; each of these two seating halls can be temporarily suppressed thanks to separating walls that disappear high up in the stage house. One of the seating areas, the largest, can further conceal a fragment of the seating through another similar device that disappears above the ceiling. Thus, the auditorium has a variable capacity to accommodate between 600 and 1,200 spectators. All these characteristics are expressed in the building's cut-out exterior lateral profile through the different height of the portions that correspond to the seating halls and the rectangular protuberances of the stage-house and the enclosure that conceals the separating device of the larger seating area.

The interior and exterior of the auditorium contrast sharply in form as well as in materials; the exterior appears as a rectangular box that contains an object with softer, gentler forms inside. The building's central lobby is an ample, profusely illuminated and beautifully detailed space that provides access to the interior of the contained object—the seating halls—and to the exhibition area. A courtyard, carved off the apparent exterior volume of the building, brings in southern natural light to the lobby's interior and its related adjacent spaces. This courtyard provides effective natural light to the partially underground level that accommodates the auditorium services, public restrooms, a small cafeteria, as well as practice and locker rooms for performing artists.

The administration wing occupies a subdued, one-story volume placed in front and detached from the large volume of the auditorium parallel to and set back from *Avenida de los Reyes Leoneses*; the space left between these two volumes configures an elongated open court that provides most of the natural light of the administration's interior. The third component and the most visible piece of the whole building is the tall volume of the exhibition area; placed at ninety degrees with respect to the extraordinary Plateresque façade of the Hostal San Marcos, which is located approximately 500 feet away, it seems to establish an architectural dialogue with it across space and time. The exhibition area is a predominantly vertical volume traversed by a ramp that links exhibition rooms placed in different levels. The volume's front façade was conceived as a deep three-dimensional screen—a giant, highly articulated window—that inevitably recalls the interior elevation of Le Corbusier's chapel of Notre Dame du Haut (Ronchamp 1955). However, it can be also read as a resonance box or an acoustic instrument which produces different sounds through a calculated distribution and placement of holes and planes within a carefully articulated box, a sort of architectural-musical instrument that generates "sounds" in the form of penetrating light and cast-shadows into the exhibition room's interiors. Reaching to a height that is similar to the protruding rectangular forms that conceal the auditorium's stage house, this tall volume provides a coherent scale to the whole as well as an urban institutional image to the whole building.

The building's structure is made in white concrete, which is exposed in various parts of the building's exterior, notably in the deep three-dimensional façade of the exhibition hall; however, the rest of the building's façades are clad with large slabs of Roman Travertine marble; most of the interior spaces are finished in white concrete, but the more public areas incorporate oak panels that provide a gentle warmth to the cleverly illuminated spaces; the seating hall interior is integrally finished in black wenge, a dark wood, provoking a sharp contrast with the predominantly white and light oak color tones of the profusely illuminated interior public spaces outside the seating hall.

The Auditorio Ciudad de León is inscribed in a series of projects designed by Mansilla and Tuñón—such as the Museum of Fine Arts in Castellón (completed in 2000), the already mentioned Center of Contemporary Art for Castilla y León (under construction) and San Fermín's Celebratory Unit (2001) that, along with the work of other Spanish architects of their generation, best represent and confirm the extraordinary high quality and creative-conceptual fertility of Spain's contemporary architecture.

Further Reading

"In Progress II." Special monographic issue, *El Croquis* 106, 107 (Madrid), 2001.
"Mansilla and Tuñón." Special monographic issue, *2G* 27 (Barcelona), 2003.

AUGUSTA EMÉRITA: PROVINCIAL ROMAN CAPITAL, MÉRIDA, EXTREMADURA

Style: Roman Architecture
Dates: Circa 25 B.C.E.–200 C.E.
Architects: Unknown; Roman and native Hispano-Roman builders

The city of Augusta Emérita (modern Mérida) was founded by the Roman Consul Marcus Agrippa in the year 25 B.C.E., as a result of the need to establish a capital for recently conquered and pacified territory. Augusta Emérita thus became the capital of *Lusitania*, the westernmost province of the Roman Empire. The significant number and splendor of buildings that were built soon after its foundation—an impressive and beautiful theater, an amphitheater for 15,000 seated spectators, a large circus two-thirds the size of Rome's own Circus Maximum, baths, temples, two remarkable bridges, and three aqueducts—testify to the importance once reached by Augusta Emérita within the large constellation of cities that conformed the Roman Empire. The city prospered and grew rapidly, becoming one of the largest of the Empire (in the fourth century it was the eleventh largest Roman city) with a wall-enclosed area of approximately 125 acres.

The bridge over the Guadiana River, which was one of the main entrances to the city (today open for pedestrian circulation only), is one of the finest examples of Roman engineering. Consisting of nearly sixty arches, its construction began in the Augustan era, that is, shortly after the city's foundation, and was completed by the year 20 C.E. Of the three aqueducts that provided water distribution to the city, ten arches of the aqueduct of Los Milagros remain standing, another fine example of the advanced engineering skills of Roman civilization. The so-called "Temple of Diana" is another well-preserved example of Augusta Emérita's glorious Roman past; however, its dedication to the Roman goddess Diana is questioned by most historians who consider that, most likely, it was part of an urban ensemble also composed of the *forum* and *basilica*; historians also agree that it may have been dedicated to an imperial cult. Its excellent state of preservation is attributed to having been enclosed within the walls of a house built in the sixteenth cen-

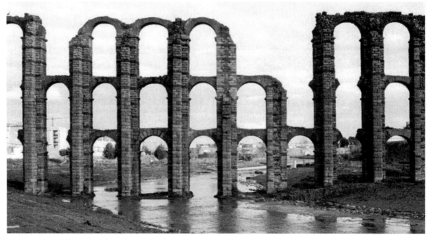

Fragment of the Roman Aqueduct known as *"Los Milagros."*

tury that in recent years was partially demolished to expose the temple's remains.

The amphitheater, built in the first decade B.C.E., the theater, and the circus (or hippodrome) constituted the entertainment district of the city. In fact, the uncharacteristic proximity of amphitheater and theater, as well as the location of the former within the city's enclosing walls, present a unique example in Roman urbanism. The amphitheater is rather well preserved, but only fragments of the circus's extensive stone seating remain. The monumental size of these two structures is living proof of Augusta Emérita's importance. Yet, and unquestionably, the most impressive Roman remain in Mérida is the theater, considered one of the finest, most elegant, and better-preserved theaters of the ancient Roman civilization.

As a building type, the Roman theater was derived and adapted from the *Greek theater*. Like its precedent, it consisted of a semicircle with tiers of seats, a slightly differentiated central space, and a stage. However, Romans implemented some interesting modifications to the original type: the central part of the semicircle, which in the Greek model was occupied by the *chorus* (or orchestra), was—in the Roman theater—reserved for seating of senators and other dignitaries; the stage, according to Vitruvius, was raised about five feet and brought closer to the audience (Vitruvius 1999, 69). This was achieved through transforming the central circular space of the Greek theater (the chorus) into a semicircular area; finally, while the Greek theater was typically carved out of a hillside, the Roman theater was, more often, partly hollowed out of a hill and partly constructed in tiers over arched galleries that, when needed, were also used as protection from inclement weather. As it evolved, the Roman theater—while remaining open to the sky—became an urban building, compact and largely introspected, somewhat isolated and independent from its surroundings, in strong contrast to the carved-out-of-the-hill, widely open and intimately related to the landscape conception of its Greek predecessor. Another unique characteristic of the Roman theater was the *scaenae frons*, the stage-front, which was a rather elaborated free-standing structure ready to accommodate a wide variety of stage designs. Vitruvius, the Roman theorist and historian of architecture, commented that the design of the scaenae frons had its own set of principles, and that temporary different stage-sets could be built on the stage depending on the type of performance to be performed: tragedy, comedy, or satire (Vitruvius 70).

The theater of Augusta Emérita is largely in accordance with this general description of the typical Roman theater. Its construction began during the reign of Augustus (23 B.C.E.–C.E. 14), that is, not long after the city's foundation; it was dedicated to Agrippa, founder of the city, and it was inaugurated in the years 16–15 B.C.E. The rows of seats (the *cavea*), which housed 6,000 seated spectators, were built-up, taking advantage of, and partially using, the hillside of Mount San Albín. As it was typical of all Roman theaters, the cavea was itself clearly separated into three parts: the lower portion was the "summa" and it was reserved for Roman dignitaries and important citizens; the central sector of tiers was called the "media," usually occupied by regular Roman citizens; finally, the upper level or "imma" was reserved for the very poor and slaves. A considerable portion of both the

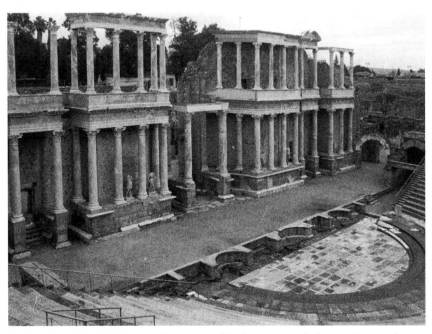

Scaenae-frons of Augusta Emérita's theater, one of the best conserved of ancient Roman theaters.

summa and the media seating tiers remains in good shape, but the upper rows, the imma, are very deteriorated.

Yet, the most impressive and architecturally dramatic component of this theater is the scaenae frons. Indeed, it remains in astonishing good shape, even if some of the original columns and sculptures have been replaced by replicas and the originals transported to the nearby **National Museum of Roman Art** built in the 1980s. Augusta Emérita's scaenae frons is a highly articulated and decorative apparatus that served as a backdrop for the wide variety of theatrical performances that usually took place in the *pulpitum*— the actual stage—of a Roman theater. It consisted of a monumental screen, approximately 230 feet wide by 33 feet deep, of two superimposed rows of marble columns, which, in style, are *Corinthian* below and *Composite* above. This structure housed a variety of service rooms and private chambers including a semicircular cavity at the center, likely the Imperial Hall, and two additional rooms for guests located to the right and left of the central cavity; these rooms also provided access to the rear side of the stage front, the *postcaenium*, where there was an open *peristyle* (a colonnaded room) that enclosed a garden ornamented with a central fountain, another element that contributed to make Augusta Emérita's theater complex one of the most refined, elegant, and impressive of the Roman Empire.

Further Reading

Arce, Javier, Ensoli, Serena, and La Rocca, Eugenio, eds. *Hispania Romana*. Milano: Electa Edizioni, 1997.

Brown, Frank E. *Roman Architecture*. New York: George Brazillier Publishers, 1961.

Chueca Goitía, Fernando. *Historia de la Arquitectura Española: Edad Antigua y Edad Media*. Vol. 1. Madrid: Editorial Dossat, 1965.

Sear, Frank. *Roman Architecture*. Ithaca, NY: Cornell University Press, 1993.

Vitruvius. *Ten Books on Architecture*. Translated by Ingrid D. Rowland. Cambridge; New York: Cambridge University Press, 1999.

Ward-Perkins, John B. *Roman Architecture*. New York: Harry N. Abrams, 1977.

ÁVILA CITY WALLS, ÁVILA, CASTILLA Y LEÓN

Style: Romanesque Architecture
Dates: Circa 1090–1100s
Architects: Raymond of Burgundy and Burgundian stonemasons

The city walls of Ávila are the best-preserved work of medieval military architecture throughout Western Europe as well as an unavoidable reference for understanding the evolution of the city in the middle ages. After the fall of the Roman Empire in the fifth century, the population of cities progressively decreased and the predominantly urban culture promoted by the Romans disintegrated; yet, cities resurged in the eleventh century thanks to organized repopulation projects launched by the Christian kings after recapturing cities from the Muslims; the development of the feudal system and the burg organization were integral parts of this process. Thus, during the late eleventh and twelfth centuries, the fortification of strategic sites became a priority of the Christian Monarchs to secure and protect their territorial advance over the lands controlled by Muslim princes. Fragments and ruins of former city walls and fortified burgs from this period—such as the Castle of **Loarre**—abound throughout Spain, but Ávila is the only city in Europe that has a standing complete original enceinte.

Ávila is located in the heart of Castilla, washed by the Adaja River at 3,700 feet above sea level. Originally a *Celtiberic* village is known as Abula in Roman times, it is the site of one of the oldest organized human settlements in Spain. In 714, the city fell to the Arab-Berber invaders who, arriving from northern Africa three years earlier, subjugated the *Visigothic* kingdom that ruled over the native Hispano-Roman population of Iberia. After more than three and a half centuries of Arab rule, the city was re-conquered in 1088 by King Alfonso VI of Castilla who, recognizing its valuable strategic location, immediately ordered the repopulation of the city and the construction of a pro-

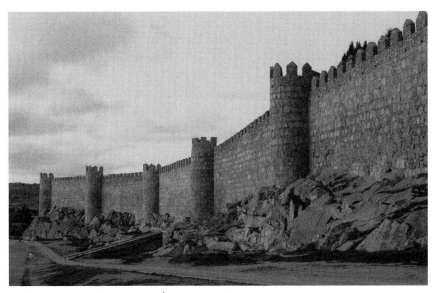

Fragment of the southern side of Ávila's city walls.

tecting enceinte. The task was undertaken by Raymond of Burgundy, husband of the king's sister (Doña Urraca, a legendary figure in Spanish history whose story is narrated in *El Cantar del Mio Cid*), with the collaboration of twenty stonemasons and twelve geometers that he had brought from France.

The city walls of Ávila are an impressive 8,250-foot-long (one and a half miles) defensive curtain wall of granite with eighty-eight towers and eight gates that enclose an approximately rectangular area. The average thickness of the walls is about 10 feet, and the average height is nearly 40 feet; they are topped by a continuous battlement rampart-walk and parapet with *merlons* and *crenels*. The walls are primarily built with irregular granite blocks of many different sizes, Roman brick and other types of stone elements; some materials were taken from the nearby Roman necropolis, from other buildings, and even from the old Roman and Visigothic walls. Whereas it is generally accepted that they were erected immediately after the recapture of the city in about 1090, the exact chronology is still debated; however, it is certain that it was completed by the end of the twelfth century. Originally, the walls were preceded by two additional defensive elements—a moat and a barbican; their objective was to impede or make difficult the approximation and deployment of charging machinery. None of these two elements remain today, although the modern *paseos* (strolling promenades located just outside the city walls), particularly the Paseo del Rastro on the south and Paseo de la Ronda Vieja on the north, may be interpreted as physical traces of the old mote.

The city walls are punctuated by eighty-eight semicircular towers disposed with certain regularity every 65 feet; virtually identical, all these towers are as tall as the walls and terminate with a similar battlement parapet. These towers had an obvious military defensive role; they are 20 feet wide and project outwardly approximately 28 feet. Their semicircular ending geometry is unusual compared to similar fortifications in other parts of Europe, constituting a typically Castilian characteristic. The battlement parapet of varied width connects all the towers, generating an uninterrupted circuit. The eight gates—or Puertas—are, without doubt, the most spectacular elements of the entire enceinte. They are formed by two towers, placed closer to each other than the regular 65-foot separation distance. There are two gates on the north side, one on the west, two on the south, and three on the east. The three eastern gates—Puerta del Alcázar on the southeast, Puerta de San Vicente on the northeast, and Puerta del Peso de la Harina at the center—are more important and older than the others. The Puerta del Alcázar owes its name to having been directly related to the no longer existing Alcázar, the political and administrative center of the city; it is the most impressive one, composed of two gigantic towers connected by a suspended rampart-arch that provided further protection to the most important entrance to the city. Two prominent brackets, placed on each of the two towers at a slightly higher level than the actual arched doorway, were likely used to support a removable wooden platform, or to accomodate structural devices of the gate's drawbridge. Further south, the Torreón del Alcázar or Torre de Homenaje, and the Torre del Baluarte, are the only physical remnants on the walls of the Alcazar demolished in the 1920s. The Torreón, with its two-level battlement parapet, the lower one supported by beautiful projecting stone brackets, is one of the highlights of the enceinte.

The Puerta de San Vicente, which owes its name to the *extramural* Basílica of San Vicente, marks the eastern extreme of this portion of the wall, while at the center of the eastern stretch is the Puerta del Peso de la Harina, the commercial—tax collecting—entrance to the city. The Cathedral of Ávila, flanking this central gate, was built within and as an integral part of the fortifications. Virtually nothing remains today of the original *Romanesque* church built by Raymond of Burgundy and his French stonemasons. The current cathedral is a remarkable Gothic example begun in the late twelfth century, thus predating other great Spanish Gothic cathedrals such as the **Cathedral of Burgos** (1222–1260) and the **Cathedral of León** (begun about 1255). A major portion of the semicircular east end of Ávila's cathedral, the *ambulatory*, is embedded in the fortified wall; known as "el cimorro," it has three successive and progressively taller machicolated parapets, creating the strongest, better protected, edge of the city. The outer parapet has a projecting gallery similar in concept and design to the Torreón del Alcázar.

The city walls of Ávila are the military architecture monument of reference of the Middle Ages because of their unmatched state of preservation, a product of a remarkable architectural and engineering quality of execution that has resisted the passage of time; it largely surpasses other similar constructions in Europe, such as the much-restored city walls of Carcassonne, France. Both the enceinte and the Romanesque churches outside the walls have been protected by UNESCO's World Heritage program since 1985.

Further Reading

Conant, Kenneth John. *Carolingian and Romanesque Architecture 800–1200*. 2nd ed. Middlesex: Penguin Books, 1978.

Fletcher, Sir Banister. *A History of Architecture*. 20th ed. Oxford: Architectural Press, 1996.

Lampérez y Romea, Vicente. *Historia de la Arquitectura Cristiana Española en la Edad Media*. Vol. 1. Valladolid: Ambito ediciones, 1999. (Facsimile impression of original 1908 edition.)

Yarza, Joaquín. *Arte y Arquitectura en España, 500–1250*. Madrid: Ediciones Cátedra, 2000.

"CASA DE LES PUNXES."
See Casa Terradas.

CASA MILÁ, BARCELONA, CATALONIA

Style: *Modernismo* Catalan
Dates: 1905–1910
Architect: Antoni Gaudí

Casa Milá, popularly known as "La Pedrera" (the quarry), is a landmark in the history of architecture, one of the most important and revered buildings of the twentieth century. The building's relevance lies in numerous converging aspects; on one hand it was designed by Gaudí at the peak of his creative career and thus regarded as his most mature work of architecture; on the other hand, yet related to the other, it was an ambitious architectural undertaking in which he applied the full spectrum of his convictions and implemented an innovative constructive, aesthetic-artistic, and typological *programme*. Moreover, it was his last secular building before dedicating all his efforts to the construction of Barcelona's *Sagrada Familia*, his most famous, still incomplete work of architecture.

Casa Milá was commissioned by the Milá family as an apartment building for Barcelona's well-established merchant class and emerging bourgeoisie. Milá's site was ideally placed at a prominent intersection of Barcelona's *Eixample*—the masterful extension of the city designed by Ildefons Cerdá in 1859. More precisely, the building occupies the north corner of Passeig de Gracia and Carrer de Provenca; the former is one of the Eixample's important arteries, an ample boulevard through which Cerdá linked the old neighborhood of "Gracia" with the Ciutat Vella (or Gothic quarter, the ancient center of Barcelona) and quickly became a fashionable street for Barcelona's wealthy elite and emerging bourgeoisie. The whole area of the Eixample became a fertile territory of exploration for the architects of the *Modernismo* Catalan: key buildings designed by the most important representatives of Modernismo—such as Domènech i Montaner's Editorial Montaner i Simon (now the Fundacion Tapies, 1880–1885), Puig i Cadalfach's **Casa Terradas** (1905), and Gaudi's own Casa Batlló (1905–1907)—are all within short distance of "La Pedrera." Yet, Casa Milá, is truly unique, universally praised as "one of Gaudí's most original works, wise and strong, a sober building . . . a song in stone" (Chueca Goitía 1965, 744).

In addition to the site's prominent location in the growing city, the orientation of the lot was ideal, with the corner of the site facing due south and the two sides facing east and west. Gaudí took full advantage of the site's nu-

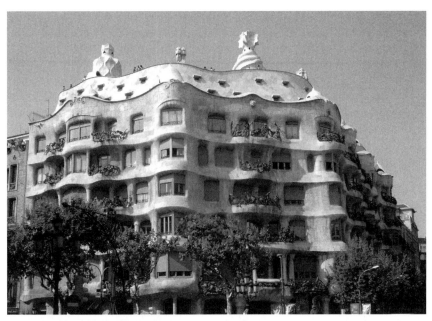

General view of Casa Milá's exterior.

merous attributes and created a building of unusual characteristics, sophisticated, audacious, and innovatively elegant. One of the more singular aspects is the brilliant dissolution of the corner in favor of a perceptually continuous façade, a fluid mass of stone. The apartments are organized behind this carefully composed stone front around two large quasi-oval courtyards that, growing wider in the upper floors, provide abundant natural light and air to the interior of the building's massive volume. The apartments are unusually spacious for the time, all different from each other and with all their main rooms organized along the undulating façades; secondary and service rooms are generally placed on the interior parts of the built volume near the circulation cores and opening to smaller ventilation shafts. This intricate design and the accomplished singularity of each apartment were only possible through the implementation of an innovative structural and architectural concept that excluded the use of walls as elements of support and, instead, employed a system of columns as the structural skeleton, anticipating by almost a quarter of a century Le Corbusier's influential "plan libre" (the "free plan," an idea based on the independence of the structural system from both the façade and interior partitions). The apartments' interiors were ample and moderately sumptuous, very luminous and rich in subtly naturalistic details; not unlike everywhere else in the building, the curvilinear line and rounded edges predominated.

The five levels of apartments are framed by a nearly double-height ground-floor level and a sculptural attic roof and roof terrace. The ground floor houses the entrances to the two main interior courts, as well as parking for carriages, among other services. At the top of the building, above the five levels of apartments, the attic roof is a marvelous space, a fully and continuously vaulted space supported by parabolic arches made in brick that reflect Gaudí's innovative constructive and structural skill, as well as his remarkable mastery of materials. Furthermore, the attic constitutes the structure that supports the building's spectacular roof; this is a magic space, a terrace accessible from strategically placed stairs that is populated by strange sculptural and surreal elements that are nothing else but ventilation chimneys and the volumes that enclose the stairs. Yet, the roof terrace is also "a place," a platform for observing the city and the distant surrounding landscape and a usable exterior space for the building's occupants. The sculptural forms on the roof terrace of Casa Milá constitute an animated artificial landscape, an idea that would be borrowed by Le Corbusier fifty years later to design the roof of the Unité d'Habitation in Marseille, France, a paradigmatic building of twentieth-century architecture. It was also the culmination of a search that Gaudí had started with his early works, such as the Palau Güell (Barcelona 1885–1889).

The innovative typological and constructive conception and its fantastic roof terrace are two very important distinctive features of Casa Milá. However, and undoubtedly, the most distinctive aspect of the building is its splendid undulating stone façade, the reason for the building's nickname of "La Pedrera." The expressiveness of the fluid curvilinear forms of the façade defy any attempt to comprehend the building as a typical sequence of floor plans enclosed by an exterior façade wall; the undulating façade of overleaping thick horizontal bands provides a sense of a continuum, a single architectural event that negotiates the corner site with ease and plasticity. Yet, on closer inspection, one can discern the points of inflexion of the building's forms, how it accommodates to the corner site and the requirements imposed by Cerdà's plan, revealing how uniquely "Barcelonan" is the building. As Josep María Montaner eloquently stated "undoubtedly, 'La Pedrera' is the most extraordinary building that has been integrated to the grid of the Eixample" (Montaner 1997, 145).

The high expressive and sculptural aspect of "La Pedrera" has provoked numerous inspired descriptions; many have referred to it as resembling primitive caves carved in a cliff, while Chueca Goitía compared it to the "reflection on the water of a geometrically organized façade that the water waves make it tremble slightly" (Chueca Goitía 1965, 744). Originally, Gaudí had proposed—and the Milá family had agreed—to crown the building with a giant image of the Virgin Mary; this is not surprising when we consider the religious devotion of the architect and of most of his Catalan clients; however, as an antireligious movement broke out in the early years of the twentieth century the idea was initially postponed and eventually withdrawn. The metal balustrades in front of many windows are also noteworthy; they were designed and built by Gaudí's young collaborator, disciple and talented architect Josep María Jujol, who also collaborated with the master in many other famous works, notably at **Park Güell**.

Casa Milá is not just a masterpiece, but a building without equal, a unique architectural creation that reflects both the originality of Gaudí as an architect, as well as the ideals that he pursued throughout his life. Further, it is also the reflection of a particularly vibrant period in the history of Barcelona and Catalonia, and a symbol of cultural identity. Today, "La Pedrera" belongs to Caixa Catalunya, Catalonia's most important financial institution. The building houses exhibition areas, offices for Caixa Catalunya's Foundation, and apartments (one has been fully restored and furnished with furniture from the period of construction), while in the attic there is a permanent exhibit of Gaudí's work and legacy. Casa Milá has been protected by UNESCO's World Heritage program since 1984.

Further Reading

Chueca Goitía, Fernando. *Historia de la Arquitectura Española: Edad Moderna-Edad Contemporánea*. Madrid: Editorial Dossat, 1965.

Curtis, William J. R. *Modern Architecture since 1900*. 3rd ed. London: Phaidon Press Limited, 1996.

Montaner, Josep Maria. *Barcelona: A City and Its Architecture*. Cologne; New York: Taschen, 1997.

Zerbst, Rainer. *Antoni Gaudí*. Cologne: Taschen, 1992.

CASA TERRADAS, BARCELONA, CATALONIA

Style: *Modernismo* Catalan
Date: 1905
Architect: Josep Puig i Cadalfach

Casa Terradas, popularly known in Barcelona as "Casa de les Punxes," is the most significant and accomplished work of Josep Puig i Cadalfach, one of the important representatives and leaders of the *Modernismo* Catalan, an artistic and architectural movement originated in Barcelona and related to similar contemporaneous developments in other European countries, such as the *Art Nouveau* in France and Belgium, the *Secessionist Movement* in Vienna (Austria), and in Scotland the work of Charles Rennie Mackintosh, to name only some among the most important. During his long and prolific life, Puig i Cadalfach excelled as an urban planner, an essayist, and a politician; also a brilliant historian, his history of Catalonia's *Romanesque* architecture entitled *L'Arquitectura Romànica a Catalunya* was published in 1918 but is still an authoritative text on the subject. Moreover, he was an eminent architect whose work, particularly Casa Terradas, is emblematic of one of the two related lines or architectural exploration—one led by Lluís Domènech i Montaner, the other by Antoni Gaudí—that evolved under the general umbrella of Catalonia's Modernismo. Puig i Cadalfach, following the footsteps of John Ruskin and Emmanuel Violet-le-Duc and Domènech i Montaner, was reportedly interested in renewing Gothic art, adapting it to the needs, practical as well as expressive, of the epoch. He firmly believed that the language of a truly Catalan architecture had to be rooted in the medieval architecture—Romanesque and *Gothic*—that had accompanied the naissance of Catalonia's national sentiment in the eleventh century.

Casa Terradas was commissioned by Bartomeu Terradas i Mont as a single residential building for his three daughters; his objective was to pass it on to them in equally subdivided parts. This rather atypical building program plus the exceptional and privileged site allowed Puig i Cadalfach to create a unique piece of urban architecture which, along with Gaudí's **Casa Milá**, Casa Batlló, and Sagrada Familia's church; Domènech i Montaner's **Palau de la Música Catalana**; and many other remarkable works, constitute a family of cherished buildings that demonstrate Barcelona's vibrant creative moment at the dawn of the twentieth century.

The building is located on an extraordinary site, an atypical triangular block at the heart of Ildefons Cerdá's grid of Barcelona's *Eixample* (a remarkable urban extension project started in 1859 that still today is the sign of identity for Barcelona's urban tissue beyond the historic Gothic quarter or Ciutat Vella). The atypical site configuration is a direct consequence of the irruption of the Diagonal Avenue (a major road that traverses the orthogonal grid diagonally from the west-southwest to the east-northeast) through the central portion of the Eixample. Thus, Casa Terradas occupies an entire city block delimited by the Diagonal, Carrer del Bruc, and Carrer del Rosselló streets which, however small, enjoys a privileged condition within the Eixample where more typical situations offered lots "between party-walls." Puig i Cadalfach took full advantage of this splendid opportunity to develop a highly expressive building, an urban landmark and an emblem of his revivalist neo-Gothic proposal.

The building occupies the site's entire buildable area, respecting the long chamfered corners imposed by Cerdá's plan at street intersections; consequently, it consists of an irregular six-sided polygonal building with two long façades—on Diagonal Avenue and Carrer del Rosselló—and four shorter sides of similar dimensions—one facing Carrer del Bruc, the other three as the result of the chamfered corners. The truncation of the side at the inter-

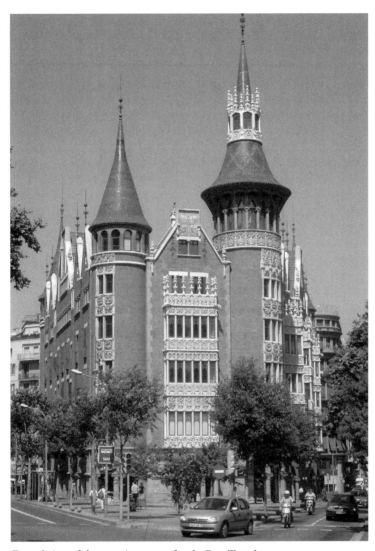

Frontal view of the most important façade Casa Terradas.

section of Diagonal Avenue and Carrer del Rosselló generates a little, but nicely scaled triangular plaza that confers more visibility and urban importance to this particular side of the building. The corners of the building are articulated by slender circular towers crowned by tall conical steeples, a characteristic that provided the building with the familiar name of "Casa de les Punxes" (House of the Steeples). The southern tower on the main façade—facing the small triangular plaza—is slightly wider and notably taller than the others, breaking the building's symmetry and emphasizing the medieval character of the whole, as if it were analogous to a medieval castle's Torre de Homenaje.

The ground floor is defined by a virtually continuous stone arcade supported by short stone columns featuring abstracted natural motifs at both their bases and their *capitals*. Above, three apparently identical levels may suggest that there was one for each of Bartomeu Terradas' daughters. However, on further inspection, the floor plans reveal differences among the various levels. Puig i Cadalfach subdivided the building both vertically and horizontally; that is, as a sequence of three identical horizontal layers as well as three independent vertical volumes masked behind a uniform envelope. The three vertical volumes of approximately equal size are separated by thick walls perpendicular to the building's longest and better oriented side—on Diagonal Avenue—making no concession to the different orientation of the other five sides; consequently, the floor plans—which otherwise show a clear disposition of generously dimensioned main rooms facing the streets (living and dining rooms, billiards and bedrooms) with a core of service rooms inside—appear as oddly subdivided into three similar but distinct internal blocks perforated by eleven vertical shafts that provide aeration and illumination to vestibules, stairs, and other service areas.

The building's six façades are primarily clad in red brick with highlighted areas in stone, mainly the corners of the façades' planes, and the framing of the projecting bow-windows of important rooms. Above the three typical floors there is another level differentiated from the other three by its fenestration of sequences of smaller arched openings; rising further, the six cylindrical towers have another level conceived as *miradores*. The towers confer a distinct neo-medieval character to the building, while the materials and details—particularly the steep roofs and stone ornamentation around windows, doors, and balconies—indicate the influence of medieval Flemish architecture, a characteristic of Puig i Cadalfach's work, as well as of some contemporaneous Dutch buildings such as Henry Berlage's Stock Exchange building in Amsterdam.

Casa Terradas is also an excellent example of the integration of the arts and crafts pursued by Modernismo, another key aspect that relates it to similar movements in other parts of Europe. The remarkable work in wrought iron, stained glass, *azulejos*, ornamental metal and wooden features—all done by skillful and talented local artisans—was coordinated by Enric Monserda who worked in collaboration with Domènech i Montaner. Overall, the building imposes a sober and elegant medievalizing presence in a prominent part of the city that reveals the architect's proposal within the Modernismo Catalan that shaped the image of Barcelona at the beginning of the twentieth century.

Further Reading

Bohigas, Oriol. *Reseña y Catálogo de la Arquitectura Modernista*. Barcelona: Editorial Lumen, 1973.

Chueca Goitía, Fernando. *Historia de la Arquitectura Española: Edad Moderna-Edad Contemperánea*. Vol. 2 Madrid: Editorial Dossat, 1965.
Permanyer, Lluís. *Josep Puig i Cadalfach*. Barcelona: Ediciones Polígrafa, 2001.

CATALONIA ARCHITECTS ASSOCIATION HEADQUARTERS.
See COAC Headquarters.

CATHEDRAL OF BURGOS, BURGOS, CASTILLA Y LEÓN

Style: Gothic Architecture
Dates: 1221–1260s (additions and alterations until 1765)
Architects: Unknown; Henri of Burgos, John of Cologne, Simon of Cologne, and Juan de Vallejo

The penetration of French ideas into Spanish territory started in the eleventh century thanks to the active development of French monasticism promoted by the *Benedictine* order first, and the *Cistercians* later. The development of pilgrimage to the **Cathedral of Santiago de Compostela** through the French-way brought in a considerable number of artisans from the neighboring kingdom of France. By the end of the twelfth century, culturally and liturgically, Spain was a virtual province of France, where ideas, trends, and techniques were developing steadily. Within this context, French oriented *Romanesque* architecture rapidly replaced and suppressed the emerging local *Asturian-Visigothic* and *Mozarabic* architectures, especially in Castilla. Romanesque architecture had such a great impact throughout Spain that it is also considered as an obstacle for the massive proliferation of Gothic architecture, for even long after Romanesque had become history in most of Europe, Christian Spain remained attached to a style that had accompanied its gradual emergence from the years of the Muslim invasion. However, the success of Romanesque architecture served to lay the foundations for the penetration of Gothic art and architecture that, in the twelfth century, emerged in and around the Ile-de-France region. The Cathedral of Burgos is—alongside the Cathedral of Ávila (see **Ávila City Walls**), the Cathedral

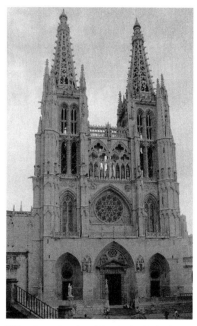

West front façade of the Cathedral of Burgos.

of Toledo, and the **Cathedral of León**—one of the landmarks of French-influenced *Gothic* architecture in Spain.

Burgos is strategically located at the heart of Castilla's plains almost halfway between the French-Spanish Pyrenean border and Santiago de Compostela. In 1075, King Alfonso of Castilla granted the land where his palace was located for the construction of a cathedral. Completed in 1096, the Romanesque cathedral became the seat of powerful bishops. One of them, Bishop Maurice, had traveled through France as the escort of Princess Beatrice of Swabia who, in the late 1210s, traveled to Spain to marry King Fernando III, "the Saint." The royal wedding took place in 1219 in Burgos' Romanesque cathedral, but, impressed by the recently built Gothic cathedrals, Maurice convinced the king to build in Burgos a new and grander cathedral in the rising, lofty and spiritual style that he had seen during his journey through France. Consequently, two years after the royal wedding the old Romanesque cathedral was demolished and construction of a new one in Gothic style began with a solemn ceremony attended by the king and the queen, in which Bishop Maurice laid the first stone of the new church. With substantial financial support from the crown and the enthusiastic filigrees, the new building was erected with unusual speed, likely under the supervision of French artisans and master builders brought along by Bishop Maurice on his return to Spain. In only ten years major parts of the east end—the sanctuary, choir, and radiating chapels—were already completed and religious services began to be offered. Bishop Maurice died in 1238—he is buried in the choir—and construction was momentarily halted. Construction resumed in 1240 and twenty years later, in 1260, the entire church was complete and thus consecrated. However, work continued in subsequent centuries with additions and alterations, some of which are remarkable artistic and technical achievements in their own right, while others have unfortunately disturbed the pure and austere thirteenth-century original.

The plan of Nuestra Señora de Burgos (Our Lady of Burgos) is cruciform—276 feet long by 194 feet wide at the transept. Following the west front, a five-bay *nave* with a central aisle flanked by two lower galleries precedes an unusually wide *transept*; beyond, the chevet, composed of a three-bay choir ending in a polygonal apse, is surrounded by the *ambulatory* gallery with, originally, five polygonal radiating chapels. Originally, the crossing was highlighted by an eight-partite *vault* supported by four circular piers with attached columns of lofty proportions; however, in the fifteenth century it was replaced by a *ciborium* built by John of Cologne, also author of the web-like towers of the front façade. John of Cologne's ciborium collapsed in 1539 and was soon replaced by an impressive new octagonal one designed by Juan de Vallejo; profusely ornamented and supported by *squinches* resting on the four central columns—significantly enlarged and reinforced as massive circular piers—the new ciborium is a singular work of architecture and sculpture. The tombs of Rodrigo Díaz de Vivar, the legendary *Cid Campeador*, and his wife are placed at the center of the crossing.

The nave's interior, except where it has been altered, stands out as pure and simple demonstration of thirteenth-century Gothic architecture. Undoubtedly, the *triforium* is, because of its large dimensions and intricate design, a unique original contribution of Burgos' cathedral to Gothic architecture probably derived from the cathedral of Bourges, France. The exterior of Burgos' cathedral has suffered many modifications and additions that completely altered the original thirteenth-century building; the façade of the southern transept—the Puerta del Sarmental—is the only one that remains closer to the original, exhibiting some resemblances to the Cathedral of Reims. The front façade, however, underwent interesting changes, notably the wonderful spires of the two towers conceived by John of Cologne in the mid-fifteenth century; the twin towers are composed of an intricate open web of stone that reaches to a height of 276 feet from the ground, matching the building's length.

In spite of the numerous additions, restorations, and modifications, the Cathedral of Burgos remains one of the most valuable and grand examples of French-influenced Gothic architecture in Spain. The mentioned resemblances of some of its parts to their peers at Bourges and Reims, as well as others that seem derived from the cathedrals of Le Mans and Coutances, also in France, demonstrate that the master builders of Burgos were well informed of the evolution of French Gothic architecture and derived the construction of their cathedral not from one single model but from various contemporaneous examples.

The Chapel of the Condestable is the most important addition made to the cathedral; it is considered a masterpiece of late-fifteenth-century religious architecture and a high point of Spanish *Flamboyant Gothic*. The chapel, designed by Simon of Cologne, son of John of Cologne, was founded by the Constables of Castilla in 1468 to house their tombs. This chapel is located at the east end of the building, slightly off the central axis of the nave; its construction demanded a drastic alteration to the central radiating chapel of the original Gothic church, which became the vestibule of the new chapel. Simon conceived a monumentally tall octagonal space—polygonal at the ground floor—crowned by a spectacular eight-point star-shaped vault with yet another star-shaped central portion of finely traced open-work in stone that permits the penetration of zenithal daylight. The exuberant and profusely decorated exterior is also characteristic of Spanish Flamboyant art and architecture. The Chapel of the Condestable had a tremendous influence throughout the region and inspired other noteworthy constructions, such as the Chapel of the Presentation, which is located off the cathedral's south aisle.

The Cathedral of Burgos, as both an original Gothic monument and a reservoir of significant later additions, is a remarkable building that exemplifies the evolution of religious architecture across many periods, from the introduction of French Gothic in the early thirteenth century, to the peak of Flamboyant art in the early sixteenth century. The whole complex was declared a UNESCO World Heritage site in 1984.

Further Reading

Bevan, Bernard. *History of Spanish Architecture*. London: B. T. Basford, 1938.

Chueca Goitía, Fernando. *Historia de la Arquitectura Española: Edad Antigua y Edad Media*. Vol. 1 Madrid: Editorial Dossat, 1965.

Grodecki, Louis. *Gothic Architecture*. Milan and New York: Electa Editrice and Rizzoli, 1978.

Lambert, Elie. *L'Art Gothique en Espagne aux XIIème et XIIIème siècles*. Paris: H. Laurens, 1931.

Yarza, Joaquín. *Arte y Arquitectura en España, 500–1250*. Madrid: Ediciones Cátedra, 2000.

CATHEDRAL OF JAÉN, JAÉN, ANDALUCÍA

Styles: Renaissance and Baroque Architecture

Dates: 1546–1660; 1667–1691

Architects: Andrés de Vandelvira, Juan de Aranda Salazar, Eufrasio López de Rojas

Spanish Renaissance architecture reached one of its higher expressions in the southern region of Andalucía, where numerous buildings—palaces and cathedrals—were designed by the most talented Spanish architects of the period such as Enrique Egas, Pedro de Machuca, Diego de Siloé, and their disciples. The **Palace of Carlos V at La Alhambra**, in Granada, and the cathedrals of Granada, Córdoba, and Jaén, among many other remarkable buildings, are the architectural highlights of the period. The Cathedral of Jaén, however smaller than its peers, is, because of its harmonic proportions, the more architecturally relevant of the three great Renaissance cathedrals of Andalucía.

Already a strategic post in Roman times, the city of Jaén emerges at the footsteps of the Cerro Santa Catalina. It was conquered by the invading Arabs in 712 and it was recuperated by Fernando III in 1246, remaining as an important strategic post, especially between the thirteenth and fifteenth centuries, when it was at the frontier between the Christian kingdoms and the

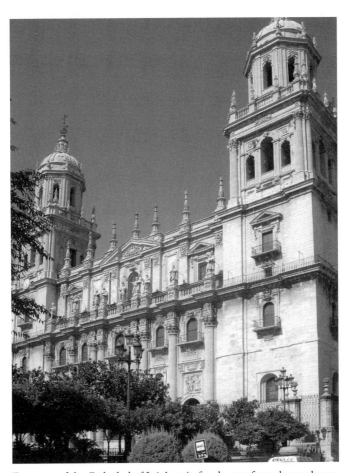

Fragment of the Cathedral of Jaén's main façade seen from the southwest.

remnants of the formerly powerful Caliphate of Córdoba; its mosque was an impressive building that testified the importance that the city had in that period. In 1492—the year that marks the end of Islamic political presence in Spain—Jaén's bishop, Luis Osorio, decided to build a new cathedral precisely on the site of the mosque, which had been used as a Christian temple between 1246 and the late fifteenth century.

The design and construction of the new cathedral was undertaken by Pedro López, and it is believed that Enrique Egas, the architect of the Cathedral of Granada, had some participation in the initial stages of the building. However, construction was halted in the early 1520s and, as a consequence, a considerable portion of the building suffered damages and was demolished in 1525. These events demanded the development of a new project for the cathedral based on the little portion that remained standing. This new project was undertaken by Andrés de Vandelvira, who resumed construction of the cathedral in 1546. Vandelvira was a disciple of Diego de Siloé, with whom he had worked in the construction of the notable church of San Salvador in nearby Úbeda, and who had already built some remarkable buildings such as the church for the convent of San Francisco, completed, precisely, in 1546, the year in which he received the commission to resume design and construction of Jaén's cathedral. Vandelvira designed the building and directed the construction until his death in about 1575; the chapter room, sacristy, and few parts of the main cathedral were then mostly complete. However, since one of Vandelvira's collaborators and disciples, Alonso Barba, undertook the responsibility of construction work, the rest of the building was continued following the architectural lines initiated by Vandelvira. In the mid-1600s, construction was carried out by Juan de Aranda Salazar, always following Vandelvira's plans, however more vaguely than his predecessor. Consecrated in 1660 after Aranda completed most of the interior work, the full building was finally finished in 1691 when Eufrasio López de Rojas completed the front façade in Baroque style almost two centuries after Bishop Osorio had decided to build the new cathedral.

The plan of Jaén's cathedral is a *latin-cross* inscribed into a pure rectangular envelope with volumes attached to the east of the *transept* on each side of the main envelope; the northern volume—an oval space inscribed within a rectangular volume known as Capilla del Sagrario—was in fact added in the eighteenth century by Ventura Rodriguez; the southern one, the sacristy, is considered Vandelvira's masterpiece because of its noble proportions and delicate architectural articulation. It consists of a 72-by-40-foot rectangle oriented east–west, of which the interior perimeter is defined by a continuous arcade resting on paired columns slightly detached from the walls; as Chueca Goitía commented, this space has an "architectural richness rarely matched" (Chueca Goitía 1965, 127). This space is associated with but independent from the actual church, accessible from a small preceding space, the "antesacristy," located at the southern end of the transept.

The church itself consists of a central *nave* with aisles flanked by lateral

chapels—two per bay—along the entire length of the building's interior except the transept. The west arm of the latin-cross plan has three bays of unequal size, while the eastern portion has two bays, also of unequal
dimensions. The bay-modulation is marked by cruciform pillars composed
of a square core with semicircular striated columns attached to each side that
raise to support the arches of the vaulting system. The different dimensions
of the bays, which increase from both ends toward the center, were carefully
and intentionally studied to transmit the perception of a constantly expanding space, an effect amplified by the utilization of vaults cut into four vertical planes that cover the central and lateral naves—one of Vandelvira's
singular contributions to the architecture of the period. The overall spatial
result is magnificent because, more than a usual church with a dominant central nave flanked by aisles, the Cathedral of Jaén's interior resembles a large
hall punctuated by vertical supports; the spatial climax is at the intersection
of nave and transept where a stilted semispherical dome with a high central
lantern that profusely illuminates the whole interior. The orthogonal east
end of the church's interior—and exterior—is another singular characteristic of this remarkable building because it contrasts with the more usual implementation of semicircular apses surrounded by ambulatories that are
extensions of the side aisles behind the altar. At Jaén, the flat end where all
three naves end further reinforces the perception of a single hall-type space
of well-proportioned but monumental dimensions.

The cathedral's main façade that faces Plaza de Santa María was started
after the temple had been consecrated. It is a remarkable piece of Baroque
architecture designed by Eufrasio López de Rojas that was built between
1667 and 1691. The façade is a generously ornamented stone mass of approximately 108 feet wide by 105 feet tall without considering the two flanking towers of obvious Italian inspiration. The abundance of sculpted images
and stone bas-reliefs, as well as the monumentality of the double-height
order of columns of the lower portion provide a sought-out theatrical effect
which was intended to communicate liturgical aspects to the filigrees. The
three entrances to the church, aligned with each of the three naves of the interior, are rather deemphasized, consisting of simple arched gateways; rather,
along with the seven balconies of the upper gallery—one for each of five unequal bays of the central plane and another for each of the towers—these entrances reinforce the scenographic aspect of the façade, a monumental stage
set that displays abundant iconography and religious imagery. The two twin
towers, while in full consonance with the rest of the façade, are significantly
less ornamented, perhaps a trace of Vandelvira's original *Renaissance* façade.

The Cathedral of Jaén underwent some additions and alterations after it
was completed. The already mentioned Capilla del Sagrario is one of them;
beginning in 1726, José Gallego—disciple of Churriguera, the designer of
the **Plaza Mayor of Salamanca**—completed the building's interior and
added a choir to the west portion of the central nave in unmistakably *Churrigueresque* style. However notable for the style, Gallego's choir encumbers the

central space, limiting and constricting the spatial amplitude conceived by Vandelvira and his followers. Yet, despite this unfortunate alteration, the Cathedral of Jaén, a national monument since 1931, is without doubt one of the purest and most accomplished manifestations of religious Renaissance architecture in Spain.

Further Reading

Bevan, Bernard. *History of Spanish Architecture*. London: B. T. Basford, 1938.
Chueca Goitía, Fernando. *Historia de la Arquitectura Española: Edad Moderna-Edad Contemporánea*. Vol. 2. Madrid: Editorial Dossat, 1965.

CATHEDRAL OF LEÓN, LEÓN, CASTILLA Y LEÓN

Style: Rayonnant Gothic Architecture
Dates: 1255–circa 1300
Architects: Unknown; Henry of Burgos

The Cathedral of León is, with the cathedrals of Toledo and Burgos, one of the three most important *Gothic* monuments in Spain outside of Catalonia, where Gothic architecture has singular and distinctive characteristics that differentiate it from works of the same period in other regions of Spain. If the cathedrals of Avila and Toledo pioneered the introduction of French Gothic in Iberia, and the **Cathedral of Burgos**—modeled after the royal cathedral of Reims—is considered as the highest exponent of Gothic architecture in Spain, the Cathedral of León is the purest and most impressive example of French *Rayonnant* Gothic in the Iberian Peninsula.

The site where the cathedral is located has a rich history. In Roman times, when León was founded by Roman veteran troops of the 7th Legion, the cathedral's site was occupied by the baths and other public buildings. In 916, after defeating the Muslim occupants, León's King Ordoño II ordered the construction of a cathedral "to thank for God's assistance" in such an important military event. This first cathedral was, most likely, a *Mozarabic* building similar to many others built in the region of León at the time; it was severely damaged by Almanzor's devastating incursions in the 990s, but restored later; however, because of the growing importance of the Kingdom of León a new cathedral was erected at the same site. Consecrated in 1073, this building was contemporary with the nearby church of San Isidoro and in all likelihood built by the same artisans and masons according to the then flour-

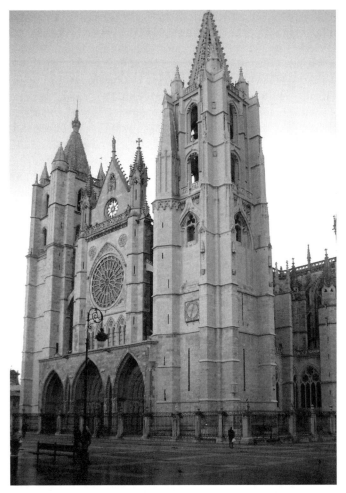

Frontal body of the Cathedral of León, seen from the southwest.

ishing *Romanesque* style as represented by, for example, the church of **San Martín Fromista**, in Palencia.

In spite of some early confusion, there is sufficient historical evidence to assert that, following the initiative of Bishop Martín Fernández, construction of the now existing Gothic cathedral began c. 1255 based on a project of Henri of Burgos, a French master mason who was then involved in the contemporaneous construction of Burgos' cathedral. The construction campaign started at the east end of the building and proceeded at remarkable speed since, by the end of the century, it was virtually completed.

The plan of the Cathedral of León is unequivocally derived from the plan of Reims (began c. 1211), one of the classical masterpieces of France's Gothic architecture. León has a *Latin-cross* plan defined by a main *nave* and *transept*—

both three-aisled—and a five-aisled choir terminating a five-sided, single-aisled ambulatory with five radiating chapels, all smaller in size but conceptually identical to its French predecessor. Yet, the Cathedral of León is about one-third the size of Reims, mostly because of its significantly shorter nave—five bays deep at León versus nine bays at Reims—resulting in a rather macro-cephalic building where the eastern end, the "head," is notably larger than the western portion, an unusual characteristic of full-size complete Gothic cathedrals. The building's full length is almost 320 feet and the main *vault* is about 100 feet high, considerably shorter than other similar buildings constructed at about the same time, such as the cathedral of Amiens.

However shorter in length and height than most of its contemporaries, the proportions of León are characteristic of classical Gothic architecture. This is altered in the western front, where the atypical location of the towers beyond the aisles adds an unusual breadth to the building's west-work (the west frontal body and main façade of the cathedral) that challenges the usual predominant verticality of *Rayonnant* architecture. The displacement of the towers beyond the aisles exposes the double flying *buttresses* of the central nave. As a result, the main, western façade of the cathedral appears as composed of three independent vertical volumes that rise behind a deep, richly sculpted, triple portal inscribed within a rather plain rectangular plane. The effect is quite singular, because neither the horizontal nor the vertical predominate despite the seemingly aspiring verticality of the two towers and their crowning steeples.

The interior is simply extraordinary, the finest Gothic building in the Iberian Peninsula and one of the most accomplished examples of Rayonnant architecture outside of France. Whereas far from the audacious height of Reims, Amiens, and Beauvais, the interior of León's cathedral leaves no doubt about the intended verticality and spatial airiness typical of Gothic architecture. At almost 100 feet from the floor, the high vault covers the nave, supported by pillars and attached uninterrupted shafts, and graceful double flying buttresses over the side aisles. Yet, the most remarkable aspect of the interior is the composition of the three-storied typical bay elevation: an arcade of *lancet* arches on the lower level, a sophisticated *triforium* on the center and a clerestory window as tall as the arcade, the whole flanked by floor-to-vault uninterrupted shafts that accentuate the four-partite vaulting of the typical bay module.

The exterior and interior elevations of the Cathedral of León also have other aspects of architectural interest. The exterior façades, especially the portals, house the most significant collection of Gothic sculpture integrated to a building in all Spain. Some sculpted motives derive from French originals—such as the "Last Judgment" scene in the central portal—while others exhibit distinctive local influences; for instance, the southern portal recalls its analogous Puerta del Sarmental in the Cathedral of Burgos, a far-from-surprising fact considering that the same masons and artisans likely participated in the construction of the two buildings. In turn, the interior elevations have a completely glazed triforium and tall clerestory windows that, because of their technical quality and narrative iconographic richness, constitute the most important collection of original thirteenth-century stained glass in all Spain.

Whereas the Gothic fabric was virtually completed by the end of the thirteen century, the Cathedral of León, not unlike many of its peers, suffered some insensitive additions and restorations in subsequent centuries, some of which contributed to the failure of the crossing's vault in the early seventeenth century. Finally, in the nineteenth century, a conscientious restoration project removed many thoughtless alterations returning the building to a rather faithful early fourteenth-century condition consistent with the date of completion of the original Gothic building. Today, the Cathedral of León stands out as the most representative Rayonnant Gothic building in Spain where the echoes of the most important French cathedrals of its time— Chartres, Reims, Amiens, Rouen—demonstrate its pure French lineage and the advanced skill and informed knowledge of the artisans and master builders who erected it in the second part of the thirteenth century.

Further Reading

Bevan, Bernard. *History of Spanish Architecture*. London: B. T. Basford, 1938.

Chueca Goitía, Fernando. *Historia de la Arquitectura Española: Edad Antigua y Edad Media*. Vol. 1 Madrid: Editorial Dossat, 1965.

Grodecki, Louis. *Gothic Architecture*. Milan; New York: Electa Editrice and Rizzoli, 1978.

Lampérez y Romea, Vicente. *Historia de la Arquitectura Cristiana Española en la Edad Media*. Vol. 1. Valladolid: Ambito Ediciones, 1999. (Facsimile impression of original 1908 edition.)

CATHEDRAL OF SANTIAGO DE COMPOSTELA, SANTIAGO DE COMPOSTELA, GALICIA

Styles: Romanesque Architecture, Baroque Churrigueresque
Dates: Circa 1070–1140s, cathedral and Pórtico de la Gloria; 1658–1750, Obradoiro façade
Architects: Unknown (original cathedral); Maestro Mateo (Pórtico de la Gloria); Fernando Casas Novoa (Obradoiro façade)

The Cathedral of Santiago de Compostela (St. James' Cathedral) is considered among the most significant representatives of *Carolingian* architecture, a work of comparable grandeur, beauty, quality, and historical importance as other important buildings of the same period such the Basilica of La Madeleine in Vézelay, France, and the Palatine Chapel in Aachen, Germany. Moreover, despite the alterations and additions that it suffered during its extended period of construction, it is one of the finest and purest architectural monuments of the eleventh century, and some additions are singular architectural achievements in their own right, such as the Obradoiro façade, a masterpiece of Spanish *Baroque Churrigueresque* architecture.

The magnificent *Romanesque* cathedral is built on the site where, allegedly, the tomb of the apostle Saint James—son of Zebedee—was found in 813. The history of the site, marked by such a remarkable event, is narrated in the *Codex Calixtinus* (a text written in the twelfth century and considered apocryphal, that is, of dubious veracity). Briefly stated, the *Codex* establishes that in 813, a peasant discovered remains of a shrine quickly recognized by Theodomiro, bishop of Iria, as the lost burial place of the apostle Saint James (Santiago, in Castilian Spanish). To celebrate the discovery of the apostle's relics, the Asturian king Alfonso II—who reigned over Asturias and Galicia in the period 792–842—immediately ordered the addition of a *nave* to the modest existing shrine. In 899, under Alfonso III's reign (866–910), a new church was built, likely in the then-mature *Asturian-Visigothic* style, a style best represented by the buildings of **Monte Naranco** and the little church of **Santa Cristina de Lena**, respectively, located in and near Oviedo, the kingdom's capital.

Situated in a remote corner of continental Europe, the valuable relics soon attracted pilgrims from all over the continent, stimulating the area's rapid growth and contributing to the development of a system of roads of communication throughout Europe that led to Santiago. As Walter Whitehill commented, in less than 200 years—that is, between the discovery of the tomb in 813 and the late 900s—a town of significant size had grown around the shrine and its related temples (Whitehill 1941, 269). In 997, the town was important enough to attract the interest of Almanzor, who—without capturing it—sacked and considerably damaged it. The Visigothic church, damaged by Almanzor, was reconstructed and consecrated again in 1003. Yet, the building was too modest and small for the growing needs and importance of the site as a major destination, perhaps even the ultimate goal, of millions of pilgrims. Therefore, a new, larger and more monumental building was envisioned by Diego de Peláez, bishop of Santiago de Compostela, who in the 1070s conceived the construction of what would become one of the most important religious buildings of all time.

One of the main issues that contributed to the rapid development of the town was the active endorsement of the pilgrimage by the *Benedictine* order of Cluny, an aspect that generated a flow of people and knowledge from throughout Europe, that arrived in Spain in the eleventh century. Thus, the evolving French ideas were then fluently carried into Spain thanks to Bene-

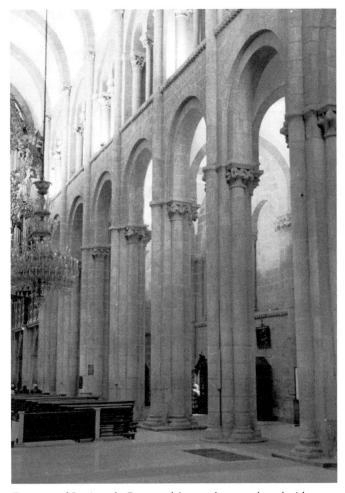

Fragment of Santiago de Compostela's central nave and south aisle.

dictine monks and to the numerous itinerant French workers and artisans who, following the Vía Francígena (the "Frenchmen road"), constantly arrived in Santiago de Compostela throughout the eleventh century. According to the always dubious *Codex Calixtinus,* the cathedral was built by fifty burgundian builders working under the supervision of a French master named Rotbertus. Consequently, Santiago de Compostela stands as a living testimony to the internationalization of architectural developments and building techniques provoked by the fluid traffic of ideas triggered by the growth of the pilgrimage to various holy sites in Europe, and particularly to Santiago de Compostela.

Built at a high elevation point of the city, the cathedral has a commanding position of the built and natural surroundings. The building is largely the work of Romanesque architects and artisans, one of the highest achievements of the period; yet, for today's exterior observer, it appears as a hybrid work, partly Romanesque, partly Baroque, depending on how it is approached. This is because of the numerous additions and transformations that it suffered, especially the original Romanesque front façade, which was covered between 1658 and 1750 by a new one designed by Fernando Casas Novoa. However, whereas the original exterior is largely lost, the interior remains virtually intact, the peak of Spanish Romanesque.

Unlike its Visigothic predecessor on the site, the Romanesque church of Santiago de Compostela has no direct built ancestors in the Iberian Peninsula. Instead, the building can be more easily associated with contemporaneous architectural developments in France, such as the pilgrimage churches of Saint-Martin in Tours (c. 1000–1120s) and Saint-Sernin at Toulouse (c. 1060s–1115). Indeed, there can be no doubt that the building is a typical "pilgrimage church," a type that originated in France with well-defined characteristics; these include a long *nave*, aisles, a generous *transept*, and an ambulatory gallery punctuated by radiating chapels around the *apse*. Kenneth J. Conant, one of the most important historians of medieval architecture, clearly described the particularities of the pilgrimage type as follows:

> Typically the 'pilgrimage church' is grand in scale. It has a long nave with aisles and a gallery, a wide transept, and a spacious sanctuary arm, all covered by tunnel vaulting carried to a uniform height. The vaults have transverse arches typically supported by square pillars with four attached shafts, one of which rises up the face of the nave to carry the transverse arch. On the ground floor two of the other arches carry their share of the arches which frame the adjoining aisle bays. The corresponding shaft in the gallery carries a diaphragm arch which separates two bays of quadrant vaulting so placed as to absorb the thrust of the high vault. In principle the aisles and galleries surround the entire building. This means an ambulatory about the apse, and a small gallery above it, beneath the clerestory windows of the apse. (Conant 1978, 160–161)

This general description of the pilgrimage church perfectly fits the Cathedral of Santiago de Compostela. The nave has ten bays, interrupted at the crossing by the transept arms, five bays long each; the sanctuary arm has three additional bays culminating in another semicircular one; together, nave, crossing, and sanctuary configure a central cross-shaped plan. All these predominantly linear spaces are surrounded by continuous aisles and galleries, generating an ambulatory space around the apse with five radiating chapels; the central one, known as the Chapel of San Salvador, is on axis with the nave and altar; it is square-ended outside but semicircular inside, flanked by niches carved in the thickness of the wall; the immediately adjacent chapels are semicircular in plan, while the plan of the two more distant ones is poly-

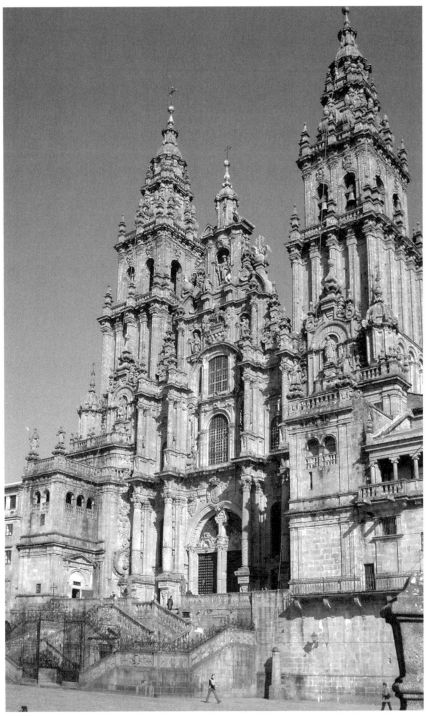

Santiago de Compostela's main façade with the stairs added in the Renaissance, and Casas de Novoa's elaborated *Obradoiro* façade.

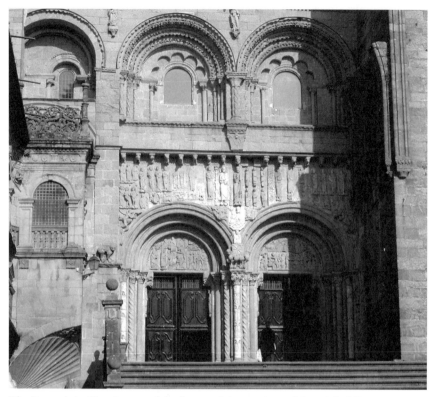

The *Puerta de las Platerías*, one of the few remaining portions of the original Romanesque exterior.

gonal (a truncated octagon). Two additional semicircular chapels are attached to the eastern side of each of the two transept arms.

The nave, transept, and sanctuary arms are magnificent, offering uninterrupted vistas from one end to the other: over 250 feet from the entrance of the nave to the apse and nearly 215 feet between the two ends of the transept arms. All these are covered by tunnel vaulting to a uniform height of nearly 70 feet that begins to spring above the gallery. The spatial climax is at the intersection of the longitudinal axis of the nave with the transversal axis of the transept where an octagonal lantern tower on *squinches* constitutes the only direct source of natural light of the central space. The narrower aisles that flank nave, transept, and sanctuary are covered by *quadrant vaults* at approximately one-half the height of the central vault; above the side aisles, the gallery—a quadrant-vaulted *triforium*—also surrounds the central cross-shaped space. The long nave and transept arms are rhythmically punctuated by square pillars with semicircular shafts attached to each of the four sides. The shafts facing the nave rise to the nave's full height, carrying the weight of transverse arches that support the *barrel vault* as well as mark the nave's rigorous modular bay composition. The other three shafts carry arches in the other three directions, generating a rhythmical and processional spatial progression toward the altar, a dignified, uplifting finale for the pilgrims' long journey.

Whereas the building suffered numerous additions and transformations, the interior—particularly the nave, transept, and adjacent aisles and galleries—remains purely Romanesque. The plans were probably originated by Diego de Peláez, bishop of Santiago, in the early to mid-1070s. In 1112, with about one-half of the building complete (apse, transept, and four bays of the nave), the old Visigothic church was demolished to allow for the completion of the new cathedral, which was probably achieved in the late 1120s. Virtually nothing of the original Romanesque exterior remains, but, according to the reconstruction made by Kenneth J. Conant, it must have been an astonishing work: a 365-foot-long by over 250-foot-wide beautifully articulated mass of brown granite, consisting of a powerful and massive west-work, nine towers, and nine protruding *apsidioles* embracing the sanctuary arm and the eastern side of the transept. As it was also typical in many other contemporaneous churches (such as Saint-Sernin in Toulouse and Sante-Foi at Conques, both in France), each of these spatial constituents—the nave, transept, apse, towers, radiating chapels, and apsidioles—were clearly identifiable from the exterior as differentiated volumes. However, at Santiago de Compostela the additions made in the seventeenth and eighteenth centuries entirely mask that rich volumetric diversity. In fact, the only remaining part of the original Romanesque exterior is the southern transept façade, completed in the early 1100s and known as Puerta de la Platerías because of its proximity to the silversmiths' shops.

The *narthex*'s portal, or Pórtico de la Gloria (masked by the Obradoiro façade since the seventeenth century) is a sculptural masterpiece of the period. Obviously inspired by the remarkable portal of the Basilica of La Madeleine in Vézelay, it was designed by a certain Maestro Mateo who carved and installed it in Santiago de Compostela between 1168 and 1188. Whereas many parts of the cathedral were still unfinished, there is no doubt that, as Whitehill remarked, "to the men of the twelfth century the cathedral—with its nine towers, its long transepts, and its triforium gallery making the full circuit around the building—was an achievement complete in itself" (Whitehill 1941, 283). Later in the twelfth century the cathedral was fortified to protect it against enemies' raids; a defensive clock tower was added to the southern transept façade next to the Puerta de las Platerías, and numerous buildings, including the archbishops' palace and pilgrims' facilities, were built adjacent to the cathedral in the following centuries. One of the more interesting additions is the *Renaissance* double stairway and platform built to provide access to the church from the plaza located about 80 feet below the nave's level (the nave was at a higher level because it was built above the relics found in the ninth century). Below the stairs, there is an interesting *crypt* that originally supported the cathedral's original Romanesque west-work and narthex.

The last consequential additions and modifications were made in the seventeenth and eighteenth centuries. In 1667, Peña de Toro designed a new south tower for the west-work, later matched by another one, on a similar style, for the north side. In 1738, Fernando Casas y Novoa added the Obradoiro façade between the two towers, thus completing an entirely new 524-foot-wide west-front for the great pilgrimage church. Both the towers and the centerfold piece are remarkable representatives of the Baroque-Churrigueresque, a regional (Spanish) architectural development named after the exuberant style of the Churriguera brothers (José, Joaquín, and Alberto Churriguera), authors of important buildings of the period such as the **Plaza Mayor of Salamanca**. The Obradoiro façade is built in front of the twelfth-century Portico de la Gloria. Thus, it replaced it as the building's façade without demolishing it. The two more than 200-foot-tall towers (one for the bells, the other for the *"carraca"* or Easter rattle) and the elaborated tripartite center piece (the Obradoiro façade), created a new silhouette for Santiago de Compostela, one that resembles more a Gothic than a Baroque cathedral. However, the attention to detail and relief, the ascending sequence of superimposed tiers of columns, pilasters, and deeply carved arched niches lodging statues, is unquestionably Baroque in character. The culmination of the ascending sequence is remarkably exuberant, with fragmented arched pediments that do not interrupt the accentuated verticality of the façade's new monumental centerfold.

Built, added to, and remodeled through the centuries, the interior of Santiago de Compostela's cathedral is a pure demonstration of the ideal Romanesque pilgrimage church, while the exterior, through the numerous additions and transformations, exhibits the importance of the site and the monument as shown by the constant desire to embellish it in successive historical periods. Today, it continues to be the spiritual goal of thousands of pilgrims who, from various points of departure in Europe, undertake the long journey to the cathedral. Architecturally, it stands as an aggregation of various architectural styles, each one of them clearly identifiable, that coexist in one of the greatest architectural monuments of all time.

Further Reading

Blunt, Anthony, ed. *Baroque and Rococo: Architecture and Decoration*. New York: Harper & Row, 1978.

Chueca Goitía, Fernando. *Historia de la Arquitectura Española: Edad Antigua y Edad Media*. Vol. 1. Madrid: Editorial Dossat, 1965.

Conant, Kenneth John. *Carolingian and Romanesque Architecture 800–1200*. 2nd ed. Middlesex: Penguin Books, 1978.

Norberg-Schulz, Christian. *Meaning in Western Architecture*. New York: Rizzoli, 1980.

Whitehill, Walter Muir. *Spanish Romanesque Architecture of the Eleventh Century*. Oxford: Oxford University Press, 1941.

CATHEDRAL OF TERUEL, TERUEL, ARAGON

Style: Mudéjar Architecture
Dates: Circa 1257–1335; 1538
Architects: Unknown; completion attributed to Yuzaf of Zaragoza

The Arab occupation of Iberia, which started with the invasion of Berber tribes in 711 and quickly expanded through virtually the entire peninsula, and the subsequent slow but relentless recuperation of the lost territories by Christian kingdoms that concluded in 1492, produced a rich variety of artistic and architectural developments unique to Iberia that were the result of the fertile crossbreeding of the two cultures—Islamic and Christian—and their different iconographic and building traditions. *Mozarabic* art and architecture, notably represented by the small church of **San Miguel de Escalada**, and the *Mudéjar* style are two characteristically Iberian developments that testify to the richness provoked by the mixture of the two different but coexisting religious and artistic traditions.

The word "mudéjar" derives from the Arab "mudayyan," which means "permitted to remain" and refers to the Muslim population that, after Christians recovered the territories formerly ruled by Muslim leaders, were allowed to remain and to continue practicing their faith. However, applied to art and architecture, the term primarily refers to Christian art produced by Muslim artisans and craftsmen for Christian works. More generally, it has been often used to describe a wider range of works that share some stylistical characteristics regardless of whether they were produced by Muslims, Christians, or Jews—the so-called "tres culturas" (three cultures) that coexisted and influenced each other throughout much of Spain in Medieval times. The thirteenth-century synagogue of Ibn Shoshan in Toledo, better known for its Christian name of **Santa María la Blanca**, is an excellent example of the crossbreeding of the three cultures.

Expectedly, Mudéjar architecture reached higher levels of development in the more arabized regions of Spain, particularly in Andalucía, Levante (the southern and central parts of the eastern coast), and Aragon, as well as in Castilla, the vast central plateau of the peninsula. The twelfth-century addition to the **Mosque of Bāb-al-Mardūm** is one small but interesting example of Mudéjar architecture in Toledo, the important and influential Castilian city. A Mudéjar architecture with unique local characteristics developed in each of these regions; often, unique regional aspects were a direct conse-

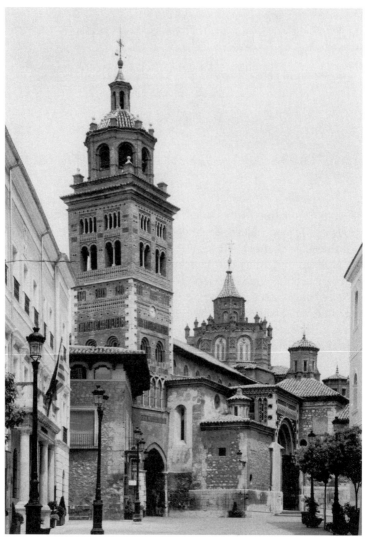

General exterior view of the Cathedral of Teruel.

quence of the importance and influence of one or more specific buildings located in the region. In Aragon where, according to Chueca Goitía, the most original and homogeneous line of Mudéjar architecture evolved, Zaragoza's **Palace of La Aljafería** played a prominent role and was very influential in the whole region (Chueca Goitía 1965, 470). Teruel, a much smaller city located in southern Aragon and founded in 1171 next to the ruins of the former Muslim village of Tirwal is, because of the wealth and quality of its heritage, the most important center of Aragon's Mudéjar architecture. The city's cathedral, the towers of San Salvador and San Martín, and the church of San Pedro are Teruel's most important Mudéjar monuments; within its area of influence, the parish church of Montalbán is yet another remarkable example of this singular architecture.

In general, Mudéjar architecture can be characterized as the implementation of typically Muslim building materials and techniques (often including ornamental elements and decorative patterns) to Christian buildings usually derived from well-known *Romanesque* or *Gothic* types, such as basilican churches and bell towers, but also to palaces and military architecture. A distinctive characteristic of Mudéjar architecture is the use of modest construction materials, primarily red-clay brick, plaster and wood; yet, a regional distinctive characteristic of Aragon's Mudéjar, especially in Teruel's area of influence, is the extensive use of colored glazed tiles creating a wide variety of decorative ways. Another typical aspect of Teruel's Mudéjar is the incorporation of structural and typological elements derived from *Almohad* models such as the turret. The beautiful towers of San Salvador and San Martín are excellent examples that feature the more salient characteristics of Aragon's Mudéjar; however, the Cathedral of Teruel is the most significant work of Mudéjar architecture.

The church of Santa María de Mediavilla, Cathedral of Teruel since 1587, is located at the heart of Teruel's historical center on the site of a formerly existing smaller Romanesque church likely built in the twelfth century. In 1257, a Mudéjar tower-gate of considerable height was added to the building's west end. Architecturally, this tower was conceived as an Almohad's turret: a tall square tower enclosing a stairs entirely built in brick and profusely decorated with a wide variety of brick-relief patterns—superimposed blind arcades, arched openings, geometrical figures, and so forth—and, in typical Teruel fashion, highlighted by a multitude of colored glazed tiles—mostly green and blue—arranged to form ribbons, colonnettes, and colonnades, and a large diversity of geometrical compositions. The tower culminates in an octagonal pavilion added in the eighteenth century; it is inscribed within the tower's square plan and crowned by an octagonal lantern and a cross that boosted the visibility of the building. The addition of the tower dwarfed the existing Romanesque church; therefore, using the Romanesque structure as a point of departure, a considerable enlargement of the church in Mudéjar style was undertaken during the second half of the thirteenth century respecting the basic outline of the building's plan but considerably increasing its height. The *ciborium* that rises over the crossing was built in 1538 in imitation of the also Mudéjar ciborium of Zaragoza's Seo. The cathedral's main portal, located on the southern side of the building, is a work from the *Modernismo* period designed by Pablo Monguió in 1909.

The cathedral's plan is rather typical and simple: a *Latin-cross* plan consisting of a four-bay central *nave* flanked by aisles, a projecting *transept*, and a polygonal *apse* surrounded by an orthogonal *ambulatory* without flanking chapels. The head of the building—transept and apse—was completed c.

1335 and it is attributed to a Moorish master known as Yuzaf of Zaragoza, while the ambulatory was added in the eighteenth century. The building's interior has aspects of architectural interest, yet, undoubtedly, the roof's structure that covers the central nave is the most salient and extraordinary element because of its innovative characteristics, enormous quality, and decorative splendor. Known as the "techumbre," this structure is a wooden armature of "par-y-nudillo" (rafter and dowel), a structural innovation imported from Seville; it is approximately 105 feet long and nearly 30 feet wide. Lengthwise, the structure is divided into nine equal modules by ten double tension wooden beams, while across its width it has three gables, each approximately 11.5 feet wide; the central one is flat and the two sides slope down following the inclination of the roof; the whole constitutes a stable tridimensional structure approximately 7 feet deep. In addition to the remarkable technological innovation that it represented, the "techumbre" is entirely painted with high-quality polychrome images featuring geometrical patterns, vegetal motifs, and epigraphic elements of undoubted Muslim influence, as well as figurative and symbolic decoration linked to Gothic representation.

The Cathedral of Teruel and the city's numerous other contemporaneous Mudéjar buildings are formidable examples of a unique architectural development, reflecting the social, political, and artistic richness and complexity of Spain's multicultural society in the Middle Ages. They have been globally protected by UNESCO's World Heritage program since 1986.

Further Reading

Borrás Gualis, Gonzalo M. *El Arte Mudéjar en Teruel y su Provincia*. Teruel: Instituto de Estudios Turolenses, 1987.

Chueca Goitía, Fernando. *Historia de la Arquitectura Española: Edad Antigua y Edad Media*. Vol. 1. Madrid: Editorial Dossat, 1965.

Corral Lafuente, José Luis, and Peña Gonzalvo, Francisco Javier, eds. *La Cultura Islámica en Aragón*. Zaragoza: Diputación Provincial de Zaragoza, 1989.

Hoag, John D. *Islamic Architecture*. New York: Harry N. Abrams, 1977.

CHURCH OF CRISTO DE LA LUZ.
See Mosque of Bāb-al-Mardūm.

CHURCH OF THE SACRED HEART, VISTABELLA, CATALONIA

Style: *Modernismo* Catalán
Dates: 1918–1923
Architect: Josep María Jujol

The Church of the Sacred Heart in Vistabella, near Tarragona, is one of the masterpieces of Josep M. Jujol, direct disciple of Antoni Gaudí and perhaps the last practicing architect whose work belongs to the artistic movement known as *Modernismo*. Jujol was also a painter, sculptor, ironworker, graphic designer, and ceramic and stained-glass artist. As an architect, he was a close collaborator of Gaudí—unquestionably the most relevant figure of Spain's Modernismo—with whom he worked in many of his masterpieces, notably Casa Batlló, **Casa Milá**, and **Park Güell**. Interestingly, some of Jujol's most famous creations are part of his collaboration with Gaudí (and often attributed to the great master), such as the ironwork of Casa Milá's balconies and the extraordinary *trencadis*-covered sinuous bench and the medallions on the ceiling of Park Güell's market. At the same time that he worked with Gaudí (which he did until the master's death in 1926), Jujol undertook architectural commissions on his own, producing remarkable buildings such as the Casa Bofarull, Casa Planells (a small apartment building on Barcelona's Diagonal Avenue), and the Teatro Metropol in Tarragona.

Not unlike Gaudí's, Jujol's work is rooted in his profound religious convictions and devotion, as well as in a careful attention to nature, as demonstrated by the extensive use of nature-related themes—air, water, animal, and vegetal motifs—throughout his work. In his architectural projects he incorporated aspects of the many other creative disciplines in which he worked—and excelled—achieving the ideal synthesis of the arts typical of late-nineteenth-century artistic and architectural trends such as Modernismo, *Art Nouveau*, and the *Arts and Crafts Movement*. As Vincent Ligtelijn and Rein Saariste sharply commented, "in the hands of Jujol the painter, sculptor, ironworker and stained-glass artist, architectural space became extraordinary, tailor-made clothing" (Ligtelijn and Saariste 53).

The small Church of the Sacred Heart is located at the intersection of three narrow streets that generate a small square, named Plaza del Dr. Josep Gaspé i Blanch, at the center of Vistabella, a small village located fifteen miles west of Tarragona that has a permanent population of barely 120 people. The project was commissioned in 1917 through Vistabella's Mr. Mallafré; construction began the following year, and the small church was finally completed in 1923. In 1924, Jujol was asked to design the adjacent rectory, but

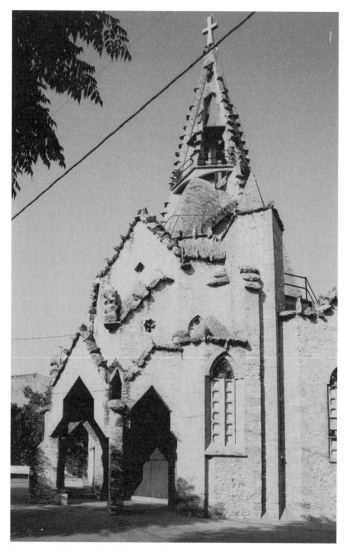

Exterior of Vistabella's Church of the Sacred Heart from the small open space that it faces.

it was only partially completed. As was typical of his work, he closely supervised the building's construction and personally executed many of its components, including interior paintings and candelabra.

The site assigned for the church was a quite small lot situated on the edge of the village's urban fabric. Jujol took as much advantage as possible of the site's small dimensions by occupying almost the entire place with a square plan oriented diagonally, that is, placing the entrance and the altar at opposite corners of the square plan; the hexagonal open porch that provides access to the church is placed at the outer corner of the square, projecting halfway beyond the square perimeter and half carved within. Inside, four rectangular pillars define a central space at the heart of the square; these pillars support two high parabolic arches that—traversing the resulting rectangular space across the two diagonals—intersect at the center of the square plan. Consequently, two distinct spatial and typological explorations converge: a linear sequence of spaces along the long diagonal of the square plan comprised of the out-projecting porch, central space, and altar; and a centralized plan defined by the clear vertical emphasis given by the high vaulted space. This may suggest that the building is Jujol's personal interpretation and synthesis of the two predominant typological models, linear and central, explored through the centuries-long history of Christian architecture.

In spite of the geometrical clarity exhibited by the plan and section drawings, the building's interior and exterior are extremely complex to the point that it is virtually impossible to discern the square shape of the plan and the conceptually symmetric cross section from either the exterior or interior of the church. The interior is simply spectacular. Beyond the compressed entrance, the vaulted central space expands vertically in all directions as if it would have been insufflated by some unknown source; at the end of the implied linear axis, the slightly elevated altar presided over by the image of the Sacred Heart, is the church's inevitable focal point. The whole is almost entirely painted, displaying natural and sacred motifs in vivid colors (blue, yellow, gold, red, white, and black) executed by Jujol himself; some of these painted images—angels, natural elements, and highly stylized texts—are absolutely delicate and beautiful, pure demonstration of his versatile artistic interests and skills. The *vault*'s ceiling is painted in deep blue, sprinkled with white and golden stars, as if the building's interior could be a natural exterior, a vast encompassing sky. The interior is illuminated through a few pointed arch windows filled in with thin translucent alabaster tiles and crowned with colorful painted glass planes. Artificial illumination is provided by candelabra designed and hand-made by Jujol with discarded tin cans.

The hexagonal porch has three main doors leading directly to the church's main *nave*; an additional door, on the extreme right side, also provides access to the interior of the building, but it opens to a small space segregated from the nave that houses the baptistery; thus, Jujol established a subtle but effective difference that complies with the old requisite of limiting access to the consecrated space only to those that had been baptized. Adjacent to the baptistery, a constricted spiral stair leads to a mezzanine level that balconies over the main nave and eventually opens onto the roof, where a narrow exterior stair that meanders over the complex roof-planes conducts to the openwork belfry.

The exterior is as enigmatic as the interior. The walls are made in exposed masonry composed of a mixture of ceramic red brick and irregular stone; bricks highlight the regular forms of the triple gate, window frames, and implied pilasters, while irregular stones fill in the spaces between. The multi-sectioned brick vault is fully exposed, resembling a medieval building that exposes the interior vaulting system to the exterior; above the vault, the open belfry reaches high, nearly doubling the vault's height. Vaults, walls, pilasters, and belfry configure a complex form; the walls' top edge is emphasized by a cornice line made of flat stones of irregular dimensions (it is said that Jujol asked the villagers to collect them in nearby vineyards) generating a building outline that recalls the skin of a prehistoric beast. In fact, the building's interior and exterior exhibit Jujol's debt to Gaudi's work, notably the unfinished church at Colonia Güell, Casa Batlló, and Casa Milá.

In 1936, Vistabella's Church of the Sacred Heart suffered a fire that partially damaged the building without challenging its overall structure. In the last twenty years, when interest in Jujol's work revived as part of a broader renewed attention to the architecture of Modernismo, many of his works, including this little church, were restored. Partially restored in recent years (only the central space and exterior were thoroughly recuperated), the little church in Vistabella has become a major point of reference as the most representative work of a talented and rather enigmatic architect who is regarded as the last master of Modernismo Catalan, one of the most vigorous creative moments of Spain's architectural history.

Further Reading

Curtis, William J. R. *Modern Architecture since 1900*. 3rd ed. London: Phaidon Press Limited, 1996.

Ligtelijn, Vincent, and Saariste, Rein. *Josep M. Jujol*. Rótterdam: 010 Publishers, 1996.

Llinàs, Josep. *Saques de Esquina*. Girona: Editorial Pre-textos, 2002.

Solà-Morales, Ignasi de. *Jujol*. New York: Rizzoli, 1991.

Solà-Morales, Ignasi de, Capitel, Antón, and Buchanan, Peter et al., eds. *Birkhäuser Architectural Guide, Spain 1920–1999*. Basel: Birkhäuser Verlag, 1998.

CITY OF ARTS AND SCIENCES, VALENCIA, COMUNIDAD DE VALENCIA

Style: Contemporary Architecture
Dates: 1991–2000
Architect: Santiago Calatrava

The City of Arts and Sciences of Valencia is the largest and most ambitious building complex undertaken to date by Santiago Calatrava, one of the world's most renowned contemporary architects. A native of Valencia, where he studied architecture, Calatrava also studied civil engineering at Zurich's prestigious ETH (Swiss Federal Institute of Technology). It is precisely in Zurich that he established a practice after winning the competition for the city's Stadelhofen Railway Station (1983–1990). Since then, he has become one of the most prolific architects of contemporary architecture, with works built throughout the world. His numerous bridges in Spain (Barcelona, Bilbao, Ripoll, Sevilla, Valencia) and abroad (Orleans, Lille, Berlin) earned him a reputation for structural audacity and expressionism that quickly extended to other types of works (museums, airports, offices, stadiums). The extension to Milwaukee Arts Museum (Wisconsin 2001) and the Olympic Stadium in Athens (2004) are among his internationally acclaimed, recently completed buildings. Calatrava's work can be inscribed as part of a fruitful tradition of twentieth-century architect-engineers such as Eduardo Torroja (creator of the **La Zarzuela Racecourse Grandstand**), Pier Luigi Nervi, Félix Candela, Peter Rice, and Frei Otto, as well as form-innovators such as Antoni Gaudí and Eero Saarinen.

The City of Arts and Sciences is a large cultural complex of buildings housing a Science Museum, a Planetarium and IMAX Theater, and a parking garage and urban garden known as the Umbráculo. These three structures are located on the dry bed of the Turia River, between the Monteolivete Bridge and another bridge that traverses the dry bed farther to the southeast, in part of a nearly ninety-acre site designated for the whole complex on the southeastern edge of Valencia, between the city's center and its seafront district and harbor. The Oceanographic, a large marine-life center housed under concrete shell structures conceived by Felix Candela and located on the other side of the bridge, is a cultural and architectural complement to

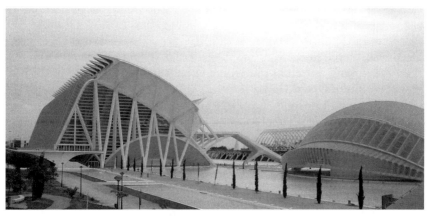

General view of the City of Arts and Sciences building complex; the museum is on the center left of the image and the Planetarium and IMAX theater on the right; the *Umbráculo* is between them on the background.

Calatrava's major architectural interventions. The project is part of a vast initiative launched by Valencia to develop a cultural institution of national and international stature at the same level of other similar institutions built in other cities in Spain such as the **Guggenheim Museum** in Bilbao, the Ciudad de la Cultura in Santiago de Compostela, and the **Kursaal Auditorium and Cultural Center** in San Sebastián, to name but a few. In fact, the history of the project is quite unusual: in 1991, Santiago Calatrava won a design competition to build a Telecommunications Tower that was to be placed on the west part of the site; that same year he received the direct commission to design a Science Center and a Planetarium in addition to the Telecommunications Tower. As a consequence of a governmental change, the Telecommunications Tower project was eventually withdrawn and replaced by a new, state-of-the-art immense Opera House and Performing Arts Center to be located in the site of the Telecommunications Tower. The latter (still under construction) is both part of the overall City of Arts and Sciences project and an independent volume of overwhelming scale.

The three buildings that have been completed so far—the Science Museum, the Planetarium and IMAX Theater, and the Umbráculo—occupy the southern half of the site, delimited by the two above-mentioned bridges, the Junta de Murs i Valls street, and the Autopista de El Saler; the park area occupies the northern half. The three are linked by axial paths and flanked by reflecting pools that recall the former presence of the river in the site and at the same time work as water reservoirs for the building's mechanical and fire protection systems. The first built structure was the Planetarium and IMAX Theater (completed in 1998); this central piece of the site's western area was conceived to resemble a human eye: the semispherical dome of the IMAX Theater is the eye's pupil, while the concrete shell and articulated (movable) glass and metal sides represent the eye's socket and eyelids, respectively. These two elements create a protecting canopy for the ambiguous interior-exterior spaces placed below, a protected outdoor space that forms a promenade around the semispherical volume of the IMAX Theater. The Planetarium and other services of this building component were accommodated below level, thus preserving the pure analogical eye form that emerges from the ground as well as preventing visual conflict with the Science Museum and future Opera House.

The Science Museum is the most important and largest completed building on the site. It consists of a large longitudinal hall almost 800 feet long by 350 feet wide composed of twenty-one identical modules that support an inclined aluminum roof and the cantilevering brackets that receive the structure of support of the immense glazed curtain-wall that encloses the long vertical space that faces the park on the entire northern side of the building. The twenty-one structural modules are created and supported by the branching off of five massive concrete pylons that also accommodate, in their interior, the vertical circulation systems of the building. These pylons are

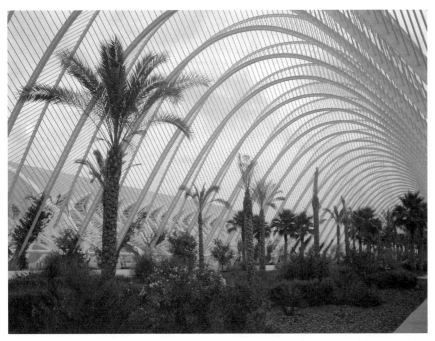

The *Umbráculo*; the southern side of the museum appears beyond and through its permeable structure.

veritable arborescent (tree-like) structural elements that punctuate the building's interior with structural rigor and sculptural plasticity.

The museum has three main levels; the lower level houses the two main entrances placed at the two ends of the volume's longitudinal extension and at same level of the ensemble's exterior spaces; this level also accommodates ticket booths, restaurants, a cafeteria, gift shops, offices, and many other building services. The intermediate level houses several exhibition galleries, while the museum's main gallery occupies the entire third floor; large, spacious, widely open and profusely illuminated by large panes of glass, this uppermost gallery is framed by the intricate and ingenious, fully exposed, structural system that supports the whole building. The two gallery levels balcony over the dynamic, fully glazed vertical space on the north side of the building. This building, like most of Calatrava's work, is a structural feat, a complex—yet extremely clear—sequence of interconnected structural elements that define every part of the building as well as the whole. The section is quite remarkable, resembling the articulated skeleton of a giant insect or of an enormous prehistoric animal. In fact, it would not be exaggerating to say that the Science Museum is a glass-enclosed skeleton, pure structure sealed by a transparent skin.

Designed in 1996 and built between 1997 and 2000, the Umbráculo is the newest portion of the large building complex. Extending alongside the Autopista de El Saler, it consists of a 1,000-foot-long by 200-foot-wide urban garden and promenade with a parking garage for seven hundred cars and twenty buses located below. The promenade, which appears as an open-air variation of the Science Musuem's glass-enclosed northern space, is slightly elevated from the street level and is covered by a high arched steel structure with open lattice work that intends to mitigate the effect of the intense Mediterranean sun. It is a graceful and elegant structure that counterpoints the formal and structural exuberance of its neighbors. The whole space is flanked by a long concrete bench and a deep concrete planter both of which are entirely covered with small and irregular fragments of white ceramic tiles that recall Gaudí's colorful bench at **Park Güell**. In fact, Gaudí's work is often cited as a precedent of Calatrava's work because of their similar interest in structural innovation and experimentation, formal audacity, and exuberant expressionism.

Santiago Calatrava's buildings for Valencia's City of Arts and Sciences are a formidable architectural ensemble in which the architect-engineer-artist has made a powerful demonstration of structural virtuosity in the design of various complex buildings. The already completed Science Museum, Planetarium and IMAX Theater, and Umbráculo await the completion of the Opera House and the construction of Calatrava's new bridge on the east end of the site to constitute a unique place where one architect was able to design and build a remarkable series of buildings of major architectural and engineering relevance, as well as of cultural and civic importance.

Further Reading

Calatrava, Santiago. "Museo de las Ciencias, Valencia." *AV Monografías* 87, 88 (January–April 2001).
Calatrava, Santiago. "Science Museum." *Lotus International* 109 (Milano), 2001.
Jodidio, Philip. *Santiago Calatrava*. Cologne: Benedikt Taschen Verlag, 1998.

CIVIL GOVERNMENT BUILDING, TARRAGONA, CATALONIA

Style: International Modernism
Dates: 1956–1964; restored in 1985–1987
Architects: Alejandro de la Sota; restoration by A. de la Sota and Josep Llinàs

The Civil Government Building in Tarragona, designed by Madrid-based architect Alejandro de la Sota, is the most important Spanish institutional work of architecture of the 1950s, an emblem of a moment in which Spain began to reopen to the rest of the world after two decades of complete international isolation following the end of the Civil War (1936–1939). The building is also a symbol of the resistance of architects to the regressive eclecticism that characterized Francisco Franco's period (1939–1975). Moreover, along with the Gymnasium of the Maravillas School (Madrid 1960–1962), the Civil Government building is one of the two most celebrated works of Alejandro de la Sota, an unavoidable reference for post–Civil War architecture in Spain.

The project was the result of a competition won by Alejandro de la Sota in 1956. However, construction began only in 1957 and the building was completed and inaugurated in 1963. The Civil Government Building is located on the north edge of Plaza Imperial Tarraco, a roundabout north of the *Ramblas* that, in the 1950s, was virtually at the edge of the city's urban

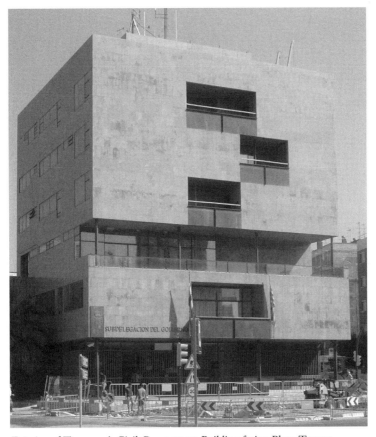

Exterior of Tarragona's Civil Government Building facing Plaza Tarraco.

core. Its function was to represent and conduct the business of the country's central government in Catalonia. The brief consisted of governmental offices and official residence for the governor, the general secretary, guests-of-honor, as well as two apartments for service staff. In general, one-half of the programmed area was for offices and governmental functions, while the remaining half was for residential purposes. The competition brief also defined the building's height at 23 meters (approximately 75 feet), required street front alignment facing Plaza Imperial Tarraco, and imposed the use of stone for the façades.

The modernity of de la Sota's winning entry was absolutely astonishing for a building of such institutional visibility in a period in which "official architecture" invariably had neo-regional eclectic or neoclassical tones. To borrow William Curtis' words, in Tarragona, de la Sota "inverted customary expectations of civic monumentality," where "official architecture would have had a solid base, a wall punctured by windows, a symmetrical façade and a crowning cornice, de la Sota's building had a transparent base, a planar wall, and a counterpoint between symmetry and asymmetry" (Curtis 1996, 487). In other words, while complying with the competition requirements, de la Sota delivered an impeccable project that challenged the status quo of governmental buildings of the period and created a landmark of Spain's twentieth-century architecture. Not surprisingly, Franco declined to attend the building's official inauguration. Beyond the anecdotic, the virtues of the building rest on its sober monumental image and the mastery with which the architect resolved a complex program that combined governmental offices with official residences without compromising the building's formal integrity and institutional image. In fact, the integration of the two main components—offices and dwellings—is truly remarkable. This is tightly and cleverly condensed in the front façade, a marvelous exercise of architectural composition that emphasizes the building's institutional role and incorporates ambiguous and ironic commentary.

The whole building is planned on a precise 6-meter-square modular and structural grid (nearly 20 by 20 feet). The overall mass of the building is conceptually symmetric, but symmetry is challenged by protruding components that embrace the main volume on the rear lower levels and by subtle displacements and decentering of elements in the main façade. Briefly stated, the building consists of a three-story base that houses governmental and office functions, a transitional one-story level for ceremonial purposes, and a four-story cube housing the "important" residences (governor, secretary general, and guests of honor). The three-level base volume takes advantage of the wedge shape of the site by occupying three 6-meter-wide bays at the front and five bays at the rear; this volume houses general building services and the two generous apartments for service staff in the semi-buried lowest floor, a magnificent lobby conceived as an enclosed public space placed in the front of the ground floor with offices in the rear side; the governmental functions, including the governor's office suite, are in the first floor. Conversely, the other five levels of the building are housed within a three-bay-square volume pushed to the front of the site to comply with the 23-meter height regulation and, especially, with the street front alignment facing Plaza Imperial Tarraco.

At the front of the building, the ground floor and the ceremonial level are enclosed by floor-to-ceiling glazed enclosures that sharply contrast with the predominantly opaque stone façade of the other floors. Deeply recessed from the frontline of the building, these two levels emphasize the hovering aspect of the stone-clad volumes; this is reinforced by four slender steel columns, clearly inspired by **The German Pavilion** designed by Mies van der Rohe and built in Barcelona in 1929. These four columns constitute the only departure from the rigid 6-meter structural grid; not only are they in steel instead of concrete as the rest of the building's skeleton, but also they are subtly displaced from the modular grid echoing the curvilinear geometry of the site's front at the circular Plaza Imperial Tarraco.

The side and rear elevations are notably softer than the front façade, responding more to the needs of providing light and ventilation to the related interior spaces than to the building's institutional image. This civic role is, however, manifestly expressed by the building's south façade. This façade exhibits an undoubtedly intended formality enriched with ambiguous and symbolic gestures; a hierarchical and symbolically empowering center is clearly marked at the first floor by the protruding loggia of the governor's suite and again in the uppermost level with the opening for the outdoor patio of the Governor's residence. Yet, between these two corresponding elements, the patio openings of the other two residences (visibly smaller) and other elements of the front façade are subtly displaced from the center, establishing clear and intentional hierarchical differences. Moreover, there is an unavoidable facial resemblance in the composition of this façade, as if the building, conscious of its role as representative of Madrid's central government in a region that had historically opposed it, indicated—through a somewhat elegant grimace—a certain discomfort in being there.

After years of poor maintenance and insensitive modifications to the original building, the building was fully restored by Barcelona-based architect Josep Llinàs, who worked in close collaboration with the original architect, Alejandro de la Sota. The restoration was commissioned by the Ministry of the Interior with the objective of returning the building as much as possible to its original condition while adapting it to the changing needs of contemporary government buildings. Llinàs' respect and careful study of the building, as well as de la Sota's participation, guaranteed a successful operation. Not surprisingly, the building quickly and easily adapted to the different needs of the democratic system that followed the end of Franco's regime. More interestingly, the building reemerged as a revered icon of Spain's middle-of-the-century modern architecture, representing more the resistance to the regime's architectural conservatism than the totalitarian government for which it was conceived. Today, it is considered as one of the seminal buildings of Spain's architectural renaissance in the second part of the twentieth century and a very influential work for younger generations of architects.

Further Reading

"Alejandro de la Sota." Special monographic issue, *AV* 68 (Madrid), 1997.

Curtis, William J. R. *Modern Architecture since 1900*. 3rd ed. London: Phaidon Press Limited, 1996.

Llinàs, Josep. *Saques de Esquina*. Girona: Editorial Pre-textos, 2002.

Saliga, Pauline, and Thorne, Martha. *Building a New Spain: Contemporary Spanish Architecture*. Barcelona: Editorial Gustavo Gili, 1992.

Sota, Alejandro de la, et al. *Alejandro de la Sota: The Architecture of Imperfection*. London: Architectural Association, 1997.

CLUB NÁUTICO OF SAN SEBASTIÁN, SAN SEBASTIÁN, GUIPÚZCOA

Style: Modern Movement—International Style
Date: 1929
Architects: Aizpurúa and Labayén

The small building for the Sailing Club of San Sebastián—known as the Club Náutico—is the most representative example of International Style Architecture in Spain. The term "International Style" was coined after a major architectural exhibition held in 1932 at New York's Museum of Modern Art that was organized by Alfred Barr, Henry-Russell Hitchcock, and Philip Johnson. This exhibit, and its accompanying book entitled *The International Style: Architecture since 1922*, eventually became a milestone in the history of architecture because of its early attempt to classify and understand the salient features of the then emerging *Modern Movement* that, in their opinion, had already developed sufficient general characteristics to be considered "a style." The authors' emphasis was on the visual and formal similarities that the work and postulates of these architects exhibited, leaving aside particular differences and the work of other notable representatives of early twentieth-century architecture that did not fit in their scheme. Thus, book and exhibit included the work of those who were then considered the most progressive architects of the then emerging Modern Movement—Walter Gropius, Mies van der Rohe, Le Corbusier, J.J.P. Oud, Richard Neutra, and many others. The Club Náutico was the only building designed by Spanish architects featured in that milestone event in the evolution of twentieth-century architecture.

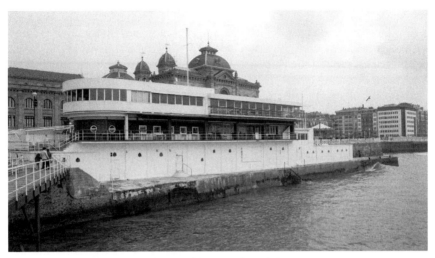

View of the Club Náutico's façade toward the Bay of San Sebastián.

The building was designed by José Manuel Aizpurúa and Joaquín Labayén, two young and emerging architects; in fact, they were the youngest of a group today known as the "1925 generation." This was not an established group of architects but a historical category that observed the efforts made by young Spanish architects—Fernando Mercadal, Manuel Sanchez Arcas, Luis Lacasa, and others—to introduce in Spain the avant-garde principles and ideals postulated by the fathers of the Modern Movement. The Club Náutico would eventually be Aizpurúa and Labayén's most significant work among their few built contributions. Today, the Club Náutico is—along with Peña Ganchegui and Eduardo Chillida's **Plaza del Tenis and Peine del Viento**, and Rafael Moneo's **Kursaal Auditorium and Cultural Center**—the earliest of three masterpieces of Spain's twentieth-century architecture that dot San Sebastián's seafront.

The Club Náutico is located opposite the late-nineteenth-century building of the Gran Casino (now the city's town hall) and perched between the seafront walls and the beach at the east end of the Paseo de Concha, a long and beautiful strolling promenade along the crescent-shaped sandy beach Playa de la Concha that is framed between two splendid rocky promontories, the Monte Urgull (immediately north of the sailing club) and Monte Igeldo, at the opposite west end. The commission given to Aizurúa consisted of extending the existing club house building that was placed below street level by the sea; in fact, its roof used to be accessible as a slightly elevated terraced extension of the seafront's promenade. The program comprised the provision of locker rooms, a members' hall, a restaurant, and the typical service areas associated with a building of these characteristics.

Aizurúa and Labayén used the existing brick building as the base for their addition, extending it lengthwise to accommodate the new locker rooms;

above, they added a two-story concrete building with evident nautical allusions. This consisted of an elongated and predominantly horizontal volume with a semicircular end; the lower floor, matching the street level on Paseo de la Concha, housed the club members' hall and office while the upper level was devoted to a members' restaurant that, through an uninterrupted horizontal band of sliding windows, provides wonderful views to the ocean, the mounts, and the crescent-shaped sandy beach. The nautical metaphor and image, which by then had become one of the formal and stylistic attributes of the Modern Movement, was more than obvious: hanging on the edge between land and sea, the building borrowed the image of a ship, consisting of a horizontally extended white volume hovering over a rather opaque base; the base's bull-eye openings, deck-like terraces, wood paneling, and extended use of metal railings reinforced the naval metaphor, which in this case was further emphasized by the building's function and location. In fact, from the sea and across the bay, the sailing club resembles a small ship anchored by the city's edge.

Aizpurúa and Labayén's building is—because of its formal characteristics and architectural vocabulary—the most distilled Spanish example of International Style architecture. The architectural language and image of the Club Náutico have been often associated with Le Corbusier's contemporaneous Villa Savoye (Poissy 1928–1931), universally recognized as one of the masterpieces of the period; however, formally and conceptually it is more closely related to the work of other architects and buildings of the period, notably the workers' housing in Hook of Holland (1924), designed by the Dutch architect J.J.P. Oud. Moreover, the building has an added significance as the most important work of the progressive period—architecturally and politically—that preceded Spain's Civil War (1936–1939) and the dictatorship of Francisco Franco (1939–1975) that had a long-lasting regressive impact on the evolution of Spain's twentieth-century architecture. The Club Náutico is regarded as the highest accomplishment of the "1925 generation" outside of Catalonia, where Josep Lluís Sert—a former collaborator of Le Corbusier—and the architects associated with the *GATCPAC* produced other significant works of the period such as the **Dispensario Antituberculoso**.

In spite of the dictatorship's hostility toward modern architecture, the building survived the Civil War and Franco's period, likely because of its small size and geographical location—in Basque country—where opposition to Franco was high. Moreover, Aizpurúa's authorship of the building should not be discarded as a reason because the building's main architect was an active supporter and local leader of Franco's *Falange Española*; Aizpurúa was assassinated shortly before the beginning of the Civil War, constituting, to some extent, a paradox because, throughout Europe and not without some notable exceptions (for example Giuseppe Terragni in Italy), the architects who subscribed to the ideas and postulates of the Modern Movement were actively opposed to right-wing fascist movements (such as the Falange Española), that flourished in Europe in the 1930s. Today, the building remains in rather good shape but it has suffered some unfortunate alterations such as the added glazed enclosure to the restaurant's terrace on the seafront side and to the entry sequence on Paseo de la Concha. Yet, despite these additions, the nautical image of the building and its rational conception remain unquestioned marks of the building's architecture, preserving its historical importance as the most relevant example of International Style architecture in Spain.

Further Reading

Chueca Goitía, Fernando. *Historia de la Arquitectura Española: Edad Moderna-Edad Contemporánea*. Vol. 2. Madrid: Editorial Dossat, 1965.

Flores, Carlos. *Arquitectura Española Contemporánea, I 1880–1950*. Madrid: Aguilar, 1988.

Hitchcock, Henry-Russell, and Johnson, Philip. *The International Style: Architecture since 1922*. New York: W.W. Norton, 1932.

Tafuri, Manfredo, and Dal Co, Francesco. *Contemporary Architecture*. New York: Harry N. Abrams, 1979.

COAC HEADQUARTERS, BARCELONA, CATALONIA

Style: Modern Architecture
Dates: 1957–1962
Architect: Xavier Busquets i Sindreu

The headquarters of Catalonia's Architects Association in Barcelona, the "COAC," is the emblematic building that represents the triumph of modern architecture, after long years of ostracism during the first decades of Francisco Franco's dictatorial regime. The need to return to a modern architectural practice had been postulated and propagated in Barcelona since the late 1940s by *Grup R* and was anticipated in buildings designed by some architects from this group, such as the **Hotel Park** (Barcelona 1950–1954) by Antoni de Moragas, the **La Marina Apartment Building in La Barceloneta** (Barcelona 1951–1955) by José Antonio Coderch, and the Agusti House in Sitges (1953–1955) by Josep María Sostres. The emblematic stance of the building is reaffirmed by every aspect related to its design; on one hand, because—as the headquarters of the Architects Association, it is considered as "the architects' home" and as the result of an open competition judged by internationally renowned personalities—it made a clear statement in favor of modern architecture; on the other hand, because it is located in Barcelona, a city reputed for the importance of architecture as an

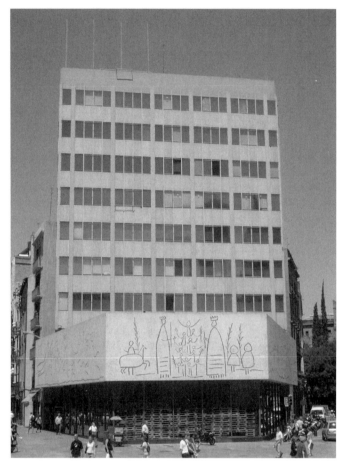

View of the COAC Headquarters exterior.

aspect of cultural pride and identity (this extends to the whole region of Catalonia), and also because of its location at the heart of the Ciutat Vella, the city's historical *Gothic* center.

The design competition took place in 1957 and it was judged by respected personalities such as Gio Ponti and J. H. Van der Broek. As Carme Rodriguez and Jorge Torres commented, "the jury granted awards in two categories according to types of projects that responded to different official positions" (Rodríguez and Torres 1994, 42). Thus, among the projects awarded there were some that postulated an unequivocal modern architectural language as well as others that proposed more traditional and monumental buildings. The competition entries of Xavier Busquets and Antoni de Moragas were among the first, while Eusebi Bona's proposal was representative of the second group. Without a declared winner, a new competition stage, with the incorporation of Alfred Roth as a member of the jury, took place the following year. Busquets' project was finally selected over the entry jointly submitted by Bohigas and Martorell and Giráldez, López Iñigo and Subias (two teams that had presented similar proposals and had been selected in the first stage of the competition), and others. The selection and eventual construction of Xavier Busquets' project in a historically charged urban context was a determinant to reassert modern architecture in Barcelona in particular and in Spain in general. The reaffirmation of modern architecture coincided with the beginning of a period in which Spain succeeded in establishing a certain financial stability and economic development after years of stagnation caused by the Spanish Civil War.

The site for the project was a small, trapezoidal lot placed at the tip of an irregular city block at a very short diagonal distance west of Barcelona's Plaça de la Seu, that is, just in front of the city's splendid Gothic cathedral. The site's trapezoidal form was open on three sides, with the fourth side—the base of the trapezoid or "rear" side—sharing a party wall with the neighboring building. The program consisted of providing a wide variety of public areas—auditorium and conference hall, exhibition area and related functions—and a considerable large surface of office space for the association's numerous activities and services. Busquets' scheme was an exemplary response to the complexities imposed by both program and site and quickly became a referent of how to insert a modern building into a dense historical urban context.

The program's public and private zones were separated and housed into two clearly differentiated intersecting volumes: public functions are accommodated in a low horizontal volume that works as the base for the building, while the offices are housed in a prismatic eight-floor tower; the entrance and main lobby are precisely and intelligently placed at the intersection of the two. The low volume takes over the site's entire available area; at the ground floor it houses the lobby at the rear of the site, accessible from the two long sides of the trapezoid, and a two-level exhibition area at the front; the conference hall-auditorium is placed on the upper floor of this low volume. In contrast with the site-determined form of the lower volume, the tower block rises as a perfect parallelepiped at the site's rear; services and vertical circulation are provided behind, between the rear wall of the tower and the neighboring building, in another predominantly rectangular block slightly displaced to one side—the less exposed side—of the trapezoidal site.

The contrast of the two volumes is further reinforced by their materials. The base has two parts: a floor-to-ceiling transparent enclosure at the street level and a windowless concrete frieze above that encloses the auditorium floor. The concrete frieze features an *sgraffiti* mural with drawings originally made by Pablo Picasso. This was an important detail that emphasized the building's allegiance with modernity because Picasso was the most important Spanish artist of the time—and probably the most famous artist alive worldwide—who was unavoidably associated with a universal idea of modernity. The vertical block leaves the building's metal structure in the façade, which, in the original project, was intended as a fully glazed curtain-wall. This aspect of the building's design echoes, at a much smaller scale, the façades of Mies van der Rohe's Lake Shore Drive apartments in Chicago (1948–1951) and had a conceptual resemblance—yet at a much smaller scale—with Arne Jacobsen's contemporaneous SAS Royal Hotel (Copenhagen 1958–1960). This is not surprising considering that Grup R had actively disseminated the ideas of Nordic modern architecture. The offices spaces of the tower were designed by a variety of architects and some of them were awarded Barcelona's prestigious FAD prize.

The COAC is an important institution in Barcelona and Catalonia, a true mirror of the social and cultural importance of architects in a city and a region that are proud of their architectural history and legacy. Moreover, the Architects Association provides a large spectrum of services to its members. Therefore, an addition to Busquets' building was necessary in the 1980s; however, the site is not adjoining the original building but is located across the street. The building, which houses more offices and the COAC's splendid library collection, was designed and built by Josep Roselló between 1988 and 1993. In contrast with the main building's apparent disregard for context and history, Roselló's extension is more contextual; in so doing, it also reflects the spirit of its own time, but more importantly, it seems to pay homage to the original building, allowing it to stand out as the most important and emblematic modern building of Barcelona's historic heart.

Further Reading

Rodríguez, Carme, and Torres, Jorge. *Grup R*. Barcelona: Editorial Gustavo Gili, 1994.

Ruiz Cabrero, Gabriel. *The Modern in Spain: Architecture after 1948*. Cambridge, MA; London: The MIT Press, 2001.

Saliga, Pauline, and Thorne, Martha. *Building a New Spain: Contemporary Spanish Architecture*. Barcelona: Editorial Gustavo Gili, 1992.

CONFERENCE AND EXHIBITION HALL, SALAMANCA, CASTILLA Y LEÓN

Style: Contemporary Architecture
Dates: 1985–1992
Architect: Juan Navarro Baldeweg

The Conference and Exhibition Hall of Salamanca is regarded as the most significant work of Juan Navarro Baldeweg, one of the most important architects—along with Rafael Moneo and Albert Viaplana and others—of a generation of architects and teachers credited as the initiators of Spain's vibrant architectural development in the last quarter of the twentieth century. Salamanca is a very important city of central Spain, famous for the history and reputation of its university—the oldest in Spain—as well as for its *Renaissance* legacy. In fact, Salamanca was one of the important centers of development and dissemination of Renaissance ideas in Spain between the fifteenth and seventeenth centuries as important buildings and institutions of this period—for instance, **La Casa de las Conchas**, the buildings of the Universidad de Salamanca, and the church of **La Clerecía**—clearly demonstrate. Navarro Baldeweg's Conference and Exhibition Hall of Salamanca is representative of the architect's search for an austere architecture that reconciles modernity with history.

Salamanca is located on a slightly elevated hill north of the Tormes River. The city's Renaissance skyline, dominated by the towers and cupolas of many extraordinary churches, is certainly imposing, and offers an extraordinary visual spectacle. The Conference and Exhibition Hall is situated within the perimeter of the old city and is adjacent to the Park de la Vaguada, a natural topographic limit of the city's historical core. The actual building site is situated between the higher, historical part of the city, and an ample avenue that runs several feet below. Thus, the Conference and Exhibition Hall had to negotiate an important level difference at the same time that it had to be a transition between the traditional urban fabric and newer parts of the historical city.

Navarro Baldeweg's design concept for such a difficult site was remark-

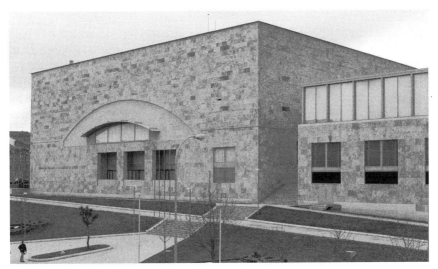

Exterior view of the Conference Center of Salamanca; the volume of the Conference Hall is to the left, while the Exhibition Hall appears partially on the right.

ably clear and simple; in his own words, the project was defined by a "three-fold characterization: as a pedestal for the city, as a wall construction which clearly highlights its profiles on the lower perimeter of the city and a passage and vestibule between the consolidated upper nucleus and the Park de la Vaguada" (*El Croquis* 2000, 108). These ambitious objectives were accomplished by separating the building program into two different components—the conference center and the exhibition hall—housed in two different building volumes and linked by an open-air plaza flanked by an outdoor amphitheater on the upper side of the site. From the outer side of the city's historical fabric, the two volumes appear as a whole, unambiguously separated by a wide *perron* of urban proportions but unified by their architectural attributes (materials, details, and volumetric relationships). They assuredly emerge as an effective stone-clad pedestal above which the vibrant historical skyline of Salamanca emerges with all its splendor.

The two volumes are accessible through the open-air plaza placed at an intermediate elevation between the low and high parts of the site. However different in size, function, and organization, the two volumes share a basic architectural idea: both are rather neutral rectangular boxes that "contain" much more articulated and hierarchically organized spatial sequences; thus a sharp ambiguity between the "container" (the exterior envelope) and the "contained" (the building's internal articulation) is established. This differentiation is also manifested in the buildings' exterior through subtle, partially disclosed, gestures and details.

The significantly larger volume houses the conference center, a facility devoted to professional conferences, conventions, and other similar activities. It consists of a rectangular envelope that encloses two auditoriums—one for 1,300 people, the other with nearly 500 places—and all the typical associated spaces and services needed by facilities of this type such as a large, welcoming, and inviting public lobby. The smaller auditorium is placed below the bigger one, while the lobby that services both of them is at an intermediate level between the two. The large auditorium is covered by a magnificent *baldaquino* structure that seems to hover over the auditorium's seating as a precious object contained within the center's enveloping walls; it is a fragment of an incomplete spherical cupola made out of concentric horizontal concrete layers with an *oculus* at the center. Designed to comply with the demanding and indispensable acoustic requirements of an auditorium, this element vests the building with spatial hierarchy, an aspect emphasized by the natural light that penetrates through the central oculus and the vertical openings cut in the perimeter walls and that illuminate the space from behind the baldaquino. The arcs of the cupola's incomplete circular plan are wittily "completed" by large implied arches on the four façades of the building's stone-clad exterior. Additionally, the cupola is taller than the apparent height of the building, but this is invisible from the exterior, an intentional decision to avoid any interference with the city's celebrated historical profile.

The much smaller volume accommodates the entrance to the exhibition area. It consists of a stone-clad box crowned by a light glass-and-steel enclosure delicately posed over the stonewalls. Inside, a zigzagging ramp links the building's three levels entirely dedicated to various exhibition areas and seminar rooms. The ramp and glazed enclosure of this volume are analogous to the baldaquino of the conference center as expressive lightweight elements contained within the austere enveloping walls. The two apparently independent volumes of the building complex are linked at the basement level, under the open-air plaza and outdoor amphitheater.

The building complex's structure is in reinforced concrete, while the façades are clad with Salamanca stone applied over a structure of support. Thus, the building's exterior image is subdued and austere, a respectful homage to its old prestigious neighbors. The austerity and simplicity of the building's volumes, its studied spatial richness, clear structure, and conceptual logic, and—especially—the inflections of its architectural vocabulary, materials, and details suggest that the work of American architect Louis I. Kahn was influential for Navarro Baldeweg, while the stark minimalism—particularly the upper portion of the exhibition areas—shows traces of a debt to the work of Mies van der Rohe. More importantly, Navarro Baldeweg's building for Salamanca's Conference and Exhibition Hall is a full-scale architectural lesson about how to insert a contemporary building with an uncompromising contemporary language within a heavily charged historical context, an aspect that projects it as one of the most important examples of Spain's architecture of the 1980s; a seminal moment in a new, vigorous period of the country's rich architectural history.

Further Reading

Curtis, William J. R. *Modern Architecture since 1900*. 3rd ed. London: Phaidon Press Limited, 1996.
"Juan Navarro Baldeweg." Special monographic issue, *El Croquis* 54 (Madrid), 2000.
Ruiz Cabrero, Gabriel. *The Modern in Spain: Architecture after 1948*. Cambridge, MA; London: The MIT Press, 2001.
Saliga, Pauline, and Thorne, Martha. *Building a New Spain: Contemporary Spanish Architecture*. Barcelona: Editorial Gustavo Gili, 1992.

DIAGONAL MAR PARC, BARCELONA, CATALONIA

Style: Contemporary Architecture
Dates: 1997–2003
Architects: Enric Miralles and Benedetta Tagliabue

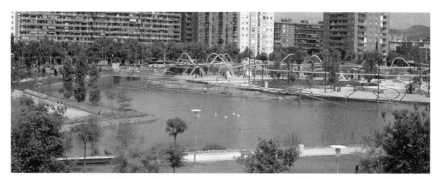

Overall view of Diagonal Mar Parc's lake and fountain.

The Diagonal Mar Parc, designed by the Barcelona-based office of Enric Miralles and Benedetta Tagliabue (EMBT Architects), is among the most important architecture-landscape ensembles built in Spain at the end of the twentieth century, a vibrant and creative period in the recent history of the country's architecture. Moreover, as one of Enric Miralles' numerous projects that were completed posthumously (he died in 2000 at the young age of forty-five), it is considered as a valuable testimony of his remarkable architectural legacy that includes celebrated masterpieces of contemporary architecture such as the **New Cemetery Park of Igualada** (1985–1991) and the Hostalets Civic Center (1992), both in partnership with Carme Pinós, and the Hamburg School of Music (1997–2000), the Renovation of Utrecht's Town Hall (1997–2001), and the Scottish Parliament in Edinburgh (1998–2004), the last three in partnership with Benedetta Tagliabue.

The park is part of an ambitious large-scale development undertaken by Hines, one of the world's biggest real estate companies. The initiative consisted of redeveloping an existing eighty-four-acre brownfield industrial area and its conversion into a mixed-use residential, commercial, and leisure zone of activity. The project revitalized the formerly unattractive east-northeastern end of the city where the Diagonal Avenue—a major artery that traverses the entire city in west-southwest east-northeast direction—approaches the seafront; the addition of a large public park as part of the development was required by the city of Barcelona; taking up an area of thirty-five acres, Diagonal Mar Parc is among the largest public parks in Barcelona, a city recognized for the quantity, variety, and quality of its parks, plazas, and other outdoor public places.

Diagonal Mar Parc occupies a large portion of a rectangular city block defined by four major streets and traversed by Passeig Taulat, an important street parallel to the sea that runs between Diagonal Avenue and Ronda del Litoral (Barcelona's seafront circumvallation roadway); some parts of this block were already assigned to high-rise residential buildings with which some areas of the park became closely intertwined. Extending throughout the site, the park appears as an exuberant display of landscaping and architectural elements that covers the entire available area as a carefully crafted tapestry. The park is composed of numerous components, including a large artificial lake and waterfall, a paved plaza, several artificial hills, playgrounds and places for various other recreational activities, an interactive fountain, pergolas, planters, a wide variety of seating areas and many other features, all related by a strolling promenade—with a bridge crossing over the lake— that links all the different parts of the park amid a large diversity of indige- nous vegetation species.

The architects' conceptual point of departure consisted of establishing a physical link between Diagonal Avenue and the sea before that important ar- tery reaches the coastline (which could happen less than a mile farther but never materializes). Thus, placed between these two important linear ele- ments of the city—the seashore and the Diagonal Avenue—the park becomes an abstract bridge that links the two, even if it still needs the "complicity" of a pedestrian overpass (projected but not yet built) to cross over the Ronda del Litoral highway and thus physically connect the park with the beach. The park's strolling promenade was conceived as a *rambla*, an eventful pedestrian route typical of Catalonia's cities. At Diagonal Mar Parc, the rambla is a lin- ear path that cuts the site diagonally across, becoming a dynamic constituent of the project that links the park's numerous zones. A secondary promenade cuts the site in a different direction, conceptually perpendicular to the first.

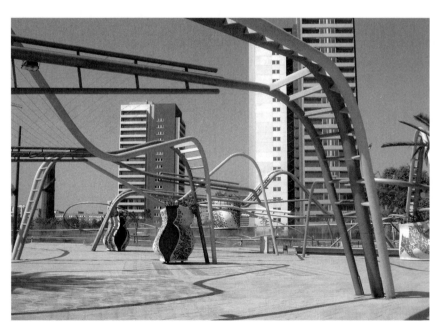

Fragment of the main paved area of Diagonal Mar Parc showing the hanging planters, the sculp- tural metallic pergolas, and, in the middle-ground slightly above the pavement, some pipes that are part of the sprinkling water fountains. Hines' multi-story buildings are in the background.

The two paths intersect near the center of the park, and farther to the west converge in an area that provides a pedestrian crossing of Passeig de Taulat before bifurcating in two new different directions; together, these two elongated paths constitute the park's main system of circulation.

The main rambla begins in the northern corner of the site, where the triple intersection of streets Carrer de Lull and Carrer Josep Plá with the Diagonal Avenue marks the most urban corner of the park. There, a large paved plaza evokes the hard surfaces of typically urban public spaces; it is populated by sculptural metal pergolas, giant hanging planters, and various seating areas, and is flanked on one side by the artificial lake. Bordering the lake's northeastern edge, the rambla cuts the site diagonally, reaching the opposite end where, in the future, the pedestrian bridge will connect the park with the beach.

The two-level lake is the central element of the park. It is located at an existing depression of the site, a trace of its former industrial condition. The north-northeast border is unbroken, marked by a hard concrete edge; instead, the opposite "shores" are made by a zigzagging line demarcated with softer materials, including various vegetation species growing both on the lake's softer edge and on the water; a waterfall placed at the southeastern portion of the lake shows the several of feet difference in the lake's two water levels, while an interactive pipe-fountain located on the edge of the paved plaza completes the water features that animate the park.

The park offers an ample variety of possibilities for playing, resting, walking, or simply enjoying a fragment of nature within an urban environment. Several artificial hills, veritable grassy truncated cones, provide higher elevation points where one can be more detached and isolated than in the more public spaces; moreover, these hills act as landscaping filters between the park as a public place and the private areas of the lower levels of neighboring high-rise buildings. Throughout, numerous seating arrangements—placed in paved areas, or directly on the grass—invite the visitor to gather in large or small groups, or simply be alone, tacit acknowledgment of the diverse needs and interests of contemporary metropolitan residents. Similarly, smaller arrangements of metal pergolas and giant planters—of similar lineage to those found in the paved plaza—reappear in other parts of the park, as if they were members of a marching parade running between the plaza and the beach. This may be indicative of a subjacent narrative, an aspect of architecture that fascinated Enric Miralles and that can be found throughout his work. At Diagonal Mar Parc, the pergolas, planters, benches, paving patterns, and metal grills provide an aura of domesticity, of homely objects found in local residential patios and terraces; but here, these same elements take on urban dimensions, becoming a domestic space at the scale of the metropolis.

As it could have been anticipated, both the real estate development and the park generated controversial criticism. In spite of this controversy, Hines' Diagonal Mar real-state initiative received the inaugural Urban Land Institute Europe Award for Excellence in 2004, while the park designed by EMBT Architects is already a lively public park that attracts users of all ages from various parts of the city; once trees and the rest of the planned vegetation grow, and the pergolas provide the needed shade to the many now unprotected seating areas, Diagonal Mar Parc will surely become an urban oasis, a luscious retreat placed between the city and the beach at one extreme of one of the world's most vibrant and architectural cities.

Further Reading

"Enric Miralles & Benedetta Tagliabue: 1996–2000." Special monographic issue, *El Croquis* 100, 101 (Madrid), 2000.

DISPENSARIO ANTITUBERCULOSO, BARCELONA, CATALONIA

Style: Modern Movement—Rationalist Architecture
Dates: 1934–1938; restoration, 1982–1992
Architects: Josep Lluís Sert, Joan B. Subirana, Josep Torres i Clavé, and the GATCPAC; restored by Corea-Gallardo-Mannino and Ramón Torres

The Dispensario Antituberculoso (Antituberculosis Clinic) is regarded as the most relevant Rationalist building in Spain as well as the most clear built representation of the ideas and postulates of the *GATCPAC* (Grupo de Artistas Técnicos Catalanes para el Progreso de la Arquitectura Contemporánea, or Catalonia's Group of Artists and Technicians for the progress of Contemporary Architecture). This group was founded by Josep Lluís Sert and others with the objective of becoming—first in Catalonia and later in the whole country—Spain's arm of the CIAM, an ad-hoc group of early-twentieth-century architects that promoted and developed the architectural and urbanistic postulates of the *Modern Movement*. While the Dispensario Antituberculoso was commissioned to the GATCPAC group and designed by a team composed of Josep Lluís Sert, Joan Subirana, and Josep Torres i Clavé, the building is generally considered as one of Sert's early masterpieces.

Josep Lluís Sert is one of the most important representatives of twentieth-century architecture, undoubtedly Spain's most important and recognized architect of the first half of the century. He was born in Barcelona in 1902; soon after graduating from Barcelona's school of architecture he moved to Paris where he worked at Le Corbusier's office between 1929 and 1930. He

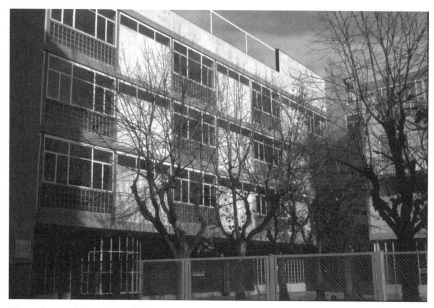

View of one of the wings of the Dispensario Antituberculoso facing the interior courtyard of the building.

returned to Barcelona to open his own office and became Spain's most active proponent of modern architectural postulates. As a founding member of the *GATCPAC* and former collaborator of Le Corbusier (the most influential twentieth-century architect worldwide) he had a key participation in the development of the *Plan Maciá* (project based on modern urbanistic principles for Barcelona undertaken, precisely, by Le Corbusier, Sert, and others in 1933). In 1937, soon after the outbreak of the Spanish Civil War (1936–1939), he returned to Paris in exile; there he designed the Pavilion for the Republic of Spain (one of the two confronted parties in the ongoing Spanish Civil War) for Paris' 1937 World Fair where he collaborated with numerous artists that supported the Spanish Republic such as Pablo Picasso, Joan Miró, and Alexander Calder; in fact, Picasso's famous monumental painting entitled "Guernica" was first exhibited in that Pavilion. In 1939— at the outbreak of World War II—he moved to New York where he associated with Paul Lester Wiener and Paul Schulz; he was president of the now legendary CIAM (International Conference of Modern Architecture) between 1947 and 1956, and dean of Harvard's School of Architecture between 1953 and 1969. At the end of Francisco Franco's dictatorship (1939–1975) he resumed architectural practice in Spain with an office based in Barcelona. The Dispensario Antituberculoso is—together with the apartment building on Carrer de Muntaner (1930–1931) and the experimental social housing building known as Casa Bloc (1932–1936), both in Barcelona, the latter in partnership with Torres i Clavé and the GATCPAC—one of the few but very influential buildings designed by Sert in Barcelona at the beginning of his long career as architect, urbanist, pedagogue, and theorist.

The building was commissioned to the GATCPAC in 1934 by the autonomous government of Catalonia with the objective of fighting and eradicating tuberculosis in the region. In addition to the typical health care functions, the program also included a center for the study of tuberculosis and offices for an association purposely formed to combat this then-decimating illness. The site assigned for the project was a small city block defined by streets Torres i Amat and Sant Bernat, in the westernmost corner of Barcelona's Ciutat Vella, the city's old, dense, and intricate "Gothic Quarter." Both program and site were ideal to make a demonstration of modern architectural and urbanistic principles: the former, because hygiene and better sanitary and health conditions leading to a better quality of life were among the postulated benefits that the promoters of modern architecture had been propagating through their writings and realizations for almost two decades; the latter, because a site in the middle of the dense city provided the opportunity to promote the dogma of modern and rationalist architectural principles at the center of the city. This particular aspect was possible by successfully challenging building regulations of that time.

The Dispensario Antituberculoso was organized in three main volumes around a central south-facing courtyard in complete disregard of the surrounding context's characteristics. The three volumes were composed of a main L-shaped multistory block, another volume that intersects the short arm of the "L" perpendicularly, and a detached, smaller two-story volume. This volumetric differentiation did not correspond with the three main functions of the building—health clinic, study center, and offices for the association; rather, the functional components of each of these were distributed throughout the two larger and interconnected volumes of the multilevel L-shaped block and the volume that intersects it, while the smallest of the three volumes houses the porter's lodging and marks one corner of the site. The whole inevitably recalls the work of Le Corbusier, notably resembling a small-scale fragment of the project for the headquarters of the League of Nations (Geneva 1927).

The clinic's functions were primarily housed in the ground floor, while doctors' offices, X-ray rooms, the study center, and the association's office were distributed in the two upper floors; the center's auditorium and conference hall occupied the entire two upper floors of the volume that intersects the L-shaped block. The vertical circulation through this complex volume is provided by three primarily blind vertical boxes placed at the ends of the L's arms, thus anchoring and framing the building to the site. The entire roof of the two main blocks was conceived as a solarium in full consonance with the building's therapeutic functions. In fact, with the whole organized around a south-oriented outdoor courtyard, the architecture accommodated to and associated with the therapeutic aspects of treating tuberculosis patients in well-illuminated and sun-bathed spaces. As Carlos

Flores commented: "From the medical as well as the architectural viewpoint the dispensary offered optimum conditions, with its extensively glazed corridors, perfectly ventilated and illuminated, its easily washable tile finishes, and even the use of color . . . contributing to the creation of a welcoming and undramatic environment" (Güell and Flores 1996, 65).

The building's structure was made of a regular modular grid of steel posts and small-brick vaulting system for floor slabs, a variation of the typical *catalan vault*. The building's enclosure is typically modern, composed of large glazed surfaces with extensive use of translucent walls of glass blocks and large unbroken opaque planes. The rational structural system and modular construction; the use of industrial and prefabricated elements for stairs, walls, and wall finishes; and the incorporation of some typically local building materials and techniques, such as colored glazed ceramic tiles, were quite unusual and innovative for that time in Spanish architecture, converting the building into an emblem of modern architecture. Yet, the Dispensario Antituberculoso remained an isolated experiment of a promising period truncated by the outbreak of the Spanish Civil War, at the end of which the conservative triumphant side blocked the development of modern architectural ideas in the country and imposed a return to more traditional vocabularies and modes of construction.

In the early 1980s the building exhibited the negative effects of many years of poor maintenance and insensitive interventions. The restoration and adaptation of the building to new needs was commissioned to the Barcelona-based office of Mario Corea, Francisco Gallardo, and Edgardo Mannino, who worked in collaboration with Ramón Torres. Between 1962 and 1967, as a young graduate student, Corea had worked at Sert's office in Boston; later, between 1976 and 1981—along with Mannino—he again worked with Sert, this time in his Barcelona-based office collaborating on the projects that the master was undertaking in Europe. The team was charged with a full-scale restoration that included repairing some problems of the building's construction (specially related to the structural system); updating and upgrading the mechanical, electrical, and telecommunications systems; and adapting the existing structure for its new use as a community health center, all while restoring the building as closely to its original condition as possible.

The restoration was undertaken with extreme care and utmost respect for the original building; the architects succeeded in re-functionalizing the existing structure into a CAP (Centro de Asistencia Primaria, a community health center) without leaving any exterior signs of the conversion, limiting their intervention to a few modifications of the interior partitioning, and always respecting the architectural postulates of the original. As they stated in their descriptive text of the project, their intention was that "the [new] program followed the building" (Corea et al. 1993, 80). Yet, the most important accomplishment was, undoubtedly, to have restored the dignified and proud legacy of the building as the paradigmatic work of Rationalist modern architecture in Spain.

Further Reading

Bastlund, Knud. *José Luis Sert: Architecture, City Planning, Urban Design*. New York; Washington, DC: Frederick A. Praeger, 1967.

Corea, Mario, Gallardo, Francisco, and Mannino, Edgardo. *Corea-Gallardo-Mannino*. Madrid: Aspan Editores, 1993.

Curtis, William J. R. *Modern Architecture since 1900*. 3rd ed. London: Phaidon Press Limited, 1996.

Güell, Xavier, and Flores, Carlos. *Architecture of Spain, Guide*. Barcelona: Fundación Caja de Arquitectos, 1996.

Rovira, Josep M. *José Luis Sert: 1901–1983*. Milano: Electa Edizioni, 2000.

EL ESCORIAL. *See* Monastery of El Escorial.

EMPÚRIES: GREEK-HELLENIC AND ROMAN SETTLEMENT, EMPÚRIES, CATALONIA

Styles: Greek and Roman Architecture
Dates: Fifth century B.C.E.–first century C.E.
Architects: Greek settlers, native populations, and veteran Roman troops and settlers

Empúries (as it is known today in Catalan language), or Ampurias in Castilian Spanish, originated as a Greek-Hellenic trading post situated on the northeastern corner of the Iberian Peninsula. The first settlement in the area, the Palaiapolis (old city), was located on what was then a small off-shore island, where the village of Sant Martí d'Empúries stands today. There are traces of human occupation on this island from the Bronze Age, but it was thanks to the presence of Greek-Hellenic settlers that a small town grew and prospered in the five centuries that preceded the Christian era.

The establishment of *Hellenic* settlements in the Iberian Peninsula was undertaken by colonizing expeditions of Greek colons from western *Phocean* towns. The first Hellenic settlers, who were probably from Massilia (modern Marseilles, on France's Mediterranean coastline), founded the Neapolis (new city) on mainland in the fifth century B.C.E., at a short distance from the Palaiapolis. The new settlement was called Emporion, which in Greek means "a place where supplies are readily available" (from where the modern English word emporium derives). In the fourth century B.C.E., Emporion became an independent and commercially powerful center that controlled trade in eastern Iberia and in a significant portion of the Mediterranean.

Roman troops arrived in Greek-Hellenic Emporion in the year 218 B.C.E., marking the beginning of Rome's military presence in the Iberian Peninsula. This was a result of the Second Punic War between Rome and Carthage. Interestingly, even before their arrival, Emporion's inhabitants had decided to align with Rome instead of Carthage, a logical decision considering that with its numerous and powerful trading centers located in southern Iberia and on the northern coast of Africa, Carthage represented a threat to Emporion's control of trade in the Mediterranean. In the late third century B.C.E., a Roman military camp—the Praesidium—was established a few hundred feet to the west of the Hellenic city. For some time, Emporion remained politically independent from Rome, but in the year 195 B.C.E., when the growing Roman colonies in Iberian territory were fully romanized and divided into two provinces (*Ulterior* and *Citerior*) the city lost its treasured independent status.

In the second century B.C.E. the city was transformed. The flourishing economy of Emporion resulted in a vast building program that included the construction of new defensive walls, several temples and sanctuaries, and a monumental public plaza (the agora) that was delimited on the north by a

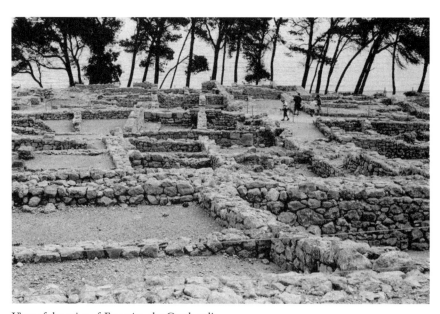

View of the ruins of *Emporion*, the Greek polis.

market (the stoa) in accordance with architectural and urbanistic Greek-Hellenic principles. The city's alignment with Rome was firm but it still remained jurisdictionally and culturally independent, reaffirming its Hellenic heritage.

However, in the early years of the first century B.C.E., stimulated by the continuous and growing presence of Roman settlers and war veterans, a new city—purely Roman—began to emerge on the same location of the old Praesidium, beyond the walled confines of Emporion. The construction of the new city coincided with the process of romanization of Emporion, which meant that the city's population became Roman; therefore, the formerly Greek-Hellenic city lost its independence to become a possession of Rome. The Roman city, clearly different from the Hellenic, was laid out according to Roman urban principles, that is, divided in rectangular blocks delimited by *cardines* and *decumani*. It occupied a rectangular area of approximately one-half of a mile by slightly less than one-quarter of a mile in north–south and east–west directions, respectively. According to some researchers—such as Xavier Aquilué (Arce 1996, 45–46)—the new city was itself divided into two parts that had different legal status: the southern portion (approximately 1,500 by 1,000 feet) was inhabited by Roman citizens who were originally from Rome or from the Italian peninsula, whereas romanized Iberian natives inhabited the smaller and more modest northern part. Expectedly, the more important buildings—forum, temples, market, amphitheater, and the houses of Roman dignitaries—were located in the southern portion.

The construction of the *forum*—the center of Roman political, religious, and civic life—was, perhaps, the last major building initiative undertaken at Emporiae (the name of the city was changed from its Greek original to a Latin form). Typically, in the Roman Republican period, the forum consisted of a hierarchical and well-organized group of buildings around an open public space that was located at the intersection of the city's main *cardum* and *decumanum* (the two main intersecting axes that characterized the layout of most Roman towns) constituting an architectural-urbanistic formal unity. Accordingly, Emporiae's new forum was a highly organized space of generous dimensions (approximately 210 feet square) dominated by the Temple of Jove (or Jupiter) and surrounded by a colonnaded plaza; the southern edge—opposed to the Temple of Jove—was closed by a line of shops (tabernae). Later, already in the age of the Empire, the forum was remodeled to incorporate two imperial temples and a large building complex composed by the *basilica* and the *curia*. The amphitheater, a very important component of Roman cities fundamentally used for entertaining the urban population, was located at the city's southern end just outside newly built defensive walls.

The standing ruins of Empúries reveal the existence of fine Roman villas, some decorated with magnificent murals and mosaics comparable to those found in Pompey. They testify to the importance and richness once attained by the city. However, the city's population was too attached to its own, but lost, glorious past; therefore, Emporiae began to decline during the Flavian

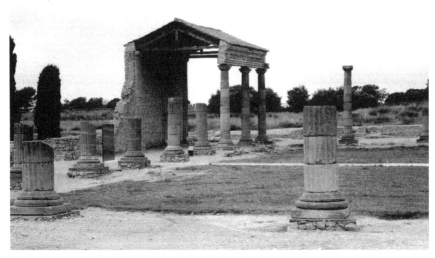

Remnants of the Roman forum at Empúries.

period (69–96 C.E.) and was eventually fully abandoned. Today, the ruins of Emporiae are part of a rich archeological site that has not yet been fully explored. Current archeological studies and excavations will shed new light on the history, life, and richness of this once important Greek and Roman port strategically situated at one corner of the Mediterranean basin, the cradle of Western civilization.

Further Reading

Arce, Javier, Ensoli, Serena, and La Rocca, Eugenio, eds. *Hispania Romana*. Milan: Electa Edizioni, 1997. (See especially the article by Xavier Aquilué entitled "Empuries Repubblicana," 44–49.)

Brown, Frank E. *Roman Architecture*. New York: George Brazillier Publishers, 1961.

Chueca Goitía, Fernando. *Historia de la Arquitectura Española: Edad Antigua y Edad Media*. Vol. 1. Madrid: Editorial Dossat, 1965.

Sear, Frank. *Roman Architecture*. Ithaca, NY: Cornell University Press, 1993.

Ward-Perkins, John B. *Roman Architecture*. New York: Harry N. Abrams, 1977.

GALICIAN CENTER OF CONTEMPORARY ART, SANTIAGO DE COMPOSTELA, GALICIA

Style: Contemporary Architecture
Dates: 1988–1993
Architect: Alvaro Siza Vieira

The creation of a Galician Center of Contemporary Art (CGAC) in Santiago de Compostela was envisioned in 1988 by the Xunta da Galicia—the regional autonomic government—with the objective of exhibiting and promoting contemporary art in the rich historical city. The design of the building was commissioned to Portuguese architect Alvaro Siza, considered the "father" of the so-called "School of Porto," as the architecture produced in the 1980s by young architects based in that city of northern Portugal is known because the affinities in their work exhibited the influence of Siza's early work and prolific pedagogic activity. By the late 1980s, Alvaro Siza had become an architect of international reputation who had already built celebrated buildings such as the Boa Nova Tea House (Leça da Palmeira, Portugal, 1963); the Borges and Irmão Bank (Vila do Conde, Portugal, 1978–1986); the Bonjour Tristesse Apartments (Berlin, Germany, 1980–1984); and many other buildings in Holland, Italy and, of course, Portugal. The CGAC was the first of an eventually long list of buildings that Siza built in Spain, such as the Meteorological Center for Barcelona's Olympic Village (1992), the School of Journalism also in Santiago de Compostela (1993), and the Rectory for the University of Alicante (1995). The selection of an internationally renowned architect from Porto as the designer of such an emblematic building of Galician culture is not surprising considering Santiago de Compostela's international projection, and the strong historical, cultural, and linguistic ties that exist between northern Portugal and Galicia. In 1992, as the CGAC was near completion, Siza received the Pritzker Prize, the world's most prestigious award for a living architect's work.

The building is situated in a densely built area just outside the limits of the city's historical center next to the old gate through which the pilgrims who took the legendary *camino francés* (the French Way) arrived to the city, about one-half mile from the imposing **Cathedral of the Santiago de Compostela**. More precisely, the art center is on the street Ramón del Valle Inclán, adjacent to the impressive *Baroque* church and convent of Santo Domingo de Bonaval; in fact, the CGAC occupies an area formerly used as the convent's vegetable garden. The lot's geometrical and topographical char-

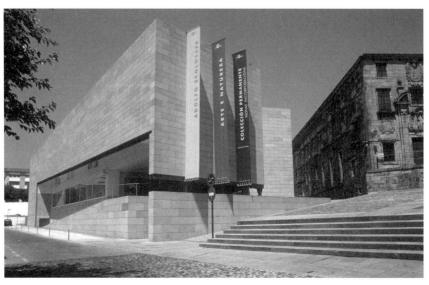

Exterior of the Galician Center of Contemporary Art; to the right is the Santo Domingo de Bonaval Church.

acteristics—a very irregular site with no dominant directions, primarily oriented west at the bottom of a steep slope partially occupied by the convent's gardens and the Cemetery of Bonaval—presented difficult challenges that the architect brilliantly resolved by arranging a series of elongated and superimposed volumes that negotiate the site's difficult conditions and the building brief's demanding requirements.

The building has more than 75,000 square feet of usable space distributed in two L-shaped volumes that, confronted and rotated with respect to each other, define at their intersection a triangular multistory space, the building's pivotal center and main public lobby. The long arm of one of the L-shaped volumes is aligned with the front street—Ramón del Valle Inclán—while the long arm of the other is parallel to the Cemetery of Bonaval situated behind the convent's church. Together, these two volumes define the building's insertion into the complex urban fabric and emerge, rather than as a compact volume, as the result of a continuous folding and intersecting of planes that simultaneously accommodate to the characteristics of the site and to the internal logic of the interior spaces. The latter is particularly interesting because during the design phase the architect had to work without the pre-existence of an art collection that would be exhibited in the building, and thus the absence of a precise program of needs. Consequently, Siza's strategy consisted of creating a flexible container that could provide a large variety of art manifestations, from traditional exhibition galleries to large volumes of unobstructed space for contemporary installations.

The front L-shaped volume contains the main lobby, administrative offices, and services; the rear one, which is markedly more irregular than the front one, accommodates exhibition areas in the long arm, and a comfortable auditorium for lectures, film festivals, and other cultural activities in the short segment. A perceptually narrow stairway runs the entire length of this volume's long arm connecting all four levels, from the service and curatorial areas in the basement to the building's roof terrace for outdoor exhibitions. However, despite the strong linearity suggested by this specific circulation element, the movement through the building is far from lineal; rather, one perceives a spiraling ascendance that gravitates around the generous triangular central and pivotal space of the whole building.

The building's exterior is uniformly clad with granite panels applied over a metallic substructure. The choice of granite, a material that predominates throughout Santiago de Compostela, seems obvious for historical and contextual reasons, but the way in which it was detailed unequivocally establishes a temporal distinction with neighboring structures, in particular with the Convent of Santo Domingo de Bonaval. In spite of using a material usually perceived as heavy, massive, and definitely grounded, the CGAC's exterior was designed to provoke ambiguous perceptions. In effect, the folded planes and pleats of the exterior enclosure, often suspended off the ground for unusually long distances or supported by intermediary steel supports, the fragmentation of pure form, and the numerous areas carved out of the building's virtual volume (for example, the two extraordinary entry sequences on Ramón del Valle Inclán street) put in evidence the use of granite as skin-enclosure rather than as an integral structural system.

In sharp contrast with the apparent opacity of the exterior, the building's interior is astonishingly bright; floors, stairs, ledges, and many other exposed surfaces in all the public areas are covered in Greek marble, while the floors of exhibition galleries are in oak and all walls are smoothly plastered and painted white. The numerous and often concealed openings, skylights, and cracks on walls and roofs create cool luminous spaces conducive to the appropriate display and observation of art work. The careful detailing of all other elements—such as natural and artificial lighting, handrails, and furniture (also designed by Siza)—and the sculptural effect of the folding walls and ceilings appear as artistic manifestations in their own right, and establish a dialog between the expressive qualities of the exterior container and what it contains, the architecture and art work, respectively.

In 1990–1994, Alvaro Siza restored the grounds and gardens of the Convent of Santo Domingo de Bonaval, creating a public park that works as an outdoor extension and complement to the CGAC. Siza restored the gardens and added a few walls, paths, and paved platforms while maintaining the original paths and highlighting some quasi-archeological remains. Thus, while independent from each other, art center, park, and convent constitute a marvelous architectural, artistic, and landscaping ensemble where past and present converge. This is, no doubt, a relevant aspect of Alvaro Siza's project; the whole area gained public visibility with the new art institution and a new civic space in perfect harmony with the neighboring buildings and with the site's rich historical and symbolical past.

Further Reading

"Alvaro Siza." Special monographic issue, *El Croquis* 68, 69, and 95 (Madrid), 2000.
Curtis, William J. R. *Modern Architecture since 1900*. 3rd ed. London: Phaidon Press Limited, 1996.
Jodidio, Philip. *Alvaro Siza*. Cologne: Taschen GmbH, 2003.
Trigueiros, Luiz, ed. *Alvaro Siza*. Lisboa: Editorial Blau, 1996.

GARDENS OF EL GENERALIFE.
See La Alhambra Palace.

THE GERMAN PAVILION, BARCELONA, CATALONIA

Style: Modern Movement
Dates: 1928–1929; dismantled in 1930; rebuilt in 1986
Architect: Ludwig Mies van der Rohe

The German Repräesentationsraum Pavilion for Barcelona's International Exhibition of 1929, more commonly known as "the Barcelona Pavilion," is one of the paradigmatic works of twentieth-century architecture, universally recognized as an all-time masterpiece. It was designed in 1928 by German architect Ludwig Mies van der Rohe—one of the masters of modern architecture—and built under his supervision with Lilly Reich, one of his close collaborators. Inaugurated on May 26, 1929, when King Alfonso XIII and Queen Eugenia Victoria of Spain visited it, the German Pavilion represents—to borrow architectural historian William Curtis' words—"the will of an epoch constructed in space" (Curtis 1996, 273). Alongside Walter Gropius' Bauhaus (Dessau, Germany 1926), Le Corbusier's Villa Savoye (Poissy, France 1928–1931), and Frank Lloyd Wright's Fallingwater (Bear

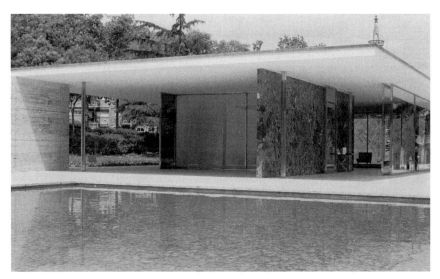

Exterior fragments of the German Pavilion with the large reflecting pool in the foreground.

Run, Pennsylvania 1935), the German Pavilion completes a celebrated quartet of canonical works of Modern Architecture.

The pavilion was one of two buildings and numerous stands that represented the *Weimar Republic* (Germany's democratic experiment between 1919 and 1933) at the 1929 Barcelona International Exhibition. As the Repräesentationsraum (Representational) Pavilion, it was the Weimar Republic's official "embassy" at the International Exhibition, representing the country's cultural and political values, which were characterized by a commitment and idealization of modernity, liberalism, and internationalism. Therefore, it should be understood that the pavilion did not have a specific function or building program, but a purely representational, honorific, ceremonial, and symbolic role. It simply was the expression of an ideal. Consequently, Mies van der Rohe's goal was to make an architectural full-scale demonstration and interpretation of the above-mentioned Weimar Republic's ideals, which—in his view—were those of the new Germany that emerged after World War I. Josep Quetglas (a contemporary Spanish architectural critic and historian) convincingly argued that the Pavilion represented the new ideal of the German house: open, effective, precise (Quetglas 1991, 29–33). In the official Bulletin of the International Exhibition, the building was presented as pursuing "only one representational objective—to document German cultural activities. This building turns out to be an interesting demonstration of modern architectural objectives put to the purposes of display—offering a set of spaces, some covered and some in the open air, that follow a new trend. Its effectiveness is principally due to the careful selection and application of the materials used, as well as to the simplicity and grandeur of its form" (Subirana i Torrent 1986, 32).

At the building's opening, Georg von Schnitzler—General Commissar of the Reich—stated: "Here, we wanted to show what we can do, what we are, how we feel and see today. We do not want anything but clarity, simplicity, honesty" (Curtis 271). Undoubtedly, these objectives were largely met, for the building stands today as one of the most revered representatives of Mies van der Rohe's famous axiom "less is more." In effect, in Barcelona, Mies van der Rohe constructed a remarkable representational and symbolic building, one whose significance largely exceeded its intended function because, sitting on its elegant travertine platform, the pavilion stands as the realization of an ideal, a manifesto where every detail is part of a precise and ambitious social, political, and aesthetic *programme*.

The Barcelona fair grounds were located on the Montjuic; they were designed by local architect Josep Puig y Cadalfach, a highly respected Catalan architect who had already produced some notable buildings in Barcelona, including the **Casa Terradas**. The fairgrounds were laid out according to some traditional Beaux-Arts planning principles, and consisted of a variety of large exhibition halls that framed an ascending axial procession towards the Palacio Nacional, centerpiece of the fairgrounds. At the bottom of the exhibition grounds, a wide plaza operated as a welcoming open-air concourse; the axis of its compositional organization was perpendicular to the main axis of the fairgrounds, and a large ornamental circular fountain marked the intersection of the two axes in typical Beaux-Arts style.

The German Pavilion was located on the west end of the concourse, just beyond a set of eight free-standing *Ionic columns* that provided a ready-made permeable visual screen. The pavilion's striking modernity, simplicity, lack of ornamentation, and rather small size were in strong contrast with the traditional and large buildings that surrounded it. Nevertheless, and in retrospect, the pavilion was as classical as the buildings with which it coexisted, yet, its classicism was of a much different nature, a conceptual one, because everywhere else the building exuded modernity and abstraction. In effect, the pavilion was the culmination of a period in which Mies searched for a synthesis of the then-emerging modern postulates with the already well-established classical principles. It also seemed to emerge as a synthesis of various aspects that impacted Mies' work of the 1920s—such as Karl F. Schinkel's work, the influence of Frank Lloyd Wright's architecture for the American prairie, the paintings of Piet Mondrian and Theo van Doesburg, and the films of Sergei Eisenstein—which he had already explored, however partially, in some previous works, most notably the project for a Brick House of 1923.

The German Pavilion occupied an area of 56.62 by 18.48 meters (approximately 186 by 61 feet). Its design and construction was based on a precise square module of 1.09 meters (3.57 feet). Broadly stated, it consisted of four major spaces: a "central" enclosed space (the ceremonial room), the

Reich's offices (small, detached, and independent from the main room), an open space dominated by a large rectangular reflecting pool, and another open-air secluded enclosed patio fully occupied by another reflecting pool. The main enclosed space was covered by a thin, purely rectangular slab delicately supported by eight cross-shaped steel columns clad in chrome. A carefully calculated disposition of marble and glazed partitions defined both the limits of the building and activated the movement around and across the interior spaces. A free-standing green-marble partition, framed by two columns, directed the visitor to the interior, where a fully glazed panel, continued by another green-marble wall that eventually forms a u-shaped enclosure, delimited the extents of the building's interior and exterior spaces. Inside, one area was highlighted by the presence of a polished free-standing partition of onyx dorée (an expensive, highly textured, and beautiful marble), which—in association with an isolated column and a thick rectangular black carpet laid over the travertine floor—defined a space where two low chairs, designed for the occasion, awaited their distinguished occupants. Diagonally across from the entrance and beyond and through the fully glazed partition that closed this space, Georg Kolbe's beautiful "Morning" bronze sculpture appeared fully visible. Delicately posed on the surface of the reflecting pool, with its image reflected on the water and on the highly polished walls of green marble that framed the secluded rear open-air space, the sculpture constituted an unavoidable focal point of attention, the aesthetic-spatial culmination of the building.

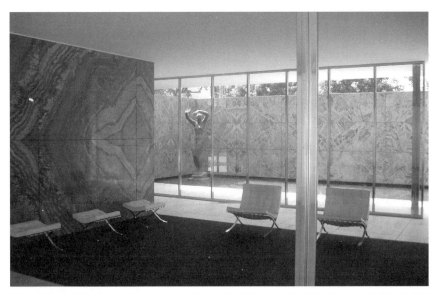

View of the building's main interior space; beyond and through the fully glazed wall of the building's rear side Georg Kolbe's sculpture seems to float over the small reflecting pool enclosed by marble walls.

Ludwig Mies van der Rohe, working with a collaborator, designed for this particular building a specific set of furniture items, including the famous "Barcelona chair," an "armless" low armchair consisting of two chrome-coated, stainless-steel, criss-crossed and slightly curved bands that support two thick and tight leather cushions held in place by thick cow-hide straps. Not unlike the role assigned to the pavilion itself, the Barcelona chair had an honorific function: two of them were placed side-by-side in the central space with the specific purpose of hosting the king and queen of Spain during their pre-scheduled visit to the Pavilion during the fair's inauguration; in other words, Mies conceived the chairs as modern versions of a royal throne. Since then, the Barcelona chair has become one of the twentieth century's most celebrated furniture designs because of its classical proportions and undisputed elegance that match the quality and historical importance of the building for which it was conceived.

The German Pavilion was originally designed and built as a temporary structure. However, already before the end of the International Exhibition— scheduled for the end of 1929—and prompted by the international acclaim that the building received, some initiatives intended to preserve the pavilion instead of dismantling it; yet, those initiatives did not succeed and the building was finally disassembled in January of 1930; the metal frame was stored in Barcelona and later sold for its weight value, while the more expensive components (marble and onyx walls, chrome-plated columns, etc.) were sent back to Germany to be reused by the companies that had sponsored the pavilion's construction. As a result, the Barcelona Pavilion entered into the history of architecture through the numerous—and revered—photographs taken during the building's short physical existence. Nevertheless, the idea of rebuilding it remained omnipresent; in 1954—thanks to the initiative of architect Oriol Bohigas—a long process that led to the eventual reconstruction of the pavilion began.

Three decades later, in 1984, through the initiative of a few enthusiastic architects and institutional sponsorship, the site where the pavilion stood in 1929 was excavated, launching a long and meticulous reconstruction of this unmatched masterpiece of architecture; in fact, it can be said that its reconstruction was the result of an archeological project of the modern times, because the team that excavated the site found the original footings of the cross-shaped columns, allowing them to rebuild the pavilion in exactly the same location that it had occupied in 1929. Moreover, the availability of original documents, the careful research selection of materials' sources undertaken before its reconstruction, as well as Germany's donation of a faithful replica of Kolbe's "Morning" sculpture produced an astonishingly convincing reconstruction. Re-inaugurated on June 2, 1986, the pavilion is a major architectural attraction not only for those who had learned to admire it through the mythical black-and-white photographs of 1929, but also to younger generations of architects—and general public—who cherish it as one of the greatest architectural creations of all time.

Further Reading

Curtis, William J. R. *Modern Architecture since 1900*. 3rd ed. London: Phaidon Press Limited, 1996.

Quetglas, Josep. *Imágenes del Pabellón de Alemania*. Montreal: Les Editions Section b, 1991.

Schulze, Franz. *Mies van der Rohe: A Critical Biography*. Chicago; London: University of Chicago Press, 1985.

Subirana i Torrent, Rosa Maria, ed. *Mies van der Rohe's German Pavilion in Barcelona, 1929–1986*. Barcelona: Public Foundation for the Mies van der Rohe German Pavilion in Barcelona, 1986.

THE GREAT MOSQUE OF CÓRDOBA, CÓRDOBA, ANDALUCÍA

Style: Umayyad Islamic Architecture
Dates: 786–990
Architects: Abdallah ibn-Falad and other unknown architects

The Great Mosque of Córdoba is the most representative religious building that testifies to the creative splendor of the Muslim occupation of Spain. With over 250,000 square feet of interior space supported by a veritable forest of columns (more than five hundred!), it was the result of successive building campaigns that contributed to the creation of a work of unusual interest, rare beauty, and historical relevance.

When the Muslim invaders seized control of Iberia, they established the Umayyad Emirate in Córdoba. After consolidating their domain of the region, they remained tolerant of the native population's religion, but needed a place of cult for their own faith. In the 750s they rented half of Córdoba's *Visigothic* Cathedral of San Vicente to use it as a mosque. In 786, Abd-al-Rahman I purchased the entire cathedral and began the construction of a new Friday Mosque, probably designed by his architect Abdallah ibn-Falad. The numerous expansions of the following two centuries attest to the growth and power of Córdoba's Muslim population.

As a building type, a mosque has some unique characteristics. The most important element is the *quibla*, a wall oriented toward Mecca that indicates the direction of prayer. Facing the quibla is the *haram* (praying hall), which is an interior space consisting of a series of aisles perpendicular to the quibla. Very often, a *sahn*—an open-air courtyard defined by enclosing walls—precedes the praying hall, while *riwaqs*—porticoes or arcades that surround a mosque or a shrine—provide a spatial transition between the sahn and haram.

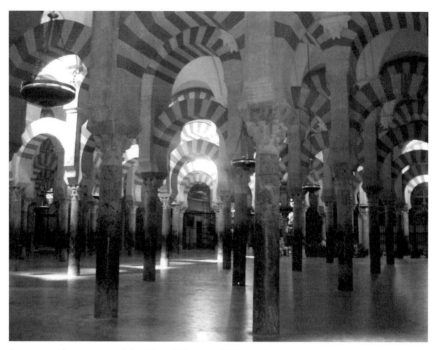

Fragment of one sector of the Great Mosque of Córdoba's interior.

Another important element is the *mihrab*, a niche carved in the quibla, which—as John Hoag explains—first appeared in the eighth century in Medina and probably derives from Egyptian Christian architecture (Hoag 1977, 77). These are the main elements; however, there are many variations of the basic type often related to regional stylistic developments of the geographically widespread Islamic culture, especially in the period of expansion during which they settled in—and for a long time dominated—a vast portion of the Iberian Peninsula.

The Great Mosque of Córdoba is, arguably, one of the most significant examples of Islamic architecture worldwide. It was built in four major building campaigns: the first was between 786 and 796, under Abd-al-Rahman I; the first addition was done between 833 and 848, during Abd-al-Rahman II's reign; the second addition and renovation of the original building took place between 961 and 975, during Al-Hakam II's period; finally, the largest expansion was done by Almanzor, *vizier* of Hisham II, between 987 and 990.

Construction began in 786 during the last years of Abd-al-Rahman I's reign (756–788). One year later it had been completed. It consisted of eleven aisles of twelve bays each, with a small mihrab carved on the quibla and aligned with the central aisle, which is slightly—yet noticeably—wider than the others. Curiously, the mihrab is not exactly pointed toward Mecca, a fact attributed to some early confusion of the invaders who believed that Mecca was to the south. This misunderstanding would also appear in many other mosques in Spain.

The entire walled complex enclosed an area of approximately 18,000 square feet; the haram occupied one-half of the square (approximately 240 feet wide by 120 feet deep), while the other half—slightly larger—was formed by the sahn. There was no riwaq in Abd-al-Rahman I's mosque, thus the transition between sahn and hall was through a thick wall parallel to the quibla and perforated by doors that accessed each of the haram's eleven aisles. The haram is the most important and architecturally significant space: it consists of eleven aisles of twelve bays each, defined by a two-tiered arcade supported on cylindrical columns. The central aisle is wider than the others (26 feet and 22.5 feet wide, respectively), suggesting a central emphasis within the haram. The arcades supported a no longer existing flat wooden roof that covered the entire hall. The upper tier is crowned by round arches, while the lower tier has *horse-shoe* arches, a feature that became associated with Islamic architecture but was already known by Spain's Visigothic builders before the Arabs arrived. The lightness of the arcades, with their alternate radial bands of white stone and red brick, probably derived from Roman architecture.

The columns that support the arcades activate the haram's spatial dynamism; most of them were surely pillaged from other Roman and Visigothic buildings, some probably located as far away as North Africa and southern France. Their different proportions, colors, materials, textures, capitals, and bases—characteristics that depended on their origin—produce a lively contrast with the regular and repetitive pattern of the arcades' white stone and red brick, generating an ethereal space unknown in Western architecture probably since the long-past and forgotten polychrome spaces of Greek architecture.

Half a century later, Abd-al-Rahman II ordered the extension of the praying hall; eight more bays were added in the direction of the quibla, matching the style and polychrome characteristics of the original arcades. However, this time, rather than pillaging columns and *capitals* from other buildings, new ones were created. All things considered, the expansion did not alter the character of the interior beyond the perceivable change in proportions— from a rectangular space to a slightly oblong square—even if the original position of the quibla was marked by the thick pillars that countered the arcades' lateral thrust.

In the following century the Great Mosque was expanded twice. In 951, Abd-er-Rahman III only enlarged the sahn (the front open-air courtyard), adding a 90-foot-square and over 100-foot-tall minaret, and riwaqs to three of the sahn's sides. Ten years later, his successor, Hakam II, made the final expansion of the Great Mosque, adding twelve additional bays, a double quibla wall, and four stone vaults. Contrary to the first major expansion,

Hakam II's addition represented a consequential stylistic shift toward more elaborated decorative patterns, and the development of a more central or focal space. This was determined by incorporating a *maqsura*—a screen or barrier that surrounds the *mihrab* and the *minbar* (a seat located to the right of the mihrab for the reading of Friday's prayer)—and the stone vaulting of the central aisle in the first three bays of the expansion.

The stylistic shift is clearly seen in the arcades: instead of employing round and horse-shoe arches with alternating bands of white stone and red brick as in the original Mosque's arcades, the architect of the extension introduced highly elaborated five-foil interlaced arches with carved *voussoirs*. This finely laced surface decoration extended to the walls above the arcades, thus de-materializing the planes, which now—as a result of the complex geometry of the *lobated arches* and the need to counter the greater lateral thrust of the added stone vaults—required significantly larger dimensions. The columns and their capitals, copied from rigid *Byzantine* models, lost the sculptural richness and variety of detail of their equals in the earlier portions of the building. In fact, the spatial and luminous effects of the lower part of the Mosque—the columns and their capitals—versus the upper part—the inter-laced five-foil arches—can not be more contrasting: the former are rigid and solid, the latter are ethereal and intricately layered.

Arguably, the stone vaults are the most innovative aspect of Hakam II's addition; they are richly ornamented by interlaced stone arches and beauti-fully carved with abstracted geometric and organic figural patterns, as well as surfaces profusely covered with mosaics. The central aisle culminates in the mihrab, which thus became a richly ornamented octagonal space at the center of the double wall of the quibla, an innovation likely adopted from the nearby mosque at Madinat-al-Zahara.

Another addition took place in 987, this time to the west because the river was an impediment for southern expansion. Almanzor added eight aisles to the entire complex matching the details and style of each of the previous three phases; this extension restored to the haram its original square proportions, while the sahn recovered its half-square proportions. It can be said that because of its absolute lack of originality, Almanzor's was the most inconsequential addition to the Great Mosque even if it was the largest. In 1238, after Córdoba was reconquered by Christian Kings, a nave of the mosque was converted and adapted for the Christian cult. Three hun-dred years later, in the 1520s, a major enlargement of this church took place, taking over an even larger portion of the mosque's interior. Certainly, this building has details of interest, yet, having emerged at the expense of more than half of the first two phases of the original mosque, it generated a lively controversy. When Carlos V, who had authorized construction of the cathe-dral, saw the new building, he said: "I did not know that it was this [that you wanted to do], otherwise I would not have authorized it; you have done what can be done anywhere else but destroyed what was unique in the world."

Further Reading

Bevan, Bernard. *History of Spanish Architecture*. London: B. T. Basford, 1938.
Chueca Goitía, Fernando. *Historia de la Arquitectura Española: Edad Antigua y Edad Media*. Vol. 1. Madrid: Editorial Dossat, 1965.
Hoag, John D. *Islamic Architecture*. New York: Harry N. Abrams, 1977.
Yeomans, Richard. *The Story of Islamic Architecture*. New York: New York University Press, 2000.

GUGGENHEIM MUSEUM, BILBAO, VIZCAYA

Style: Contemporary Architecture
Dates: 1991–1997
Architect: Frank O. Gehry

Completed in 1997, the Guggenheim Museum in Bilbao, designed by American architect Frank O. Gehry, is one of the most important buildings of the end of the twentieth century not only in Spain but also worldwide, a work that marked the last decade of the century. Furthermore, this project became inevitably associated with the festive spirit that surrounded the turn of the millennium, which coincided with the city's celebration of its seven-hundredth anniversary. This major work of architecture was the product of an intelligent collaboration between the Basque Country Administration and the Solomon R. Guggenheim Foundation; the former provided the site, logistics, and financing, while the latter contributed with its wonderful contemporary art collections and highly regarded experience as one of the most important art institutions in the whole world. The museum was part of an ambitious large-scale redevelopment of Bilbao that included other major public works designed by internationally renowned architects, such as a new airport terminal and a footbridge (the latter virtually adjacent to the museum), a new light-rail transit system, and a Conference Hall and Auditorium, commissioned to Santiago Calatrava, Norman Foster, and Soriano & Palacios, respectively.

The Guggenheim Foundation already owned a famous and splendid art museum in New York City, an unquestionable landmark of 1950s architecture designed by famous American architect Frank Lloyd Wright. At Bilbao, as part of the partnership agreement with the Basque Country Administration, the Guggenheim Foundation reserved the right to select the architect. After a competition held among a selected list of international architects, the commission was given to Frank O. Gehry, one of the most innovative and

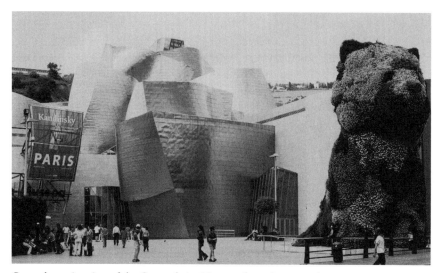

General exterior view of the Guggenheim Museum from the entry plaza.

talented architects of the second half of the twentieth century. By 1991, Gehry had already completed numerous celebrated works of architecture in the United States and abroad—for instance, his own home in Santa Monica, California (1978); the Los Angeles Aerospace Museum and Theater (1984); and the Vitra Design Museum in Weil-am-Rhein, Germany (1989)—while many others, such as the American Center in Paris, France (1988–1994) and the Walt Disney Concert Hall in Los Angeles (1989–2002), were in different stages of design and completion.

The building's program included permanent and temporary exhibition spaces, a large auditorium, administrative offices, museum support and curatorial services, a restaurant and small café, and the usual retail spaces that have become an integral part of cultural institutions of this magnitude; a public plaza and a water garden were also part of the project's programmatical requirements. The site was a challenging piece of land on the south bank of the Ria de Bilbao, in the city's former warehouse district; the actual extents of the site were adjacent to a freight yard and were traversed by the *Puente de la Salve*, a motorway bridge that constitutes one of the main vehicular entrances to Bilbao's center. Literally located between the river bank and the city's urban fabric, the museum building had to negotiate a 52-foot elevation difference between the two. The somewhat chaotic nature of the site was ideal for Frank Gehry, and architect who is famous for his signature nontraditional, sinuous, and fragmented forms that create vibrant and dynamic spaces of undoubted sculptural characteristics. Moreover, Gehry's previous collaborations and associations with many avant-garde contemporary artists guaranteed an architectural work of high artistic quality in its own right.

An impressive 256,000-square-foot sculptural mass clad in titanium, glass, and limestone, Gehry's Guggenheim Museum in Bilbao is a fabulous container of art, a "vessel of ideas," anchored between the river and the city. The building is brilliantly inserted in the complex site, equally integrated to the fabric of the city and the riverfront, successfully opening the building on the two fronts and negotiating the 52-foot elevation difference between them. This was accomplished by means of a public paved plaza that detaches the building from the street front and by a strolling promenade along the riverside that eventually leads to a gently stepped stairway that links the riverfront with the public plaza. The main entrance to the building is, precisely, from the public plaza, facing the city side, where it becomes a focal point at the end of Calle Iparraguirre, an important street that bisects the center of Bilbao diagonally. There, Jeff Koons' floral sculpture entitled "Puppy" pro-

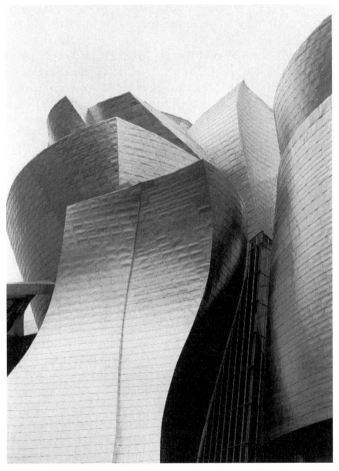

Detail of the Guggenheim Museum's exterior skin on the side facing the river.

vides a soft counterpoint to the building's angular volumes in glass, stone, and metal. The actual entrance to the museum's interior is below the level of the plaza, at the end of an ample descending stairway that constitutes an interesting, site-specific reversal of the usual ascending stairs of monumental public institutions; the plaza level, however, provides direct access to the public parts of the building—auditorium, restaurant, and retail—and becomes a natural outdoor expansion for the museum's cafeteria. More importantly, the plaza has become an active and vibrant civic space that serves as a connection between the riverfront and the recently renovated Museum of Fine Arts in the neighboring *Parque de Doña Casilda*, located approximately one-quarter of a mile west of the Guggenheim Museum.

Frank Gehry organized the building around a central 160-foot-tall glazed atrium; the permanent exhibition galleries are distributed around this pivotal space, linked by suspended curving walkways and glass elevators. The temporary exhibition space, especially conceived to welcome large-scale art installations, is the horizontal counterpoint to the vertical atrium space; it consists of a large and elongated column-free space—almost 450 feet long by 100 feet wide!—that passes under the La Salve bridge and culminates, on the exterior, in a twisted and split open-work tower that became one of the visual signs of the project and the city. Most exhibition areas are on the river side of the building housed in curvilinear sculptural volumes built in steel and clad with a paper-thin titanium skin; the other areas—restaurant, café, service, and offices—are, instead, turned to the city's side and housed in slightly more conventional concrete volumes pierced with rectangular openings and clad in Spanish limestone or painted in deep blue.

The innovative architectural forms and materials used by Frank O. Gehry in designing this building required the implementation of state-of-the-art computer technology to transfer the ideas conceived in three-dimensional models to the more conventional two-dimensional documents used by the building industry; likewise, the manufacturing of many building components was possible thanks to the use of the most advanced technological processes, such as robotics and computer-assisted fabrication techniques. Expectedly, for a building of this size and importance, the most advanced and sophisticated technology was also used for the galleries' artificial illumination, temperature and humidity control, and other key aspects of the museum.

The building was inaugurated on October 3, 1997, only six years after the birth of the idea. Long awaited, discussed, and published, as well as celebrated and controversial even before the first stone was laid, the Guggenheim Museum had an immediate impact not only in Bilbao, but also throughout the world, becoming an instant landmark, an architectural icon of the end of the millennium. Gehry's masterpiece immediately proved that an expressive sculptural and fragmented architecture was not necessarily at odds in a dense city fabric with a rich historical past; in fact, quite the opposite, because thanks to its remarkable architectural attributes, the building was the catalyst for recuperating a rather difficult area in the center of the city. Above and beyond, the Guggenheim Museum in Bilbao is much more than just a great or interesting building; not unlike Antoni Gaudí's Sagrada Familia in Barcelona or Jørn Utzon's Opera House in Sydney, Gehry's building has already become a powerful visual symbol of Bilbao.

Further Reading

Bruggen, Coosje van. *Frank O. Gehry: Guggenheim Museum Bilbao*. New York: Guggenheim Museum Publications, 1997.

Curtis, William J. R. *Modern Architecture since 1900*. 3rd ed. London: Phaidon Press Limited, 1996.

Dal Co, Franceso, and Forster, Kurt. *Frank O. Gehry: The Complete Works*. New York: The Monacelli Press, 1998.

Ferguson, Russell, ed. *At the End of the Century: One Hundred Years of Architecture*. Los Angeles; New York: The Museum of Contemporary Art and Harry N. Abrams, 1998.

HOTEL PARK, BARCELONA, CATALONIA

Style: Modern Architecture
Dates: 1950–1954
Architect: Antoni de Moragas i Gallissà

The Hotel Park is one of the most significant buildings of the revived Spanish interest in the principles of modern architecture, which began to develop in the late 1940s and 1950s—that is, in the post–World War II period, and a decade after the end of the Spanish Civil War (1936–1939) and the instauration of Francisco Franco's dictatorial regime (1939–1975). In that period, the dictatorship had suppressed the country's promising early twentieth-century developments of modern architecture, especially in Catalonia, such as the work of architects affiliated with the *GATCPAC*, notably Josep Lluís Sert and others, and favored a more traditional approach to architectural design and practice.

Hotel Park was designed by Antoni de Moragas i Gallissà, a Barcelona-based architect who in the late 1940s was in the early stages of his career and whose previous work—especially his first two schemes for the Hotel Park—was a reflection of the predominance of more traditional architectural design ideas and language. At the same time, as a member of the Collegi d'Arquitectes de Catalunya (the local and highly influential professional association of architects), Moragas organized lecture series with the participation of con-

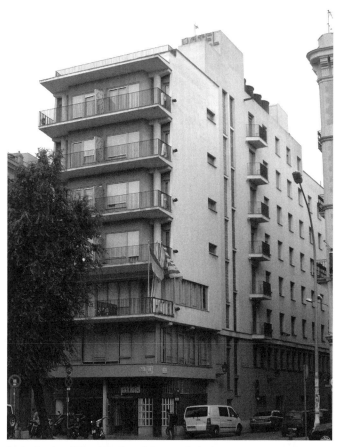

Main façade of Hotel Park on Marques de la Argentera Avenue.

temporaneous renowned figures such as Alvar Aalto, Bruno Zevi, Nikolaus Pevsner, and Gio Ponti. These lecture series marked a turning point in Moragas' work which, beginning in 1950, exhibited an architectural language clearly influenced by the modern work of Nordic architects (Asplund, Aalto) and by the then emerging Italian Organicism postulated by Italian architectural critic Bruno Zevi. Thus, Moragas' third and final scheme for the Hotel Park, developed precisely in 1950, marked a shift in the architect's work and stands as a symbol of the reemergence of modern architecture in Catalonia, as demonstrated in the work of architects such as José Antonio Coderch, José María Sostres, and other relevant figures of Barcelona's architecture in the mid-twentieth century. In 1952, these Barcelona architects—Moragas, Coderch, Sostres, with Oriol Bohigas, Joaquim Gili, Francesc Basso, Josep M. Martorell, Josep Pratmarsó, and others—founded the *Grup R*, an ad-hoc association of architects considered responsible of reintroducing modern architecture in Spain. Hotel Park is regarded as the first completed work done by a member of the Grup R, and is Moragas' most relevant architectural work.

The building is located on Marquès de l'Argentera Avenue just opposite the Estación de Francia railroad station, then the most important surface connection of Barcelona with the rest of the world; the city's harbor and Marina are also within a short walking distance. Literally on the edge but still within the physical limits of Barcelona's Ciutat Vella (the old "Gothic quarter"), the hotel occupies a rather small, constricted, and unusually elongated city block that has a very narrow front of about 23 feet on Marquès de l'Argentera street, the only side that offered an ample exposure to the exterior. Moragas used the entire available site to create a single structure yet subtly articulated in a few different parts. The most obvious differentiation is the building's frontal part that cantilevers out to maximize the available floor area for rooms; the articulation and design of this particular volume exhibits very interesting characteristics: while the side and rear façades are simple and austere, inspired in the sober architecture of Gunnar Asplund or Adolf Loos, the frontal part is much more dynamic, a wonderful composition of large extensions of wall surface, floor-to-ceiling glazing, cantilevering balconies, and exposed columns that establishes a language rich in formal oppositions—opaque versus transparent, open versus closed, permeable versus concealed—and recalls aspects of Alvar Aalto's Sanatorium in Paimio (Finland 1929), one of the masterpieces of early twentieth-century architecture.

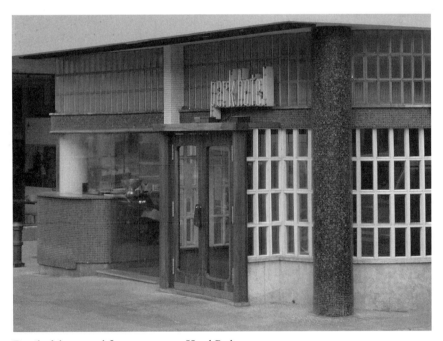

Detail of the ground floor entrance to Hotel Park.

The building's vertical extension is clearly divided into two differentiated sections: the bottom two levels house the hotel's public and service areas, and six stories that accommodate a total of 100 hotel rooms; the rooms are distributed along a double-loaded central corridor; the first five of these six floors are virtually identical (nineteen rooms per floor), while the smaller sixth level houses fewer rooms and is frankly set back at the front and rear of the site likely as a result of code restrictions. The two sections are cleverly and elegantly differentiated by subtle detailing, changes of fenestration, and material texture; this is clearly marked on the two long sides, and particularly on the façade facing Iñiguez de San Juan street. The vertical band of fenestration that provides natural light to the internal stairs resembles a "stitch" that connects the two sections placed just before the beautiful façade articulation of the frontal volume. This frontal block appears as the building's prow or "the front wagon," and constitutes the formal synthesis of the project. The exposed cylindrical columns that cut through the cantilevering balconies of the rooms placed at the front seem to anchor the whole building to the site, while they remain partially concealed behind the glazed enclosure of the first floor's lounge. Finally, at ground floor there is a remarkable and sophisticated composition that reveals the ambiguities of the building's formal language through a few gestures: the enclosing walls are slightly set back from the building's outline; on the southern corner of the site, the wall that encloses the hotel's cafeteria—covered in translucent glass blocks and glazed ceramic tiles—wraps around the corner column concealing it in a similar fashion as in the floor above; yet, in the other corner, the curvilinear wall made of glass blocks leaves the column exposed to the exterior, as a symbolic guardian of the hotel's carefully detailed entrance. These simple and fine formal and material articulations break the overall symmetry of the building and create a dynamic street-level façade that echoes some of Alvar Aalto's material expressivity of the late 1940s.

Inside, the distribution of rooms and detailing are as simple as carefully conceived: set back doors preserve privacy, smoothly plastered walls with rounded edges, and soft and warm materials throughout provide a welcoming atmosphere for hotel residents. The gentle and continuous stairway with a spiraling parapet topped by a wooden handrail is a little masterpiece in its own right, a testimony of Moragas' attention to detail, texture, and color. After suffering many years of neglect and poor maintenance, Hotel Park was fully remodeled in 1990 by Antoni de Moragas i Spa (the original author's own son) and Irene Sanchez. The restoration project consisted in adapting the structure to fulfill the requirements of the current building code, upgrading the technical facilities, and modernizing the hotel services while preserving the architectural and historical integrity of the original building. The participation of the original architect's own son surely guaranteed the successful return of this masterpiece of Catalonian twentieth-century architecture to its nearly original condition, recognizing its historical role as one of the buildings that inaugurated a new fruitful period of modern architecture in Spain.

Further Reading

Flores, Carlos. *Arquitectura Española Contemporánea, I 1880-1950*. Madrid: Aguilar, 1988.

Rodríguez, Carme, and Torres, Jorge. *Grup R*. Barcelona: Editorial Gustavo Gili, 1994.

Ruiz Cabrero, Gabriel. *The Modern in Spain: Architecture after 1948*. Cambridge, MA; London: The MIT Press, 2001.

HOUSE OF SHELLS. *See* La Casa de las Conchas.

KURSAAL AUDITORIUM AND CONGRESS CENTER, SAN SEBASTIÁN, GUIPÚZCOA

Style: Contemporary Architecture
Dates: 1990–2000
Architect: José Rafael Moneo

The Kursaal Auditorium and Congress Center of San Sebastián is one of the most important buildings of the final decade of the twentieth century. The project was the result of an invited design competition that counted with the participation of several renowned international architects. Designed by Rafael Moneo, winner of the international competition, the building is a relevant example of end-of-century architecture worldwide, a period in which Spain's architecture played a significant role and that had been inaugurated by another building designed by Moneo, the **National Museum of Roman Art** in Mérida. The building complex is located at the mouth of the Urumea River on what was a generous piece of unbuilt land left when the old casino was torn down, a hybrid site between the city and the ocean. A celebrated work since announced as winner of the design competition, the Kursaal was completed in 2000 and soon received the Mies van der Rohe Award for Eu-

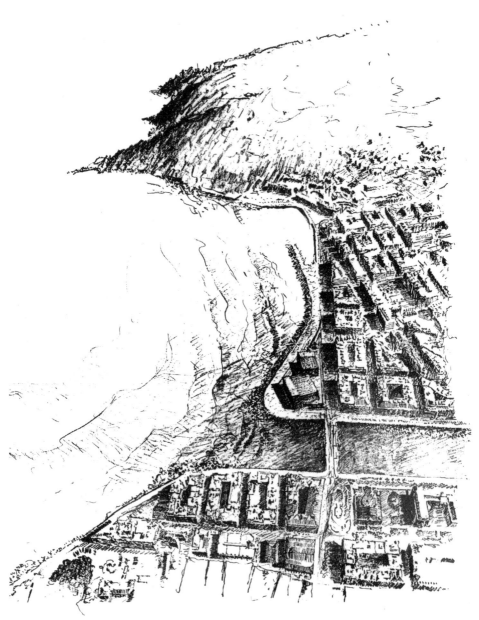

Drawing by Rafael Moneo showing the implantation of the Kursaal building complex with the context of the city and its surrounding landscape. *Drawing courtesy of architect Rafael Moneo.*

ropean Architecture, the most important distinction for works of architecture built in the European Union by an architect from the Union, and one of the most distinguished awards worldwide.

The site's natural and imposing beauty and its ideal location between city and sea inspired the architect to approach the building's design as an abstract artificial landscape rather than as an extension of the city. In so doing, Moneo established a conceptual and architectural dialogue with Eduardo Chillida's environmental sculpture "**Peine del Viento**," situated at the other end of San Sebastián's bay. This strategic design decision was likely a decisive factor for obtaining the first place in the competition and the commission to build the project.

The original competition program called for the design of a Music Complex, but—as a result of the increasing resources needed to maintain ambitious cultural public buildings like the Kursaal—the programmatical requirements continued to evolve and change throughout the final design stages. Eventually, the building had to satisfy the requirements of a multi-purpose complex to house a wide variety of musical performances, festivals, conferences, and conventions. All these factors contributed to the enrichment of the building's role in the city, even if—as built—the abstract image of the project's seminal concept is, at times, spoiled by the iconography of commerce, spectacle, and tourism.

The project's concept is extremely simple and clear: two asymmetric irregular crystals emerging from a low and horizontally extended stone platform. However, as it is typical in Moneo's work, beyond this apparent simplicity there lies a complex system of spatial relationships, ambiguities, and subtle site gestures. The two prisms are clad in translucent glass panels

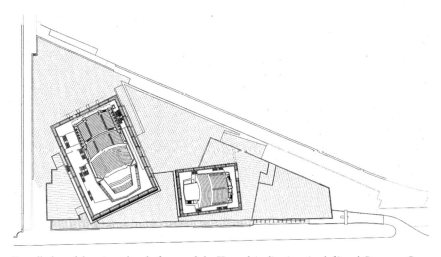

Overall plan of the triangular platform and the Kursaal Auditorium (on left) and Congress Center (on right). *Drawing courtesy of architect Rafael Moneo.*

and house the two large seating halls, the Auditorium and the Congress Center; the platform, roughly triangular in plan, accommodates the various differentiated entrances, exhibition halls, conference meeting rooms, restaurant, cafeteria, shops, offices, and services. Two levels of parking are provided underground.

Undoubtedly, the volumes of the Auditorium and Congress Center are the architectural and formal protagonists of the whole complex. They emerge through the platform with powerful sculptural presence as two crystalline rocks stranded at the intersection of sea and river. Their assertive formal profile against the coastline echoes Sidney's Opera House (Sydney 1957–1973), designed by one of Moneo's mentors, the Danish architect Jørn Utzon.

The Auditorium itself is a slanted prismatic volume (approximately 200 by 160 feet and 90 feet tall) that houses a seating hall with capacity for 1,800 seated spectators. The Congress Center is formally similar but smaller (140 by 105 feet and 66 feet tall). Both are resolved according to similar design strategies and the same construction system. They are clad with a double wall of plemented translucent glass panels supported by a steel structure that generates a large translucent container within which the volumes for the seating areas are contained asymmetrically. This is more evident in the Auditorium, where the seating hall *floats* within its translucent container clearly biased toward one of the long edges, creating an interstitial space between the glass walls and the hall's enclosures that becomes the main lobby. The generous dimensions of this space, its beautiful materials and textures, and the multiplicity of stairs and ramps that provide access to the various levels of the seating hall create a dynamic space, a scenographic ambiance where the public takes on the main performing role. A similar relationship of container–contained, with virtually identical formal strategies and materials, was implemented in the Congress Center but, because of its smaller dimensions, the asymmetry between the two is much less pronounced.

The various accesses to the building's components are housed within the triangular platform, which stretching along Avenida Zurriola is frankly oriented toward the city side of the site; the long, low wall creates an urban edge while allowing views of the ocean from the existing buildings on the opposite site of the street. Moreover, it also generates the extension of the walking promenade along Paseo de la Zurriola that connects Mont Ulía (on the east) with Mont Urgull (on the west). The platform's upper level is accessible by strategically placed ramps and stairs from the beach's side, becoming a privileged place for observation and contemplation of the imposing landscape. All the entrances to each of the numerous distinct functional components of the building complex are located at street level, under the platform, 31 feet above sea level. The access to the two main areas—Auditorium and Congress Center—are also clearly differentiated, but both are located within a generous space carved out of the platform, a transitional space that is both a covered exterior vestibule and an extension of the civic space of the street. Thus, the visitor is led from the street-level promenade to the con-

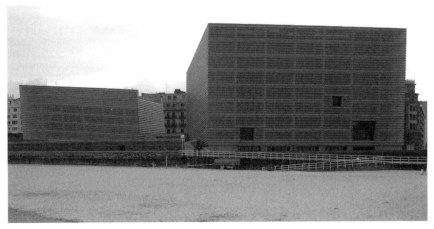

General Exterior view of the Kursaal from the beach with the Congress Center on the left and the Auditorium on the right.

trolled spaces of the seating halls through a sequence of transitional spaces—first a compressed and darkened exterior vestibule, then a multistory, expansive, luminous and spatially vibrant lobby—that gradually prepare the spectators for the performances. Additional clearly differentiated entrances provide access to the other functional independent areas housed under the platform (restaurant, cafeteria, exhibition halls, meeting rooms, administrative offices, and all the services).

The building's relationship with the surrounding landscape is certainly memorable. The two prisms are enclosed by translucent glass panels that profusely illuminate their respective lobbies with carefully studied filtered daylight. However, the direct visual relationship with the marvelous exterior through transparent planes is highly controlled, limited to a few selected instances. Nonetheless, these are spectacular, consisting of large clear-glass planes deliberately placed to frame views to the sea and the surrounding landscape at the vestibule level of the two main volumes. Each one of them offers a selected view of each of the two mounts, Urgull and Ulía, that delimit *Playa de la Zurriola* (Zurriola's beach). Yet, the most spectacular views of the building are at night when, with the interior fully illuminated, the two sculptural crystals stand as two phosphorescent rocks placed between city and sea that irradiate an enigmatic light and animate the coast line.

Further Reading

Curtis, William J. R. "Rafael Moneo: The Structure of Intentions." *El Croquis* 98 (2000): 28–41.

Moneo, Rafael. "Kursaal Auditorium." *Assemblage* 14, 8–13.

Moneo, Rafael. "Seis Propuestas para San Sebastián." *El Croquis* 43 (June 1990): 7–23.

Ruiz Cabrero, Gabriel. *The Modern in Spain: Architecture after 1948*. Cambridge, MA; London: The MIT Press, 2001.

LA CASA DE LAS CONCHAS, SALAMANCA, CASTILLA Y LEÓN

Style: Plateresque Architecture
Dates: Circa 1480–1493; rehabilitation, restoration, and transformation 1984–1993
Architects: Unknown; partially attributed to Rodrigo Arias Maldonado; rehabilitation and transformation, Víctor López Cotelo and Carlos Puente Fernández

La Casa de las Conchas ("House of Shells") is one of the most representative examples of the *Plateresque*, a style that flourished during the reign of the Catholic Kings as a transition from the *Gothic* period to the *Renaissance*. It is characterized by a libertine mixture of different styles which, with complete disregard of the building's structure and architectural articulation, often approached aesthetic anarchy. The Plateresque reflects the endurance of Gothic traditions, the high level of impregnation of *Mudéjar* decoration, and the slow appropriation of Renaissance ideas. The open-air interior courtyard and the façades of La Casa de las Conchas are outstanding examples of the Plateresque style. Along with the **Palace of El Infantado** in Guadalajara, and the **Universidad de Alcalá de Henares**, it is one of the relevant civil monuments of that period.

The building is located at the intersection of Calle de la Rúa and Calle de la Compañía, at the heart of Salamanca, just opposite **La Clerecía**. It was built in the late fifteenth century by Rodrigo Arias Maldonado (known as Dr. Talavera), a professor of the then already reputed University of Salamanca and a member of the Catholic Kings' Royal Council. Originally, the building was a Gothic town palace, a then emerging type with rather well-defined characteristics. La Casa de las Conchas has many of these typical features such as a central courtyard surrounded by a two-story arcade, a rather closed exterior with few small window openings, exterior walls profusely decorated with heraldic symbols, and towers in the corners, of which only one remains.

The building is rather introspected, very closed to the exterior but opened around the outdoor courtyard. It is accessible from Calle de la Rúa, where one doorway—eccentrically located at the northwest corner of the west façade—leads to a rather constricted and austere vestibule. The door is crowned by a *mixtilinear* heavily decorated *pediment* that profusely displays

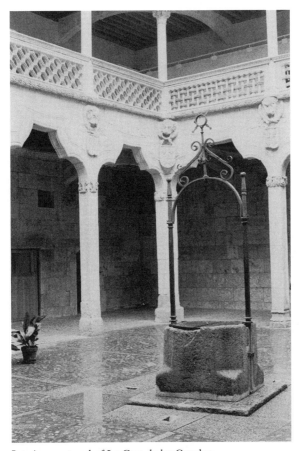

Interior courtyard of La Casa de las Conchas.

the fleur-de-lis (heraldic symbol of the Maldonado family). The entry sequence through the doorway, vestibule, and courtyard is not straight, presenting, instead, a zigzag path. This misalignment of associated spaces was typical of Gothic town palaces. Access to the courtyard is on the right side of the vestibule, where a low platform negotiates the different level of the entry vestibule and the courtyard, the latter located at a higher elevation than the street.

All the main rooms of the building are placed around the slightly irregular rectangular courtyard, which is enclosed by arcades and galleries in the two levels. The arcades are exuberantly decorated with various motifs and the mixture of styles typical of Plateresque art. The lower-level arcade is composed of five-centered mixtilinear arches supported by square pillars; the arches of the upper-level gallery are also mixtilinear but they only have three centers and are much lower and extremely flattened; they are supported by round marble columns crowned with Plateresque *capitals*. A honeybee-comb

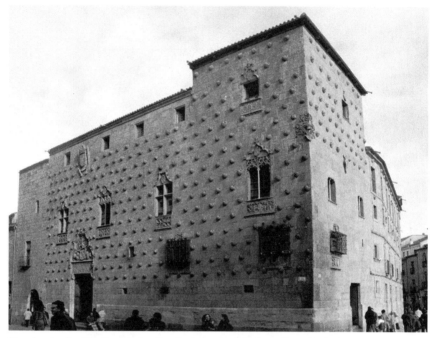

Exterior detail of La Casa de las Conchas's façade with the wall profusely decorated with shells in stone relief.

balustrade articulates the transition from one level to the other. The exotic richness, variety, and complexity of details confirm the influence of Mudéjar architecture and decoration left by the centuries-long Muslim occupation of Spain. The courtyard has a water-well—which has a beautiful granite curb-stone—located off-center and slightly rotated with respect to the courtyard's dominant directions. The water-well proves the wealth and social importance of the owners, for in that epoch only the very wealthy could afford the luxury of having provision of potable water within their premises.

The exterior façades are the architectural highlight of the building, illustrating the liberty with which ornament was applied. They are virtually covered over with more than 300 conchas de vieira (sea shells) distributed in a typically Mudéjar diamond pattern. Their presence and purpose is still the subject of much debate: one belief is that they were applied as a symbol of the owner's membership to the Orden de Santiago (Order of Saint James); another one attributes it to fashionable uses because they were widely used in the late Gothic period; however, considering that the display of heraldic symbols as façade decoration was one of the most prominent characteristics of the Plateresque, the most believable theory is that it is related to the celebration of the marriage between Maldonado and Juana Pimentel Benavente (the shells were the heraldic symbol of the Benavente family). In fact, the abundance of shells and fleur-de-lis in the two façades of the building may be interpreted as symbolizing the union through marriage of the two families. Whichever their origin, they provide a decorative exuberant gracefulness to the building's exterior and contribute to the rather chaotic coexistence of divergent styles, all typical characteristics of the palaces built in urban centers by the powerful nobility of the period. Yet, at the same time, they provide a certain plastic unity to an otherwise architecturally unremarkable exterior.

Other noteworthy aspects of La Casa de las Conchas are the beautiful and intricate design of the iron grill-work in lower-level windows (attributed to Fray Francisco of Salamanca and considered as the finest example of this period), the opening of some larger windows on the street façades that replaced preceding smaller openings more typical of the Gothic period—reflecting the arrival of Renaissance ideas even if the partitioning of windows still exhibits the characteristics of Gothic building traditions—and the beautiful coffered wood ceilings.

Curiously, the owners only occupied the building for a short period, for already in 1529 it became a rental property. In the late 1600s and 1700s the building underwent some modifications with the rebuilding of the arcade on Calle de la Rúa and the removal of twenty-three courses of stone from the only remaining tower to lighten the load on the already suffering foundations. In 1929, La Casa de las Conchas was declared a national monument. Later, in 1984, Salamanca's town council handed over the building to Spain's central government with the purpose of converting it into a public library. The building was then in disrepair; stonewalls and foundations were in poor shape, the courtyard had decayed, and the beautiful coffered ceilings had severely deteriorated. The restoration of the original building and its transformation into a public library was commissioned to Víctor López Cotelo & Carlos Puente Fernández. This demanded delicate tasks such as the stone-by-stone disassembling and reassembling of the courtyard and its adjacent stairs, and the provision of large portions of missing foundations to the existing walls. López Cotelo's and Puente's work was extremely sensitive, preserving and reviving the historic character of the building while making alterations and additions of undeniable cleverness and austere elegance. The uses and functions of the new public library were organized around the existing courtyard, reasserting its role as the spatial center of the whole. Moreover, the addition of new stairs improved the circulation throughout the building, while a new reading room in what used to be an open-air space, covered by a skylighted shed-roof, contributed to the overall effectiveness, warmth, and good natural illumination of the building's new life.

Further Reading

Barcia Merayo, Luis. *Castillos y Palacios de España*. Barcelona: Editorial Salvat, 1994.

Chueca Goitía, Fernando. *Historia de la Arquitectura Española: Edad Antigua y Edad Media*. Vol. 1. Madrid: Editorial Dossat, 1965.

López Cotelo, Víctor, and Puente, Carlos. "Lectura Gótica: Biblioteca en la Casa de las Conchas." *Arquitectura Viva* 33 (November–December, 1993); 50–55.

LA CLERECÍA, SALAMANCA, CASTILLA Y LEÓN

Style: Baroque Architecture
Dates: 1617–1754
Architects: Juan Gómez de Mora; Pedro Matos; Andrés García de Quiñones

The church of La Clerecía in Salamanca, with its associated and adjacent Colegium Regium (Royal College), is considered to be among the most relevant architectural monuments of Felipe III's (1598–1621) and Felipe IV's (1621–1665) reigns, which broadly correspond with the beginning and climax of the *Baroque* period in Europe. Initiated in 1617, the construction of this large religious building complex elapsed over a period of almost one and a half centuries; it was originally commissioned by Felipe III to his official royal architect, Juan Gómez de Mora, later continued by Pedro Matos, and eventually completed by Andrés Garcia de Quiñones. Juan Gómez de Mora was, undoubtedly, one of Spain's most important architects; he succeeded Juan de Herrera—Felipe II's royal architect and one of the authors of the influential **Monastery of El Escorial**—and was involved in numerous significant architectural and urban projects such as the **Plaza Mayor of Madrid** and the church and monastery of La Encarnación (Madrid 1611–1616).

La Clerecía and the Colegium Regium were founded at the instigation of Queen Margarita de Austria (Felipe III's wife) as Salamanca's *Jesuit* College. The complex occupies a large city block facing Calle de la Compañía at the heart of Salamanca, one of the most important Spanish cities of the time; its renowned university, with its splendid *Plateresque* and *Renaissance* buildings, is one of the oldest and most reputed in Europe and was the center of Spain's intellectual activity in the sixteenth and seventeenth centuries. La Clerecía and Colegium Regium are actually placed at a short distance from the university buildings, just opposite **La Casa de las Conchas**, a relevant representative of Plateresque architecture. The Colegium Regium houses the facilities for the Jesuit College, while La Clerecía is the college's church and constitutes the most visible element of the immense, rather introspected complex; its dome and towers stand out among the many beautiful domes and towers that characterize Salamanca's skyline.

The plans for the project were made by Juan Gómez de Mora closely fol-

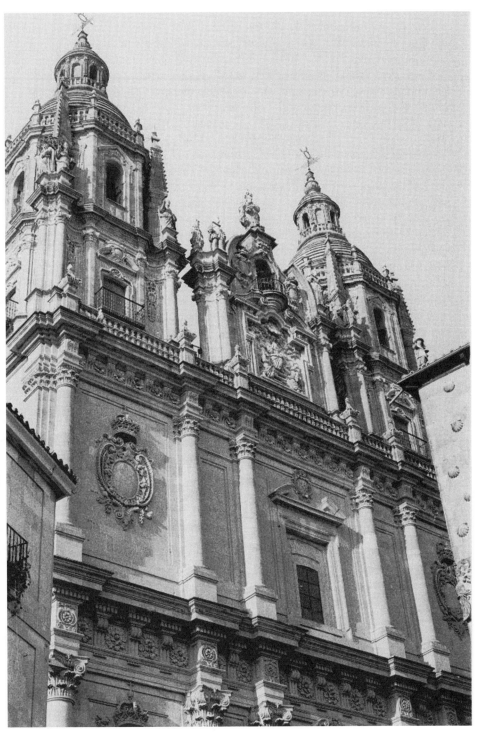

Fragment of the main façade of the church of La Clerecía.

lowing the example of the Jesuit's mother home in Rome, Il Gesú, designed by Vignola (c. 1568) and considered one of the most influential works of Baroque architecture. As Chueca Goitía observed about La Clerecía in relationship to Il Gesú, "the church is placed in similar relationship to the rest of the Colegium, the position of the cloister and porter's house is virtually identical and, if one ignores the differences imposed by the different characteristics of their respective sites, the similarities are obvious" (Chueca Goitía 1965, 255). The multilevel college buildings are organized in strictly linear wings around square courtyards connected by ample corridors. The complex's rigorous plan organization and overall severity reflects the influence of the austere and rigid architecture imposed by Herrera at El Escorial. In fact, Juan Gómez de Mora was Herrera's successor not only in his role as royal architect but also as the continuator of his severe architecture, a hardly surprising thing considering that Juan Gómez de Mora had been trained by his uncle—the well-known architect Francisco Gómez de Mora—who had worked with Herrera at El Escorial.

In plan, the church of La Clerecía is a *Latin-cross* composed of an aisleless *nave* and a *transept* ending in a shallow rectilinear sanctuary. The church's interior is certainly beautiful, one of the grandest Baroque interiors in Spain; the vaulted nave consists of four identical bays marked by arches placed between severe *Doric* fluted pilasters topped by a full-scale entablature that runs along the entire perimeter of the interior space composed by nave and transept; side chapels open on each side of the nave's arcades, as well as on the sanctuary's sides. The whole is wrapped within a regular, unarticulated rectangular envelope that conceals the form of the interior space, a characteristic of Baroque architecture.

At the center of the space, a majestic dome of fine proportions covers the *crossing*; it is slightly stilted and supported on ornamented *squinches* below a row of rectangular openings that generates a short cylindrical drum that detaches the actual dome from the vaulting; this detail eventually became a typical feature of Spanish Baroque. The dome was likely built by a Jesuit sculptor, Pedro Matos, who in 1644 had succeeded Gómez de Mora as the architect in charge of the complex's construction. However, it is generally agreed that Matos followed plans left by Gómez de Mora; yet, he left significant traces of his intervention in the dome and the façade, both of which show a higher interest in sculptural relief and ornament which, according to some historians, manifests the influence of Francisco Bautista's work, considered as one of the most important Castilian architects of the mid-1600s.

In spite of the modifications introduced by Pedro Matos, the whole building remained faithful to Juan Gómez de Mora's original project. Its resemblance to Vignola's Il Gesú is certainly striking: the plan is conceptually identical, except that La Clerecía ends with a rectilinear bay beyond the crossing and Il Gesú ends in a semicircular *apse* added to the bay that creates the short arm of the Latin-cross plan. The articulation of the interior, and the sections through the nave and crossing are, despite some evident differences, remarkably similar. The main distinction is in the exterior façades, likely because they were redesigned by the architects who succeeded Gómez de Mora in the construction of this monumental work.

The church's originally planned main façade was, most likely, a rather flat and unornamented front piece in the lines of Vignola's façade for Il Gesú and consistent with the severe and austere style that characterized post-Herrerian architecture in Spain, of which Juan Gómez de Mora was the most important representative. However, the construction of the church's façade began long after de Mora's death and the stylistic preferences had, by then, evolved to more elaborated designs and profuse ornamental programs. The two lower portions are attributed to Pedro Matos, while the two towers and central piece of the façade's coronation are unquestionably the work of Andrés García de Quiñones, one of the more prominent Spanish architects of the first half of the eighteenth century. The two lower portions—the first corresponding with interior's nave and the second with the vaulting and roofing systems—are articulated as a sequence of superimposed giant orders of columns that animate the surface of the façade with a plasticity typical of Baroque architecture; Quiñones' coronation begins above the horizontal cornice of the central portion and consists of a complex and profusely ornamented central pediment-belfry flanked by two symmetrical towers that rise high up to double the overall height of the façade, providing a sculptural and monumental silhouette to the building. Quiñones was also involved in the Colegium, where he completed the cloister of the Espiritu Santo in which, as in the towers of the façade, an ascending vertical movement predominates over the preferred horizontal lines of Gómez de Mora's Herrerian architectural lines. The arcaded corridors that run along the college's rooftops are a distinct characteristic of this large building.

The Jesuit's Colegium Regium and church of La Clerecía encapsulate, in the sequential work of Juan Gómez de Mora, Pedro Matos, and Andrés García de Quiñones, the evolution of Spain's Baroque architecture before the development and emergence of the peculiar and exclusively Spanish *Churrigueresque* style. Therefore, the whole complex—which today's houses Salamanca's Universidad Pontificia—but especially the church of La Clerecía, marks an important and extended period of the country's architectural history as an indisputable landmark of the Baroque.

Further Reading

Blunt, Anthony, ed. *Baroque and Rococo: Architecture and Decoration*. New York: Harper & Row, 1978.

Bottineau, Yves, and Butler, Yvan. *Baroque Ibérique*. Fribourg: Office du Livre, 1969.

Chueca Goitía, Fernando. *Historia de la Arquitectura Española: Edad Moderna-Edad Contemporánea*. Vol. 2. Madrid: Editorial Dossat, 1965.

Luz Lamarca, Rodrigo de. *Francisco de Mora y Juan Gómez de Mora: Cuenca, Foco Renacentista*. Cuenca: Diputación de Cuenca, 1997.

LA MARINA APARTMENT BUILDING, LA BARCELONETA, BARCELONA, CATALONIA

Style: Modern Architecture
Dates: 1951–1955
Architects: José Antonio Coderch de Sementat; with the
collaboration of Manuel Valls Vergés

The apartment building in La Barceloneta, designed by the Catalan architect José Antonio Coderch with the collaboration of Manuel Valls Vergés in the 1950s, is an undisputed landmark of Spain's modern architecture. Commissioned by the Social Institute of La Marina for retired fishermen, the building is located at the intersection of Paseo Joan de Borbó, or Paseo de la Marina, and Cervera Street in La Barceloneta, a low-cost housing neighborhood for fishermen east of Barcelona's Marina, developed in the 1750s and composed of unusually elongated city blocks oriented north–south. More precisely, Coderch's building occupies a rectangular lot at the north end of a city block placed just in front of the harbor that affords ample vistas to the city's seafront. The brief required two apartments for six people in each floor level and general building services, a challenging task considering the site's reduced dimensions and existing building regulations.

La Marina apartment building was Coderch's first multifamily urban commission and is regarded, along with the superb Casa Ugalde (Caldes d'Estrac, Spain 1951), as one of his major masterpieces. Moreover, it is a distinguished representative of the resistance of mid-century architects, particularly in Catalonia, to accept the regressive eclectic architecture favored and imposed in Spain during Franco's rule (1939–1975), as well as of the moment—within that period of political and cultural isolation—in which Spain began to reopen to the rest of the world. Architecturally, the building is noteworthy because of its remarkable contextual insertion into the urban fabric, intelligent functional distribution of the apartments, and innovative conception of the exterior that recuperated elements from traditional architecture but used them in an unusual, almost surreal, way.

The building consists of a two-storey base, a vertical development of six typical floor levels and a crowning at the top marked by an overhanging canopy. The unequivocal manifestation of these three parts and the vertical emphasis infused to the six-level vertical development bring echoes of Sullivan's own skyscrapers such as the Wainwright Building (Saint Louis, Mis-

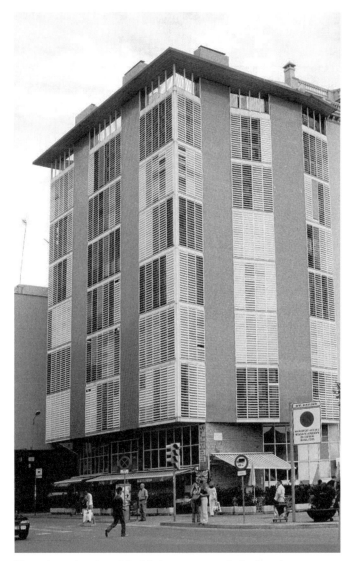

General exterior view of La Marina apartments in La Barceloneta.

souri 1891) and the Guarantee Building (Buffalo, New York 1895). Interest-ingly, the nonorthogonal geometry of the floor plans, the cantilevered slabs, and the vertical emphasis also have similarities with a contemporaneous building of Frank Lloyd Wright—the Price Tower (Bartlesville, Oklahoma 1952–1956)—an architect who influenced Coderch's work. However, despite these "American echoes," the building materials, specifically the ceramic tiles and louver-blinds of the façade, and the organization of the floor plans are firmly rooted in Catalonia's Mediterranean traditions.

The resolution of the project's programmatic requirements (two three-bedroom apartments per typical floor) is extraordinary considering the site's exiguous dimensions and unfavorable predominant orientation (widely open vistas to the north and west but severely confined on the east and definitely blocked on the south). The typical plan is divided into two equal halves, each half accommodating a three-bedroom apartment, with the central circulation core placed at the center of the block. The two resulting apartments are virtually identical; the only actual difference is their orientation; while the one that occupies the western half opens to the seafront, the eastern unit has more confined vistas, especially in the bedrooms; however, the architect intelligently placed the living areas on the north end where both units can afford, even if in unequal terms, the attractive views of the Marina and the city's seafront. Yet, the most interesting aspect of the typical level resolution is the complex, elegant, and informal geometry of the floor plans, key of the project's intelligent conception that reverberates throughout the whole building.

The plan is defined by concrete pillars of large dimensions that necessarily fall within the boundaries of the site, and cantilevering slabs that project beyond those boundaries to increase the floor area of each apartment; the cantilevering portions, which occupy most of the undulating exterior of the building's vertical development, are articulated by alternately tile-clad and louver-blind vertical bands, two materials typically found in Mediterranean architecture but used in a novel and abstract manner by Coderch; the ceramic-tile-clad bands mask fireplaces, kitchen walls, and closets, while the louver-blinds screen fully glazed interior spaces and exterior terraces. The use of these two materials generates wonderful effects, not only on the exterior of the building but also in the apartments' interiors. Outside, the alternation of vertical bands provides a vertical emphasis to the whole only softened by the rhythmic punctuation of the movable louvers, especially when they are in open (horizontal) position. Inside the apartments the light effects are different in the bedrooms and livingrooms; it is precisely in the fully glazed living areas that the effect of the louvers reaches a maximum potential, providing a rather intriguing "exterior ambiance," suddenly becoming a shaded porch or an enclosed courtyard.

Below the undulating and cantilevering volume of the building's main body, the two-storey base accommodates the entrance to the apartments' lobby and—originally—a few nonresidential spaces, while the porter's apartment was located in a semiburied level. The base is enclosed by an alternating system of fully glazed and opaque enclosures, but these are not in alignment with the vertical bands of the upper volume; their material expression is also different (regular unglazed brick and mullioned glazed planes instead of glazed ceramic tiles and louver-blinds, respectively); yet, they share the nonorthogonal geometry that does not follow the site's property lines, counterpointing each other to emphasize a seemingly floating aspect to the upper portion. At the opposite vertical end, the building is crowned by an overhanging canopy, an abstract cornice that protects the building's top floor terrace and provides an appropriate horizontal line that culminates the volume's vertical development. As it cantilevers out of the vertical mass it provides a clever counterpoint to the recessed ground floor.

Coderch's apartment building in La Barceloneta was quickly recognized as a typological breakthrough that used a modern architectural vocabulary while revitalizing regional traditions and materials. It is not surprising that the architect, conscious of this important step, revisited the themes explored in this building in numerous other opportunities such as the Apartment Block on J. S. Bach Street (Barcelona 1961), the house for the sculptor Antoni Tapies (Barcelona 1963), and a beach house in Tamariú (near Palafrugell 1965). But, and perhaps more importantly, the building pioneered the emergence of a new paradigm for multistory residential buildings in a Mediterranean setting followed and reinterpreted elsewhere in subsequent years by other architects who understood the potential of Coderch's innovative contribution.

Further Reading

Curtis, William J. R. *Modern Architecture since 1900*. 3rd ed. London: Phaidon Press Limited, 1996.

Flores, Carlos. *Arquitectura Española Contemporánea, I 1880–1950*. Madrid: Aguilar, 1988.

Frampton, Kenneth, ed. *Contemporary Spanish Architecture: An Eclectic Panorama*. New York: Rizzoli, 1986.

Rodríguez, Carme, and Torres, Jorge. *Grup R*. Barcelona: Editorial Gustavo Gili, 1994.

"LA PEDRERA." *See* Casa Milá.

"LA PEINETA." *See* Sports Complex and Track and Field Stadium of Madrid.

LA ZARZUELA RACETRACK GRANDSTAND, MADRID, COMUNIDAD DE MADRID

Style: Modern Architecture
Dates: 1934–1936; 1940–1941
Architects: Carlos Arniches, Martín Domínguez, and Eduardo Torroja

The grandstand for Madrid's Hipódromo de La Zarzuela (the city's horse racetrack) is Eduardo Torroja's masterpiece and one of Spain's most important architectural works of the 1930s. The building complex was in fact designed by the architectural office of Carlos Arniches and Martín Domínguez in collaboration with the internationally well-known civil engineer Eduardo Torroja, who along with Robert Maillard, Eugene Freyssenet, and Pier Luigi Nervi is considered a pioneer in the design of concrete structures. The Grandstand for La Zarzuela Racetrack is the best-known work of Arniches and Domínguez, as well as Torroja's most important architectural work—among many other brilliant structures he conceived—to the point that it is often credited only to him.

The building is the result of a competition organized in 1934 and won by the team composed of Arniches, Domínguez, and Torroja for designing Madrid's new horse racetrack that was to replace the city's old Hipódromo Real (Royal Horse Racetrack), which had been demolished as a consequence of the implementation of Secundino Suazo's winning competition for Madrid's Expansion Plan of 1929 and the prolongation of the Avenida Castellana. The site for the new horse racetrack was established in the area of the Quinta de El Pardo, a large park adjacent to the Royal Palace of El Pardo (one of the main palatial residences of the kings of Spain) located approximately ten miles northwest of Madrid's center. The racetrack facilities, which since then are known as the Hipódromo de La Zarzuela, are actually located very near to the royal palace, less than half a mile to the west and on the other side of the nearby Manzanares River.

The building's completion has an interesting history. Construction began in 1935, the year after the competition was awarded, and the whole complex was nearly completed in 1936 when the Spanish Civil War broke out; the area of La Zarzuela, just outside of the country's capital, was an active war front; as a result, the partially completed building was severely damaged, its parts lying in ruined condition. Fortunately, after the war ended (1939), the damaged areas were quickly restored and the rest of the building complex was completed in May 1941 when the Hipódromo de la Zarzuela was effectively inaugurated.

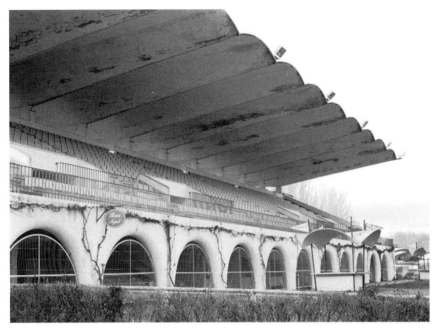

View of the La Zarzuela grandstand cantilever and ground level arcade.

The brief of the design competition—in which only nine teams partici-pated—consisted of a complex set of requirements that included a large grandstand, offices, and various services, but also demanded a careful plan-ning of separated areas and facilities for the main racetrack and for training and taking care of horses. The team of Arniches, Domínguez, and Torroja resolved the spatial and functional complexities of the program with extreme clarity and simplicity, placing the main racetrack and its public facilities apart from the stables and other service areas. Undoubtedly, the beautiful concrete canopies that cover the three public grandstands—elegant and audacious double-curvature cantilevering shells—are the whole complex's more archi-tecturally relevant characteristic.

Concrete shells structures had already been used in numerous buildings; however, a cantilevering canopy of this magnitude represented a major struc-tural innovation and achievement. Another rather innovative aspect was the use of a bare concrete shell as the representative image of a building that had an institutional character. In effect, the building's image relied entirely on the elegance and audacity of the structural solution, an aspect that was at the heart of Torroja's understanding of architecture as he eloquently stated in one of his writings: "The structure should be beautiful in itself, without needing ad-ditions or frills. As there is an attempt, at the same time, to eliminate super-impositions and ornamental freedom, success is more difficult to achieve than ever" (quoted by Fernández Ordóñez and Navarro Vera 1999, 89). Arniches and Domínguez, who worked with Torroja on numerous projects, understood that at La Zarzuela the structure was the key of the project, and let it stand out. This factor surely contributed to the credit given mainly to the engineer of the team. However, their important contribution to the project is quite visible in the arched gallery at the foot of the stands and around the paddock (the enclosed area where racehorses are saddled and shown before a race), and demonstrated the architects' eclectic architectural style.

The seating portion of the stands is supported by a linear sequence of structural porticoes put at five-meter intervals (a little less than 16.5 feet) connected by double-curvature concrete vaults that house a grand hall for accommodating the users' betting activities and related betting offices. The stands are sheltered by the laminar concrete canopy that cantilevers off the line of concrete vertical supports. The concrete canopy consists of a double curved *hyperboloid* shell that cantilevers over 14 feet off the central line of supports; at the anchoring point, the shell is almost 6 inches thick, but at the outer extreme it is less than 2 inches thick, thus creating a graceful and extremely elegant profile. While seen together they appear as a sequence of vaulted modules; structurally, these modules are not actual vaults; rather, they are independent and self-supporting modules consisting of a rigid vertical support and double-curvature hyperboloids; as they extend off the central supports their profile resembles a gull's wing. Thus, hovering over the stands, the canopy provides the indispensable shelter from sun and rain for the seating areas without creating any visual obstruction for the seated spectators, a remarkably functional and elegant solution that has transcended time and influenced many similar structures built later in other parts of the world.

As it has been said, the Grandstand for La Zarzuela Racetrack is "one of the most unique and attractive works of Modern architecture in the Madrid of the thirties. It became an emblem of modernity, as expressed in the bold engineering of its repeated white, airy vaulted canopies" (Solà-Morales et al. 1998, 239). It was awarded Spain's national architectural award and its cantilevering canopy has also been declared a monument of national interest. After a decade of declining activity in the 1980s and 1990s, the Hipódromo de La Zarzuela closed in 1997. Consequently, the building was virtually abandoned; yet, efforts to save and restore what is considered a masterpiece of Spain's twentieth-century architecture abounded. These efforts were finally rewarded in 2003 with the signature of an agreement that will permit the reopening of the racetrack after repair, restoration, and rehabilitation of the built structure is completed in 2005.

Further Reading

Chueca Goitía, Fernando, Sambricio, Carlos, Capitel, Antón, Ruiz Cabrero, Gabriel and Hernández de León, Juan M. *Arquitectura de Madrid, Siglo XX*. Madrid: Tanais Ediciones, 1999.

Fernández Ordóñez, José Antonio, and Navarro Vera, José Ramón. *Eduardo Torroja, Engineer*. Madrid: Ediciones Pronaos, 1999.

Solà Morales, Ignasi de, Capitel, Antón, and Buchanan, Peter, et al., eds. *Birkhäuser Architectural Guide, Spain 1920–1999*. Basel: Birkhäuser Verlag, 1998.

LOARRE: CASTLE AND FORTIFIED WALLS, LOARRE (NEAR HUESCA), ARAGON

Style: Romanesque Architecture
Dates: Circa 1070–1200s
Architect: Unknown

The castle of Loarre—a National monument since 1906—is considered not only the oldest but also the most significant fortified castle in the Iberian Peninsula and one the most important examples of *Romanesque* architecture in Europe. Its historical relevance is based on the rich history of the site and on the building's unusual architectural characteristics, for Loarre is a rare standing case in which we find an excellent combination of eleventh-century military, religious, and civil architecture. Its construction began in the early years of the eleventh century, but some important parts were built as late as in the fourteenth century. Interestingly, as we ascend through the built complex, we encounter components that belong to older building campaigns, the opposite of what we would normally expect.

Loarre is a natural fortress located at an altitude of more than 3,000 feet above sea level on a steep and rugged rock with commanding and strategic views of the Gallego valley. The site was already used as a bastion by Caesar's generals during the period of Roman conquest and occupation of the Iberian Peninsula. It is believed that the *Iberos* (indigenous tribes that populated the region) had already built a military fortress on the site, for—in their language—"Loarre" means fortified castle on the rock.

In the early years of the eleventh century, Loarre was a small burg that responded to the Kingdom of Aragon; in 1062 the burg was captured by the Arabs who used it as a strategic point in a defensive line of containment of the small Christian kingdoms that were concentrated near the Pyrenees. In 1070, Aragon's King Sancho el Mayor (r. 1063–1094, also known as Sancho Ramírez) recuperated Loarre and installed a community of *Augustinian* canons. Moreover, he immediately began an ambitious building campaign that would convert Loarre into a strategic military site in the long process of recuperating the Iberian Peninsula from the Arabs.

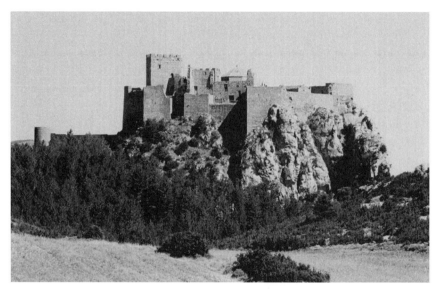

General distant view of Loarre Castle emerging over an inexpugnable natural rock formation.

The architects who conceived Loarre created a virtually inexpugnable precinct using the site's natural conditions willfully and skillfully; high up on the rocky formation, the burg was protected by a complicity between natural elements and man-made construction. In effect, the steep and rugged rock provided a natural defense on a wide arc on the west of the site, while a defensive wall, probably built in the thirteenth century, protected it from the other cardinal directions where a less steep slope exposed Loarre to invasions and attacks. The beautifully built defensive wall, a paradigmatic example of stone-wall construction of that period, extends for approximately 600 feet, punctuated by eight hollow semicircular towers distributed at irregular intervals. An additional tower of cubical proportions located on the southeast portion of the wall, known as "Torre de los Reyes" (Kings' Tower), framed the only entrance to the burg. This entrance led to the fortress' plaza, a large area open to the sky that was dominated by a more than 72-foot-high prismatic tower—the "Torre del Vigía" or "Torre de Homenaje"—that used to serve as a defending bastion for the monastery and castle before the fortified wall was built. Now free-standing, this tower used to be connected to the castle by a no-longer existing wooden *pasarelle*.

The castle and, particularly, the church that it contains are the most remarkable architectural components of the whole built complex and are considered among the more sophisticated examples of Spanish Romanesque (Whitehill 1941, 244). The entrance to the walled precinct is through an arched portal flanked by columns. The portal opens directly to a great monumental stairway covered by a stone *barrel vault*; halfway up, small arched gateways open on each side of the stairs without a transitional landing that would articulate the passage from the stairs to the spaces they lead to. The right side opening leads to a small semicircular *crypt* covered by a half dome and a short barrel vault, while five short arches rhythmically modulate the semicircular portion of the wall. Two extremely narrow stairs, carved out of the massive thickness of the wall that separates the great stairway and the crypt, lead up—through trap-doors set on the floor—to the main floor one level above.

The church itself is the architectural jewel of the complex. It consists of three parts that various authors interpret differently; for example, Walter Whitehill explains it as consisting of a semicircular *apse*, a domed *crossing* and an irregular *nave* (Whitehill 1941, 246), while Kenneth J. Conant sees it as a three-bay space where each bay has distinct spatial characteristics—apse, dome, and vaulted nave (Conant 1978, 314). The church may be simply described as a linear sequence of three differentiated spaces—apse, central domed space, and nave—covered by different stone vaulting systems. The three spaces have a uniform width of approximately 32 feet and their respective vaults spring at approximately the same height; however, the three remain as autonomous spatial entities. Curiously, the nave is the shortest of the three components. Its trapezoidal plan form is due to the unusual angle of the west-end wall, likely a result of having to adjust to the presence of an existing adjacent construction.

The nave is covered by a barrel vault whose highest point is approximately 44 feet above the floor. The two lateral walls are punctuated by tall and wide blind arches that provide a modular cross axis to the short and unusual nave configuration. The semicircular apse—located exactly above the already mentioned crypt—is at the east end of the linear spatial sequence, vaulted with a rather smooth and unarticulated half-dome. In sharp opposition to the flatness of the nave's wall surfaces, the apse's walls are articulated by two superimposed arcades; the lower has thirteen interconnected arches, while the upper one consists of five arches in exact vertical alignment with the five openings of the lower-level crypt, bringing diffused natural light to the church's interior.

The central bay is the architectural and spatial climax of the building. It is covered by a semispherical dome that reaches a height of more than 65 feet from the floor at its center point. The dome rests on four full-width arches that mark the square plan of this central space; the transition from the square plan of the four supporting arches to the dome's circular plan is a remarkable structural and plastic achievement consisting of two superimposed *squinches*. The linear sequence of the three components and the vertical emphasis of the central bay generate spatial ambiguity, for it seems that the three spaces resolve the tension of their different spatial characteristics at the vertical axis of the central dome, while the articulated wall surface of the semicircular apse resolves the east-west axis.

The unusual and eccentric location of openings in all three spaces largely accentuates the spatial ambiguity. Besides the three windows of the apse, there are four shafted windows in the central bay—three on the south wall and one on the north—as well as four bull's-eye openings between the top of the arches and the spring of the dome on each of its four sides. In the nave there is only one window, on the southern wall, set at very unusual low level, and there are no openings on the northern side. The main entrance to the church is from the castle's interior; it consists of a small door framed by a stone arch flanked by two semicircular attached columns. The reduced dimensions of the opening and its eccentric position contrast with the spatial grandeur of the church's interior; disengaged by scale and location, it also emphasizes the ambiguity—central versus linear, horizontal versus vertical—of the church's space.

The exterior of Loarre's castle is rather simple and austere: a stone-clad mass of aggregated volumes. The modulated and plastic profile of the church's volume is, perhaps, the only exception to the dominant austerity and severe volumetric composition. However, the building has some other architectural and ornamental details of interest such as the arched portal and the shafted windows of the church, as well as columns, capitals, and bas-reliefs of extraordinary sculptural quality. Other dependencies of the castle included facilities related to the castle's monastic and military functions. A tower—the "Torre de la Reina" (Queen's Tower)—is located within the castle's interior at the peak of the rocky formation. The absence of big rooms and separated areas for monks, military personnel, nobles, and laymen demonstrates the high level of promiscuous proximity in which they lived.

The unusual Romanesque purity of the castle's church, the richness and quality of its severe and austere architecture, the astounding aesthetic complicity between the castle and its surrounding landscape, and its rather well-preserved condition almost 1,000 years after it was built, are living proof of the importance that Loarre once had as a strategic military, religious, and noble settlement for the emerging Christian kingdoms of Spain, which had launched a centuries-long quest to recuperate the territories lost in the eighth-century Muslim invasion of Iberia.

Further Reading

Barrat i Altet, Xavier. *Le Monde Roman: Villes, Cathédrales et Monastères*. Cologne: Taschen, 2001.

Conant, Kenneth John. *Carolingian and Romanesque Architecture 800–1200*. 2nd ed. Middlesex: Penguin Books, 1978.

Whitehill, Walter Muir. *Spanish Romanesque Architecture of the Eleventh Century*. Oxford: Oxford University Press, 1941.

MONASTERY OF EL ESCORIAL, SAN LORENZO DEL ESCORIAL, CASTILLA Y LEÓN

Style: Renaissance Architecture
Dates: 1563–circa 1584
Architects: Juan Bautista de Toledo and Juan de Herrera

The Monastery of El Escorial is one of the most important architectural as well as political monuments in the history of Spain, a landmark in the history of humankind. It is deservedly considered as the paradigm of Spanish architecture, a faithful reflection of Spain's ideals during the reign of King Felipe II, a period that marked the consolidation and development of its imperial objectives and shaped in stone the kingdom's assertive religiousness that would have a lasting influence in the history of the country. This immense building is not only a monastery, but also a royal palace, a pantheon, a church, and a college as envisioned by Felipe II and his two remarkable architects Juan Bautista de Toledo and Juan de Herrera.

Reportedly, El Escorial was founded as Felipe II's thanksgiving offering for Spain's victory over French troops at Saint Quentin in 1557. However, this seems to have been an appropriate pretext to materialize Felipe II's old idea to build a royal mausoleum to bury his father, Emperor Carlos V, who had turned over the vast kingdom of Spain to him in 1556, before retiring to a *Hieronymite* monastery at Yuste until his death. The project began to take final form after Carlos V's death in 1558 when Felipe II appointed a committee of wise men—mathematicians, physicians, artists—to select the site; after three years of search, a low hill on the southern foot of the Guadarrama Mountains was finally selected as the appropriate location for the ambitious project. Profoundly devout as he was, Felipe II soon decided that El Escorial would be a Hieronymite foundation, an order that Carlos V had particularly favored; it was also decided to dedicate it to San Lorenzo (St. Lawrence) because the victory of St. Quentin had occurred on the feast day of the Spanish saint who had been martyred on a gridiron. At a political level, the creation of this royal monastery-palace-pantheon-college was a key aspect of Felipe II's centralist political project at a critical historical moment of the increasingly powerful kingdom of Spain that also included moving the royal court from Toledo to the then rather small and unimportant village of Madrid thirty-five miles southeast of El Escorial.

Felipe II was an avid consumer of art and was well informed of the most advanced theoretical developments and realizations of Italian Renaissance,

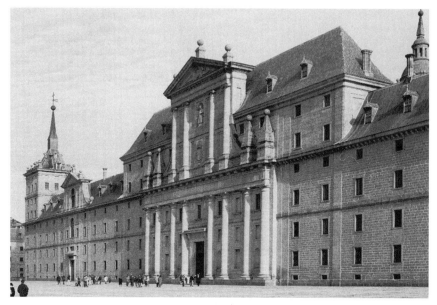

Main entrance to the Monastery of El Escorial building complex.

such as the work of Bramante and Vignola. As Peter Murray commented, "his Italianate artistic sympathies and his personal character—rigid, devout and almost morbidly conscientious . . . attracted him to the severity of the Vignolan style practiced in Rome from the 1550s" (Murray 1971, 346). Juan Bautista de Toledo, Toledo was a Spanish architect who was then in Naples (one of the important possessions of Felipe II's kingdom) and, according to some historians, had probably collaborated with Michelangelo at Saint Peter in Rome. In 1561, Felipe II recruited Toledo back to Spain. The king officially appointed him as Royal Architect and, among other things, asked him to lay out the plans for El Escorial according to the complex program that, as he had envisioned it, included a monastery for fifty monks, a royal palace, a palatial church, a pantheon, and a college all within the same built structure. The inclusion of a college as part of the complex was quite unusual for the Hieronymite order and raised a lively controversy between the king and the order's monks and prior, but Felipe II was quite determined, and he prevailed. Juan Bautista de Toledo was the master architect in charge of designing the vast complex, but the king was also very involved in the design process, participating in meetings and, according to some testimonies, making important decisions that had significant influence in the final project regarding aspects of both organization and architectural style.

Toledo's project was impressively simple and sober, dominated by a stark austerity of detail and formal restrain. It consisted of a giant rectangular enceinte—680 feet wide by 530 feet deep—with a dominant east-west axis and a protruding square form—the royal palace—at the east end. The conceptually symmetric plan was subdivided into three major parts, with the church and royal palace aligned along the central east-west axis flanked by the monastery on the south and the college and other dependencies of the palace on the north, all organized around more than a dozen courtyards of varied size. This was Toledo's "traza universal" (universal plan) and it resembled a gridiron, the instrument with which San Lorenzo had been martyred, a symbolic metaphorical reference to the saint to whom the vast complex was dedicated. The influence of well-known Italian Renaissance precedents and ideas is obvious; as Catherine Wilkinson-Zerner remarked, Toledo's traza universal "looked a little like Diocletian's palace at Spalato . . . Filarete's hospital in Milan (Italy), a French chateau, and Raphael's and Sangallo's designs for St. Peter's all rolled in one" (Wilkinson-Zerner 1973, 89). However, the scheme may also be seen as derivative of Spanish hospitals, for example, the Royal Hospital at Santiago de Compostela, built in the late fifteenth century during the reign of the Catholic Kings.

The east-west axis—constituted by the sequence of the Patio de los Reyes (Kings' Courtyard), church, and royal palace—was the organizing spine of the building complex. The church—an unusual case in which it was both a palatine chapel and a monastic church—is the central feature of the sequence, preceded by the Patio de los Reyes that simultaneously works as the church's atrium and as ceremonial entrance to the whole building; behind the church, the nearly square volume of the palace's state apartments projects beyond the rectangular form of the overall plan, resembling the "handle" of the gridiron. The church's plan is a *Greek-cross* inscribed into a square form, with an

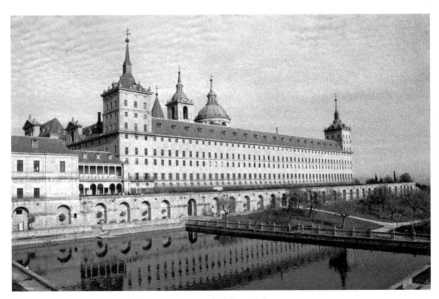

View of the south façade of the Monastery of El Escorial.

additional western bay for the "coro" (choir), a characteristically Spanish typological feature. Two large open spaces, the Patio de los Evangelistas (Evangelists' Courtyard) and the palace courtyard, flank the dominant volume of the church on the southern (monastery) and northern (palace) sides of the building, while to the west, groupings of buildings around smaller courtyards—the monks' cells on the south and the college on the east—flank the open space of the Patio de los Reyes. Toledo had conceived these western (frontal) components as lower volumes than those behind, demonstrating his mastery of hierarchical and balanced composition. However, this part of Toledo's initial project would be modified later to accommodate significant additions to the original program.

Juan Bautista de Toledo died in 1567 when the lower portions of El Escorial were already under construction. He was initially succeeded by Juan Bautista Castello, an Italian master brought especially from Italy by Felipe II to confront the increasing technical complexities that building El Escorial demanded; however, he died two years later and Felipe II appointed Juan de Herrera, a remarkable architect who had been working as Toledo's assistant since the early stages of the project. Herrera's main role was to carry to completion Toledo's traza universal, which he eventually accomplished in record time, completing the immense building in 1584. He is also credited with having resolved and designed some important portions of the building that had not been fully defined before Toledo's death, such as the church's splendid cupola, the western portions of the enceinte with its beautiful gate, the central piece of the Patio de los Evangelistas and, most importantly, the distinctive roofs that are one of the unique and innovative aspects of the whole building. Herrera also confronted the program's enlargement of the monastery and the college, which he resolved by enlarging the two frontal west volumes, matching the height of the rest of the building in Toledo's original plan.

El Escorial is a remarkable, simple, and austere building, dominated by severe forms and an astonishing lack of decoration. The extended façades are unusually flat and undecorated, animated only by the pattern of regularly distributed windows that appear as simple rectangular openings practiced on the surface of the wall; only some portions of the walls are treated with a higher sculptural emphasis, notably the gates that mark the main and numerous subsidiary entrances to the enceinte; however, the emphasis is always minimal, reduced to most severe and simple decorative expression. The most distinctive forms of the building's exterior are the four corner towers, the two western towers of the church, and, especially, the church's magnificent cupola that reaches to a maximum height of near 300 feet from the ground and presides over the entire structure. Only Herrera's remarkable pyramidal slate roofs crowned with a spire ending in a sphere and cross animate the silhouette of the otherwise simple form of the whole complex.

The building's exterior is entirely built with large-size monolithic blocks of yellow-gray granite. In spite of its renowned simplicity, it was erected using the most advanced available technology of the time by the most skill-ful artisans and builders; many building components were actually created and manufactured in other parts of the widely spread kingdom. For example, the altar piece was done in Milan, paintings and metal work in Flanders, and silverwork in Toledo. Not unlike the building's exterior, the interiors are rather austere and unornamented; yet, they house a superb collection of paintings especially done for Felipe II by some of the most famous artists of the time, such as Titian, Ribera, and Tibaldi. The latter is also the author of many splendid paintings that decorate the library's *barrel vault*. In fact, the library is an important legacy of Felipe II's vision for the large building com-plex, both architecturally and spiritually, because he conceived it as symbol-ically representative of the union of the sacred and secular worlds, a remarkably modern idea for the time. Architecturally, it is a huge gallery cov-ered by a painted barrel vault and lined up with shelving custom designed by Herrera; the shelves house an impressive collection of nearly 5,000 illumi-nated manuscripts and over 40,000 printed books.

Even though the building was officially completed in September 1584 with a ceremony that celebrated the placing of the last stone, work continued in other unfinished areas, such as the Royal Pantheon located under the church's *chancel*. Later, some parts of the building suffered some modifications. The Borbons dynasty that succeeded the Hapsburgs altered parts of the palace with their characteristically sumptuous environment, creating a sharp con-trast with the humble severity and modesty of Felipe II's original building.

The Monastery of El Escorial is today a protected World Heritage Mon-ument. As designed and built by both Juan Bautista Toledo and Juan de He-rrera the large building complex is a faithful representative of Felipe II's objective to create a distinguished and majestic, yet austere and sober royal and religious complex. El Escorial's imposing simplicity of form and re-strained use of decorative expression became the distinctive architectural characteristic of Felipe II's period as well as of Herrera's work that eventu-ally had a tremendous influence and projection in Spanish architecture. In fact, Herrera is considered the father of the "estilo desornamentado" (unor-namented style) that suppressed the widely spread *Plateresque* that had char-acterized Spain's official architecture; as renowned *Renaissance* historian Peter Murray stated, Herrera's style "was to continue to exert great influence on official architecture in Spain" (Murray 1971, 350). The building is deservedly considered a paradigm and a masterpiece of world architecture, while the ar-chitect, Juan de Herrera, is regarded as one the most important architects of the period and one of the greatest of Spain's architectural history.

Further Reading

Chueca Goitía, Fernando. *Historia de la Arquitectura Española: Edad Moderna-Edad Contemporánea*. Vol. 2. Madrid: Editorial Dossat, 1965.
Murray, Peter. *Architecture of the Renaissance*. New York: Harry N. Abrams, 1971.

Rodríguez Ruiz, Delfín, ed. *Palacios Reales en España: Historia y Arquitectura de la Magnificencia*. Madrid: Fundación Argentaria-Visor Distribuciones, 1996.
Wilkinson-Zerner, Catherine. *Juan de Herrera: Architect to Philip II of Spain*. New Haven, CT; London: Yale University Press, 1993.

MONTE NARANCO: PALACE OF RAMIRO I AND CHURCH OF SAN MIGUEL DE LILLO, OVIEDO, ASTURIAS

Style: Asturian-Visigothic Architecture
Date: Circa 848
Architect: Unknown

After the Muslim invasion of the Iberian Peninsula in the early eighth century, the then widely spread and dominating *Visigothic* kingdom of Spain, which had established its capital in Toledo, had to retreat north, finding refuge behind the Cantabrian Mountains, where they succeeded in consolidating a resisting stronghold. The kingdom's sovereign, Alfonso II (known as Alfonso the Chaste), who reigned between 791 and 842, established his capital in Oviedo and inaugurated a campaign of reconquest that would lead, after seven centuries, to the recovery of the territory lost to Muslim invaders. Already in the sixth and seventh centuries, the Visigoths had developed an original art style derived from the Roman architecture examples that abounded in the Iberian Peninsula. This rich and varied style achieved a mature stage of development in the ninth century before being suppressed and displaced by the increasing internationalization of French-influenced *Carolingian* and *Romanesque* architecture sponsored by the Burgundian *Benedictine* monks of Cluny, which quickly spread thanks to the rapid development of the pilgrimage to Santiago de Compostela.

The splendid buildings built on the southern slope of Monte Naranco during the reign of Ramiro I (842–850) represent the architectural apogee of the *Asturian-Visigothic* pre-Romanesque architecture. The royal complex was completed and consecrated in 848, and probably consisted of more buildings, but two important ones remain standing: the Palace of Ramiro I (also known as Santa María del Naranco) and the church of San Miguel de Lillo. The palace remains virtually intact, but only one-third of the original church of San Miguel de Lillo stands today. Both buildings are built with calcare-

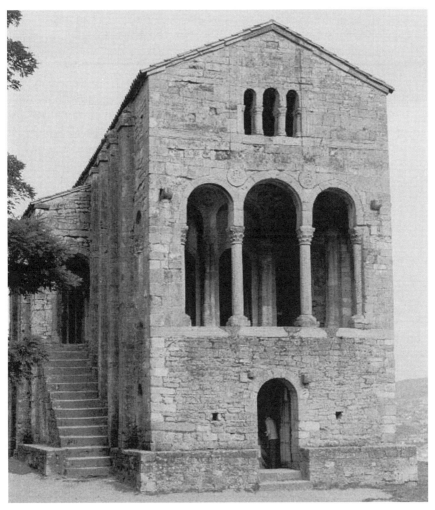

The Palace of Ramiro I at Monte Naranco.

ous tufa stone quarried uphill. Of the two monuments, the palace is more interesting, not only because it is more complete, but also because—unlike its neighbor—it is a singular building type, previously unknown and unrepeated later.

The precise function and use of the Palace of Ramiro is unknown. For a long time it was believed to have been a religious building, probably because in the tenth and eleventh centuries, that is, after the end of Visigothic rule, it was used as a church (Santa María del Naranco). However, more recent research provided evidence that is was used as a recreational and/or ceremonial residence for the king and queen. In this case, the neighboring church likely was the palatine chapel.

The building is a predominantly vertical rectangular box—approximately 70 feet long by 20 feet wide—emerging from the steep slope of the hill. It has two levels independent from each other, that is, they are not directly communicated. Instead, access to the upper level is provided through protected porch-like exterior stairs placed at the center of each of the two long—north and south—façades (only the northern one remains intact; the other has partially survived). The lower level is covered by a low *barrel vault* (approximately 8 feet at the highest point) supported by four ribbed arches. Its original function is unclear, but it was probably used as a royal bath or as a chapter hall; it is also believed that it might have been a *crypt*, yet the absence of burial remains questions this conjecture. Two additional rooms are located on each side of this hall.

The upper level is definitely more important, undoubtedly the architectural gem of the entire complex. It is a symmetrical rectangular hall accessible on the center of the long sides from exterior porched stairs. This double-high room (approximately 15 feet deep by 40 feet wide, considered from the entrance) is covered by a barrel vault reinforced by seven transversal ribbed arches, three on each side of the room and one at the center. Medallions, featuring relief sculpture with animal motifs, and relief straps deliberately aligned with the ribbed arches, reinforce the rhythmical modulation of the interior walls and provide a decorative prolongation and termination to the arches' ribbed structure.

The nearly 3-foot-thick walls of the two long sides are in effect composed of seven unequal arches that rest on clusters of four thin, spirally striated columns topped by ornamented capitals. The unequal distance between the supports for the arches—the central one is wider, and the other diminish as they get farther from the central arch—seems to have been premeditated, probably to produce the optical illusion of a higher volume at the center of the rectangular *nave*. There are three openings symmetrically distributed on each of the two sides: the doorway on the central bay (framed by the widest of seven arches), and two arched window openings two bays farther from the central arch on each direction. All other arches are filled in with stone work.

The two short ends are closed by a three-bay arcade where the central arch is slightly wider than the other two. Likewise, the arches are supported by clusters of four spirally striated columns topped with carved *capitals*. However, unlike the two long sides, the arcades of the short ends are completely open, leading to two-bay-deep screened exterior tribunes, veritable *belvederes* that afford splendid views to the landscape and the town below. Like the interior hall, the two exterior tribunes also have barrel vaults, supported by a similar system of arcades; however, contrary to the interior arcades, which are filled in with stone work, the tribunes' arches are open, supported either by clusters of four columns or by a single, richly striated column. As simple as this may sound, this is a remarkable architectural detail that articulates the difference between interior and exterior at the same time that it provides an undeniable plasticity to the interior walls and a vigorous look to the exterior façades.

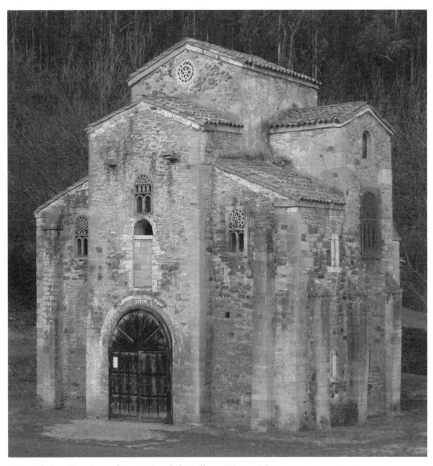

General Exterior view of San Miguel de Lillo at Monte Naranco.

The building's exterior is simple and astonishingly beautiful, an emerging vertical mass of lofty and delicate proportions. The short ends have a tri-partite organization consisting of a rather heavy base (approximately 10 feet tall), a central portion dominated by the three large open arches, and a stone-faced top punctuated by a *triforium* at the center. On the two long sides, the thick, lightly striated and projecting pilasters or *buttresses*—continuous from floor to eave—are another remarkable feature of the building. Aligned with the ribbed arches that support the vaults of the main hall and its exterior tribunes, these pilasters counter the lateral thrust of the vault, thus antici-pating by at least a century the development of exterior buttresses, a typical feature of Romanesque and *Gothic* architecture. Undoubtedly, this was a tech-nical innovation developed by Ramiro I's architect, because the same feature is also found in both San Miguel de Lillo and **Santa Cristina de Lena.**

San Miguel de Lillo, surely built at the same time, is situated at a very short distance (less than 1,000 feet) from the Palace of Ramiro I. Originally, it was a 70-foot-long *basilica* with a *narthex*, a three-bay central nave flanked by aisles and a one-bay *transept*; the central nave and the two galleries ended in rectangular *apses* or chapels, thus generating a triple-apse east end, a distinctive feature of Visigothic basilicas such as **San Juan de Baños**. However, two-thirds of the original church were lost in the thirteenth or fourteenth century, probably as consequence of a land movement. Only the western half of the church—the narthex with its two adjacent rooms and the nave's first bay—survived the natural incident. Soon later, a new apse was built to close the remnants and continue using it as a church. The characteristic Visigothic royal tribune, the place where the king and queen attended religious ceremonies, usually located above the vestibule and accessible by narrow stairs, also survived. It is flanked by two small rooms that were probably used for the dignitaries' rest during long ceremonies.

The building is carefully articulated as an addition of protruding forms, in sharp contrast with the simple volumetric form and permeable exterior of the neighboring Palace of Ramiro I. The interior is also much more complex, for it is covered by alternating transversal and longitudinal short barrel vaults that reach a maximum height of 36 feet. Yet, like its contemporaneous neighbor, the exterior walls also feature the innovative system of buttresses to counter the lateral thrust of the interior vaults.

The remarkable high quality and richness of the church's decoration is, unquestionably, the most important aspect of the building's remains. The tall, round columns that support the arches of the nave and aisles are richly decorated with various motifs. Also, there is evidence that the interior may have been fully covered by frescoes—a possible *Byzantine* influence—some of which were particularly beautiful. One of the frescoes' noteworthy characteristics is the representation of human figures, previously nonexistent in Spanish Christian art. But the most interesting decorative elements are the delicate and imbricate stone lattice work of the small arched windows, and the beautifully carved doorjambs of the main doorway. The latter is of particular interest for it is a beautiful stone relief copy of a known Eastern Roman *diptych* from the sixth century, representing scenes of a circus performance. This stands as evidence of the Oriental influence in Spanish pre-Romanesque art and architecture. Kenneth Conant also mentions a possible Germanic influence in the "agglomeration of aspiring and intersecting forms" (Conant 1978, 91), which may be attributed to the fluid relationship between Ramiro's predecessor (Alfonso II) and Charlemagne.

Together, the Palace of Ramiro I and San Miguel de Lillo, along with the small church of Santa Cristina de Lena (located in Pola de Lena, approximately twenty-five miles south of Oviedo), are living testimony of the originality and quality of the Asturian-Visigothic architectural and artistic style. Also known as "Ramirense," this regional-national style matured toward the middle of the ninth century and, in some aspects, anticipated some innovative developments usually attributed to the architecture of the high Middle Ages.

Further Reading

Bevan, Bernard. *History of Spanish Architecture*. London: B. T. Basford, 1938.

Chueca Goitía, Fernando. *Historia de la Arquitectura Española: Edad Antigua y Edad Media*. Vol. 1. Madrid: Editorial Dossat, 1965.

Conant, Kenneth John. *Carolingian and Romanesque Architecture 800–1200*. 2nd ed. Middlesex: Penguin Books, 1978.

Lampérez y Romea, Vicente. *Historia de la Arquitectura Cristiana Española en la Edad Media*. Vol. 1. Valladolid: Ambito Ediciones, 1999. (Facsimile impression of original 1908 edition.)

MOSQUE OF BĀB-AL-MARDŪM, TOLEDO, CASTILLA-LA MANCHA

Style: Umayyad Islamic Architecture (Mudéjar Architecture)
Dates: Circa 999–[1187]
Architect: Attributed to Muza, "son of Ali" (Hospitaliers)

In the year 929, Abd-al-Rahman III proclaimed the political independence of the Umayyad Emirate of Córdoba, which, created by Abd-al-Rahman I in 756, he ruled between 912 and 961. The independence meant raising the status of his domains from an emirate—dependent on a central caliphal authority based in Baghdad—to an independent Caliphate or empire. Consequently, the process of "Islamization" of the Iberian Peninsula, which had begun in the eighth century when the Muslim rulers consolidated control of the territory, accelerated in the second quarter of the ninth century with the arrival of a wave of Muslim artists and educators.

Accordingly, a large percentage of the population converted to Islam, demanding the construction of mosques throughout *al-Andalus*. Following the example and typological characteristics set by the **Great Mosque of Córdoba** (786–990), large new mosques, some actually splendid, were built in Sevilla, Toledo, Granada, Jaén, and Almería. However, and unfortunately, when the Christian kingdoms recovered the cities, most of the mosques—for instance in Sevilla, Toledo, and Jaén—were replaced by Christian cathedrals. Therefore, with the exception of major parts of the Great Mosque of Córdoba, there remain few standing buildings that faithfully testify to the artistic splendor reached by the Caliphate of Córdoba at the peak of its intellectual and creative activity in the Iberian Peninsula.

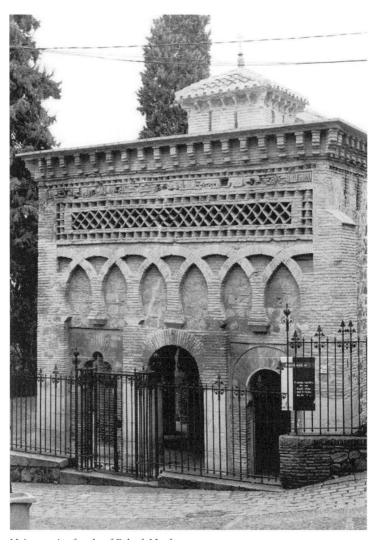

Main exterior façade of Bāb-al-Mardūm.

However, in Toledo—the former capital of the *Visigothic* kingdom and one of the cultural centers of al-Andalus—the mosque of Bāb-al-Mardūm is a little masterpiece of the end of the caliphal period, one of these rare buildings of reduced dimensions that often appear as a perfect synthesis of the artistic aspirations and realizations of a time. Bāb-al-Mardūm is a significant building for many reasons, but two stand out: the excellent use of brick as both structural and decorative material and the system of proportions and dimensions that regulates its overall design and composition. The first of these aspects would be later marvelously explored and mastered by *Mudéjar* architects; the second is just the consequence of the high level of development and sophistication of the Caliphate, particularly in the areas of mathematics, geometry, poetry, and natural sciences, that distinguished it as the most advanced and better organized culture in western Europe. However, at approximately the same time that Bāb-al-Mardūm was built, the Caliphate began to disintegrate into smaller regional principalities, or *taifas*, that would not be able to resist the Christian kingdoms' intention to recuperate the old Visigothic capital. This little mosque was built near the gate of Bāb-al-Mardūm, that is, within Toledo's walls but on the edge of the city, at approximately 1,000 feet from the center where the great mosque was located.

The delicate balance and carefully studied relationship of the building's plan, section and elevations, that is, the proportional system that regulates its composition, is one among many aspects that demonstrate the high level of sophistication of the Caliphate's culture. Indeed, the proportions are delightful: the plan is an almost perfect 27-foot-square building enclosed by thick brick walls (3 feet thick on average) that generate a 19-foot-square interior space; the interior is further subdivided into a three-by-three module system that generates nine regular squares defined by four central columns. The columns, which like its capitals were surely appropriated from existing Visigothic buildings, mark the center of the space. The eastern side of the square, the *quibla*, was a solid continuous wall that likely housed a no longer existing *mihrab*, while the other three sides are permeable arcades defined by brick pillars carrying a diversity of complex brick arches.

The tripartite modulation of the plan and its general dimensions are also carried on in section: the lower layer corresponds with the open areas of the arcades and the four central columns; the second spatial layer is formed by the intersection of the *horse-shoe* arcades that traverse the building in the two directions emphasizing the nine-square partition of the plan; finally, the third layer is considerably more dense, occupied by nine ribbed stone vaults, all different from each other and clearly inspired on the vaults that cover the *maqsura* of the Great Mosque of Córdoba; the vault of the central module rises higher than the eight of the perimeter, illuminating all of them through small but effective openings.

All facades of Bāb-al-Mardūm are somehow similar in concept but different in detail. The eastern side of the square, the quibla, used to be a continuous wall with a mihrab at the center that probably protruded outwards. The other three sides are defined by three-bay partly open, partly blind, exquisitely designed arcades; the north façade is composed of three semicircular arches that rest on articulated brick pillars of approximately square proportions; the open part of the arcade features recessed horse-shoe arches that are in correspondence with the intersecting arcades that divide the interior space into nine squares; above the semicircular arches there is an uninterrupted line of six *mixtilinear* heavily pointed arches—two for each bay—with recessed small horse-shoe arches crowned with *voussoirs* below an ornamental cornice made out of brick that wraps around the entire building.

The west façade is quite different; the three bays are marked by three different arches—a horse-shoe arch to the right and a *mixtilinear lobated arch* on the left that flank a central, wider, and taller horse-shoe arch cut out of a slightly protruding plane that suggests a central east-west axis; expectedly, these arches are in spatial and dimensional correspondence with the interior arcades. Yet, the most interesting aspect of this façade is the intricate layering and articulation achieved through the masterful utilization of brick as both structure and ornament. The highlight is a band of intersecting horse-shoe arches set over a blind stone wall placed above the arches that grant access to the interior of the building; this beautiful sequence of arches is crowned by an ornamental band composed of diamonded shapes within a relief-frame below the building's *kufic* inscription, all cleverly done by using brick of various dimensions in diverse positions and patterns.

In 1085, Toledo was finally recaptured by King Alfonso VI. One century later, the growing Christian population demanded the adaptation of the former mosque into a Christian church, renaming it as Church of Cristo de la Luz. The transformation, undertaken in 1187 by the *Hospitalers*, implied the demolition of the quibla wall on the east and the addition of an *apse*. Interestingly and fortunately, this was done without altering the existing building's character. Rather, the addition was respectful of the former Muslim temple both in the utilization of materials and details (exposed brick, blind arcades with cusped lobated arches, brick cornice, ceramic roof-tiles). In fact, the addition is itself a good example of the Mudéjar architectural style that developed in central Spain after the *Reconquista* and is well represented by buildings such as **Santa María la Blanca** in Toledo and the **Cathedral of Teruel** in Aragon.

Further Reading

Chueca Goitía, Fernando. *Historia de la Arquitectura Española: Edad Antigua y Edad Media*. Vol. 1. Madrid: Editorial Dossat, 1965.

Hoag, John D. *Islamic Architecture*. New York: Harry N. Abrams, 1977.

Yarza, Joaquín. *Arte y Arquitectura en España, 500–1250*. Madrid: Ediciones Cátedra, 2000.

MUSEO DEL PRADO, MADRID, COMUNIDAD DE MADRID

Style: Neoclassical Architecture
Dates: 1785–1819
Architect: Juan de Villanueva

The building for the Museo del Prado is the culminating work of Juan de Villanueva, arguably the most important architect of *Neoclassical* architecture in Spain and a pioneer and innovator for the development of this style in the rest of the world. In effect, educated in Madrid and Rome, Juan de Villanueva was the dominant architect of the late eighteenth–early nineteenth centuries in Spain, a difficult period marked by the French Revolution in the powerful neighboring country (1789), the Napoleonic expansion that eventually occupied Spain, the eventual War of Independence (1808–1813), and the surging movements of independence in Spain's territorial possessions in the American continent. However affected by this multitude of events, the work of Villanueva in general, and the building for the Museo del Prado in particular, represent a great testimony to the efforts made by the Spanish crown to sustain the splendor and grandeur reached in previous centuries.

The Museo del Prado was inaugurated in Villanueva's building on November 19, 1819; however, until then, the building and the institution had had a separate and parallel history. In the last decade of the eighteenth century, and surely inspired by the recent creation of the Louvre Museum in post-revolutionary Paris, Spain's King Carlos III, had envisioned the creation of a museum of paintings and sculptures; yet, this did not go further than a statement of intentions. Later, in 1809, already during the French occupation and the War of Independence that battled against it, King José I Bonaparte (Napoleon's own brother) signed a decree creating the "Museo Josefino" that did not materialize. Finally, after returning to Spain in 1814, the grandson of Carlos III and new King Fernando VII—who after a brief liberal constitutional period tried to reinstate an absolute monarchy—gave

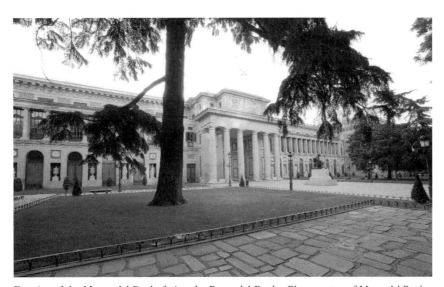

Exterior of the Museo del Prado facing the Paseo del Prado. *Photo courtesy of Museo del Prado.*

final shape to the creation of a royal museum of paintings and sculptures, likely at the instigation of his second wife María Isabel de Braganza.

The initial intention was to house the royal collections in the Palacio de Buenavista, located in Plaza Cibeles, at the north end of the Paseo del Prado that had been created during Carlos III's reign. However, the idea of using a partially completed building that had been designed by Juan de Villanueva and stood near the southern end of the Paseo del Prado eventually prevailed. In effect, in 1785, Villanueva had designed the building for the Academy of Natural History that, along with the adjacent Botanical Garden, was both part of a complex devoted to the study of natural sciences and an ambitious urban development program dedicated to elevating the architectural and urbanistic character of Spain's still young capital.

Urbanistically, Villanueva conceived the building for the Academy of Natural History as a long urban screen that provided scale to a long stretch of the Paseo del Prado between the Botanical Garden and Neptune's Fountain. This long building is composed of three solid primary volumes—one on the center and another at each end—linked by significantly narrower and more permeable galleries. The two volumes of the extremes are cubical, very similar to each other exteriorly but very different in their internal organization. The southern cube is organized around an open central square, while a central rotunda is the dominant space of the northern volume. Villanueva conceived these two cubical volumes to house the different offices and cabinets of study for the Academy of Natural History; between them, a central volume, connected to the two cubes by linear galleries, was envisaged as a large assembly hall for discussions and meetings of scientists and scholars. This is housed in a linear volume placed perpendicular to the dominant direction of the building at the center of the composition.

Neoclassicism, that is, the recuperation of the purest forms of classical Greco-Roman architecture, is breathed throughout, in the building's architectural conception as well as in its vocabulary of classical elements. Thus, the central square of the southern volume is reminiscent of the typical roman house, while the domed rotunda of the northern cube is evocative of a classical circular temple, and the plan of the assembly hall is obviously inspired by the Roman *basilica*. The strict implementation of a classical architectural vocabulary and syntax strengthens the architect's Neoclassicist position. This is more evident in the splendid *Ionic* composition of the circular rotunda and upper-level colonnade of the galleries, as well as in the giant *Doric* hexastyle portico of the main entrance.

The building's brick and stone façades are proof of Villanueva's masterful knowledge of the classical language that he had learned in six years of residence in Rome as the winner of Spain's first Rome Prize fellowship in 1758. As a renowned historian of Spain's architecture who made a profound study of this building observed, the smooth transition from the Doric order of the main portico to the Ionic order of the galleries reflects an unusual familiarity with the compositional principles of the classical orders (Chueca Goitía

1965, 623). Yet, there are two aspects that stand out as notable innovations introduced by Villanueva. First, the façades of the two cubical end volumes are turned to the sides offering their main façade to the sides of the site, instead of being oriented toward the Paseo del Prado like the main façade; this establishes a certain volumetrical and compositional independence for each of the three volumes without questioning the building's architectural integrity. The second notable innovation of Villanueva is the flat crowning—that is without a triangular *pediment*—of the central hexastyle portico that operates as main entrance to the building and formal extension of the central assembly hall; the flat crowning is attributed to Villanueva's subtle understanding of classical language and its signification; for Villanueva, using a triangular pediment was appropriate for the façade of a temple but would be improper for a civic and scientific building such as the Academy of Natural History. All things considered, as again Chueca Goitía pointed out, the building designed by Juan de Villanueva is one of the most innovative works of the late 19th century in Europe (Chueca Goitía 1965, 622).

The construction of Villanueva's building was rather advanced but still partially incomplete when between 1808 and 1812 it was taken over by the occupying French army, who used it as stables and for gunpowder storage. Later, after the War of Independence that had left some severe damage to the building, the standing structure was pillaged by the local population, who needed readily available building materials to restore their own homes. Fernando VII ordered the restoration of the damaged sections and the completion of the unfinished portions of the building according to Villanueva's plans (he had died in 1811). Thus, in 1819, the Museo Real de Pinturas—early denomination of the modern Museo del Prado—was finally inaugurated with a display of little more than 300 paintings. The building was a faithful construction of Villanueva's conception; only the exteriors were enhanced through a decorative program of sculptures created by a committee specially appointed for that purpose; the most important piece of this final part of the building's construction was the frieze that crowns the main portico and features an allegory of Fernando VII as supporter and protector of the arts, sciences, and techniques represented by mythological gods.

After 1868, the Museo Real was nationalized to become the Museo Nacional del Prado; shortly after, the collections grew enormously as a result of merging the Museo del Prado with the Museo de la Trinidad. By the end of the nineteenth century the splendid building designed by Villanueva had become largely insufficient to house and display the museum's rich collections. The first expansion consisting of the addition of a line of rooms parallel to but separated from the linear gallery on the east side of the building was made in 1918; this addition provoked the creation of two elongated courtyards between the central and the two cubical volumes of the original building. In the 1950s another line of rooms was attached to those built in 1918, and in the 1960s the courtyards were closed.

As the museum's collections continued to grow, other neighboring buildings were appropriated (the Casón del Buen Retiro in 1971 and the Palacio de Villahermosa in the 1980s). In 1996 a major architectural competition for expanding and reorganizing the museum's various buildings was organized. Ten finalists were selected but no single proposal was declared as the winning entry to be implemented. Currently, Rafael Moneo—one of the finalists—is working on a vast and ambitious extension of the building that resolves the urban articulation of the building's rear (eastern) side and, extending beyond, creates a structure that embraces the neighboring cloister of the Convento de los Gerónimos. Once completed (by the end of the decade), the Museo del Prado will finally have a building facility according to the richness of its collections. Moreover, the building will unite the talents of two undisputable masters of the architecture of their time, the Neoclassical Juan de Villanueva and Rafael Moneo, one of the most important contemporary Spanish architects who, with his **National Museum of Roman Art** in Mérida, inaugurated one of the most vibrant periods in the history of Spain's architecture.

Further Reading

Bevan, Bernard. *History of Spanish Architecture.* London: B. T. Basford, 1938.
Chueca Goitía, Fernando. *Historia de la Arquitectura Española: Edad Moderna-Edad Contemporánea.* Vol. 2. Madrid: Editorial Dossat, 1965.

NATIONAL MUSEUM OF ROMAN ART, MÉRIDA, EXTREMADURA

Style: Contemporary Architecture
Dates: 1980–1986
Architect: José Rafael Moneo Vallés

Romans first arrived on the Iberian Peninsula around the year 295 B.C.E. Initially, they occupied and colonized former *Hellenic* and *Phocean* settlements on the Mediterranean coastline, but as the occupation progressed inland, new towns, fully Roman, were founded throughout the peninsula's territory: Tarraco, Barcino, Hispalis, Cesarea Augusta (Roman names of modern Tarragona, Barcelona, Sevilla, and Zaragoza), and Itálica, Sagunto, and many others, were prosperous Roman settlements, some of which reached a size and splendor comparable to the most important cities of the geographically spread Roman Empire. As a result of the long Roman occupation of the Iberian Peninsula, both Spain and Portugal have a large number of cities in which there are important Roman remains (e.g., aqueducts, bridges, theaters). Modern Mérida—ancient capital of the Roman province of Lusitania—is, without doubt, the Spanish city that holds the largest number of significant standing buildings and sites of archeological interest from the Roman period. Already in 1838, the city of Mérida created a Museum of Roman Art with the objective of preserving the archeological heritage of **Augusta Emérita** (modern Mérida). Originally, the collections were housed in the church of Santa Clara, but that structure proved inadequate and insufficient and thus the creation of a National Museum of Roman Art was decided upon in 1975. Years later the project for the new museum was commissioned to Rafael Moneo, a Spanish architect of international reputation who had already built some recognized buildings in Spain such as the Bankinter (Madrid 1973–1976) and Logroño's town hall (1973–1981).

Designed in 1980 and completed in 1985, Moneo's building quickly attracted international recognition, not only as the architect's first major masterpiece, but also as a building that inaugurated a fruitful period in which Spain's architectural production suddenly moved to the center of attention of architects and critics worldwide. The architect's primary intention was that the museum achieved the character and presence of a Roman building. At first inspection, this museum may appear as a simple work, yet, beyond the apparent simplicity of the scheme there lies a complex architectural conception rich in historical associations, subtle spatial articulations, and intelligent scale adjustments.

The museum occupies an entire, slightly irregular city block delimited by three vehicular streets—José Ramón Mélida on the south, Pedro María Plano on the east, and Calle del Museo on the north—and a pedestrian passageway—Travesia del Museo, the western edge—becoming a detached and carefully articulated urban block fully clad, inside and out, in Roman brick applied over a concrete structure. This site is located just opposite the well-conserved remains of Augusta Emérita's Roman Theater and Amphitheater; together, the ruins and the museum constitute a pole of archeological, museographic, and architectural interest within the structure of a city under which Roman ruins certainly abound. The most important façade, the building's unequivocal front and entrance, is on José R. Mélida Street, natural link between the center of the city and the Roman archeological site.

A more than 32,000-square-foot accessible crypt is located under the entire building. It houses and displays archeological remains—fragments of a Roman street, buildings' foundations, frescoes and mosaics of an *extramural* roman home, fragments of an *Early Christian* style of *basilica* and tombs— found in the site during the excavation to build the foundations. The contrasting orthogonal and rhythmically punctuated geometries of the two spatial components of the *crypt*—the Roman remains and the new building's arched structure—generate a dynamic and vibrant space where two clearly different time-periods establish an *architectural dialogue* with Roman undertones through the use of materials, structure, and formal elements. Also at

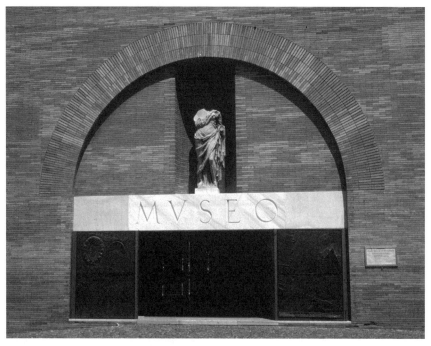

View of the main entrance to Merida's National Museum of Roman Art.

the crypt's level, a corridor-tunnel passing under Pedro María Plano Street provides direct access to the site of the adjacent Roman ruins.

The complex consists of two main volumes connected by a bridge. The most important volume, placed parallel to Jose R. Mélida Street, houses the exhibition areas, while the other one, located at the intersection of the two streets but frankly facing José R. Mélida Street, accommodates the public access, auditorium, services, administration, and the vertical circulation elements that connect the two volumes. Architecturally, the two volumes are different: the block housing the exhibition areas consists of a series of parallel walls that define three types of exhibition spaces; the other volume is composed of a series of smaller functional wings—the bridge that connects the two volumes being one of them—around a courtyard that separates public from private areas. In spite of these differences, both volumes are clad in Roman brick constituting an undifferentiated architectural whole.

An unmistakably Roman arch inscribed on a large planar brick wall marks the entrance to the building. The arch not only demarcates the access but also introduces the building's main formal theme, anticipating the spectacular sequence of arches of the museum's main space. Once inside, a somber vestibule houses ticket and information booths, a bookstore, a ramp, and stairs. The ramp provides access to the exhibition area and to the crypt, both located below the entry level; the stairs lead to the upper levels, where the auditorium and offices are located.

The volume that houses exhibition areas is, expectedly, the most important and architecturally charged. It is defined by a series of transversal parallel brick walls that generate three differentiated exhibition areas: a high sky-lit longitudinal *nave*, a series of high subsidiary exhibition spaces, and a sequence of multistory galleries. The whole takes the form of a roman basilica, with reminiscences of other roman building types such as thermal baths and aqueducts. The brick-clad walls constitute an appropriate and intentional support for the objects displayed, one that generates staged scenographical and associative effects.

The nave is the synthesis of the project, the organizational spine that supports all the other elements. It is architecturally defined by means of a large arch, hollowed out of the brick walls, that generates a longitudinal space transversal to them. Only a few items are on display in the nave, notably a partly reconstructed full-size Roman column, and the three most important sculptures rescued from the nearby Roman Theater. These sculptures and other important exhibited items are displayed against the rear wall, dramatically illuminated by direct sunrays that penetrate through a high clerestory window. Thus, the nave is a virtually empty space, a covered-street or

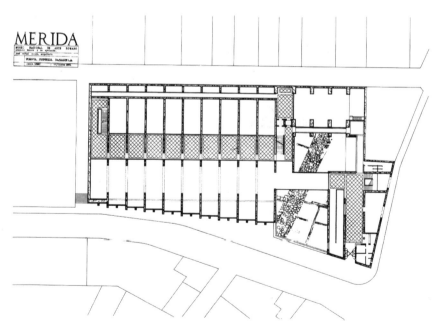

Entry level floor plan of the National Museum of Roman Art. *Drawing courtesy of architect Rafael Moneo.*

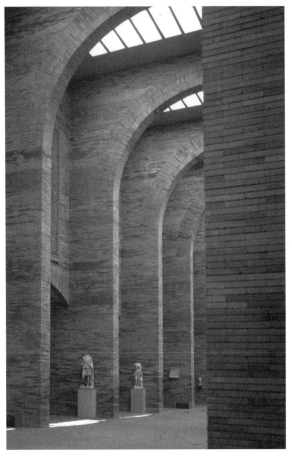

Interior fragment of the main nave-like space of the National Museum of Roman Art looking toward the south wall.

promenade open to the sides, where the museum collections are thematically displayed.

The transversal brick walls establish a rigorously rhythmical partition of spaces, defining ten bays on each side of the nave. On the south side, there are nine triple-height subsidiary small rooms, resembling chapels, where large-size exhibit items are on display, effectively illuminated by indirect natural light coming from large clerestory windows invisible to the observer. As the building accommodates to the site's slightly curvilinear and irregular profile of the southern edge, the depth of the chapels progressively shortens; consequently, the last bay's chapel was suppressed; here, a witty architectural moment takes place: the large clerestory window becomes fully visible, allowing the penetration of direct sunlight that profusely bathes the nave's rear brick wall; the exhibit items displayed against this wall become the museum's inevitable focal point.

On the north side of the main nave there are ten three-story lateral galleries, framed between the parallel brick walls that house other components of the museum's collection. Large-size items are displayed in the galleries' lower level, while other collections—thematically organized—are exhibited in the two additional floors. These are generated by light *pasarelles* that occupy only one-half of the bays' width, yielding triple-height void spaces and vast wall surfaces generally used to display large mosaics. The light and elegant stairway that provides access to the upper levels is placed in the last of the sequence of ten bays, thus forcing the visitor to complete the promenade along the nave. The galleries' first upper level houses the collection of pottery, glass, and coins; the second houses exhibits related to Augusta Emérita's social and political structure, art, culture, and history.

Another notable aspect of the building is the positioning of the nave and its adjacent exhibition spaces one full story below the entry level. In placing the nave below street level, Rafael Moneo negotiated several issues, notably the control of the building's scale and its impact within the city fabric. But, in making this important decision, the architect also triggered a multiplicity of meaningful associations, such as the subliminal perception of descending into an archaeological site—an excavation that uncovers remains of an ancient civilization—and brought echoes from the architecture of industrial naves. This is heightened by the lightness of the pasarelles that traverse the brick walls and from where the main nave—understood as full-size archeological archival display—can be observed.

The forms, materials, construction system, and organization of the building certainly transmit the Roman essence that the architect intended. As architectural historian and critic William Curtis pointed out, the Museum of Roman Art "is the critical work in Moneo's development, and, some would argue, the seminal building of the period in Spanish architecture as a whole" (Curtis 1994, 57). Its significance exceeds the geographical borders of Spain, having become a paradigmatic building of the late twentieth century, one that synthesized the period's architectural debate and discourse about the role of history and context, typology and design method, construction, texture and materiality, and the dialectical oppositions between regional and universal, abstraction and representation, and theory and practice.

Further Reading

Allegret, Laurence. *Musées*. Paris: Editions du Moniteur, 1987.

Curtis, William J. R. "Rafael Moneo: Pieces of City, Memories of Ruins." *El Croquis* 64, 1994, 47–66.

"Rafael Moneo." Special feature. *Architecture and Urbanism* 8, no. 89 (Tokyo), 1989.

Ruiz Cabrero, Gabriel. *The Modern in Spain: Architecture after 1948*. Cambridge, MA; London: The MIT Press, 2001.

Saliga, Pauline, and Thorne, Martha. *Building a New Spain: Contemporary Spanish Architecture*. Barcelona: Editorial Gustavo Gili, 1992.

Solà-Morales, Ignasi de, ed. *Contemporary Spanish Architecture: An Eclectic Panorama*. New York: Rizzoli, 1986.

NAVIGATION PAVILION AT EXPO '92 SEVILLA, SEVILLA, ANDALUCÍA

Style: Contemporary Architecture
Dates: 1989–1992
Architect: Guillermo Vázquez Consuegra

The Navigation Pavilion is the emblematic building of the exhibition grounds for the "Expo '92 Sevilla," the Universal World Fair with which the city, and Spain, celebrated the five-hundredth anniversary of Christopher Columbus' discovery of America. This was a most unusual event, which, in conjunction with the Summer Olympic Games held in Barcelona in that same year of 1992, put Spain at the center of attention in the international community. Expectedly, these two events had tremendous impact on the architecture of the two cities because it was an opportunity for both to update, renew, and revitalize their urban infrastructure.

Sevilla is one of the largest cities in Spain; throughout its long history it enjoyed periods of remarkable affluence, but it also confronted poverty and decadence. The most prosperous time was after the discovery of America because the city was the center of exploration and exploitation of the New World and controlled trading with the Americas. After a long period of economic decline, the five-hundredth anniversary of Columbus' adventure was an ideal opportunity to relaunch the city's growth. Thus, Expo '92 was the catalyst for undertaking a major renovation of Sevilla's transportation and communication facilities, as well as for developing a large area on the west side of the Guadalquivir River designated as the World Fair's grounds. The most important buildings were commissioned to renowned Spanish architects such as Rafael Moneo, Cruz and Ortiz, and Santiago Calatrava, who designed the airport, a new railroad station for new high-speed trains, and the Alamillo bridge, respectively (to name only three of the most relevant works). Moreover, historically, universal World Fairs had been a showcase of international architecture and, considering the architectural caliber of many pavilions and the reputation of their designers, Expo '92 was not an excep-

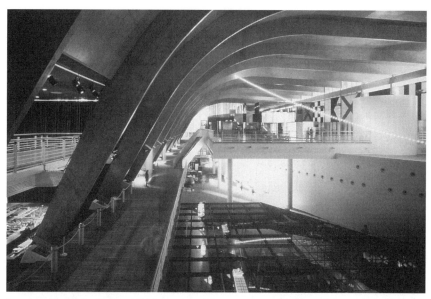

Interior view of the large exhibition space of the Navigation Pavilion. *Photo courtesy of architect Guillermo Vázquez Consuegra.*

tion. The pavilions of Finland, Italy, and Japan, designed by Monarc, Gae Aulenti, and Tadao Ando, respectively, confirmed the expectations.

Many of the city's new or renewed infrastructure and cultural facilities were placed in various parts of the city, while many new bridges linked the historical center of the city on the east side of the Guadalquivir with the exposition grounds located in the more than 1,000-acre newly developed area, which is known as La Cartuja Island, just northwest of the city's center on the opposite side of the river. As deserved homage to the importance of navigation in Sevilla's history—from the city's crucial role as the dominant harbor during the Spanish exploration and exploitation of the Americas to the more recent importance of the city's shipbuilding industry—the Navigation Pavilion became the insignia building of the World Fair's grounds. It was designed by Guillermo Vázquez Consuegra, one of the most prominent contemporary architects from Andalucía, author of numerous historical and typological studies, as well as of very important buildings of Spain's recent architecture such as the Apartment Complex on street Ramon y Cajal (Sevilla 1984–1987), a new waterfront promenade (Vigo 1999), and the Museum of Enlightenment (Valencia 2001). The Navigation Pavilion is, because of its architectural quality and international projection, his most renowned contribution to Spain's late-twentieth-century architecture.

The building is situated on the southern edge of the exhibition grounds, framed between two new bridges—the Pasarela de la Cartuja and the Puente de Campina—and facing the center of the city on the opposite side of the

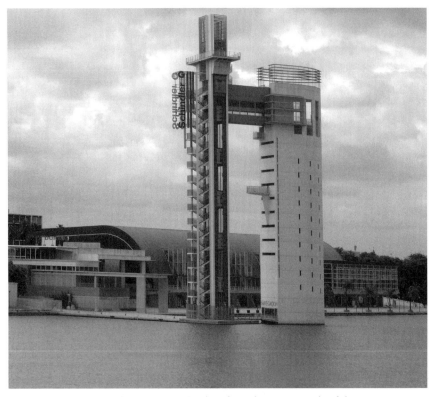

Overall exterior view of the Navigation Pavilion from the opposite side of the river.

river; on the other side, it faces the Plaza de los Descubrimientos, the central open space of the World Fair. The pavilion consists of two predominantly linear elements; one, low and horizontally extended along the riverfront, is more than 500 feet long and houses the building's programmatical components; the other is a 200-foot-tall *belvedere* tower anchored on the edge of the river; however different in form and function, they share conceptual and formal characteristics, notably their constitution in two parallel components separated by an interstitial space.

The low volume was conceived as a neutral but architecturally precise and significant container that housed, during Sevilla's Expo '92, a large exhibition hall that was planed to accommodate a new Maritime Museum after the fair's end. It is placed alongside the river, between the quay and the Plaza de los Descubrimientos, the latter located at a 15-foot-higher elevation that the building negotiates through an intelligent stepping configuration covered by a large, encompassing curved roof. This volume is organized in two parallel components linked by a narrow and very high pathway; the larger portion, on the river's side, houses a spacious exhibition area surrounded by ramps and stairs, while the other part, facing the Plaza de los Descubrimientos, accommodates three stories of building services, offices, and storage areas.

A precise module of 7.20 meters (approximately 23.5 feet) governs the building's construction. This modulation is marked by a structural system composed of concrete elements on the two sides of the volume that support long-span (130 feet long) curved beams built in laminated wood echoing old shipbuilding techniques. This structure supports a copper roof that, on the river side, becomes an integral enclosure system as well as a powerful formal and symbolic element; as the architect commented, "the curving metal roof, which takes on the role of the main façade offering its convex surface to the historic city, evokes resonances of old waterfront sheds and warehouses" (Vázquez Consuegra 1992, 82). The continuous curved surface of the copper roof is interrupted by five slender and fully glazed boxes that bring natural light to the exhibition hall's interior, and by a five-bay-wide projecting glazed volume—the temporary exhibitions gallery—on the north end of the building.

The 200-foot-tall observation tower is the vertical counterpoint to the low volume; not unlike it, it is composed of two parallel linear elements: a white concrete tower anchored in the river and a lightweight prismatic metal structure placed at the end of the pier. The former houses ascending ramps and elevators, the latter accommodates the descending stairs; the two are separated by an interstitial space analogous to the long corridor that separates the two linear components of the lower volume and connected only at the top levels by a fully glazed bridge. The keel form of the white concrete tower's plan inevitably recalls the section of a ship, triggering a variety of metaphorical and formal associations related to the building's function as well as to the forms and materials used in the exhibition hall. Moreover, the formal, textural, and material differences established by the diverse materials and structural conception used in the two towering elements reaffirm the building's presence on the site and take on an emblematic and symbolic role not only for the Expo '92 World Fair but also as a new landmark of Sevilla's skyline.

The Navigation Pavilion complex also incorporated a large stepping platform that related and negotiated the elevation difference between the Plaza de los Descubrimientos and the riverfront. This stepping platform is flanked by yet another linear element, perpendicular to the river, that houses a restaurant and a cafeteria that provide magnificent views of the river and the historical city. Unfortunately, after Expo '92, the building remained open for only a short time, featuring the Expo's exhibit, but the eventual destination of the building as the city's new Maritime Museum was not yet fulfilled. Today, the Navigation Pavilion awaits a use according to its high architectural quality and short history as the architectural emblem of a milestone celebration of Spain's history.

Further Reading

Rispa, Raúl-Alonso de los Rios, and César-Aguaza, María José, eds. *Expo '92 Seville: Architecture et Design.* Paris: Gallimard/Electa, 1992.

Saliga, Pauline, and Thorne, Martha. *Building a New Spain: Contemporary Spanish Architecture.* Barcelona: Editorial Gustavo Gili, 1992.

"Spanish Architecture 1992." Special monographic issue, *El Croquis* 55, 56 (Madrid), 1992.

Vázquez Consuegra, Guillermo. *Vázquez Consuegra.* Introduction by Peter Buchanan. Barcelona: Editorial Gustavo Gili, 1992.

NEW CEMETERY-PARK OF IGUALADA, IGUALADA, CATALONIA

Style: Contemporary Architecture
Dates: 1985–1992
Architects: Enric Miralles and Carme Pinòs

The New Cemetery-Park of Igualada is one of the most important representatives of the high quality and diversity of Spain's architecture during the last quarter of the twentieth century. Moreover, it is the most important and celebrated work of the Barcelona-based practice of Enric Miralles and Carme Pinòs, then a team of young architects who, in the mid-1980s, made a sudden emergence into Spain's architectural scene by winning several important competitions for public buildings such as the Hostalets Civic Center (1986–1992), the Boarding School in Morella (1986–1994), and the Eurythmics Sports Center in Alicante (1990–1993). Their architectural proposal, presented in elegant and precise drawings that often resembled maps of architectural ideas, came as a breath of fresh air in the middle of the 1980s international architectural debate dominated by the polemics between so-called *Postmodernist* and Deconstructivist trends.

The city of Igualada is located approximately forty-five miles northwest of Barcelona. It is primarily an industrial city that has experienced a notable growth in recent times. Like most of the team's projects of the mid-1980s, Miralles and Pinòs received the commission to build the New Cemetery-Park of Igualada after winning the design competition called by the city to build a new cemetery. The site was placed far from the city's urban center, near a developing industrial zone. The architects' winning original scheme consisted of a large Z-shaped incision into the ground flanked by embankments containing overlapping rows of casket chambers that generated an introspected space, an appropriate setting for the emotive grieving and remembrance that a cemetery requires. However, as it would become typical of Miralles and Pinòs' design process, the architects refined their original project throughout the final design phase, softening the abstraction of the initial scheme in favor of a more sophisticated and intimate relationship of the different architectural elements with the surrounding natural setting.

Only one part of the original competition scheme has been built to date; the rest will be possibly added as the need to expand the cemetery increases in forthcoming years. Yet, the small portion that has been completed is largely sufficient to understand and appreciate the profound architectural poetics of the whole. The architects conceived the cemetery as a ceremonial descent into the earth, an intentional and artificial erosion of the ground that configures a tree-shaded descending route charged with the ritual and symbolism of a procession, an analogy to life and burial. The processional route begins at the entrance to the site, where an elliptical space placed at the same level with the street and lightly punctuated by trees is reserved for public parking and for the funeral vehicles. A concrete retaining wall and an almost calligraphic iron gate mark the beginning of the descending *promenade*, a tree-shaded gentle and ample ramp flanked by long concrete embankments that lodge three overlapping rows of casket-size individual burial chambers. The vertical overlapping of burial chambers is, in fact, a typical solution for cemeteries in Spain and other European countries; however, in Miralles and Pinòs' project this is reinterpreted with remarkable subtlety, using this element as a retaining wall that engenders the perception of a ground burial as

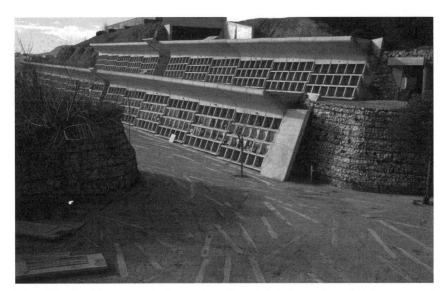

View of the tiered concrete embankments from the elliptical plaza at the end of the ceremonial promenade.

the coffins are symbolically interred into the sloping sides of the concrete embankments.

Organized in two tiered platforms, the concrete embankments converge to another elliptical area, echoing the first, located at the lowest level of the linear incision created in the site, where no signs of the immediate exterior are visible; only the distant landscape appears as a silent witness and grieving companion. This elliptical space, framed by walls made out of rock fragments contained by metal mesh, houses a series of crypts and family pantheons carved out of the artificially created layers; these pantheons offer a similar conception of interment manifested with the long concrete embankments that differs from the more familiar "monument-type family pantheons" of a typical cemetery. Service and religious facilities are housed at the highest level of the site near the entrance. The triangular chapel, still unfinished, promises to be a highly evocative and intimate space conceived for the emotional services that will take place in it. Adjacent to the chapel, a long stairway provides access to an even higher level, a place for contemplation where both the cemetery and the immediate context seem to disappear under the vast skies and the distant presence of the mountains.

The New Cemetery of Igualada is also a demonstration of Enric Miralles' interest in architectural narratives and metaphor, that is, the ability of architecture to convey meaning by establishing spatial, thematic, and/or cultural relationships. These metaphors are often subtle, sometimes abstract, and sometimes quite literal; for instance, the whole cemetery is conceptually buried into the ground, while the overall site plan of the project, the "drawing" of the site, appears as a figural metaphor of a dismembered body, a series of loosely connected fragments along a spine that resembles a human figure. Also, the pavement made out of railroad ties seems to metaphorically allude to a river of souls, while the concrete embankments may be interpreted as stranded ships. In addition to developing narrative aspects derived from the project's function and the site's characteristics, it seems that the architects incorporated intentional narrative allusions into their architectural sources. In this regard, **Park Güell** appears as an inevitable reference because many of its characteristic elements—the elliptical space, the inclined processional route, the tilting planes, the rusticity of materials and details—resonate in Miralles and Pinòs' complex in Igualada; however, where Parc Güell is exuberant, exciting, and playful, an ascendance of platforms and ramps to discover the city from the top of the hill, the cemetery is serene, austere, and solemn, a slow descent toward a space of introspection and reflection. Distant echoes of other religious masterpieces, such as Le Corbusier's church at the convent of La Tourette and Vistabella's **Church of the Sacred Heart** designed by Josep María Jujol, are also visible in the unfinished chapel.

Much more than a building complex, the New Cemetery-Park of Igualada is "a place" in the highest possible sense where architecture, landscape, topography, and sculpture converge to create a spatial narrative of undis-

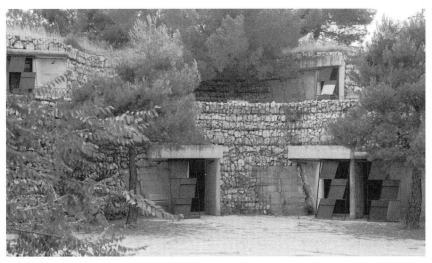

View of the crypts in the elliptical area at the end of the cemetary's processional route.

putable allegorical and emotive character. Further, it is a memorable place, at once peaceful and eventful, carefully conceived for remembrance and contemplation, in remarkable consonance and complicity with the impressive natural landscape that surrounds it. Enric Miralles, arguably one of the most talented and leading international architects of the late twentieth century, died on July 3, 2000, at the early age of forty-five, after a sudden incurable illness. He is buried in a crypt at the New Cemetery-Park of Igualada that he designed.

Further Reading

Buchanan, Peter, ed. *The Architecture of Enric Miralles and Carme Pinòs*. New York: Sites-Lumen, 1990.

Curtis, William J. R. *Modern Architecture since 1900*. 3rd ed. London: Phaidon Press Limited, 1996.

"Enric Miralles & Benedetta Tagliabue: 1996–2000." Special monographic issue, *El Croquis* 100, 101 (Madrid), 2000.

"Enric Miralles-Carme Pinòs." Monographic issue, *El Croquis* 49, 50 (Madrid), 1991.

PALACE OF CARLOS V AT LA ALHAMBRA, GRANADA, ANDALUCÍA

Style: Spanish Classical Renaissance Architecture
Dates: 1527–1568; 1600s
Architects: Pedro de Machuca; Luis de Machuca

The fifteenth century witnessed the emergence of a movement that questioned the formal precepts and technological methods of previous centuries and developed a new language inspired by ancient Greco-Roman art and architecture. This movement, known as the *Renaissance*, started in Italy and soon extended through central Europe. In Spain, the production of architecture was still heavily dependent on medieval forms of architectural practice; variations of *Romanesque* and *Gothic*, with their own architectural languages and construction techniques, persisted as the dominant modes of architectural practice and production. However, a transition from Gothic to Renaissance slowly began to take place in the late 1400s and eventually matured toward the beginning of the sixteenth century. Initially, Renaissance ideas impacted only the surface of buildings, appearing as ornament applied to the façades of otherwise typically medieval buildings; these hybridizations provoked the development of singular Spanish styles, "deviations" of the true Renaissance, known as the *Isabelline* and *Plateresque*. **La Casa de las Conchas** in Salamanca, and the **Palace of El Infantado** in Guadalajara are excellent examples of these hybrid architectures.

Eventually, a pure Renaissance architecture arrived in Spain in the early 1500s mostly thanks to artists and architects who had been trained in Italy. The Palace of Carlos V at La Alhambra is the first and, without doubt, the most important Classical Renaissance building in Spain as well as a relevant example of Italian Renaissance outside of Italy. The building was designed by Pedro de Machuca, an excellent painter who had been educated in Italy, likely in Rome, during the first two decades of the sixteenth century. As an architect, the Palace of Carlos V is his first and only work (his only two other constructions, the Puerta de las Granadas and the fountain named Pilar de Carlos V, also in La Alhambra, are of minor magnitude compared to the palace.)

The commission was made by Holy Roman Emperor Carlos V (grandson of the Catholic Kings and therefore king of Spain) who, in 1526 spent a summer at the **Palace of La Alhambra** with his new wife Isabel, daughter of the king of Portugal. Delighted by the wonderful architectural and landscape setting, Carlos V asked Pedro de Machuca—then a renowned painter who had already produced extraordinary works in Granada, Toledo, and Jaén—to design a large palace for him and his royal court within the premises of La Al-

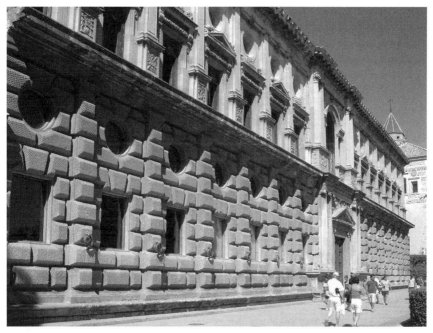

Exterior façade of the Palace of Carlos V at La Alhambra.

hambra. The project began the following year and continued well after Pedro de Machuca's death in 1550; eventually, the palace would be unfinished and never used by Carlos V and his court. Curiously, the enterprise was financed with funds provided by *moriscos* in exchange for permission to reestablish some of their old customs.

The building is adjacent to the Court of Myrtles and Court of Lyons of the formerly *Nasrid* palatial complex. In fact, Machuca had to sacrifice a portion of the Court of Myrtles—the southern wing—to make room for Carlos V's palace which irrupts as a foreign, over-scaled, and massive object into the intricate sequence of intimate courts and gardens of the fourteenth-century Nasrid royal residence. Yet, despite the, today, questionable impact that it had in the magnificent creation of the Muslim rulers, the palace is a remarkable work of architecture, an unequaled example of Italian Renaissance.

The two-storey building is almost 205 feet square in plan that encloses a large open-air circular court. The influence of Italian Renaissance architecture, particularly Bramante's, is obvious in both the overall conception of the building—a large square mass pierced by a large circular open space—and the classical architectural language of the exterior and interior façades. In plan, the building has no additional aspects of interest—a sequence of sometimes oddly proportioned rooms along the four façades—except for the beautiful octagonal chapel placed on the northeastern corner (at the hinge with the two Nasrid royal courts), which was going to be covered by a dome (never

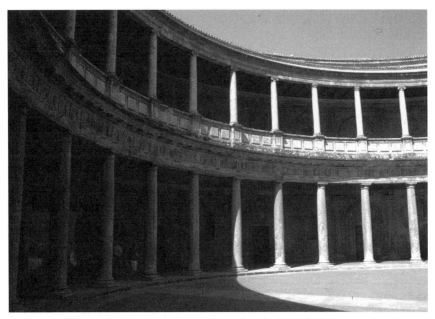

Fragment of the circular courtyard of the Palace of Carlos V with the two overlapping surrounding galleries.

erected). Access to the palace is provided through portals leading to vestibules placed at the center of each of the four façades and leading directly to the circular gallery that surrounds the central court; the west entrance—opposite the Alcazaba—is the more important and ceremonial of all four.

The exterior façades are distinctly Renaissance, inspired by fifteenth-century Florentine models. The lower level is in rusticated stone with *Doric* pilasters marking a constant rhythmical modulation that frames rectangular windows, below, and oeil-de-boeuf (bull's-eye) openings above, the latter used to illuminate a mezzanine level. Above the first floor, the hierarchically more important *piano-nobile* is composed in *Ionic* order, in accordance with ancient Greco-Roman classical tradition; Ionic pilasters frame rectangular windows perfectly aligned with those of the lower level and crowned by alternately triangular and flattened-arch *pediments*. The central bay of each façade that marks the entrances to the palace is clearly emphasized by carefully articulated portals. The most important one, on the west side of the building, features pairs of attached fluted columns on pedestals, Doric on the lower level and Ionic on the upper floor. Conversely, the southern façade's portal, built long after and probably inspired in Italian *Mannerism*, presents interesting alterations of the orders' sequence, with pairs of Ionic and *Corinthian* half-columns below and above, respectively, framing a more complex arched opening.

The circular courtyard is, architecturally, the salient component of the building. As Chueca Goitía stated, "it is the most original and ideologically Renaissance" element of the whole (Chueca Goitía 1965, 115). In effect, the circular colonnaded open court was a cherished typological and formal search initiated by Italian Renaissance architect Bramante (for example, his nonbuilt court around the Tempietto in the cloister of San Pietro in Montorio). Interestingly, in the early 1500s two geographically distant buildings materialized Bramante's concept; one was Antonio da Sangallo's and Vignola's Palazzo Farnese in Caprarola, Italy; the other was the Palace of Carlos V. Machuca's court is 100 feet in diameter, enclosed by a fully *trabeated* gallery supported on thirty-two columns, Doric below and Ionic above, that echo the classical orders' sequence of the exterior façades. The lower-level gallery, completed before Pedro de Machuca's death, is covered by a ring *vault* in which the vault's lateral thrust is absorbed by its own curvature, an undoubted technical feat for the period. The accomplished perception of lightness of the interior court contrasts strongly with the apparent massiveness of the building's exterior and constitutes one of its prominent characteristics.

The construction of the palace progressed slowly; when Pedro de Machuca died in 1550 only some parts had been completed. Work was continued, first by his son Luis de Machuca, who closely followed his father's project; later, after a long interruption that started before and extended beyond the 1570s, work was resumed by other architects under the overall supervision of Juan de Herrera, architect of the then contemporaneous **Monastery of El Escorial**, who completed the west façade and other parts of the interior always according to Pedro de Machuca's project. However, with the upper-level gallery and the chapel's dome unfinished, construction was halted and the project to complete the royal residence abandoned. Eventually, the building was finished for use but without some of what could have been wonderful Renaissance features, such as the chapel's dome. In spite of it, it is purely Renaissance in its conception, an unmatched emblem of the penetration of Italian ideas in Spain. Today, it is part of the extraordinary architectural complex of La Alhambra, a monumental, multicultural site protected by UNESCO's World Heritage program since 1984.

Further Reading

Bevan, Bernard. *History of Spanish Architecture*. London: B. T. Basford, 1938.

Blunt, Anthony, ed. *Baroque and Rococo: Architecture and Decoration*. New York: Harper & Row, 1978.

Chueca Goitía, Fernando. *Historia de la Arquitectura Española: Edad Moderna-Edad Contemporánea*. Vol. 2. Madrid: Editorial Dossat, 1965.

PALACE OF EL INFANTADO, GUADALAJARA, CASTILLA-LA MANCHA

Style: Isabelline Architecture
Dates: 1480–1483; partially reformed in 1569; restored in 1963–1970
Architects: Juan Guas; reformed by Acacio Orejón; restored by José González de Valcárcel

The Palace of El Infantado is one of the most relevant buildings of the rich and singular period of transition from *Gothic* to *Renaissance* architecture in Spain. The fundamental characteristics of this period are the endurance of medieval architectural practices, the slow introduction of Renaissance ideas in Spain, and the parallel emergence of a variety of hybrid architectural languages generally referred to as the *Isabelline* and *Plateresque* styles; these two originated in the central region of Castilla and had a certain predominance throughout Spain toward the end of the fifteenth and beginning of the sixteenth centuries. Other important examples of this period are **La Casa de las Conchas** in Salamanca, the Medinacelli Palace in Cogolludo, and the main buildings for the **Universidad de Alcalá de Henares**. More importantly, the Palace of El Infantado is among the most important civil works of architecture of the Isabelline period, a building regarded as a perfect synthesis of Spanish *Flamboyant Gothic* and *Mudéjar* architecture, as well as a precursor of Renaissance architecture in Spain.

The building was commissioned by the 2nd Duke of El Infantado, Iñigo López de Mendoza, who ordered the demolition of the existing fourteenth-century residence built by his predecessors and the construction of a new, splendorous palace. Thus, the Infantado Palace became a visible sign of the importance attained by the city of Guadalajara in the fifteenth and sixteenth centuries—when it was the seat of the Duchy of El Infantado—as wells as of the influential role and power of the Mendoza family. The design of the palace was entrusted to Juan Guas, considered the most important Isabelline architect, author of other masterpieces of the period such as the monastery of San Juan de los Reyes in Toledo (about 1478), commissioned by Queen Isabel la Católica in 1476, and the Real Castle at Manzanares (c. 1470s), the first commission he received from the powerful Mendoza family.

As it was increasingly typical of residential palaces of the period, the building is organized around a rectangular courtyard fully enclosed by a two-level

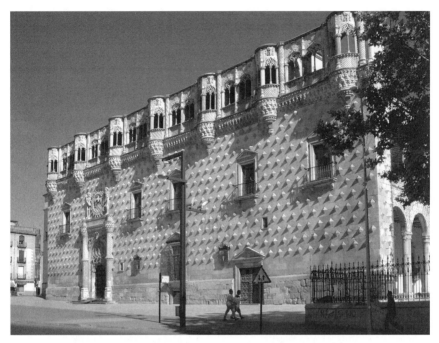

West front of the Palace of El Infantado; on the right is a small glimpse of the south side arcade.

gallery. This courtyard and its enclosing gallery are relevant contributions of Juan Guas; its rectangular form is defined by a regular modulation of five-by-seven bays marked by arcades supported by columns crowned by *mixtilinear ogee* arches and a profuse decoration in high-relief that defies any attempt at a tectonic understanding of the building's structure. This court-yard is known as the "Patio de los Leones" (Court of Lions) because of the high-relief lions featured on the arches' *spandrels*. In Guas' original building, the two superimposed arcades were likely supported by superbly carved *helicoidal* columns; however, only those of the upper level subsist; the lower-level columns were replaced by others of *Tuscan* inspiration in a major re-form of the building undertaken in the sixteenth century by Acacio Orejón. The gallery provided access to a series of aligned and generously dimen-sioned rooms that used to be covered by splendid Mudéjar *artesonados*; once a sign of the palace's magnificence, these Mudéjar ceilings were fully de-stroyed by fire in the twentieth century.

On the west side of the palace there is an additional linear sequence of rooms attached to the west wing that flanks the courtyard. This imposing west body that housed the palace's more important rooms, which were also covered by Mudéjar artesonados, constitutes the building's front, the cere-monial façade that establishes the palace's urban presence and civic impor-tance. In 1496, Lorenzo Trillo added rooms to the southern side of the original courtyard building; however, contrary to the west body, this is a permeable two-level arched gallery that was functionally, as well as ceremonially, related to the long open hall that occupies most of the piano-nobile's southern wing; the gallery opened to a beautiful Mudéjar garden decorated with mythological motives.

The great west front is, without doubt, the most remarkable aspect of the building. It consists of an imposing urban façade entirely built with *ashlar* stone from Tamajón; the large planar surface may be interpreted as a sign of the arrival of Italian Renaissance ideas, yet, everything else reveals the almost obsessive predilection for heavily textured and decorated surfaces typical of Isabelline and Plateresque architecture. The plane is subtly subdivided in six modules implied by the projecting "garitones" (sentry boxes) placed at the building's top; below this richly articulated band, the façade is a virtually unbroken surface in which the six modules are barely suggested by the existence of five window openings on the middle level (these are not original but part of a sixteenth-century reform that replaced formerly existing smaller openings) and the building's main doorway. As was typical of buildings of this period, the main doorway is off-center, displaced to the central module of the façade's left half. This entrance leads to an ample vestibule adjacent to the northwest corner of the interior courtyard. The exterior stone doorframe is flanked by two richly textured semicylindrical columns crowned by a mixtilinear ogee arch. The abundance of heraldic symbols associated with the owners' family within and above the rectangular frame defined by the two columns was a typical characteristic of noble residences of this period.

Yet, the two more relevant aspects of the façade are the rich relief texture of the planar surface and the top-level gallery of "garitones." The former is created by a pattern of projecting diamond figures displayed regularly at the intersection of the blocks of ashlar stone in a typically Mudéjar diamond-grid arrangement; this textured effect was typical of contemporaneous buildings—for instance, La Casa de las Conchas—and it may have been conceived by Juan Guas to soften, articulate, and dignify the large and predominantly bare front façade. The gallery of "garitones"—elements borrowed from military architecture—constitutes a richly decorated horizontal band, originally an open gallery, that crowns the building. The demarcation and highlighting of the uppermost band of frontal façades is, in fact, a typical and genuine characteristic of Spanish architecture of the period that reveals the influence of Mudéjar architecture.

In 1570, the 5th Duke of El Infantado ordered a major reform that severely altered the original building. The renovation was commissioned to Acacio de Orejón who replaced the original small windows of the front façade for larger Renaissance openings crowned by triangular *pediments*, and replaced the helicoidal columns of the courtyard's ground-floor gallery with Tuscan-inspired columns. In 1936, during the Spanish Civil War (1936–1939), the building was badly damaged by bombs and a subsequent fire destroyed some of its most remarkable features such as the wonderful interior

Mudéjar ceilings. The building was largely reconstructed in the 1960s by José González de Valcárcel, who restored the palace's former grandeur; however, the reconstruction was only partial, focused on recuperating the building's imposing west façade and urban presence; the Mudéjar interiors could not be recuperated. Today, the Palace of El Infantado houses a provincial archive, library, and museum, and remains the indisputable historic landmark of this once powerful city.

Further Reading

Bevan, Bernard. *History of Spanish Architecture*. London: B. T. Basford, 1938.

Chueca Goitía, Fernando. *Historia de la Arquitectura Española: Edad Moderna-Edad Contemporánea*. Vol. 2. Madrid: Editorial Dossat, 1965.

Herrera Casado, Antonio. *El Palacio del Infantado*. Guadalajara: Aache Ediciones, 2001.

PALACE OF LA ALHAMBRA AND GARDENS OF EL GENERALIFE, GRANADA, ANDALUCÍA

Style: Nasrid Islamic Architecture
Dates: 1309–1354
Architect: Unknown

The Alhambra is one of the greatest building ensembles in the history of architecture. A place that inspired writers, poets, and artists, attracted rulers and vassals, the initiated and the profane; a place where myths, legends, dreams, poetry, mystery, and history converge. Situated in a wonderful enclave, at the footsteps of Sierra Nevada and dominating the valley of the Darro River, the Alhambra stands out as the high point, and final act, of almost eight centuries of Muslim presence in the Iberian Peninsula.

After the disintegration of the Caliphate of Córdoba early in the eleventh century, al-Andalus faced internal confrontations; the once independent Caliphate was fragmented into regional *taifas* governed by local princes. Thus, in the late eleventh century and through the 1100s, important cities—for instance Toledo, Avila, Zaragoza—fell to the ambitious *Reconquista* campaign launched by Christian kings. However, in the twelfth century, the Marrakech-based *Almoravids* succeeded in reunifying what remained of al-Andalus. In 1147, the *Almohads* captured Marrakech and eventually conquered Muslim Spain but were defeated in 1212 by an alliance of Christian armies in the famous battle of Las Navas de Tolosa. The internal divisions of al-Andalus, and the relentless territorial advance and clever repopulation projects of the Christian kingdoms forced the Muslims to retreat south where, in 1238, a new dynasty—the *Nasrids*, led by Muhammad I—seized control of the remnants of al-Andalus; while independent from other Muslim states, they were tributary vassals of the king of Castilla.

Centered in Granada, the Nasrids restored the old splendor of the Caliphate of Córdoba by welcoming Muslim refugees from other parts of the peninsula. However, politically isolated and confined to a reduced territory along the southern coast of the Mediterranean (the current provinces of Almería, Granada, and Málaga), they survived only as tributaries of Castilla but, toward the mid-1400s they no longer resisted the reunification project led by the Catholic Kings Fernando and Isabel. Boabdil, the last of the Nasrid rulers, finally surrendered in 1492, bringing to an end almost eight centuries of Muslim political presence in Spain. In the two and a half centuries that they ruled Granada, they left an incomparable cultural legacy. La Alhambra and its related buildings are the highlights of that wonderful testament.

The building complex of La Alhambra is composed of the Alcazaba, the Royal Palaces, the gardens of El Generalife, and various other structures such as Arab Baths, "El Partal," many patios, and towers. The origin of the name is a Castilian transformation of the palace's name in Arab, "Cal'at al-Hamrá," which means the Red Castle, an allusion to the red-colored clay of the hill, which was also the base material for building the walls. The history of the site started when the first Nasrid Sultan—Muhammad I (1238–1273)—repaired "La Acequia Real," an irrigation channel that takes water from the Darro River three miles uphill from the site, and began the construction of a military structure and a protecting enceinte. His successors added buildings and facilities, but the major construction impulses were during the sultanates of Yusuf I (1333–1354) and Muhammad V (1354–1391).

The Alcazaba and the Royal Palaces are surrounded by a thick fortified wall flanked by high towers that—as Chueca Goitía stated—"encloses the precinct of La Alhambra which, more than a fortress with a palace, is a walled-in city" (Chueca Goitía 1965, 439). This enceinte is accessible through five gates, each one of them featuring different characteristics. The "Puerta de la Justicia" (Gate of Justice) for example, has a beautiful pointed *horse-shoe* arch marking the entrance to an inverted S-shaped passageway that leads into the citadel. Now in ruins, the Alcazaba is the oldest part of the built complex; its construction began in 1238 and, despite some literary chronicles that claim it was completed in only one year, it was probably completed during the reign of Muhammad II (1273–1302). Originally, it was a military facility containing houses, store areas, a *hammam*, and other quarters organized around a trapezoidal court.

Nasrid architecture is not concerned with the building as object or as an addition of well-articulated volumes (a characteristic of Western architecture); instead, it favors the dissolution of the building into several autonomous components organized around courtyards in which the use of water features—fountains, channeled streams, basins—is a central aspect of the conception. Courtyards are a central aspect of Nasrid's architectural ideas because they work both as spatial organizers as well as sensorial stimulators. In effect, the exploitation of visual effects (bright versus shaded, open versus concealed), the subtle sound of circulating water (fountains, reflecting pools, channels), the aromas emanating from gardens, and the tactile contrasts (cold marble floors, warm stucco), are all elements that unequivocally pursue the users' sensual stimulation.

La Alhambra is the highest expression and paradigmatic example of the Nasrids' sensual architecture. Originally, it had four courtyards: a small square court (now in ruins) that served as the ceremonial entrance to the palace and had a small mosque on the southeastern corner; farther east, another square but larger courtyard (partially in ruins) is flanked by the Tower of Machuca on the north while on the east it is framed by the "Mexuar," the center of the monarch's administrative and judicial activity; farther east, the two other courts—the Court of Myrtles and the Court of Lions—are almost intact and constitute the unquestionable highlights of Nasrid architecture.

The Court of Myrtles is the largest of the four; it was built toward the mid-fourteenth century during the reign of Yusuf I; it has pleasant rectangular proportions and is dominated by a large reflecting pool flanked by low hedges of myrtles that cover the entire longitudinal length of the courtyard from north to south; a seven-bay gallery of arches supported by slender columns provides permeable enclosures on the north and south ends. These galleries precede shallow halls stretching the whole width of the court with alcoves on each end. The northern hall, which in turn antecedes the Tower of Comares, is known as Sala de la Barca (Hall of the Boat) because of its wonderful wooden ceiling that resembles an inverted ship. The Tower of Comares houses the Hall of Ambassadors, also known as the Hall of the Throne. This is a remarkable space, the largest and most ceremonial of the whole complex. The proportions and characteristics of this room are exquisite; it is a 37-foot-square by 60-foot-high space enclosed by a 9-foot-thick wall with nine low alcoves carved into the wall thickness on three of the four sides. The lower portion of the interior walls are completely covered by a combination of colored faience arranged in complex geometric patterns; above, finely laced stucco carvings dematerialize the walls and convey a certain lightness unknown in Western architecture. Outside, from the courtyard, the Tower of Comares rises behind the seven-bay arched portico, while beyond the enceinte the tower appears as an inexpugnable bastion, the formal center of the ensemble. The stark austerity and simplicity of the exterior walls is in sharp contrast with the complex and richly decorated interior.

The Court of Lions was built during the Sultanate of Mohammad V, constituting the last significant addition to the royal palace. Like its neighboring Court of Myrtles, it is a nicely proportioned rectangular court (94 by 52 feet). The court is presided by a magnificent fountain featuring twelve lions

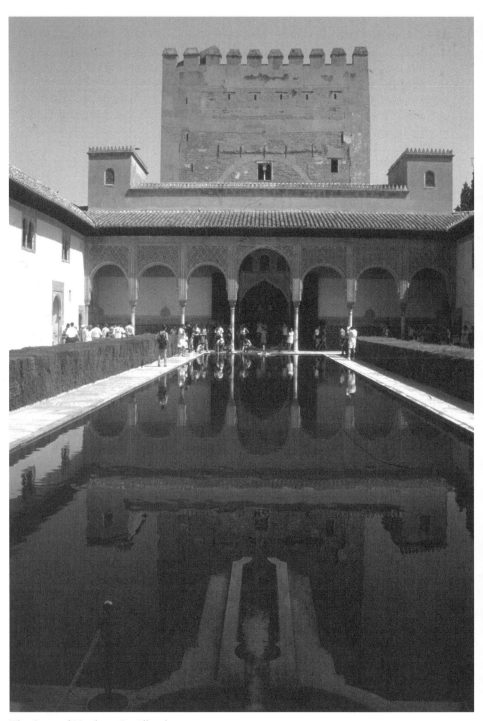

The Court of Myrtles at La Alhambra.

that collects the water of a cruciform channel that traverses the courtyard in all four directions; these channels end in small round basins placed beyond the court's physical boundaries as defined by a continuous gallery composed of alternately twin and single columns that support a decorative arcade. The colonnade's north and south ends include square kiosks, or *belvederes*, that project into the courtyard. The continuous gallery provides formal unity to the courtyard and operates as a screen behind which a wide variety of residential wings are housed: the Hall of Kings on the east, the Hall of the Abencerrajes on the south, and the Hall of the Two Sisters on the north side. Whereas the east and west arms of the water channel that traverses the court end on small circular basins at the center of the gallery, the north and south arms penetrate into both the Hall of Abencerrajes and the Hall of the Two Sisters to end in larger circular basins placed at the center of each hall. Thus, these rooms, as well as the colonnaded gallery become extensions of the court, interior spaces of a spatial unity dominated by the lions' fountain.

Each of the three wings that enclose the Court of Lions has unique architectural characteristics; however, the Hall of the Two Sisters, on the north side, is the spatial climax of the court's ensemble, a veritable interior courtyard presided by a central basin. Architecturally, the most interesting aspect of this hall is the ascending octagonal honeycomb-vault made out of stucco that reveals the Muslim interest in designing delicate and intricate patterns, as well as the remarkable skill of their craftsmen. On the opposite end, the Hall of Abencerrajes is covered by a star-shaped dome of *mocarabes*, yet another extraordinary testimony to the decorative richness of Muslim architecture.

While the Court of Myrtles and Court of Lions are the highlights, La

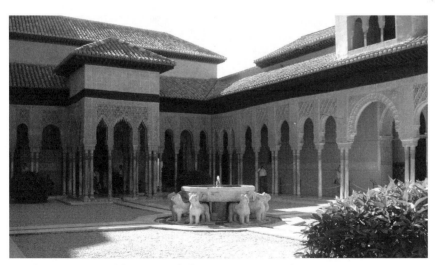

La Alhambra's Court of the Lions with the Lions Fountain at the center.

Alhambra has many other notable architectural components such as the Mirador de Daraxa, the Harem's court, El Peinador de la Reina, the garden of Lindaraja, and El Partal. Among them, the gardens of El Generalife stand out as the ideal landscape complement to the outstanding Nasrid palaces. They are located beyond the enceinte but are an integral part of the complex, a masterpiece of garden design and a sublimely sensual space. El Generalife is also a fruit garden and a relaxing compound where the presence of water and the aroma of plants play central roles. The central piece is the Court of the Acequia, an elongated rectangular court traversed

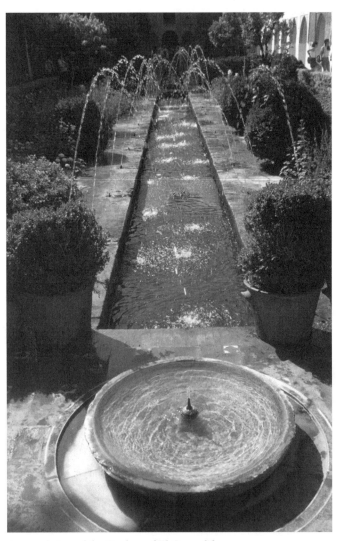

A general view of the Gardens of El Generalife.

from north to south by the Royal Acequia (actually an exposed portion of the irrigation channel that takes water from the Darro River) flanked by fruit gardens, fountains, and other water features culminated by arcaded pavilions on both ends. Farther east, the Patio de la Sultana has a U-shaped water basin with a square central fountain. In its northeast corner begins the famous stairway flanked by channels with cascading water that links the gardens with a marvelous uphill belvedere. The geometrical and formal design of gardens, the abundance of water features, the built pavilions for leisure, and the overall conception of El Generalife anticipated by more than three centuries Le Notre's gardens at the Chateau de Versailles (Versailles 1680s). However, beyond their similar compositional and purpose aspects, they have a significant difference: while in Western gardens (as epitomized at Versailles) space opens toward infinite vistas and a vast extension of land, the Muslim garden seeks to enclose space and generate intimate places for sensual stimuli.

Other notable aspects of La Alhambra include the magnificent design and geometrical patterning of colored faience throughout the built structures; the almost textile character of the stucco decoration; the *kufic* inscriptions and the verses of Ibn Zamrak carved in stucco; the use of religious metaphor, astrology, and symbolism in the conception of virtually every component of the complex; and the remarkable craftsmanship and care for detail throughout. The royal building complex and palace of La Alhambra, as well as the gardens of El Generalife are universally considered as unique works of architecture and landscape design that mark the climax of Nasrid art in Spain and one of the greatest achievements of Islamic architecture worldwide. In recognition of their importance and uniqueness they have been protected by UNESCO's World Heritage program since 1984.

Further Reading

Antequera, Marino. *The Alambra and The Generalife*. Granada: Editorial Padre Suárez, 1953.

Chueca Goitía, Fernando. *Historia de la Arquitectura Española: Edad Antigua y Edad Media*. Vol. 1. Madrid: Editorial Dossat, 1965.

Hoag, John D. *Islamic Architecture*. New York: Harry N. Abrams, 1977.

Stierlin, Henri, and Stierlin, Anne. *Alhambra*. Paris: Imprimerie Nationale, 1991.

Yeomans, Richard. *The Story of Islamic Architecture*. New York: New York University Press, 2000.

PALACE OF LA ALJAFERÍA, ZARAGOZA, ARAGON

Style: Mudéjar Architecture
Dates: Circa 1031–1100s
Architect: Unknown

In the early years of the eleventh century, the once powerful Caliphate of Córdoba that ruled over the territory of al-Andalus began to disintegrate. After years of chaos and anarchy, the political unity of the Caliphate dissolved, breaking up into almost thirty *taifas* governed by local chiefs who had gained power through the network created by the great *vizier* al-Mansur (981–1002). Naturally, the most important cities of al-Andalus—Seville, Toledo, Valencia, Badajoz, and Zaragoza—became the capitals of powerful and independent taifas, a system that lasted until their isolation and rivalry; consequently, their political independence made them succumb to the growing interests of Christian kings who, from their stronghold in the north of the Iberian Peninsula, had launched military campaigns to recover *Hispania*. However, before that, liberated from the influence of Córdoba, some taifas reached high levels of artistic sophistication and economic prosperity.

The Palace of La Aljafería is the most important full-scale standing example of the taifas' period, the best representative of the high creative level attained by Islamic culture throughout Spain as demonstrated in numerous other existing fragments of buildings. La Aljafería is located in Zaragoza, the ancient Cesarea Augusta of the Romans, former capital of the northernmost portion of the Caliphate of Córdoba; its construction was undertaken by the second governor of Zaragoza's taifa, Abu Ja'far Ahmad ibn Sulayman al-Muqtadir (r. 1049–1082), who brought the regional kingdom to a cultural and political pinnacle. The building's name derives from the Arabic "al-Ja'fariyya," but, originally, the building was known as "Dār-al-surūr" (House of Happiness); a lavish recreational luxurious palace and a highly protected fortress in the Islamic period, the building continued to be the center of regional political power after the city fell to Christian armies in the twelfth century. Originally situated outside the city walls, the palatial complex is surrounded by a fortified defensive wall that encloses a slightly irregular rectangular area of approximately 270 by 220 feet. The wall's defensive role is emphasized by sixteen bastions and a tall tower—Torre del Trovador—that, built in the previous century, was incorporated as an integral part of the building complex.

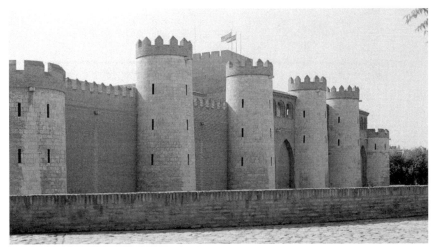

Exterior defensive walls of the Palace de la Aljafería.

Access to the walled-in area is on the east side of the building through a *horse-shoe* arched gate placed between two bastions near the northeast corner of the fortification. Beyond the walls the enceinte is subdivided into three transversal portions. Considering the numerous alterations that the building suffered through the centuries, it is difficult to establish the exact configuration of the eleventh-century Islamic building, but it is clear that al-Muqtadir's private quarters occupied the central portion, organized around an open-air courtyard now known as Patio de Santa Isabel. This court is enclosed on all four sides by arcades that generate permeable spatial screens. The arcades of the long sides—east and west—are composed of wide *multi-lobated* arches supported on pillars and semi-attached columns. The southern screen is much more elaborated, comprised of a four-bay sequence of intricately laced *mixtilinear* arches resting on pillars and slender columns topped with palm *capitals* attached to each side of the pillars. The whole resembles a delicate embroidery made out of plaster and stone that dematerializes the wall planes; this dematerialization of the plane is further emphasized by a reflecting pool that, cutting across the entire southern end of the courtyard, mirrors the complex superposition of the arcade's elaborated geometrical patterns.

The northern portico is the spatial climax of the building. It is composed of a sequence of screened spatial layers across the full width of the northern edge. The first layer is made of slender and rather unelaborated pillars that generate a four-bay permeable screen; beyond, another four-bay arcade resting on sturdier cruciform pillars constitutes the southern edge of a space that used to house a semi-enclosed rectangular pool; finally, the more interior arcade, which framed the rectangular pool on the north, east, and west, is the

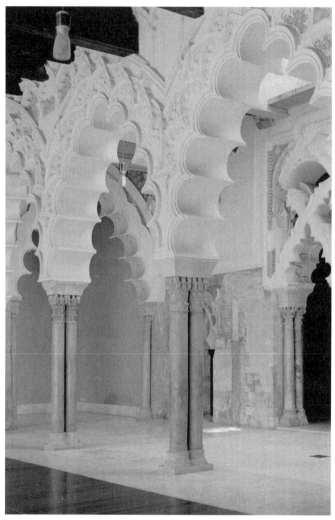

Interior fragment of the northern portico's arcade of interlaced arches.

most sophisticated of all, consisting of highly detailed mixtilinear pointed arches resting on twin marble columns crowned by palm capitals. The little oratory, located on the southeastern corner of the space, marks the importance of this sequence of carefully screened spaces. Beyond, on axis with the courtyard, a narrowly spaced four-bay arcade composed of an even more complex sequence of interlaced mixtilinear arches, all purely decorative, marks the entrance to the palace's private chambers.

The little oratory is the architectural gem of the building. It consists of a small octagonal room located on the north side of the palatial hall and likely intended for the exclusive use of the governor, his family, and close collaborators. The walls are lavishly decorated with blind arcades composed of exuberantly fragmented mixtilinear arches resting on short columns and virtually entirely covered with "atauriques" (ornamental plaster work based on vegetal motifs). In the oratory's upper portion there is an arcade composed of small but highly complex interlaced lobated arches. The innovative palm capitals that top columns throughout the building are of particular architectural interest because they represent a genuine attempt to create a new capital type instead of making degenerate variations of the known ancient classical orders. Originally, the oratory was covered by a polychrome *artesonado* (wooded paneled ceiling), but today it is covered by a *vault* inspired by the *mihrab*'s vault of the **Great Mosque of Córdoba**. Conversely, the beautiful mihrab's sectional horse-shoe dome is authentic, a constructive jewel of the period. The mihrab's horse-shoe triumphal arch, pointing to Mecca on the southeastern side of the octagon, is the only different arch in the space; featuring alternatively carved and plain *voussoirs* and supported by twin columns on each side of the opening, it introduces a visual pause to the oratory's exuberant decoration.

In 1118, the Christian king Alfonso I captured Zaragoza, bringing to an end the once powerful and sophisticated taifa. He appropriated the building as the seat of his Kingdom of Aragon, beginning a process of modifications, additions, and transformations to adapt the building to Christian uses. Whereas some were worthy of the palace's glorious past, others were insensitive to its architectural quality. Later, between the twelfth and fourteenth centuries, the building underwent the construction of the Chapel of San Martín, the west arcade of the Patio de Santa Isabel, and the *Mudéjar* rooms added during King Pedro IV's reign. Other important additions were made near the end of the fifteenth century when the Catholic Kings added a monumental stair and polychromatic painted woodwork. In 1593, an exterior wall with pentagonal bastions in the corners and a moat were built around the palace by express order of King Felipe II, transforming the site into a citadel. In the eighteenth and nineteenth centuries, the building suffered even more substantial transformations to become a military barracks. Finally, in 1931 it was declared a National Historic Monument, but it would still take a half century to restore its artistic past. Since 1987, a considerable portion of La Aljafería houses the seat of Aragon's autonomic government. Thus, after centuries of cultural neglect and abuse the building finally recuperated its role as the center of regional political authority as well as its original architectural splendor.

Further Reading

Chueca Goitía, Fernando. *Historia de la Arquitectura Española: Edad Antigua y Edad Media*. Vol. 1. Madrid: Editorial Dossat, 1965.

Corral Lafuente, José Luis, and Peña Gonzalvo, Francisco Javier, eds. *La Cultura Islámica en Aragón*. Zaragoza: Diputación Provincial de Zaragoza, 1989.

Hoag, John D. *Islamic Architecture*. New York: Harry N. Abrams, 1977.

Yarza, Joaquín. *Arte y Arquitectura en España, 500–1250*. Madrid: Ediciones Cátedra, 2000.

PALACE OF RAMIRO I.

See Monte Naranco.

PALACE OF SOBRELLANO, COMILLAS, CANTABRIA

Styles: Eclectic, Neo-Gothic Revival Architecture
Dates: 1881–1890
Architect: Joan Martorell i Montells

The nineteenth century was, throughout Europe, marked by difficult and often tumultuous episodes that originated as a consequence of the radical social, political, and technological changes that had begun to occur in the last part of the previous century. The French Revolution (1789) and the Industrial Revolution are two among the most important of those drastic episodes that market the evolution of the century. Expectedly, these events had ramifications that impacted and influenced the development and evolution of artistic and architectural ideas. Architecturally, the century—especially the second half—was dominated by a proliferation of proposals for renewal and stylistic trends that, on one hand, represented a reaction to *Neoclassicism*, and on the other, attempted to reconcile the discipline with the radical changes that were taking place in all aspects of life and social organization. *Romanticism*, *Eclecticism*, and the *Revivalism* of historical styles were some of the more widespread avenues of exploration that architects of the nineteenth century followed in the attempt to apply in architecture the ideas and technical progress that marked the period, preparing the discipline for the breakthrough of the *Modern Movement* that surged in the early decades of the twentieth century.

The virtually pan-European emergence of regional styles—*Art Nouveau* in France and Belgium, *Jugendstil* in Germany and Austria, *Liberty Style* in Italy, the *Arts and Crafts Movement* in Britain, and the *Modernismo Catalan* in Spain, all of which originated with some independence from each other

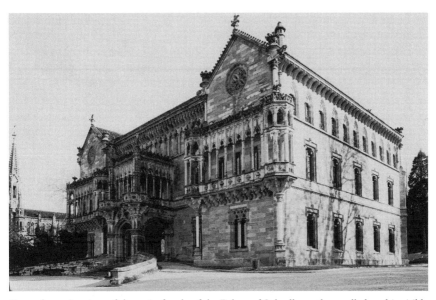

General exterior view of the main façade of the Palace of Sobrellano; the small chapel is visible on the far left.

in the final years of the nineteenth century—that shared some stylistic, technological, and theoretical postulates does not necessarily represent a culmination of the diverse and often opposed explorations of nineteenth-century architecture, but it appears as the chronological link between these explorative movements and the radical rupture presented by twentieth-century architecture. The Palace of Sobrellano, in Comillas (Cantabria), which can be considered as a representative of Eclecticism and Revivalism, is one of Spain's most interesting buildings of that period, and at the same time it links late-nineteenth-century architecture with the emergence of the Modernismo Catalan, one of the most vibrant and fecund chapters in the history of Spain's architecture.

The building was commissioned in 1878 by Antonio López y López, a native of Comillas who, in his early youth, had emigrated to Cuba. He eventually amassed a moderate fortune with which he returned to Spain, more precisely to Barcelona, where he eventually became a wealthy and influential shipping magnate. In recognition of the material and financial support that he provided to suffocate the Cubans' insurgence for independence, King Alfonso XII awarded him the title of Marquis of his native city of Comillas where Antonio López y López already owned a large piece of property located on a slightly elevated site just west of the town's center. He used to spend the summer season in Comillas and had built a few residential buildings in the site. However, the buildings were not in accordance with his newly attained social status; therefore, as the first Marquis of Comillas, he decided to build a monumental architectural ensemble consisting of a sumptuous palace and a chapel and family pantheon.

He trusted the conception of the project to Joan Martorell i Montells, a prominent architect from Barcelona who can be considered as a precursor of Modernismo Catalan. Martorell put the two buildings aligned at a high part of the site with their fronts facing north; while aligned, both were kept at considerable distance from each other to be perceived as individual architectural objects; however, they were supposed to be connected by a subterranean passage that was never built. The chapel and family pantheon was conceived as a small-scale *Gothic* church with a single slender tower at the front crowned by a high-reaching spire, Gothic arches and tall buttressed walls. The whole vaguely recalls the style of English perpendicular Gothic churches of the thirteenth century, as well as some religious works of Augustus Pugin, one of the most important architects and theoreticians of England's *Gothic Revivalism* of the mid-nineteenth century. The chapel was completed in 1881 in time for King Alfonso XII's memorable visit to Comillas. Fundamentally, while it also served as a chapel, the building is a family pantheon, the burial place for the family of the Marquis of Comillas.

Farther west, at virtually the same elevation, emerges the sumptuous palace with its massive imposing volume alleviated by the complex filigreed elements attached to its frontal façade. Like its neighboring chapel, the palace has echoes of Pugin's work (for example Scarisbrick Hall in Lancashire, c. 1845) in the utilization of elements typical of Gothic architecture such as pitched roofs, pointed arches, stained-glass windows, and circular openings with inscribed laced stone work. Yet, the Palace of Sobrellano is definitely less pure in its Gothic Revivalism, incorporating elements and organizational principles more typical of other typically Spanish architectural styles (*Almohad*, *Mudéjar*, *Isabelline*) that are clear reflections of Martorell's sophisticated eclecticism. The interiors display an even more extravagant diversity of decorative styles, combining motives and elements derived from various periods and regions. The main room, located at the opposite (south) end of the central axis of the building, is simply grandiose, a triple-story vertical volume with spectacular stained-glass windows featuring neo-Gothic motives and fully decorated walls. This room was reserved for social events and receptions and it was linked to other rooms on the west side of the building that served similar purposes. The more domestic living areas—living room, billiard, dining rooms—were located on the east side of the central axis. The interior decoration was made with the participation of renowned Catalan artists such as Joan Roig and Eduardo Llorens, while Cristóbal Cascante—a classmate of Antoni Gaudí who supervised the building's construction until its completion in 1888—contributed designs for many furnishing items.

Under the patronage of the Marquis, Comillas became a fertile laboratory of exploration for the then-incipient Modernismo Catalan. Joan Martorell also designed the splendid and imposing building for the Universidad Pontificia in which Lluís Domenech i Montaner—author of the **Palau de la**

Música Catalana (Barcelona 1905–1908)—added numerous parts; also, within the premises and park of the Palace of Sobrellano is "El Capricho," the small summer residence of Antonio López's brother-in-law and one of the first celebrated works of the young Antoni Gaudí, the unquestionable leading figure of Modernismo Catalan. Finally, Cascante, in addition to supervising the construction of the buildings designed by his fellow Catalan colleagues, designed the town's hospital.

Today, the Palace of Sobrellano is owned by the regional government of Cantabria, which has converted it into a museum and exhibition hall often used for official receptions. The building stands as a testimony to a glorious period in which Comillas underwent a rapid process of modernization and transformation (it was the first city in Spain to have electrical power). Architecturally, the palace is the best representative of the strong link that existed between some neo-Gothic explorations of late-nineteenth-century architecture in Spain and the inherent and progressive Gothicism embraced by the Modernismo Catalan as part of a full-scale linguistic, artistic, social, and political search for a national identity.

Further Reading

Chueca Goitía, Fernando. *Historia de la Arquitectura Española: Edad Moderna-Edad Contemporánea.* Vol. 2. Madrid: Editorial Dossat, 1965.

Middleton, Robin, and Watkin, David. *Neoclassical and 19th Century Architecture.* Milan and New York: Electa and Rizzoli, 1980.

Russell, Franck. *Art Nouveau Architecture.* London: Academy Editions, 1979.

PALAU DE LA MÚSICA CATALANA, BARCELONA, CATALONIA

Style: Modernismo Catalan
Dates: 1905–1908; restoration: 1982–1989; 2000
Architects: Lluís Domènech i Montaner; restoration and addition:
Oscar Tusquets, Lluís Clotet, Carlos Díaz, and Ignacio Paricio

Lluís Domènech i Montaner is considered, with Antoni Gaudí, to be one of the two greatest exponents of the *Modernismo Catalan*. He is the leader of one of the two parallel lines of exploration in this architectural movement, primarily based in Barcelona and related to analogous contemporaneous developments in other European countries, such as Belgium and France's *Art Nouveau*, Austria's *Secessionist Movement*, and Germany's *Jugendstil*. His architectural work is characterized by an intelligent conception and orchestra-

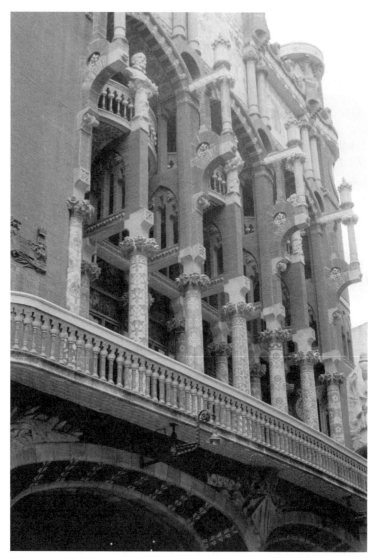

Fragment of the deep street façade over the entrance to the Palau de la Música Catalana.

tion of all the elements that constituted the project's *programme* (in its widest meaning) and the implementation of the newest available technology and methods of construction. His architectural legacy includes remarkable building complexes, such as the Café-Restaurant building for Barcelona's Universal Exposition and the Hospital de San Pablo, also in Barcelona (1910). The Palau de la Música Catalana (Palace of Catalan Music) is regarded as Domènech i Montaner's masterpiece.

The Palau de la Música Catalana was commissioned in 1904 by the Orfeó

Català, an independent private choral association founded in 1891 by Lluís Millet and Amadeu Vives, two recognized Catalan musicians. The programme included a major auditorium for approximately 2,000 spectators, a practice room for the Orfeó Català choir, the association's offices and services. The site was quite small, located at the intersection of two narrow streets—today named as Carrer Sant Pere Més Alt and Carrer Amadeu Vives—within Barcelona's historic quarter, the Ciutat Vella, not far from the old Roman road now known as Via Laietana. The neighborhood is characterized by a dense and intricate fabric of narrow and constricted streets in a nongrid organization.

Construction was achieved with amazing rapidity, completed in slightly more than three years (it was inaugurated on February 15, 1908). This was possible thanks to the architect's intelligent and audacious use of a reticular iron skeleton (one of the earliest uses in Europe for buildings of such institutional caliber) and of prefabrication methods for nonstandardized components; an interesting example is the ceramic-covered columns that were built in off-site workshops and delivered to the building site for final assemblage.

Domènech i Montaner's conception of the project for such a large building in such a small site was remarkable, taking full advantage of the limited visual exposure that the site offered for an important institution by developing a monumental, highly ornamented, and complex three-dimensional façade structure behind which the rest of the building, notably the large auditorium, unfolds with outstanding constructive and conceptual clarity in both plan and section. In plan, the building has four distinct zones organized in linear succession: an ample and spacious entrance hall, a monumental stairway that connects all the building's levels, the auditorium, and a rear service and vertical circulation zone; each of these zones extends across the full width of the site. The spacious vaulted foyer is placed on the ground level along Carrer Sant Pere Més Alt; access from the exterior is through a fully glazed enclosure framed by a flattened arch over two massive cylindrical pillars; the architect intelligently liberated the corner pillar to articulate the building's corner emplacement, a gesture further emphasized by Miquel Blay's exuberant stone sculpture attached one level above. Immediately after the foyer, an approximately 12 feet deep space accommodates a stone double stairway leading up to the *piano-nobile* that provides access to the main auditorium floor, and farther up to the mezzanine and the auditorium's upper seating platform.

The auditorium hall is, expectedly, the largest and most important space. It consists of a lusciously decorated multistory oval space framed by a continuous colonnade made of short columns supporting two levels of lateral booths. The space is crowned by a splendid stained-glass leaded skylight, a reverse cupola designed by Domènech i Montaner, featuring a bright yellow sun that illuminates the seating hall with vibrant multicolored light. The stage is framed by a large stone arch with attached allegorical sculptural groups (a bust of Beethoven and the Valkyries' cavalcade inspired by Wagner's famous work). An intense and luminous polychrome decoration based on floral and other vegetal motifs abounds throughout the hall's interior, as if a beautiful flowery garden grew under the skylight's presiding sun.

The spatial distribution is equally clear in section. The ground floor accommodates the already mentioned entrance hall (in the original building), the offices of the Orfeó Català below the auditorium seating, and a choral room under the main stage. The upper floors house the seating hall's various levels, and at the building's front, a beautiful double-story room—now bearing Lluís Millet's name—used as the upper-level foyer and gathering hall. This large room is exactly above the ample entrance hall and opens to a deep, multistory, highly articulated, multilayered, and spatially complex balcony— the distinctive feature of the building's exterior—punctuated by two lines of polychrome ceramic-clad columns topped with floral *capitals* (designed by Lluís Bru, an assiduous collaborator of Domènech i Montaner); the columns support brick pointed arches placed perpendicular to the building's front, which, in turn, support semicircular projecting balconies two stories above. Thus, the façade—which with similar motifs wraps around the building's corner along street Amadeu Vives—appears as an independent element with its own spatial and constructive logic. This was a distinctive characteristic of Domènech i Montaner, who had developed a whole theory based on the structural and volumetric independence of the façade.

Reminiscences of *Mudéjar* and neo-Gothic architecture are inevitable when one observes the vibrant coloration of the façade and the intricate work in brick, ceramic, and stone. At the Palau, as in most works of the Modernismo Catalan (for example, Gaudí's Casa Vicens-Montaner and **Park Güell**, and Puig i Cadalfach's **Casa Terradas**, all three located in Barcelona), this revival of historical sources was associated with a wider sociopolitical and cultural project, which, under the auspices of the *Renaixença*, aimed to reassert a Catalan national identity. This was already noted by renowned historian Manfredo Tafuri, who commented that the Palau's "Mudéjar, neomedieval and neobaroque roots burst in a visual feast in which, especially in the sophisticated interior of the Palau—the community is invited to recognize itself" (Tafuri 1979, 89).

In the early 1980s, along with a revived interest in the architectural legacy of Modernismo Catalan, the building began a long process of restoration and adaptation to contemporary needs that demanded an important addition to Domènech i Montaner's original masterpiece. The project was commissioned to the well-known Barcelona-based architect Oscar Tusquets and his collaborators Lluís Clotet, Carlos Díaz, and Ignacio Paricio. The addition was done in two major phases completed in 1989 and 2000, respectively. The first phase included the addition of a library, archives, classrooms, offices, and many other support functions for the Orfeó Català; this was accomplished by adding a small building at the building's rear—the western corner—as wells as shortening the *nave* of the adjacent church of Sant Francesc de Paula. The truncation of the church's nave permitted the generation of a small public outdoor area for the new exit from the Palau. In the second phase, the church was finally removed and transferred to another site and a new annex building put in its place. The annex, which roughly occupies the same area where the church was, houses an underground auditorium for 600 people and a restaurant. The exit plaza on the side of the building was enlarged, generating an elegant contemporary exit to the early twentieth-century building. The annex's façade on Carrer Sant Pere Més Alt was aligned with the short façade of the adjacent Plaza Lluís Millet, generating a more generous visual and physical space for the main approach to the building from the city's historic center. The materials and details of the added structures—glass, brick, and steel—establish an interesting dialogue with the original building, harmonizing without competing with the luscious ornamentation of Domènech i Montaner's work. Tusquets' and his partners' intelligent addition, and their exceptional restoration of Domènech's building, revitalized the area and gave new relevance to the outstanding structure and cultural activity of the Orfeó Català. The original 1908 building has been part of UNESCO's World Heritage program since 1997.

Further Reading

Borras, Maria Lluïsa. *Lluís Domènech i Montaner*. Barcelona: Ediciones Polígrafa, 1970.

Montaner, Josep María. *Barcelona: A City and Its Architecture*. Cologne; New York: Taschen, 1997.

Sack, Manfred. *Lluís Domènech i Montaner: Palau de la Música Catalana*. Stuttgart: Edition Axel Menges, 1995.

Solà-Morales, Ignasi de. *Minimal Architecture in Barcelona: Building on the Built City*. Milan: Electa Edizioni, 1986.

Tafuri, Manfredo, and Dal Co, Francesco. *Contemporary Architecture*. New York: Harry N. Abrams, 1979.

PALLARS HOUSING COMPLEX, BARCELONA, CATALONIA

Style: Neorealist Modern Architecture
Dates: 1958–1959
Architects: Oriol Bohigas and Josep María Martorell

The small housing block located on Carrer de Pallars is the most significant Spanish work of the critique of modern architecture's urban postulates launched toward the end of the 1950s by some critics and theorists.

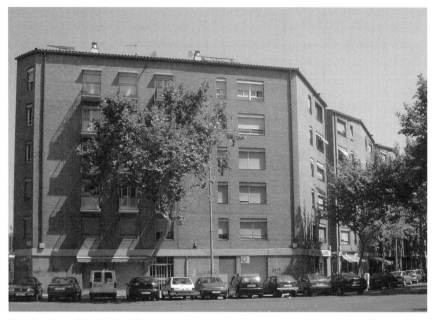

Exterior view of the Pallars Housing Complex at the intersection of Carrer de Pallars and Carrer Lope de Vega.

This critique had immediate acceptance in many avant-garde circles that believed that the application of the principles and strategies put forward by modern architecture for designing cities and social urban housing had been exhausted. One of the most interesting critiques of modern architecture originated in Italy, where architects and theorists such as Gio Ponti, Ludovico Quaroni, and Mario Ridolfi initiated a movement that had strong links with contemporaneous Italian Neorealist explorations in cinema and literature. These propositions were followed with interest in many parts of the world where similar concerns with the dogmatic postulates of modern architecture had began to surface, especially among emerging professionals. Oriol Bohigas and Josep María Martorell, the younger founding members of Barcelona's *Grup R* and authors of the Pallars Housing Complex, belong to this generation of young architects who pioneered the social and urban critique of the universalizing precepts of modern architecture in Spain. Later joined by David Mackay and Albert Puigdomènech, their partnership eventually became a leading and highly influential architectural practice in Barcelona and Spain, especially in the post-Franco era.

As is often the case with nonspeculative real estate housing developments, the project for this housing development was the consequence of a governmental initiative launched during Francisco Franco's dictatorial regime (1939–1975), which stimulated private industry to provide housing for em-

ployees in exchange for tax benefits. The Pallars Housing Complex was commissioned by a metallurgical company that originally intended to build
apartments for its employees in an entire city block demarcated by the Carrer de Pallars, Carrer Lope de Vega, Camí Antic de Valencia, and Carrer
d'Espronceda in Barcelona's popular neighborhood of Poblenou. Originally,
the project envisioned the development of a complete city block defined
along the lines of Ildefons Cerdà's praised urban plan for the extension of
Barcelona (1859).

Bohigas and Martorell conceived the rental housing project as a system of
repetitive built modules along the street that, through a specially designed
corner unit, would be replicated in all four street fronts of the city block to
constitute a coherent and uniform complex consisting of street-front apartment blocks with a central open court; however, only one of the four street
segments, the side of the city block facing Carrer de Pallars, was completed.
The segment of apartments is comprised of six independent blocks—four in
the center framed the two special corner blocks at the extremes—aligned
along the street front. The four typical blocks are separated by five recessed
stairways that provide individual access to a cluster of twenty-two side-to-
side and back-to-back apartments organized at split-level intervals; there are
five levels of apartments on the street side and six on the rear side, that is,
ten apartments face the street and twelve face the unaccomplished central
court. The split-level concept optimized the efficiency of the vertical circulation and increased the privacy of the bedrooms placed on the interior side
of the unit that are organized around a closed internal court—a vertical shaft
for air and illumination—of reduced dimensions. The corner units were specially designed to conform with the chamfered corner of Cerdà's typical city
block for Barcelona; the corner units accommodate two apartments per floor
that are accessible from nonrecessed central stairs. The ground floor on the
street side of the entire segment was destined for neighborhood-scale commercial activity.

As determined by the building regulations for this type of initiative, each
housing unit (the individual apartment) has 60 square meters (slightly less
than 650 square feet) that include a rather open living-dining-kitchen area
and three small bedrooms. The living areas and the larger of the three bedrooms receive direct natural light and ventilation through windows that open
to the exterior of the block, either to the street side or to the (intended) open-
air central courtyard; instead the two smaller bedrooms open to the enclosed
vertical shaft for air and illumination pierced at the center of each cluster of
four apartments. The split-level disposition of apartments helped to control
visual privacy from one apartment to the other across the reduced dimensions of the internal court.

In addition to its radical departure from mainstream housing typologies
of the period, the salient characteristics of the building are the studied volumetric articulation of the individual blocks and the intentional use of tra-

ditional and domestic materials and construction technology. The front plane of each of the four typical blocks that constitute the central portion of the street-front forms has a central fold that generates a soft "V" shape matching the soft pitch of the roof that covers it. This—along with the recessed stairways that separate the blocks—modulates and activates the plane of the façade with a remarkable economy of gestures. The use of red brick, standard windows, exposed downspouts, and ceramic roof tiles, all materials typically used in traditional construction in Spain, are the technological correlate of the architects' Neorealist proposal. The subtle modulation of the exterior planes, which was also implemented on the inner side of the city block; the continuous horizontal concrete cornice that demarcates a difference between the commercial and residential portions of the street front; and the balconies that project out on the south-facing corner of the block appear as the architects' only formal gestures in an otherwise extremely austere building.

Bohigas and Martorell's building demonstrated that the city could still grow according to Ildefons Cerdà's celebrated plan for Barcelona, originated exactly 100 years before; it also proved that it was possible to make an engaged, discursive, and critical architecture that continued knitting the traditional social and urban fabric of the city using traditional construction materials and techniques. The relevance of the project was immediately recognized by local critics and professionals who distinguished the Pallars Housing Complex with the 1959 "Premio FAD," one of the most important architectural awards in Barcelona and Spain.

Further Reading

Drew, Philip. *Real Space: The Architecture of Martorell, Bohigas, Mackay, Puigdomènech*. Tubingen-Berlin: E. Wasmuth, 1993.

Frampton, Kenneth. *Martorell, Bohigas, Mackay: Treinte ans d'Architecture, 1954–1984*. Milan and Paris: Electa-Moniteur, 1985.

Rodríguez, Carme, and Torres, Jorge. *Grup R*. Barcelona: Editorial Gustavo Gili, 1994.

Ruiz Cabrero, Gabriel. *The Modern in Spain: Architecture after 1948*. Cambridge, MA; London: The MIT Press, 2001.

PARK GÜELL, BARCELONA, CATALONIA

Style: Modernismo Catalan
Dates: 1900–1914
Architect: Antoni Gaudí

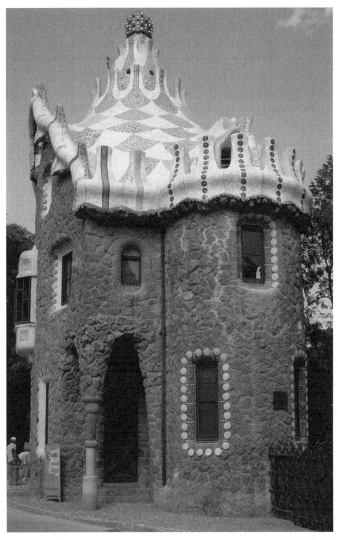

Exterior view of one of the pavilions that frame the entrance to Park Güell.

Park Güell is one of the most astonishing, enchanting, and lyrical creations of all architecture in Spain and worldwide, as well as a unique—yet unaccomplished—twentieth-century experiment in architecture, planning, and landscape. Today, it is a municipal public park owned by the city of Barcelona, but in its origins it emanated from the long and fruitful association between Catalan magnate Eusebio Güell and his favorite architect, Antoni Gaudí. Together, Güell and Gaudí conceived the park as a residential development for Barcelona's cultivated and wealthy elite, detached from the increasingly industrialized center of the city.

Eusebio Güell (1846–1918) was a prosperous industrialist and merchant who had inherited the successful textile business of his ancestors. He was a key member of a group of Catalan businessmen, thinkers, and artists who had a very definite project: the development of a political, religious, and cultural movement known as the *Renaixença* (Renaissance in Catalan language), deeply rooted in Catalonia's past, traditions, and national sentiment. Antoni Gaudí was not only a member of the Renaixença but also one of Barcelona's better-known architects who had already realized celebrated buildings such as the Casa Vicens-Montaner (1878–1880), a summer house in Comillas (known as "El Capricho," c. 1883), and the Palau Güell (1885–1889). More significantly, along with Lluís Domènech i Montaner and Josep Puig i Cadalfach, he was one of the referents of the by then well-established *Modernismo Catalan*, a primarily Catalan architectural movement somewhat related to other contemporaneous European developments such as Belgium and France's *Art Nouveau*, Germany's *Jugendstil*, and Vienna's *Secessionist Movement* with which shared formal characteristics and a desire for renewal of architectural language.

Güell and Gaudí shared the core of beliefs and ideas of the Renaixença and had already collaborated in numerous opportunities. In 1884–1887, Gaudí designed and built the stables and gatehouse for Güell's family property on Barcelona's Avenue Pedralbes. Later, Gaudí built Güell's new urban residence in Barcelona (Palau Güell 1885–1889), and in 1898 they collaborated on the ambitious project for the Colonia Güell—a textile workers' community created by Güell in Santa Coloma de Cervelló—of which only fragments were completed, notably Gaudí's crypt for the church (1908–1916) and other buildings designed by Gaudí's followers and disciples.

Park Güell was envisioned as a model residential garden city equipped with modern facilities such as electricity, a sanitation system, and a private reserve of water. The overall idea echoed English garden cities that Güell knew very well; his main intention, however, was to create an idyllic setting as a reaction to overcrowded cities that resulted from the sharp increase in urban industrial activity. As Conrad Kent and Dennis Prindle convincingly stated, originally "Park Güell was a residential retreat from urban chaos into an enclave that would reconcile traditional Catalan culture with the wealth and technical innovations of the machine age" (Kent and Prindle 1993, 27). Gaudí elaborated the Park's masterplan—the land subdivision—and designed and built the necessary infrastructure facilities such as roads, paths, and service and community buildings, which were fundamental components of the overall design. Expectedly, the whole was to be infused with the ideals of the Renaixença that Güell, Gaudí, and others to whom they directed their initiative shared profoundly.

The development is located in a rugged and stepped site known as the Muntanya Pelada ("Bald Mount") on the hillsides of the Collserola Mountains. More precisely, it is approximately two miles north of the center of the city. The slightly more than thirty-seven-acre site is completely enclosed by an approximately 9-foot-tall stone wall interrupted only by the seven entrance gates that are placed at strategic locations. The main gateway is at the lowest part of the stepped site, on Carrer d'Olot (formerly known as Carrer de Milans). It is flanked by two small pavilions integrated to the surrounding wall and originally intended as the concierge's house and the park's administrative building, but today used as a small exhibition pavilion and a gift shop. However small, they are architecturally marvelous, two plastic volumes entirely built in stone and covered by complex roofs—one of them featuring a double-helix tower crowned by a cross—fully covered by a magnificent ceramic skin made out of small and irregular fragments of colorful glazed tiles—a technique known as *trencadis*—arranged in geometrical patterns and creating forms that stimulate symbolic associations.

Beyond the gate lodges and the enclosing wall the park houses a large va-

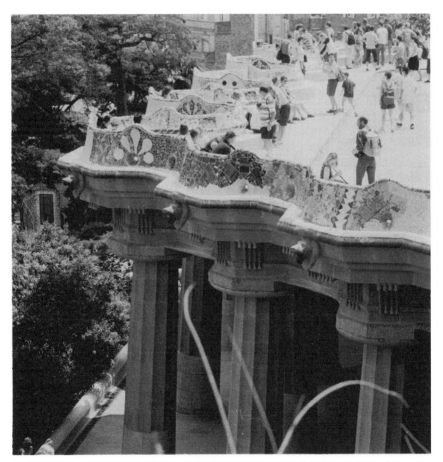

Defined by the sinous bench, the open-air theater at Park Güell is placed above the market place, which consists of a dense space punctuated by hollow columns inspired in the Doric order.

riety of buildings and structures conceived by Güell and Gaudí for community use. They consist of a market hall, an open-air theater, an ascending promenade partially covered by arcades, secondary paths, and a chapel. All of them were intended to service the sixty private residences—one in each of the sixty triangular lots into which the residential portion of the site was subdivided—that were to be built in the residential development. More importantly, the service and infrastructure buildings were indispensable for Güell's and Gaudí's social, religious, and cultural *programme*. In effect, the layout of the park, with its iconic imagery, theater, market, and sinuous paths that would have culminated in an unbuilt chapel at the peak of the site combined the secular and the sacred, that is, the cultural and religious intentions that were deeply rooted in the Renaixença's objectives to promote a Catalan national sentiment.

Immediately past the main gate, an ample exterior hall dominated by the suggestive presence of a trencadis-covered dragon-lizard fountain in front of a monumental stairway, collects and redistributes the numerous circulation systems that traverse the park. To the right, a winding vehicular road climbs up the hill servicing the sixty triangular lots of the projected residential portion; to the left, a sinuous walkway leads uphill and eventually reaches "the Calvary," a path that would have led to the chapel. The steep level differences are often negotiated by marvelous rough stone constructions—bridges, viaducts, grottos, galleries, colonnades—rich in evocative associations and mysterious meanings.

The climax of the park is, without doubt, the complex structure that, opening directly in front of the exterior hall and on axis with the main gate, accommodates the open-air theater and the covered market. The latter is a *hypostyle* open hall composed of thick striated columns suggestive of a *Doric* order supporting a large terrace above. The columns are hollow and contain drainage conduits that collect rain water and conduct it to a cistern, a reserve of water used for irrigation purposes placed below the market's floor; remarkably, the sculptural tile-covered dragon-lizard—reminiscent of Python, the mythical serpent—is nothing else but a device to control the cistern's overflow. The market space is approximately 130 feet wide by 140 feet deep. Above the market, and doubling its depth, the open-air theater, also known as the "Greek theater," is an ample gathering platform conceived for a wide variety of community activities that offers panoramic views of the city and the Mediterranean beyond. The frontal part of the theater, the portion located exactly above the market, is framed by a beautiful and evocative serpentine bench entirely covered by trencadis in a large variety of arranged compositions, a work personally undertaken by Gaudí's talented young collaborator Josep María Jujol. The intricate design patterns and vivid colors are somewhat reminiscent of the profusely tile-covered surfaces of Islamic palaces such as the **Palace of La Alhambra** and the *Alcazars*, as well as of *Mudéjar* architecture.

Güell's intention to develop a residential garden city failed because it did

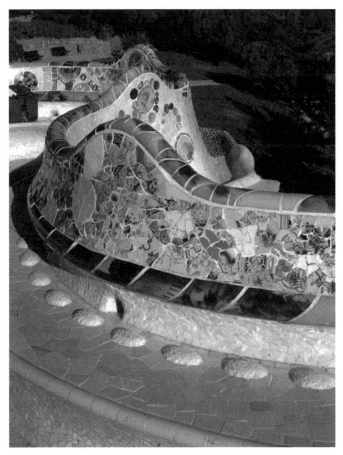

Detail of the sinuous bench covered by *trencadis* at Park Güell.

not find the expected response from Barcelona's elite. Even though he lived in one of the park's residences between 1906 and 1918, and Gaudí lived, between 1906 and 1925, in the model house designed by Francesc Berenguer, only two other lots of the original sixty were sold and only one additional house was built. Thus, the park as an idealized residential enclave never materialized, becoming, instead, an over-scaled private park for only three family groups (Güell, Gaudí, and the Trias family, close friends of Eusebio Güell). Paradoxically, the buildings and infrastructure conceived to service the residences were completed, but they hardly served their purpose. Today, they are testimony to Güell's failed intentions, but also to his incomparable patronage of his architect, the brilliant Antonio Gaudí, who—like the great masters of architecture and landscape that preceded him, such as the creators of La Alhambra, or Le Notre in Versailles (France)—domesticated an inhospitable site and transformed it into a delightful garden and an extraordinary architectural jewel.

Once abandoned as a garden-city project or as a private park, the property was purchased by the city of Barcelona in 1922 and one year later became a municipal park; however, it soon fell into disrepair and neglect, partly as a result of the suppression of Catalan national expressions imposed by Spain's dictatorial governments of the first half of the twentieth century. Partial restoration began after the 1950s, but it would not be until the mid-1980s, when the park was selected for inclusion in UNESCO's list of World Heritage sites (1984) that a more strict and thorough restoration of the park began. Today, Park Güell is one of the most revered, famous, and visited parks in the world, a sublime and enchanting site, an ascendance through extravagant paths, platforms, and ramps toward the top of a hill where one can observe the city from which its mentors wanted to escape. It is a delightful park that, day after day, attracts thousands of local visitors and tourists from all over the world who enjoy the site conceived as a singular enclave, a synthesis of landscape and architecture, nature, and artifice.

Further Reading

Chueca Goitía, Fernando. *Historia de la Arquitectura Española: Edad Moderna-Edad Contemporánea*. Vol. 2. Madrid: Editorial Dossat, 1965.

Curtis, William J. R. *Modern Architecture since 1900*. 3rd ed. London: Phaidon Press Limited, 1996.

Giedion-Welcker, Carola. *Park Güell de A. Gaudí*. New York: George Wittenborn, 1966.

Kent, Conrad, and Prindle, Dennis. *Park Güell*. New York: Princeton Architectural Press, 1993.

Montaner, Josep María. *Barcelona: A City and Its Architecture*. Cologne; New York: Taschen, 1997.

Zerbst, Rainer. *Antoni Gaudí*. Cologne: Taschen, 1992.

PEINE DEL VIENTO. *See* Plaza del Tenis and Peine del Viento.

PLAZA DEL TENIS AND PEINE DEL VIENTO, SAN SEBASTIÁN (DONOSTIA), GUIPÚZCOA

Style: Contemporary Architecture
Dates: 1975–1977
Architects: Luis Peña Ganchegui; Sculptor, Eduardo Chillida

The architectural-sculptural ensemble of the Plaza del Tenis and Peine del Viento, located on the western extreme of the bay of San Sebastián (known in Basque language as Donostia) is a wonderful public space where architecture, sculpture, and landscape—both natural and artificial—converge to create a place of singular evocative and poetic characteristics. The ensemble is the result of the collaboration between two natives of the Basque Country, the architect Luis Peña Ganchegui, and sculptor Eduardo Chillida. The latter is one of the most important and internationally famous artists of the second half of the twentieth century; his work is characterized by abstract sculptures in iron, alabaster, and granite, and large-scale site-specific sculptural ensembles, usually in public places. Commissioned by the San Sebastián City Council, the intention of the Plaza del Tenis (the name derives from its location adjacent to San Sebastián's Royal Tennis Club) was to provide a backdrop for Chillida's monumental sculptural ensemble called "Peine del Viento," a project completed in 1977 on which the sculptor had been working since the 1950s. Peña Ganchegui was commissioned for this project largely as a consequence of his highly successful previous urban project for the Plaza de la Trinidad, also in San Sebastián.

The bay of San Sebastián configures a large, crescent-shape sandy beach known as Playa de la Concha, which is framed by two rocky promontories—Mounts Urgull and Igeldo—on the east and west, respectively. The old part of this royal city is concentrated around the Mont Urgull but, since the beginning of the twentieth century—when the city became a fashionable seafront destination for the royal family and Spain's aristocratic class—it has expanded westward toward the rocky edge of Mont Igeldo; thus, a long urban promenade (nearly two miles long), known as the Paseo de la Concha, developed alongside the beach linking the two promontories. The Plaza del Tenis marks the end of the promenade constituting a civic space that works as a prelude for Chillida's breathtaking sculptural group.

Peña Ganchegui developed the project as a carefully studied sequence of "spatial events" that prepare the visitor for the contemplation of the vibrant seafront landscape and the confrontation with Chillida's triad of "wind-combs," an assemblage of three twisted and warped rust-iron elements that

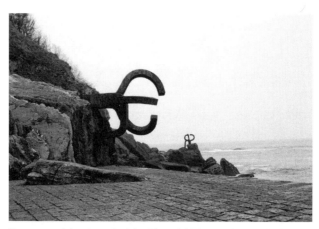

Fragment of the tip-end of the Plaza del Tenis with two of Chillida's sculptures emerging from the rock.

are embedded in the stone and seem, indeed, to "comb" the wind around Mount Igueldo. Thus, the long open-air space works in relationship with the sculptural group but does not incorporate it within its physical limits.

The sharp vertical edge of the promontory is both a limit and a point of departure for the architectural proposal. This richly textured and vertically stratified natural wall constitutes the site's irregular western border, while the ocean marks the eastern and northern limits materialized through a wide and low granite parapet-wall that wraps around the northeastern corner to eventually become the platform that precedes the sculptural ensemble. The plaza itself consists of a series of platforms entirely paved with rectangular granite cobblestones from far away Porrino's quarries. There are two main platforms: one at street level directly linked with the strolling promenade, and a higher platform that stretches along the western edge of the site defined by the promontory's natural vertical wall. The lower platform is further subdivided into three components: an ample space that operates as an open-air "vestibule," a considerably larger gathering space at the opposite end of the promenade, and a long narrow corridor framed—on the ocean side—by the low parapet wall and, on the opposite side, by sitting-height stepping-up platforms; this corridor connects the two larger spaces. Conceptually, yet not formally, the whole echoes a Greek amphitheater, a place carved against the rock in intricate and intimate relationship with the surrounding landscape.

The more elevated platform offers privileged vantage points to contemplate the sea, the nearby islands, the rocky promontories, and the city's seafront facing Playa de la Concha; conversely, the three areas of the lower platform offer differentiated experiences to the visitor. The "vestibule," a polygonal space framed by steps and the vertical edge of the higher platform, is more related to the city, connected to the end of the promenade, the Royal Tennis Club, and the sandy shoreline. The other gathering space, at the other end of the promenade and defined by similar elements, is clearly related to the infinite spectacle of the ocean's horizon, the rough waves colliding against the rocky promontory, and the impressive presence of Chillida's sculptures. Between the two, a long corridor-like area reinstates the strolling promenade as linkage between city and landscape.

Subtle details abound throughout the project: fragments of bare rock that jut out on the surface of the platforms; saw-tooth pavement edges that amplify the visual and textural relationship between the paved platforms and sharp walls of vertically stratified rock; and a faint, yet visible, line "drafted" on the floor by the convergence of different planes of same-material pavement marking two rotating crosses connected by a long line that splits in half the long corridor space, which is nothing but a clever device to guide the drainage of water through the paved areas. Perhaps the most astonishing detail is the group of seven "mysterious" holes cut on a few pavers that project out on the northeastern quadrant of the larger gathering space at the corner of the site; these orifices work in complicity with nature as blow-holes that, in stormy weather, shoot up jets of water that penetrate through an old unused water pipeline that existed in the site.

The Plaza del Tenis is a wonderful architectural intervention in a breathtaking landscape; a minimal work of architecture that revalorizes the natural beauty of the place and creates a perfect setting for Eduardo Chillida's splendid Peine del Viento. Together, the two independent but closely related works—a granite-paved plaza as culmination of a strolling promenade and an extraordinary sculptural group—establish a great formal dialogue in which the contribution of nature as energetic participant is an additional circum-

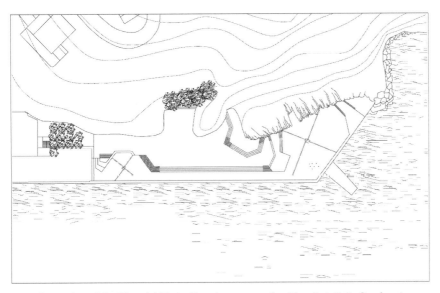

Overall site plan of the Plaza del Tenis. *Drawing courtesy of architect Luis Peña Ganchegui.*

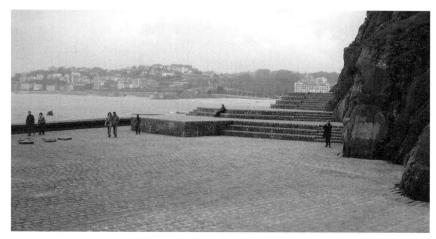

General view of a large fragment of the Plaza del Tenis with the bay of San Sebastián and the city skyline on the background.

stance that activates the changing atmosphere in which they are placed. The Plaza del Tenis and Peine del Viento ensemble are justly regarded as one of the most accomplished collaborations between an architect and a sculptor, not only in Spain but also throughout the world.

Further Reading

Curtis, William J. R. *Modern Architecture since 1900*. 3rd ed. London: Phaidon Press Limited, 1996.

Ruiz Cabrero, Gabriel. *The Modern in Spain: Architecture after 1948*. Cambridge, MA; London: The MIT Press, 2001.

Saliga, Pauline, and Thorne, Martha. *Building a New Spain: Contemporary Spanish Architecture*. Barcelona: Editorial Gustavo Gili, 1992.

Solà-Morales, Ignasi de, Capitel, Antón, and Buchanan, Peter et al., eds. *Birkhäuser Architectural Guide, Spain 1920–1999*. Basel: Birkhäuser Verlag, 1998.

PLAZA DELS PAÏSOS CATALANS, BARCELONA, CATALONIA

Style: Contemporary Architecture

Dates: 1981–1983

Architects: Helio Piñón and Albert Viaplana, with the collaboration of Enric Miralles

Also known as Plaza de la Estació Sants (Sants Railroad Station Plaza), the Plaza dels Països Catalans is one of the most innovative, controversial, and celebrated twentieth century public spaces of Barcelona in particular, and Spain in general. Designed by the Barcelona-based office of Helio Piñón and Albert Viaplana, with the collaboration of the then young Enric Miralles, this plaza has become a paradigm of end-of-the-century minimalist architecture as well as a building that stands as a symbol and point of departure for the vigorous role of Barcelona's architecture through the 1980s and 1990s. This protagonist position was the consequence of many factors, such as Catalonia's historically demonstrated passion for architecture as a manifestation of cultural identity, and the recuperation of a regional form of government after the end of Francisco Franco's dictatorial regime (1939–1975); but especially, it was the result of the cultural, urbanistic, and political vision of Oriol Bohigas—principal of Martorell, Bohigas, and Mackay, one of the most prestigious architectural firms of the second part of the twentieth century—who, from his influential position as Director of Planning at Barcelona's City Hall, initiated a process of urban and architectural renewal of the city that peaked with the celebrated works built for the Olympic Games of 1992. The Plaza dels Països Catalans was among the first group of small-scale urban inter-

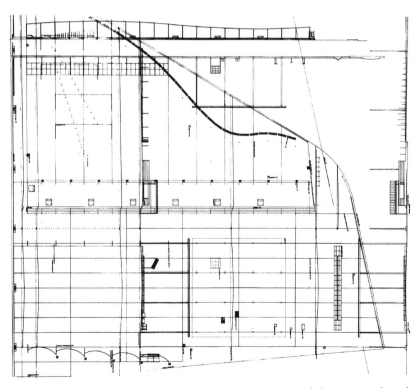

Ground floor plan of the Plaza dels Països Catalans, with sections and elevations overlapped. *Drawing courtesy of architect Albert Viaplana.*

ventions with which Bohigas started the process of recuperation, renovation, and modernization of Barcelona's public spaces.

Originally, the commission was for designing two trapezoidal open spaces located on the frontal sides of Estació de Sants, Barcelona's largest and most important railroad station. The architects—Piñón and Viaplana—developed a scheme for the two spaces, but in agreement with Oriol Bohigas, they concentrated their efforts and allocated financial resources to complete one of the two spaces—the front side, considering the location of the station with respect to the city's center—leaving the completion of the other for a later date (Buchanan 1984, 36). The Estació de Sants is in the west part of the city and is the point of convergence of numerous communication systems (railroad, subway, short and long distance buses); in turn, the Plaza dels Països Catalans is located on the northeastern front of the station, at the intersection of numerous wide and heavily circulated avenues. The existing urban and architectural context consisted of a disconnected accumulation of buildings from various periods, and whose only shared characteristics were their proximity to the train station and a certain disregard for configuring a place of civic significance or a coherent architectural ensemble. Furthermore, since the railroad tracks ran under the space of the plaza, there were severe limitations to the load that the site could bear. Evidently, the task given to Piñón and Viaplana was certainly challenging; this was immediately perceived and commented on by the architects: "At first we felt desolate. Everyone who knows the place where we had to work would understand it . . . we consider that, from that moment on, only the project had to sustain the feeling that the place would initiate" (Piñón and Viaplana; project description).

The architects' conceptual reaction to their "desolation" and to the severe limitations imposed by the site conditions was exemplary, and they succeeded in creating a place of undoubted civic significance and scale that echoes the abstract work of minimalist and conceptual artists. This was accomplished—to borrow Ignasi de Solà-Morales' precise description—"by using a common repertory of architectural elements" (Solà-Morales 1986, 18). These consist of a large uninterrupted paved surface, an over-scaled square canopy, an undulating pergola, and an ample variety of fixed urban artifacts—a clock, benches, lampposts, a fountain, and more—that together engendered a place of wonderful evocative characteristics. The restricted repertory of materials (mainly granite and steel), forms (square, rectangle, sinuous curve, slanting posts), and colors (the pale grayish pink of granite, black and grey painted steel) contributed to the coalescence of the chaotic spatial surroundings.

The limitations imposed by the low load-bearing capacity of the site determined several aspects of the project. As was typical of their work, the first design decision Piñón and Viaplana made was to define the entire extension of the site as a unified area of intervention, a virtually continuous, smooth, horizontal surface that reaches all the way over to the streets' curb. This *mineral surface* paved in pink granite constitutes an abstracted territory subtly demarcated by a directional pattern of parallel lines—a basic ordering principle—that originated

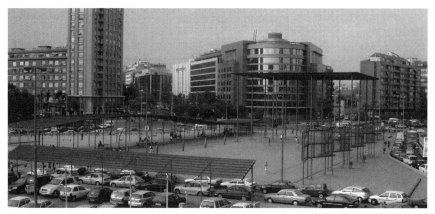

Ensemble of the Plaza dels Països from the rooftop of the *Estación de Sants*.

in borrowing one dimension of the station's own constructive modulation. How-ever, even if perceived as a continuous abstract plane, the continuity of the paved surface is altered by subtle differences, "topographical" accidents of the planar surface. The site's roughly trapezoidal form is subtly divided into two different halves—left (southeast) and right (northwest) as one looks toward the station's front—by an imaginary line originated in the station's central axis.

The tall, intentionally over-scaled canopy that presides over the plaza at the eastern quadrant of the site gives a recognizable identity to the place. It consists of a 30-meter (almost 100-foot)-square roof that hovers over 15 me-ters (nearly 50 feet) above the horizontal surface of the plaza supported on sixteen ultra-slender metal posts. Peter Buchanan referred to this element as a "palio" (a temporary awning to shade visiting dignitaries); thus considered, this canopy is a fundamental element of the plaza that dignifies and democ-ratizes the place and its occupants, the everyday citizen who, passing under it, becomes, even if temporarily, a dignitary. Placed at a short distance from the large square canopy, the undulating pergola runs along the central axis that divides the plaza in two. The materials are the same as those of the canopy—steel posts, metal mesh roofs—but the spatial characteristics are different: in contrast to the static nondirectional square form and flatness of the canopy's roof, the undulated form and the evident directionality of this element engenders a dynamism that seems to evoke the rhythmical linear movement of the trains that run directly below; in fact, the pergola can be read as an extension of the station's quays into the open fabric of the city.

All the other elements of the plaza—another linear canopy with an in-clined mesh roof that faces the station's façade; an elegant clock on a curved steel post; a long bench in pink and black granite; a free-standing wall with an opening; a long, sinuous sequence of wooden benches; granite tables on steel structures; a beautiful fountain in stainless steel; a steel structure that supports a battery of reflectors that illuminate the canopy's roof from below;

and short, enigmatic slanted posts that mask floodlights put at floor level—help to reinforce the uncompromised abstraction and rigor of the project. Perhaps, the most interesting aspect of Piñón and Viaplana's intervention is that without having attempted to mask the chaotic and disconnected surroundings (in fact, the visual permeability of the different elements does quite the opposite) and the plaza's location at an busy intersection of various transportation systems, the Plaza dels Països Catalans is a place in which time and space are suddenly suspended, even if temporarily, equally at day and night, when the shadows cast by the various elements or the floodlights and reflectors draw a different space on the extended horizontal surface of pink granite and the metal mesh roofs.

As soon as it was completed in 1983, the Plaza dels Països Catalans became a celebrated work; its hard surfaces, the virtual absence of vegetation or softening devices, its monumental horizontality, and the precise design and scale of the few elements that populate it converted it into a paradigmatic example of an urban intervention, a minimalist expression that transformed a visually charged environment into a new, significant public space.

Further Reading

Buchanan, Peter. "Regenerating Barcelona with Parks and Plaza." *Architectural Review* 175, no. 1048 (June 1984): 32–46.

Curtis, William J. R. *Modern Architecture since 1900*. 3rd ed. London: Phaidon Press Limited, 1996.

Piñón, Helio, and Viaplana, Albert. Project Description and Documentation (courtesy of the architects).

Ruiz Cabrero, Gabriel. *Espagne Architecture 1965–1988*. Milan and Paris: Electa-Moniteur, 1990.

Saliga, Pauline, and Thorne, Martha. *Building a New Spain: Contemporary Spanish Architecture*. Barcelona: Editorial Gustavo Gili, 1992.

Solà-Morales, Ignasi de. *Minimal Architecture in Barcelona: Building on the Built City*. Milan: Electa Edizioni, 1986.

Solà-Morales, Ignasi de, ed. *Contemporary Spanish Architecture: An Eclectic Panorama*. New York: Rizzoli, 1986.

PLAZA MAYOR OF MADRID, MADRID, COMUNIDAD DE MADRID

Styles: Baroque Architecture; Neoclassical Architecture
Dates: 1617–1619; circa 1790–1853
Architects: Juan Gómez de Mora; Juan de Villanueva

The Plaza Mayor is the most important public space in Madrid's histori-cal center, as well as a relevant architectural and urbanistic work in its own right. Madrid, the capital of Spain and the seat of the royal court, is lo-cated at the virtual geographic center of the country's extended territory bor-dered by the seas. Contrary to many other European capitals (Paris, for instance, was the Romans' ancient Lutetia and already in the early Middle Ages was the seat of the French kingdom), Madrid does not have ancient or royal origins to claim, but it was the result of a political decision; the oldest known trace of an organized settlement assigns it the role of a small fortifi-cation created in the 800s by the occupying Muslim rulers. This outpost was part of a defensive line that protected the very important city of Toledo, his-torical capital of the old *Visigothic* kingdom, located only forty miles south of Madrid. In 1085, the Castilian king Alfonso VI conquered the Muslim garri-

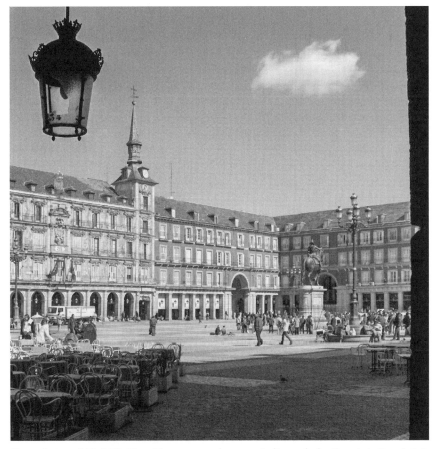

General view of Madrid's Plaza Mayor across the square's diagonal; the *Casa de la Panadería* is on the left. *Photo courtesy of Parsa Khalili.*

son as part of a large strategic plan to recuperate the territories of central Iberia, including the important city of Toledo. In the Middle Ages, Madrid evolved as a typical small medieval town with an overcrowded center of narrow streets and internal disputes. Until the sixteenth century its status and importance as a settlement of the expanding kingdom was marginal at best.

In 1492, with the conquest of Granada and the expulsion of the last Muslim rulers, the Catholic Kings Isabel and Fernando finally succeeded in unifying the entire territory under Christian rule, inaugurating a period that would eventually reach Imperial status in the sixteenth century with their grandson the Holy Roman Emperor Carlos V. Yet, even in that expanding period, the Kingdom of Spain did not have an established capital; the kings and their court were rather itinerant, temporarily settling in some of the territory's most important cities such as Granada, Toledo, and Santiago de Compostela. However, in 1561, Felipe II (son and successor of Carlos V), appointed underdeveloped Madrid as the permanent seat of his royal court and capital of the kingdom. The decision was part of his political centralist project and was partially based on the town's potential for expansion. Expectedly, the small town grew rapidly and in less than one century its population multiplied by six.

Focused in the construction of his ambitious and emblematic monastic and palatine complex of the **Monastery of El Escorial**, Felipe II did not necessarily pay much attention to the needs and development of his kingdom's new capital. However, the earliest attempts to provide urban order to the chaotic center of the city date from his reign and were planned by his favorite architect, Juan de Herrera, who in the mid-to late-1500s made some interventions in the medieval fabric of the city to create the city's Plaza Mayor as a large, open public space of rectangular proportions, in the location of the former Plaza del Arrabal and market dating from medieval times. It did not take long for the new space to become the center of the city's civic, social, and festive activity. The Casa de la Panadería (headquarters of the powerful Bakers' guild) was built on the plaza's northern side in 1590. Herrera's successor as royal architect, Francisco Gómez de Mora, continued working on the organization of the plaza. However, it was his successor and nephew, Juan Gómez de Mora, who between 1617 and 1619 gave final urban and architectural form to Madrid's Plaza Mayor.

Based on the work of his two predecessors, Juan Gómez de Mora conceived the Plaza Mayor as a rectangular space—approximately 300 by 360 foot—entirely paved and enclosed by a rather uniform façade. Typologically and architecturally, the Plaza Mayor is related to Paris' almost contemporary Place des Vosges (or Place Royale 1605–1612); however, while both are relevant examples of *Baroque* architecture and urbanism, there are some considerable differences. The Parisian model triggered a reordering of the surrounding portion of the city, while in Madrid, when Herrera and Gómez de Mora carved off a fragment of the medieval city fabric to create a space, it had negligible impact on the urban reordering of its surroundings. Moreover, the French royal square had a political and ceremonial role; the Spanish Plaza Mayor was, and still is today, a center of festivities, popular celebrations, and demonstrations. In old days it even hosted bullfights and executions.

As was typical of Gómez de Mora's work, the façades that enclosed and defined the Plaza Mayor of Madrid were likely built with the architectural austerity that characterized all of Spain's post-Herrerian architecture. However, and unfortunately, the Plaza Mayor suffered numerous fires that caused considerable damage to Gómez de Mora's original buildings. In its current configuration, the Plaza Mayor of Madrid, and especially the façades that define its architectural character, are the work of Juan de Villanueva, the most important *Neoclassical* architect of Spain and author of the **Museo del Prado**. Villanueva's intervention began in 1790, after the last fire that affected a good part of the plaza. The most important aspect of this work is the closing of the four sides of the plaza to create a continuous envelope around the rectangular open space; the ground-level gallery is also typical of Villanueva, who replaced the arcade by a *trabeated* colonnade made of restrained and powerful square pillars supporting a continuous horizontal lintel. The continuity of the colonnade and its related horizontal element is only interrupted by two-story arches that provide physical connection with the streets which, behind the façades, converge to the Plaza. Above the colonnade, the continuous façade is three stories high, with regular fenestration and displaying an extremely austere architectural language typical of Gómez de Mora's but also of Villanueva's work. The whole is crowned by a simple slate roof that reaffirms the ensemble's severe, uniform, and calm monumentality.

Largely restored and rebuilt as a result of fires, La Casa de la Panadería on the northern side of the square provides the only architectural difference to the whole. It was originally built by Diego Sillero in 1590 and incorporated as part of the plaza by Gómez de Mora; it was rebuilt in 1672 after a major fire and its façade was decorated by José X. Donoso. The 1790 fire left it badly damaged, but Villanueva restored it, respecting its general architectural character and leaving it as a singular façade within the uniform envelope of the plaza. While in harmonic scale with the rest of the space, the arches of the ground-level's gallery, the Baroque decoration of the façades, the two towers of the façade's extremes and their Herrerian pyramidal roofs, and its walls fully covered with painted allegoric murals, add a note of restrained color and movement that animates the spatial envelope.

The Plaza Mayor of Madrid exerted an enormous influence throughout Spain, and many were built in subsequent decades and centuries; the **Plaza Mayor of Salamanca** designed by Alberto de Churriguera (1729–1755), is just one of the most famous and beautiful among them. The importance of Madrid's Plaza Mayor lies in its significant role as the first urban intervention in a city that was ready to confront a major transformation as a result of having suddenly and unexpectedly become the capital of the most extended Western kingdom (large parts of Europe and vast colonized territories in the

Americas and Asia). Furthermore, the caliber and historical importance of the architects who designed it—Juan de Herrera, Francisco and Juan Gómez de Mora, and Juan de Villanueva, all undisputable masters and leading figures of their time—make of the Plaza Mayor of Madrid one of the most important public spaces of architectural and urban significance throughout Spain.

Further Reading

Bertrand, M. J., and Listowski, H. *Les Places dans la ville*. Paris: Dunod, 1984.

Escobar, Jesús. *The Plaza Mayor and the Shaping of Baroque Madrid*. Cambridge: Cambridge University Press, 2003.

Luz Lamarca, Rodrigo de. *Francisco de Mora y Juan Gómez de Mora: Cuenca, Foco Renacentista*. Cuenca: Diputación de Cuenca, 1997.

PLAZA MAYOR OF SALAMANCA, SALAMANCA, CASTILLA Y LEÓN

Style: Baroque-Churrigueresque Architecture
Dates: 1729–1755
Architects: Alberto Churriguera; Andrés García de Quiñones

The Plaza Mayor of Salamanca is one of the most splendid urban spaces of Spain, a masterpiece of *Baroque* architecture and the most interesting work of architecture and urbanism in the peculiar style known as *Churrigueresque*, which evolved mainly in central and northern Spain, and especially in Salamanca, in the first half of the eighteenth century. The term Churrigueresque was coined to refer to the work of "the Churriguera brothers"—José, Joaquín, and Alberto—who are considered to be major exponents of this Spanish variant of late Baroque architecture. This is characterized by a tendency to treat wall planes with exuberant and elaborated surface decoration often with complete disregard of the structure of support. As such—as some historians and critics have pointed out (Chueca Goitía, for instance)—it has a relationship with the country's *Plateresque* architecture of the fifteenth and sixteenth centuries that, as a "style," was also peculiar and typically Spanish.

Churrigueresque architecture probably originated as a consequence of having transposed to the scale of architecture the language and ideas originated and explored in interior works, fundamentally highly elaborated and profusely decorated altarpieces. This was typical of José de Churriguera, the elder of the three brothers and pioneer of the family's style, who had designed numerous splendid altarpieces, notably one for the Dominican church of San Esteban in Salamanca (1690). José transposed his sculptural explo-

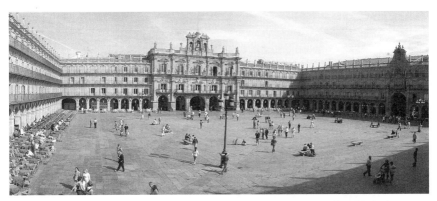

General view of Salamanca's Plaza Mayor. *Photo courtesy of the Tourism Office of Salamanca.*

rations to his architectural commissions, thus inaugurating the architectural Churrigueresque. Centered in Salamanca, Churrigueresque expanded throughout central Spain—there are fine examples in Madrid, Toledo, and Valladolid—and reached Galicia, in the northwestern corner of the Iberian Peninsula. The Obradoiro façade of the **Cathedral of Santiago de Compostela**, designed by Fernando Casas Novoa, is the most relevant example of late Baroque-Churrigueresque outside of Salamanca.

The two younger brothers, Joaquín and Alberto, were assiduous collaborators with José, often working under his direct supervision; eventually, both worked independently, continuing the style of their elder brother, a fact that triggered the association of the characteristic style with the Churriguera family. The *ciborium* and the *choir* for the Cathedral of Salamanca (c. 1715) and the Colegio de Calatrava (Salamanca 1717) are Joaquín's most important contributions; yet, Alberto—the youngest of the three Churriguera brothers— is the one who has left the most important architectural legacy. His architectural career began with his inheriting unfinished works initiated by his two older brothers. First, he completed Joaquín's Cathedral of Salamanca and the Colegio de Calatrava; later, he began to receive direct commissions. The Plaza Mayor of Salamanca is, without doubt, among his most important contributions, a restrained yet emblematic example of Churrigueresque, and a capital work of Spain's late Baroque.

Salamanca is one of the greatest historical and artistic centers of Spain, seat of the world famous Universidad de Salamanca (founded in 1218), as well as the *Jesuit*'s college and church of **La Clerecía**, among many important religious and civic institutions and buildings. The Plaza Mayor—or Plaza Real (Royal Place)—is an urban space typical of the period that generally consisted of a rectangular or square plan enclosed by uniform façades that create a rather controlled and uniform centralized space. One of the best-known examples is Paris' Place des Vosges (originally named Place Royale), built in the early years of the seventeenth century. In Spain, there abound fine examples of this urban type; the **Plaza Mayor of Madrid** (1617–1619), designed by Juan Gómez de Mora, is virtually contemporary with Place des Vosges, while Barcelona's Plaza Real was built as late as the mid-nineteenth century.

The Plaza Mayor of Salamanca is located in the center of the city, at the convergence point of numerous narrow streets dating from medieval times and within a few hundred yards of the university and Jesuit's buildings. It consists of an open space of generous and carefully studied proportions; the plan is rectangular, almost square, entirely paved and enclosed by a continuous four-storey façade integrally built in golden sandstone. Historically, this was a place of commerce, transactions, cafes, and gathering, the center of the city's febrile student, artistic, and political life.

A continuous arcade of eighty-eight arches supported on vigorous pillars encloses the plaza at the ground level, providing a semi-covered arcaded extension to the paved plaza. Above the arcade, the profusely ornamented plane of the façade envelops the plaza, creating a rather uniform and grandiose urban space, rightly considered as one of the most beautiful in Spain. The horizontal lines of cornices and shallow balconies reaffirm the continuity of the enveloping façade; between them, the regular spacing of rectangular openings framed by pilasters and aligned with the arches of the ground floor's arcade provides a rhythmical modulation to the richly ornamented wall surfaces. This continuous decoration consisting of pilasters, blazons, medallions, and a wealth of other relief motives dematerializes the walls, transforming them into plastically sculpted planes. The elements of ornamentation are generated by a system of overlapping cut-out *placas* (plates or plaques) that create fractured frames. Contrary to other similar spaces where the top level is made by visible slate roofs (for instance Paris' Place des Vosges and Madrid's Plaza Mayor), Alberto Churriguera crowned the Plaza Mayor of Salamanca by a continuous horizontal line—a short *balustrade*—and pinnacles that emphasize the rhythmical bay modulation of the ground-floor arcades and regular fenestration of the façades.

The east side of the plaza is dominated by the Pabellón Real (Royal Pavilion) and its central two-story open arch flanked by a giant order of pilasters that, known as the Arco de Toro, is one of the main entrances to the open public space. This arch is crowned by a piece that manifests a higher and sophisticated development of decorative elements and a belfry that breaks the horizontal continuity of the uppermost line of the uniform enclosure. The Ayuntamiento (Town Hall) dominates the plaza's south side, emphasized by a slightly taller and protruding five-bay central body crowned by an elaborated belfry above the wider central bay. The façade of the Ayuntamiento was completed by Andrés García de Quiñones in the 1750s after Alberto de Churriguera had left Salamanca (c. 1738). Quiñones was a remarkable Baroque architect who at that time was also working on the towers for the neighboring church of La Clerecía and its adjacent *cloister* for the Jesuit's Colegium Regium. While in general harmony with the rest of the plaza, the

Ayuntamiento's façade is even more exuberant than the rest of the plaza's enclosure, taking the Churrigueresque's typical characteristic of treating the wall as a continuously ornamented surface one step further; in fact, the work of the followers of the Churriguera brothers—for example, the already mentioned Quiñones and Casas Novoa—is generally more exuberant, even "more Churrigueresque" than the founders' work.

After 250 years of existence, the Plaza Mayor continues to be the most important urban space of Salamanca, the prime place of gathering, civic activity, and festive celebrations in a city where Baroque and Churrigueresque architecture testify that it was the most important center of artistic production of Spain in the seventeenth and early eighteenth centuries.

Further Reading

Blunt, Anthony, ed. *Baroque and Rococo: Architecture and Decoration.* New York: Harper & Row, 1978.

Chueca Goitía, Fernando. *Historia de la Arquitectura Española: Edad Moderna-Edad Contemporánea.* Vol. 2. Madrid: Editorial Dossat, 1965.

PREHISTORIC CAVES, CANTABRIAN COAST, CANTABRIA AND ASTURIAS

Style: Prehistoric Architecture
Date: Paleolithic Age
Architects: Unknown (natural rock formations used and transformed by prehistoric humans)

At the dawn of their existence, humans began to gather in social groups and soon developed codes, beliefs, myths, tools, languages, and an unsurpassed ability to conceptualize, transform, and create. Architecture is one of the wonderful creative quests of humankind, a synthesis of technological and intellectual progress, art and science aimed at satisfying our physical and metaphysical needs and aspirations. At one point men identified the need to pause, to settle and find shelter to protect themselves—even if temporarily— from adverse conditions, occupying readily available refuges, generally caves, that nature generously offered. It is precisely in these caves that, more than 15,000 years ago during the Late Upper *Paleolithic* period, humans initiated the transcendental journey of artistic production and the creative appropriation and transformation of space.

Admittedly, the men and women of the Paleolithic neither built nor created the spaces that they used and inhabited; therefore, if we consider "ar-

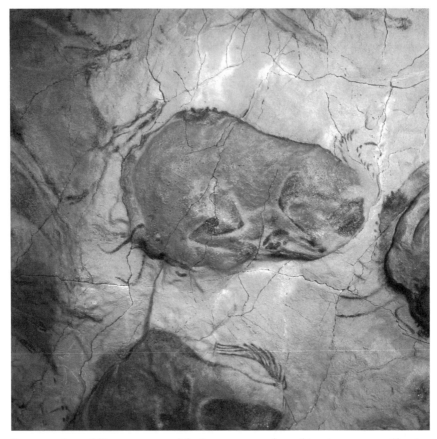

Representations of Bison are some of the images among the prehistoric cave art at Altamira. *Photo courtesy of Museo de Altamira.*

chitecture" as what is built, or further, as what is built with the intention to transcend, these caves would fail to qualify as works of architecture. However, the appropriation and occupation of these caves mark a seminal moment when by taking possession of space, defining and differentiating areas, segregating functions, and leaving physical evidence of his acts, that is, in transforming undefined space into habitat, Paleolithic man wrote the first chapter of the history of architecture.

The northern regions of Spain, specially Asturias and Cantabria, house a large number of caves from the *Aurignacian* and *Magdalenian* periods. On the walls of these caves, some of them still unexplored, there abound idiomorphic signs, symbols, paintings, engravings, and other evidence of how primitive men inhabited space, their early rites and customs. The caves of "El Pindal," "Tito Bustillo-Ribadesella," "El Buxu," "Candamo" (in Asturias), and "El Castillo," "Chufín," and "Altamira" (in Cantabria) are just some in which the most relevant vestiges of early human occupation were found. These vestiges often include layers of prehistoric deposits (debris, tools, burials, and skeletons), but the art work—animal and anthropomorphic figures, ideograms in the form of undecipherable signs and symbols, and a large range of stenciled forms—left on the stone walls and ceilings stands out. The meaning of these paintings is unknown and speculative theories abound; some specialists believe that they were related to magic or hunting rituals, while others attribute them to a particularly benign period in which the abundance of food provided spare time that man invested to develop and explore artistic expressions.

In general, these caves have a vestibule and a series of communicated halls and galleries that penetrate deep into the core of the rock. For instance, the cave of "El Pindal" (Asturias), located at Cape of San Emeterio on the Cantabrian coast, has a 30-foot-wide vestibule followed by a single gallery where fragments of prehistoric art are clearly visible. Also in Asturias, the cave of San Román de Candamo has a magnificent sequence of rooms: the usual vestibule, followed by a large hall known as "Sala de los Signos Rojos" (Hall of Red Signs) with plenty of undeciphered idiomorphic signs, and a Great Hall with one wall featuring an abundance of paintings of horses, cervids, goats, and other animals. Another room, known as "El Camarín," is believed to have been used as a magic, religious, or ritualistic chamber. The caves of "Tito Bustillo" in Ribadesella (Asturias) and "El Castillo" in Puente Viesgo (Cantabria) are two other important caves with vestiges of human occupation and paintings from the Paleolithic. However, the cave of Altamira—known as "The Sistine Chapel of Prehistoric Art" in reference to Michelangelo's painted ceiling at the Vatican—is the most important and impressive of all. It was discovered in 1868 by a hunter and years later visited by a local resident, Marcelino Sanz de Sautuola, who noticed strange and cryptic black signs on the walls. Yet, it was not until three years later, in 1879, that his daughter discovered the fantastic ceiling covered by polychrome images in what today is known as "The Great Hall."

The cave of Altamira is nearly 1,000 feet long and is divided into various chambers and halls, "rooms" naturally carved by erosion of the stone. Immediately following the mouth of the cave (a low but wide opening) there is a rather ample space known as the "kitchen" because it was where the occupants likely gathered around a fire used for heat but also to "cook." The galleries penetrate deep into the rock formation, creating a sequence of strangulated passages and ample rooms before ending in a very narrow gallery—6 to 12 feet wide—known as the "Horse Tail." Each of these passages and halls were probably used for various and differentiated activities; however, it is impossible to establish them with certainty based on the vestiges found.

Inscriptions, engraved marks, "masks," hands, and other symbols, all of confirmed prehistoric origin, are visible in various locations of the large cave; but the most impressive images are painted on the ceiling of "The Great

Hall"—a space of approximately 60 by 32 feet and (originally) a variable height of 4 to 9 feet—located at the end of a narrow bifurcation not far from the cave's entrance (about 150 feet from the mouth). The irregular ceiling features eighteen remarkable bison, a horse, and a hind all painted in ochre, red, and black tones. Some figures were created by taking advantage of the natural convexity and concavity of the stone to provide a three-dimensional depiction of the animals. Scholars proposed numerous interpretations of these paintings; yet, without any possibility to historically document them, these theories will remain forever speculative.

Initially, Sautuola's claim about the authenticity of the cave as a prehistoric site was questioned by late-nineteenth-century scholars. In the early twentieth century the validity and relevance of his discovery was no longer disputed. The splendid ceiling became an immediate attraction for thousands of people who for decades visited the cave; this had a negative impact on the preservation of the paintings and the cave had to be closed to the general public. In the year 2000, with the support of the most advanced tridimensional digital modeling systems, an identical replica of the cave's vestibule and Great Hall (known as "The Neocueva") was incorporated as part of a new Museum of Altamira built adjacent to the *real* cave. Designed by Juan Navarro Baldeweg, the new museum—a rather minimalist building—carefully respected the setting of the prehistoric landmark. Today, the cave of Altamira—a UNESCO World Heritage site since 1985—is one of the better-protected places in the world. Whereas the prehistoric men and women who once lived in that cave did not build it, the powerful abstract and graphical scenes that they left imprinted on the walls and ceilings of the cave are the living testimony to the transcendental moment in which humankind produced the first act of architecture.

Further Reading

Breuil, Henri. *La Cueva de Altamira en Santillana del Mar*. Madrid: Tip. de Archivos, 1935.

Chueca Goitía, Fernando. *Historia de la Arquitectura Española: Edad Antigua y Edad Media*. Vol. 1. Madrid: Editorial Dossat, 1965.

Saura Ramos, Pedro A. *The Cave of Altamira*. New York: Harry N. Abrams, 1999.

PUENTE DEL DIABLO. *See* Roman Aqueduct at Segovia.

ROMAN AMPHITHEATER AT ITÁLICA, ITÁLICA-SANTIPONCE, ANDALUCÍA

Style: Roman Architecture
Date: Second century C.E.
Architects: Roman builders (Imperial period)

The Roman city of Itálica was founded by Cornelio Scipione in the year 205 B.C.E., for veteran Roman legionaries who had participated in the wars against Carthage in *Hispania*. It is considered to be the first Roman-founded settlement in Spain. It became a *municipium* in the Augustan era (27 B.C.E.–14 C.E.), a status that granted some privileges over other Roman settlements; eventually it became a very influential, wealthy, and rather large Roman city until it began to decline in the third century C.E. The Emperor Trajan, the first non-Italian Roman emperor, who ruled in the period 98–117, was born in Itálica, and the family of his successor and cousin Hadrian was also native of this once highly influential city. It was precisely under the rule of these two emperors, especially under Hadrian, that the city was significantly enhanced through the construction of numerous public and private buildings.

The standing ruins of Itálica are clear and indisputable proof of the beauty, splendor, and wealth that the city enjoyed during Roman Imperial time. Fragments of a magnificent temple complex called the Traianeum, built by Hadrian in Trajan's honor, as well as of a villa known as "The House of the Exedra," baths (or thermae), a small theater, defensive city walls, and many other structures still remain; but none of them is as impressive as the amphitheater. In fact, Itálica's amphitheater is among the larger preserved Roman remains in Spain, only surpassed by the bridge over the Alcántara River in Cáceres, the marvelous standing ruins of **Augusta Emérita**, and the well-preserved **Roman Aqueduct at Segovia**.

As a building type, the amphitheater was a genuine Roman innovation as it was unknown to the Greeks, from whom the Romans borrowed and transformed many other building typologies such as temples and theaters. Amphitheaters were buildings primarily destined for entertainment, the arena in which the gladiators proved their skills and strength. However, their use was not limited to gladiatorial combats; for instance, many of them could be intentionally flooded and used for naval exhibitions. Typically, they had an elliptical form, with tiers of seats—the *cavea*—raising several levels to accommodate large crowds; in the center of the arena there was a large pit—the *fossa arenaia*—covered by a wooden structure that accommodated areas for service and storage of machinery, as well as cells for slaves and wild beasts used in the games.

While their seminal concept has often been explained as two back-to-back

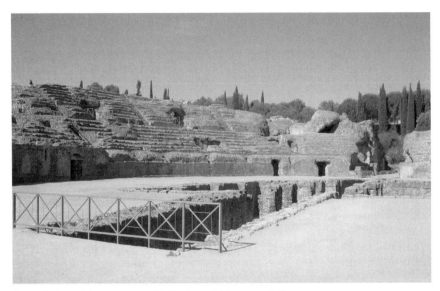

General view of the remnants of Itálica's amphitheater at Itálica.

theaters—where rows of seats configured a semicircle—their elliptical form may have derived from the Romans' marked preference for bi-axial and hierarchical planning systems composed of major and minor axes intersecting at right angles, and thus defining a strong center. Their urbanism, in which two major axes—the *cardum* and *decumanum*—are both the center and the origin of Roman-founded cities, is the clearest demonstration of this manifested preference for bi-axial systems. In any case, the oval plan presented a novel challenge that demanded great building ingenuity, an aspect in which the Romans excelled. The amphitheaters did not have a roof, but were not directly exposed to the sky either; rather, they were covered by a canvas-like membrane supported by a system of cables, an ancient predecessor of the tensile structures that cover many modern sporting facilities.

Remains of amphitheaters in varying degree of preservation can be found in most of the Empire's largest cities, such as Capua, Pompey, Pozzuoli, Verona (Italy), Arles, Nîmes (France), Tarragona, Itálica, Mérida (Spain), El-Djem (North Africa), and many others as well. The largest was Rome's still-standing Flavian Amphitheater, better know as the *Colosseum* because of its colossal dimensions; its oval's major axis is 620 feet long, while the minor axis measures 513 feet. Some amphitheaters—for example, those of Verona (Italy) and Arles (France)—are still in use, more than 2,000 years after their construction, even though the nature of the performances that take place in them has greatly changed. The Spanish Plaza de Toros (bullring) may be considered as having directly derived from the Roman amphitheater; in fact some of the well-preserved Roman originals—Arles in France, for example—are nowadays used as bullrings.

Itálica's amphitheater was likely built during the reign of Hadrian in the early years of the second century. It was located extramuros (outside the city walls), which was rather typical in Roman urbanism, although there are some provincial amphitheaters that were built within the city walls, notably that of Augusta Emérita (modern Mérida), the imperial capital of *Lusitania*. With a capacity for seating up to 40,000 people, Itálica's is considered to be the fourth largest of the entire Roman Empire; only the amphitheaters of Capua, Pozzuoli, and Rome's own Colosseum (all three within the Italian peninsula) were larger.

Not unlike the typologically related Roman theater, the amphitheater's seating area—the cavea—had three differentiated sectors: imma, media, and summa cavea. The differentiation was based on the spectators' social status and rank. The lower rows—the summa cavea—were reserved for the most important citizens and dignitaries; the central portion, or media cavea, was for regular Roman citizens; finally, the upper tiers—imma cavea—were for the poor and slaves. The rows of seats were built in stone quarried nearby and transported to the site by slaves and prisoners.

Italica's is not only the best-preserved large Roman amphitheater in Spain, but also one of the most complete ones throughout what once was the vast territorial extension of the Roman Empire. In the center of the oval there still remain parts of the central pit that was used for servicing the arena. However, it is not fully complete; only the two lower sectors of the cavea— summa and media—have partially resisted the passage of time.

Further Reading

Arce, Javier, Ensoli, Serena, and La Rocca, Eugenio, eds. *Hispania Romana*. Milano: Electa Edizioni, 1997.

Brown, Frank E. *Roman Architecture*. New York: George Brazillier Publishers, 1961.

Chueca Goitía, Fernando. *Historia de la Arquitectura Española: Edad Antigua y Edad Media*. Vol. 1. Madrid: Editorial Dossat, 1965.

Sear, Frank. *Roman Architecture*. Ithaca, NY: Cornell University Press, 1993.

Vitruvius. *Ten Books on Architecture*. Translated by Ingrid D. Rowland. Cambridge; New York: Cambridge University Press, 1999.

Ward-Perkins, John B. *Roman Architecture*. New York: Harry N. Abrams, 1977.

ROMAN AQUEDUCT AT SEGOVIA, SEGOVIA, CASTILLA Y LEÓN

Style: Roman Architecture
Dates: First and second century C.E.
Architects: Roman engineers

The Romans' initial occupation of *Hispania* began with military camps that settled on the coast of the Mediterranean Sea. However, they did not take long to realize that the Iberian Peninsula was a rich reservoir of raw materials, particularly metals. Thus, the colonization and occupation of the peninsula's interior developed rapidly and steadily to exploit the abundant availability of ores. Not unlike what they had done in many other of their provinces, Roman settlers soon established a vast system of roads that connected the most important towns (such as **Augusta Emérita**, Tarraco, Hispalis, Barcino, Cesarea Augusta, and others, modern names of Mérida, Tarragona, Seville, Barcelona, and Zaragoza, respectively) to assure the transportation of goods to and from Rome. Therefore, bridges and aqueducts—extraordinary engineering accomplishments—figure among the most significant examples of Roman architecture that today remain standing in Spain. The bridges over the Tagus and Guadiana rivers, in Alcántara and Mérida, respectively, and the aqueducts of Segovia, Mérida, and Tarragona are among the better-preserved works of Roman engineering in modern Spain and Europe.

The purpose of a Roman aqueduct was to bring water to a town from a distant river or other fresh-water source. Its conception was based on the hydrostatic principle that water rises to its own level when conducted in pipes. When it was necessary to cross a deep valley, the cheap labor provided by slaves made it less costly to build giant stone and masonry arched structures to carry the water rather than use lead or bronze conduits. The arched struc-

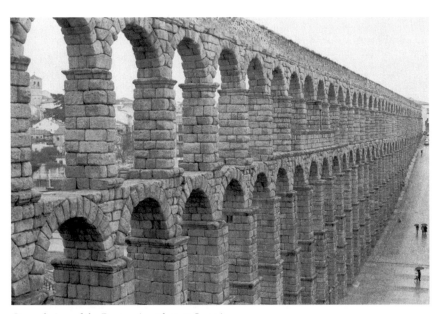

General view of the Roman Aqueduct at Segovia.

tures were topped by a smooth channel lined with cement that kept the water flowing at an appropriate slope (often a 6-inch drop per 100 linear feet) until it reached the water reservoirs usually located in the city. Thus, aqueducts traversed the landscapes of the Roman world, imposing their powerful presence across the valleys, bringing the necessary water to the urban centers where it was abundantly consumed by the Romans' lifestyle.

The aqueduct of Segovia is—because of its long span, architectural beauty, uncharacteristic slenderness, and dramatic presence in the center of a dense urban fabric—the most impressive Roman structure in Spain, and one of the most famous among the numerous aqueducts built by the Romans throughout their vast Empire. Construction probably began in the first century c.e., and it was possibly completed during the first decade of the following century, that is, during Trajan's ruling of the Roman Empire. A native of Itálica (near modern Seville) and the first non-Italian emperor, Trajan gave great impulse to the construction of roads and bridges in Iberia; the abovementioned remarkable bridge in Alcántara was also built during his rule of the Empire.

Segovia's aqueduct takes water from the Frío River, which is located approximately ten miles from the center of the city. To serve the town's need for fresh water, in the last half mile (813 meters), the aqueduct traverses a deep valley, negotiating it with a truly magnificent two-tier bridge-like structure comprised of 118 arches. The channel that carries the water is, at its highest point, almost 100 feet above ground. The proportions of the upper tier's arches are not unlike those of the typical arched structures of Roman architecture; however, the lower tier's arches are unusually high and the piers that support them are, in appearance, much more slender than usual, an aspect that distinguishes it from other similar Roman structures.

It was built with unmortared rough granite stone blocks; they are supported through the precision with which the blocks of stone transmit structural load to each other, establishing a perfect equilibrium. Some historians and observers, such as Frank Sear, consider that the builders' intention in leaving the stone blocks rough-finished was to provide a sense of strength and solidity to this otherwise, yet only apparently, light structure. Auguste Choisy, a renowned French architecture historian of the late nineteenth century, pointed out that most works of Roman civil engineering in Spain share unique characteristics that differentiate them from similar works in other Roman provinces. A comparison between the aqueduct known as the Pont du Gard (in southern France) and that of Segovia shows that the former consists of a series of superimposed arched bridges, while the latter is a series of regularly spaced vertical pillars linked by arches that both brace and provide vertical stability to the whole; while subtle, it is precisely this difference in the form of construction that provides the appearance of lightness to this massive structure, in sharp contrast with the Pont du Gard's perceptible solidity.

The central part of Segovia's aqueduct, which according to a popular legend is known as the Puente del Diablo (Devil's Bridge), covers a distance of almost 920 feet. It has an imposing and impressive structural presence at the very heart of the city. Some arches were destroyed by Al-Mamún's conquest of the city in the ninth century, that is, during the Muslim occupation of the Iberian Peninsula, but they were restored in the fifteenth century by express order of the Catholic Kings.

Having endured the passage of two millennia and the erosive effects of natural phenomena, such as storms and inclement weather, and the often damaging effects of progress (noise, vibration because of vehicular traffic, etc.), the aqueduct of Segovia continues to faithfully perform the function for which it was created; still today, it plays an important role in the provision of potable water for Segovia. In 1985, UNESCO included the old town of Segovia and its aqueduct in the list of sites protected under the World Heritage agreement. After resisting the passage of time and its related effects for almost 2,000 years, it recently began to show signs of deterioration due to increased air pollution and traffic, which combined with the normal passing of time, accelerates the process of erosion of the stone.

Further Reading

Arce, Javier, Ensoli, Serena, and La Rocca, Eugenio, eds. *Hispania Romana*. Milano: Electa Edizioni, 1997.

Brown, Frank E. *Roman Architecture*. New York: George Brazillier Publishers, 1961.

Choisy, Auguste. *Histoire de l'Architecture*. Paris: Gauthier-Villars, 1899.

Chueca Goitía, Fernando. *Historia de la Arquitectura Española: Edad Antigua y Edad Media*. Vol. 1. Madrid: Editorial Dossat, 1965.

Sear, Frank. *Roman Architecture*. Ithaca, NY: Cornell University Press, 1993.

Ward-Perkins, John B. *Roman Architecture*. New York: Harry N. Abrams, 1977.

RONDA PROMENADE AND BASTIONS, PALMA DE MAJORCA, BALEARIC ISLANDS

Style: Contemporary Architecture
Dates: 1983–1991
Architects: José Antonio Martínez Lapeña and Elías Torres Tur

The years that followed the transition after the end of Francisco Franco's dictatorship saw a veritable boom of architectural development throughout Spain, particularly in some regions. The design of public spaces and the recuperation and restoration of the architectural heritage occupied a prominent position in the country's dynamic architectural activity of those years, especially in Catalonia—a region traditionally proud of its architecture—and its area of political and cultural influence. The **Plaza dels Països Catalans** (Barcelona 1983), designed by Helio Piñón and Albert Viaplana, and José L. Mateo's restoration of Ullastret's streets and public spaces (a small medieval town in the Province of Girona) are only two examples (at the two ends of the spectrum) of the fruitful activity of that period.

The Barcelona-based office of José Martínez Lapeña and Elías Torres Tur had an important role in restoring numerous historical buildings and designing public spaces, especially in Catalonia and the Balearic Islands. Architectural critics who have followed their trajectory have referred to their work as "characterized by a playful poetic inventiveness" (Buchanan 1996, xx), or as a "controlled but poetic Rationalism that was responsive to the [Mediterranean] maritime environment, to the lush vegetation and to straightforward techniques of construction in brick and concrete" (Curtis 1996, 680–681). Indeed, the poetic and evocative nature of their architecture, often sprinkled with witty and humorous details, is an important characteristic of their proposal, which is also focused on a careful attention to materials, textures, and details. The Plaza de la Constitucion in Girona (1993), the interventions in the Bellver Castle at Palma de Majorca (1983–1993), and the celebrated rehabilitation of a *Romanesque* landmark, the Monastery of Sant Pere de Rodes in Port de la Selva (1979–1993), are among their more important and celebrated works.

The rehabilitation of the Ronda promenade and Bastions at Palma de Majorca is considered one of their masterpieces as well as one of the most interesting public spaces built in recent times. This project, which is part of a larger initiative that envisioned the design of an area of approximately nine acres located near the city's seafront, consisted of rehabilitating the area known as "Ses Voltes" (vaulted bastions) transforming it into a public promenade with an outdoor theater, a bar-café, gardens, and various services. The site, as beautiful as it is charged with history, is located just below the an-

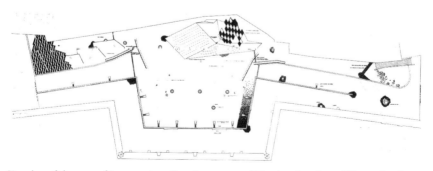

Site plan of the area of intervention. *Drawing courtesy of Martínez Lapeña and Torres, Arquitectos.*

cient city walls, an extraordinary *belvedere* toward the Mediterranean; furthermore, it is at the southern foot of Palma de Majorca's cathedral, a landmark of Catalan Gothic in which Antoni Gaudí and Josep María Jujol—two icons of Catalonia's architecture—made well-known interventions in the early decades of the twentieth century. The architects' strategy consisted of restoring and redefining the area's existing city walls, pavements, tunnels, and ramps, creating new service networks, and designing a series of spatial fragments that can be understood as having both specific and generic purposes; each of these fragments can be read as a singular intervention or as part of the whole complex.

The most visible fragment is the outdoor theater that is located at the physical center of the intervention. It consists of seventeen unequal rows of teak benches placed on an irregular diamond-shaped and softly sloping plane; the slightly elevated stage area is placed against a corner of the rampart walls and is paved with diamond-shaped marble slabs; a light screen—humorously designed as an over-scaled model of the Town Hall's *balustrade*—provides an unobtrusive and sculptural protection to the stage platform. The whole outdoor theater area is covered by a tent-like canopy made of diamond-shaped plastic pieces supported by a network of cables that trigger a large number of metaphorical associations; this blue-and-yellow canopy (the colors of the Balearic Merchant Marine) resembles a battery of flying kites, or the awning-sail of a medieval ship, or even a harlequin's costume, leaving fragments of the sky visible through the gaps of the cable structure. More impressive and profoundly poetic is the pattern of diamond-shaped shadows cast on the pavement, teak benches, and rampart walls; these constantly changing patterns of shadows, which as the architects teasingly commented "were not planned" (*El Croquis* 1993), animate the surfaces that enclose the area, recording the rhythm of the day and the seasons.

The layout of the paved areas was done with extreme care to make subtle differentiations of zones through changes of texture, color, and pattern of the pavement. Most of the promenade—except the more defined areas of the stage, theater-seating, café, and others—is fully covered by specially designed pavers made in concrete matching the color of the local marés stone of the bastion's walls; the actual form of the custom-made concrete pavers is a small-scale version of the bastion's plan form. The small vaulted rooms housed under the bastion's highest platform accommodate a wide variety of uses including exhibition areas, public rest rooms, changing rooms for performers, and other services. At the west end of this element, there is a small bar-café housed in the vaulted space with exterior seating areas subtly demarcated by soft changes of level and delimited by the high walls of the cathedral and of one of the ramps that leads to the city's higher levels. The bar's cleverly designed extensible counter is accommodated under a *baldaquino* copper roof structure supported on solid teak columns. At the other extreme—the east end of the promenade—a newly created stairway climbs along the medieval wall without ever touching it, allowing access to the Ronda's upper-level plat-

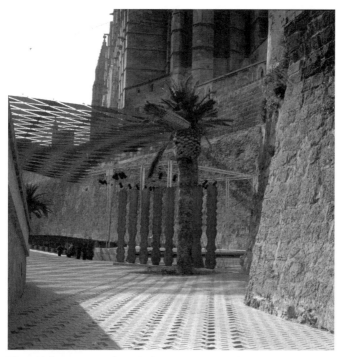

View of the canopy and amphitheater area at the foot of Palma de Majorca's Cathedral. *Photo © Gabriel Ramon.*

form; the stairway's handrail was made with an irregular pile-up of deteriorated marés stones.

The stairs are in direct spatial relationship with a new pedestrian tunnel created to facilitate the connection of the promenade with a reused old tunnel (formerly used by trains) that links this area with the city and the seafront park. The new pedestrian tunnel is filled with witty architectural details such as the tunnel's longitudinal section that alters the perception of perspectival space; its cross section as the negative profile of an oversized *Ionic* column; and an open light cannon in the form of a quarter-size striated classical column. These details recall the work of, and seem an homage to, Italian architect Carlo Scarpa, whose work was obviously influential for Torres Tur and Martínez Lapeña, while the recycling of deteriorated ashlar stones may be an homage to Josep María Jujol's innovative habit of reusing discarded materials for designing important elements of his buildings. Finally, the baldaquino roofs that cover the theater and cafeteria may be "an eye's blink" to Gaudí's own intervention over the altar of the neighboring Cathedral of Palma de Majorca.

Martínez Lapeña's and Torres Tur's rehabilitation of the Ronda and Bastions of Palma de Majorca was a careful and inventive work of architecture.

As William Curtis noted, "it was a delicate intervention . . . [an] evocative use of a polychrome tent-structure, palm trees and surreal incidents to intensify the experience of a historical place" (Curtis 1996, 681). This work has become a canonical example of a sensitive, uncompromisingly contemporary rehabilitation, restoration, and revitalization of a complex, richly layered historical site.

Further Reading

Buchanan, Peter. "Renewal of Buildings and Culture." *Architecture and Urbanism* 96, n. 12 (Tokyo), 1996.

Curtis, William J. R. *Modern Architecture since 1900*. 3rd ed. London: Phaidon Press Limited, 1996.

"Elías Torres & Martínez Lapeña 1988–1993." Special monographic issue, *El Croquis* 61 (Madrid), 1993.

Güell, Xavier, ed. *M. Lapeña-Torres*. Barcelona: Editorial Gustavo Gili, 1990.

Saliga, Pauline, and Thorne, Martha. *Building a New Spain: Contemporary Spanish Architecture*. Barcelona: Editorial Gustavo Gili, 1992.

ST. JAMES' CATHEDRAL. *See* Cathedral of Santiago de Compostela.

SALAMANCA PUBLIC LIBRARY. *See* La Casa de las Conchas.

SAN JUAN DE BAÑOS, BAÑOS DE CERRATO, CASTILLA Y LEÓN

Style: Early Visigothic Architecture
Date: Circa 661
Architect: Unknown

The once powerful Roman Empire began to decline in the late 300s; taking advantage of the situation, Germanic and barbarian tribes constantly undermined the Empire's borders. Several of these peoples—Vandals, Alans, and Suevi—eventually crossed into Gaul (modern France) and later moved into *Hispania*. A Germanic group, the *Visigoths*, initially established an alliance with Rome, but by the end of the fifth century they had succeeded in dominating the Hispano-Roman population and half a century later became the new rulers of the Iberian Peninsula, establishing their capital in Toledo. However, the two populations were not integrated and maintained a certain degree of independence. Hispano-Romans held administrative positions and were governed by Roman law, while the Visigothic king had legal jurisdiction over the Visigothic population that responded to a Visigothic Code completed by King Euric in about 475.

The Visigoths, who were originally from the land of the Danube River, in modern Germany, were Christians who ascribed to *Arianism* but were tolerant of the much larger population of Hispano-Romans' Christian Catholicism. Visigoths had been exposed to Roman culture for a long time; however, their absorption of the Romans' culture was superficial, and they remained substantially different in social and religious organization. As Jerrilynn Dodds observed, quoting renowned historian E. Panovski, "to speak of Visigothic Spain is to refer to the oligarchic rule of eight million indigenous Hispano-Romans by a governing class composed of perhaps few more than 200,000 Visigoths" (Dodds 1989, 8). A major crisis took place under the reign

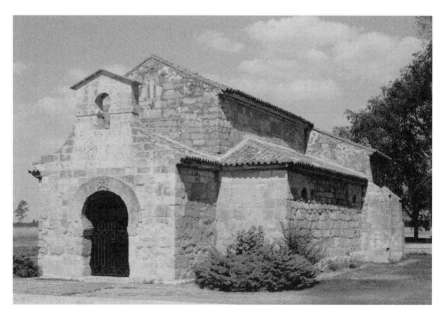

General exterior view of San Juan de Baños.

of Leovigild (r. 568–586) when he unsuccessfully pretended to force Hispano-Romans to convert to Arianism (the Arian heresy). Curiously, it would be his son—Recared (r. 586–601)—who would take the first step toward integrating the two diverse populations when he converted to the Catholic faith of the native Hispano-Romans. The process of integration initiated by Recared was accelerated in the second half of the seventh century when Recceswinth (r. 649–672) promulgated a code of law based on Roman law and applicable to the two populations.

Visigoths were not builders, but the Hispano-Roman population had certainly inherited the skill and building ingenuity of the Romans; therefore, with religious and legal integration finally underway, they undertook building campaigns, especially churches. Thus we know—through written testimony and scarce but useful archeological remnants—of the great *basilicas* that were built in Visigothic urban centers such as Toledo, Mérida, Córdoba, and Evora (the last one in modern Portugal). Unfortunately, none of these great churches resisted the period of war and anarchy that followed the early eighth century Arab-Berber invasion. The only standing relevant buildings of early Visigothic architecture are small churches, often located away from large cities. Two are of particular importance: San Juan de Baños and **San Pedro de la Nave**. Both are the best extant representative of each of the two typological developments of Visigothic churches: the transformed Roman basilican plan (San Juan de Baños), and the combined cruciform plan inserted within or overlapped over with a rectangular envelope (San Pedro de la Nave).

San Juan de Baños is located in the small village of Baños de Cerrato, near Palencia. The history of the church is well documented and quite singular: it was founded in 661 by King Recceswinth who, returning from a military campaign to suffocate an indigenous rebellion in the north, was cured by the allegedly therapeutic powers of a nearby water source already known to the Romans. The king dedicated the small church to San Juan Bautista (St. John the Baptist) in what might have been an intentional and allegorical association with the purifying and redeeming power of water. Its architectural history is also singular because, originally, the east end of the church was rather different from its current configuration. Nevertheless, and despite the alteration of some parts, San Juan de Baños is considered the finest and better-preserved of the few standing Visigothic churches. It has a basilican plan of three *naves* separated by a four-bay arcade of *horse-shoe* arches supported by splendid monolithic marble columns—probably recuperated from nearby Roman buildings—topped by typically Visigothic degenerate *Corinthian capitals*. The entrance to the church is through a protruding rectangular porch; the outer gateway is highlighted by a beautiful horse-shoe arch on nicely carved rectangular capitals. A typical Visigothic cross sculpted over the arch's keystone emphasizes the longitudinal central axis of the building (the belfry above the arched gateway was, most likely, added in the mid- to late-nineteenth century during one of the building's numerous restorations).

As mentioned, the east end of San Juan de Baños as it exists today is substantially different from what it was originally. This, which was demonstrated through careful and conscientious archeological excavations and research, adds an unusual level of historical interest to the building. The original seventh-century building had an outward-projecting crossing that, corresponding with the last arcade of the nave, created a separation—probably for liturgical reasons—between the sanctuary (or *apse*) and the naves. Two additional eastern chapels flanked the sanctuary on each side, but, rather than being immediately attached to the central apse, they were located at the extremes of the abutting *crossing* beyond the side aisles, that is, leaving an empty "bay" or space between the volume that enclosed the apse and those that enclose the side chapels. This resulted in an unusual floor-plan configuration in which the east end had a trident form, a feature that may have been typical of early Visigothic churches, as recent research at Santa Lucía de El Trampal in Alcuéscar demonstrates (Dodds 1989, 18). However, as it stands today, San Juan de Baños still has three eastern chapels, but the two flanking the central apse occupy the space formerly left empty between them. Consequently, the current configuration is more similar to a traditional basilica without crossing.

Whereas the three chapels and the bay that used to correspond with the crossing are stone *barrel-vaulted*, the nave and aisles are roofed with a timber structure. The apse or sanctuary has approximately square proportions (roughly 12 feet wide), covered by a well-done horse-shoe *vault*; the triumphal arch that faces the nave rests on massive stone walls, its keystone again emphasized with a Visigothic cross similar to that on the exterior porch. A narrow horse-shoe opening with an astonishingly beautiful *transennae* composed of geometrical motifs brings eastern light through the apse. The other sources of natural illumination are also narrow, vertical arched openings cut on the two walls of the central nave that project over the roofs of the side aisles.

San Juan de Baños and the buildings of this period are regarded as the seminal examples of a truly Spanish architecture, the seed of a style with noticeable national characteristics that would flourish in the ninth century near Oviedo (see, for example, Chueca Gotía 1965, 56). Its beautiful proportions and extraordinary construction—unmatched by contemporaneous buildings in France and other parts of the former Roman Empire—put it in a prominent position when studying *Early Christian* architecture beyond the confines of Italy and the *Byzantine* empire. In spite of the transformations and restorations suffered, it remains the most important standing building of early Visigothic architecture.

Further Reading

Bevan, Bernard. *History of Spanish Architecture*. London: B. T. Basford, 1938.

Chueca Goitía, Fernando. *Historia de la Arquitectura Española: Edad Antigua y Edad Media*. Vol. 1. Madrid: Editorial Dossat, 1965.

Dodds, Jerrilynn D. *Architecture and Ideology in Early Medieval Spain*. University Park, PA; London: Pennsylvania State University Press, 1989.

Lampérez y Romea, Vicente. *Historia de la Arquitectura Cristiana Española en la Edad Media*. Vol. 1. Valladolid: Ambito Ediciones, 1999. (Facsimile impression of original 1908 edition.)

Yarza, Joaquín. *Arte y Arquitectura en España, 500–1250*. Madrid: Ediciones Cátedra, 2000.

SAN MARTÍN FROMISTA, FROMISTA, CASTILLA Y LEÓN

Style: Romanesque Architecture
Dates: Circa 1060s–1070s
Architect: Unknown

The monastic complex of San Martín Fromista was founded in 1066 by Doña Mayor, the widow of Sancho the Great, the Visigothic king who reigned between 1000 and 1035. Sancho unified the northern Christian kingdoms against the Muslim invaders, and introduced into Iberian territory the *Benedictine* order of Cluny, two aspects—particularly the latter—that would have durable influence in the evolution of Spanish culture. Doña Mayor left a will in which, upon her death, all her belongings were to be used for the completion and growth of the Benedictine monastery of San Martín Fromista.

San Martín Fromista is located in the rather small town of Fromista, twenty miles north of Palencia. Architecturally, the building is a paradigmatic example of the provincial pilgrimage church that emerged in northern Spain as a result of the rapidly growing development of pilgrimages to Santiago de Compostela, and of the impact and expansion of French monasticism into Spanish territory during the eleventh century. In effect, the strong influence exerted by the Benedictine monks of Cluny, who from the beginning of the eleventh century received substantial support and monetary contributions from Sancho the Great, was so determinant that within a very short period of time Spain's Christian territory virtually became—culturally and religiously—a French province. French influence included the replacement of the old Spanish and *Mozarabic* liturgy by the Roman Catholic liturgy favored by Cluny; a massive penetration of French volunteers to fight against the Muslim occupants; and a steady flow of French artisans and builders who, attracted by the numerous building campaigns and religious fervor, arrived to work in Spain in the eleventh and twelfth centuries. The penetration of

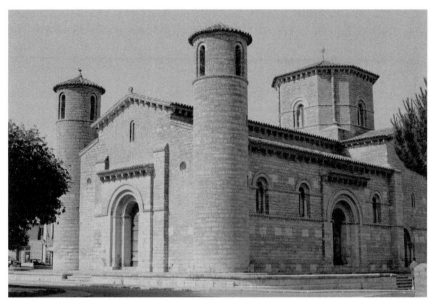

Exterior of San Martín Fromista from the southwest.

French builders and artisans played such a determinant role that the then advanced and evolving *Asturian-Visigothic* and Mozarabic architectural styles were suppressed, with every building of significance, particularly churches, built along the contemporaneous developing lines of French Romanesque architecture. It is no exaggeration to say that, architecturally speaking, the eleventh century marked the beginning of a four-century period of French domination of Christian Spain.

Based in models imported from France, Spain's pilgrimage churches developed some typical features: a *nave* generally flanked by aisles of similar height without *triforium* or clerestory, a fully developed or incipient *transept* that did not project beyond the aisles, and a three-apsidal east end composed of three parallel *apses*—one for each aisle and one for the nave—that either abutted directly on the transept or were separated by a single bay.

At San Martín Fromista we find all the typical aspects of the evolving *Romanesque* pilgrimage style before it reached maturity and full monumental development at the **Cathedral of Santiago de Compostela**. As Bevan stated, even in France it would be hard to find a building of this period of the same architectural caliber, so perfectly proportioned, advanced, and coherent (Bevan 1938, 58).

The overall plan form is almost rectangular; however, the articulation of the different spaces denotes an implicit *Latin-cross* plan: a four-bay nave flanked by lateral aisles of narrower dimensions, a transept that does not project beyond the rectangular envelope, and three parallel semicircular apses at the east end. The intersection of nave and transept is reinforced by a domed octagonal lantern. Both the nave and the aisles are completely *barrel-vaulted*, with arches supported on cruciform pillars that rhythmically punctuate the length of the nave. Both the building's plan and the articulated barrel vaulting of the three naves reflect the implementation of a *Poitevin* system; however, the presence of the dome is unusual, suggesting oriental (Byzantine) influences. The vaults of the nave and aisles spring at approximately the same height leaving no room for a triforium or a clerestory; but, since the nave is considerably wider than the aisles, the nave's vault is higher; thus, a considerable quantity of natural light penetrates through the three clerestory windows opened on the outer side of each aisle, the four openings carved in the lantern, and the radial windows of the three apses.

The naves' arcades are supported by square pillars with semicircular columns attached to each of the four sides configuring a cruciform support that lightens their massive form. The columns are topped by richly carved *capitals* displaying a wide variety of naturalistic and narrative motives, demons, monsters, and other elements of medieval imagery. At Fromista, the richly decorated narrative capitals are of particular importance not only because they constituted a novel aspect introduced by French-influenced Romanesque architecture, but also because they were marvelously executed. Unfortunately, most of the more valuable ones no longer remain in the building.

The exterior is a didactic demonstration of Romanesque architecture. It is composed of an additive system of volumes—an important characteristic of Romanesque architecture—that expresses the building's interior articulation: a higher volume clearly shows the Latin-cross plan of the central nave and transept; a much taller octagonal drum adds vertical emphasis to their intersection and constitutes the spatial climax of the building; the west arm of the Latin-cross is flanked by two slightly lower volumes on the north and south sides that cover the lateral aisles, while the east end exhibits the three semicircular parallel apses attached to the east side of the transept. The central one—the main apse—is expectedly wider and taller, constituting the east arm of the implicit Latin-cross of the plan form. Two cylindrical turrets of slender proportions—visibly taller than the main masses of the building but shorter than the octagonal drum—frame the west façade of the building. They constitute unusual components of this otherwise canonical work of Romanesque architecture.

The façades are austere and admirably proportioned, simply punctuated by clerestory windows on the north and south façades, plastically modulated by vertical pilasters at the transept's ends and by semicircular columns attached to the three apsidal volumes on the east end. The façades are also encircled by horizontal moldings carried throughout the building but interrupted by the vertical masses of the two turrets and three portals. The latter are located on the west (main entrance), north, and south sides; the three arched entryways are placed at the center of the portals and highlighted by slightly protruding rectangular planes; however, only the west portal is centered on the plane of the façade; the other two are placed eccentrically and misaligned with respect to each other. The northern entrance plane is further emphasized by the presence of two beautiful thin columns crowned by carved capitals, while the other two remain austere and undecorated. Inside, the three entrances were corresponded with a heavier concentration of narrative capitals on the columns that directly faced the portals, suggesting that they may have been conceived as interior gates.

The lantern at the crossing of nave and transept is so remarkable and unusual for the time that it deserves special consideration. It represents a notable and well-articulated transformation of the square plan of the crossing to the circular plan of the dome. On the inside, above the level of the nave's vault, the volume of the lantern begins as a square plan supported by larger pillars; *trumpet squinches* at the four corners of the crossing provide a transition from the square plan to an octagonal drum that climbs to a much higher elevation. The eight resulting walls are punctuated by arched windows which, placed at alternating intervals, reinforce the two intersecting dominant axes (east-west and north-south) of the building; a semispherical dome of dignified proportions and precise stone construction crowns the lantern's interior. Outside, the lantern emerges on a square platform that, slightly projecting over the roofs of the nave and transept, appears barely visible from the exterior and quickly transforms into an octagonal volume pierced on four sides by arched windows; the other four sides of the emerging octagonal volume are marked at the center by very slender attached half-columns that rise to the eave of the octagonal roof.

San Martín Fromista suffered some unfortunate additions and alterations in subsequent centuries, but in the early twentieth century it was restored nearly to its original condition; however, some of the building's most valuable capitals and *corbels* that constituted one of its highlights were unfortunately removed. Nevertheless, as it exists today, San Martín Fromista is living proof of the influx of contemporaneous French architectural developments into Spanish territory and one of the most significant and representative examples of Romanesque architecture worldwide.

Further Reading

Bevan, Bernard. *History of Spanish Architecture*. London: B. T. Basford, 1938.

Chueca Goitía, Fernando. *Historia de la Arquitectura Española: Edad Antigua y Edad Media*. Vol. 1. Madrid: Editorial Dossat, 1965.

Conant, Kenneth John. *Carolingian and Romanesque Architecture 800–1200*. 2nd ed. Middlesex: Penguin Books, 1978.

Lampérez y Romea, Vicente. *Historia de la Arquitectura Cristiana Española en la Edad Media*. Vol. 1. Valladolid: Ambito Ediciones, 1999. (Facsimile impression of original 1908 edition.)

Whitehill, Walter Muir. *Spanish Romanesque Architecture of the Eleventh Century*. Oxford: Oxford University Press, 1941.

SAN MIGUEL DE ESCALADA, ESCALADA (NEAR LEÓN), CASTILLA Y LEÓN

Style: Mozarabic Architecture
Dates: Circa 913–914
Architects: Attributed to Abbot Alfonso and Mozarabic monks

In the year 711, forces led by Tariq, Muslim governor of Tangier, penetrated into Iberia through the Strait of Gibraltar and quickly dominated the vast territories ruled by the *Visigothic* kingdom that had emerged after the fall of Rome 250 years earlier. Muslim rulers established the independent Caliphate of Córdoba and were tolerant of the Christian religion of the native Hispano-Roman population, allowing them to profess their own religion in exchange for paying a small poll tax. Nevertheless, as a natural consequence of the Muslim occupation, Christians progressively assimilated Arabic culture; the term *Mozarabic*, which means "arabized," refers, precisely, to the Muslim-influenced native Christian population that lived in *al-Andalus*. This cultural assimilation had an impact on all aspects of Christians' lives; thus, when allowed to build new places of worship, they spontaneously incorporated elements that were typical of Muslim buildings, engendering an architecture that evidences Arabic influence.

Mozarabic architecture spread widely across the Iberian Peninsula, especially during the years of religious tolerance; however, even if tolerable, conditions were adverse; thus, Mozarabic architecture expanded but never distilled a synthesis of elements to constitute a uniform style. Yet, as a result of mounting tension between Muslim and Christian populations, the Muslim leader Muhammad I (r. 852–886) launched persecutions of Christians. The late ninth century was a convoluted period in which the peninsula was in a virtual state of anarchy, with constantly fluctuating frontiers between Christian and Muslim territories; local Muslim princes were fighting each other for territorial control, and Visigoths succeeded in establishing a stronghold in the north, behind the Cantabrian Mountains. Naturally protected by the mountains, the *Asturian-Visigothic* kingdom flourished in and around Oviedo, giving birth to the development of an original and innovative regional architectural style, of which the royal complex at **Monte Naranco** and the little church of **Santa Cristina de Lena** are the best standing examples. It was therefore natural that persecuted *Mozarabs* (Christians who had lived under Muslim rule) emigrated north, seeking refuge in Christian-controlled territory.

The centuries-long struggle between Christians and Muslims for control of Iberia, and their mutual religious persecution, has left little evidence of noteworthy Mozarabic buildings. The more interesting developments emerged in the safe northern Christian states, especially in and near León, new capital of the Asturian-Visigothic kingdom. The most significant standing example of Mozarabic architecture in Spain is the little church of San Miguel de Escalada, located approximately twenty miles east of León.

A now famous inscription left by the church's patrons recounts its singular history and origin as follows:

> This place, of old dedicated in honor of the archangel Michael and built with a little building, after falling into pieces, lay long in ruin until Abbot Alfonso, coming with his brethren from Cordoba his fatherland, built up the ruined house in the time of the powerful and serene prince Alfonso. The number of monks increasing, this temple was built with admirable work, enlarge in every part from its foundations. The work was finished in twelve months, not by imperial imposition or oppression of the people, but by the insistent vigilance of Abbot Alfonso and the brethren, when García already held the scepter of the realm with Queen Mumadona in (913) and consecrated by Bishop Genedius on November 13. (Dodds 1989, 50)

The inscription implies that the building was erected in only twelve months; however, this is hardly believable for the time despite the building's small size. Instead, historians agree that, most likely, Abbot Alfonso and the monks who had arrived with him from Córdoba completed a partially abandoned and unfinished existing building applying the knowledge and skills they learned as Mozarabs in al-Andalus.

San Miguel de Escalada is a building of rectangular plan derived from the classical *basilica*. It has a central *nave* flanked by two lateral galleries, a non-protruding *transept* separated from the nave by an *iconostasis*, and three eastern *apses*. Each one of these spatial components exhibits characteristics of undoubted Mozarabic origin. Yet, the building also features elements that derive from Visigothic architecture. The central nave is separated from the two flanking aisles by a graceful five-bay arcade composed of *horse-shoe* arches supported on marble columns topped by degenerate *Corinthian capitals*. These two arcades provide a hint of the hybrid Mozarabic-Visigothic origin of the building: the horse-shoe arches, while already known by Visigothic builders before the Muslim invasions, recall, because of their extreme lightness, the arcades of the **Great Mosque of Córdoba**. The marble columns were most likely appropriated from other buildings; the capitals that crown them have typical Visigothic features and probably belonged to the ruined building that previously existed on the site. The central nave is approximately 15 feet wide, while the two aisles are about 8 feet wide. The iconostasis is composed of three horse-shoe arches (similar in concept but narrower than

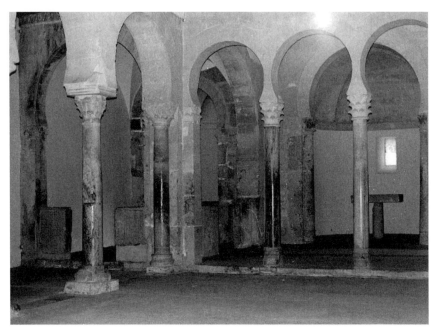

Interior fragment of San Miguel de Escalada; to the right are the three arches of the central nave's iconostasis with the central altar behind.

the arcades' arches) creating a frank separation between nave and transept. Cruciform massive pillars mark the intersection of the central nave with the transept. Here again elements of different origin seem to converge: iconostases were usual in Asturian-Visigothic churches of this period while the cross-shaped pillars, which anticipated those profusely used in *Romanesque* architecture, were already known by the Muslim architects who had built Córdoba's Great Mosque, a hardly surprising influence considering that Córdoba was the homeland of the monks who built San Miguel de Escalada.

The east end has three apses in alignment with each of the three naves; in spite of this alignment the apses are more spatially related to the transept than to the naves. Rectangular in plan outside, the three apses have horse-shoe plans; the triumphal arch that opens in front of each of them is also a horse-shoe arch; the central one is supported by two columns attached to thick masonry walls. The central nave is significantly higher than the two lateral galleries, with walls built in masonry and plaster that rise far above the two arcades; five small arched vertical openings bring measured natural light to the interior. The two lateral naves have lower roofs, and no openings were practiced on the thick side walls with the exception of one horse-shoe arched doorway centered on the southern wall of the nave that constitutes the only entrance to the church. There are additional openings at the transept's south and north ends, while vertical arched openings on each of the three apses bring in eastern natural light. Interestingly, the naves and transept are not vaulted even though the technique had been already mastered by Visigothic architects from previous centuries. Instead, the wooden roof structure is exposed, relating the building more directly to some older Visigothic predecessors, such as **San Pedro de la Nave**, than to the more recent buildings in nearby Oviedo. Some traces of paint indicate that the exposed roof structure was possibly ornamented with painted motifs.

The exterior southern portico is another singular characteristic of San Miguel de Escalada. Composed of a beautiful and elegant arcade of horse-shoe arches resting on graceful marble columns, it was built at a later date than the main body of the church. The first portion of this arcade, built in 930, consisted of seven arches; six more were added to the east at a later date. The portico's precise function is unknown; some historians see it as a place for *conversos* (Lampérez y Romea 1979, 221), while others believe that it might have been a burial gallery (Yarza 2000, 99). Regardless of its function and considering that the only possible access to the church is through a doorway located on the southern wall, this arcaded portico acts as an exterior vestibule, a transition between the open-air luminous outdoors and the rather somber interior of the building.

San Miguel de Escalada is a protected National Monument since 1886. The building's spatial lightness and the gracefulness of its horse-shoe arcades evoke the astonishing spatial amplitude of the Great Mosque of Córdoba applied to a basilican plan, as needed for Christian liturgy. This hybridization produced a unique monument that demonstrates the artistic and technical

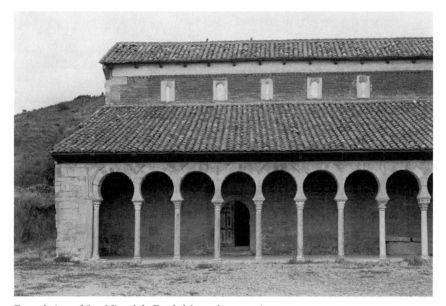

Frontal view of San Miguel de Escalada's southern portico.

diversity of Mozarabic architecture as the crossbreeding of the two dominant cultures—Islamic and Asturian-Visigothic—that cohabited in Iberia toward the end of the first millennium.

Further Reading

Conant, Kenneth John. *Carolingian and Romanesque Architecture 800–1200*. 2nd ed. Middlesex: Penguin Books, 1978.

Dodds, Jerrilynn D. *Architecture and Ideology in Early Medieval Spain*. University Park, PA; London: Pennsylvania State University Press, 1989.

Lampérez y Romea, Vicente. *Historia de la Arquitectura Cristiana Española en la Edad Media*. Vol. 1. Valladolid: Ambito Ediciones, 1999. (Facsimile impression of original 1908 edition.)

Yarza, Joaquín. *Arte y Arquitectura en España, 500–1250*. Madrid: Ediciones Cátedra, 2000.

SAN MIGUEL DE LILLO. *See* Monte Naranco.

SAN MIGUEL, SAN PEDRO, AND SANTA MARÍA TARRASA, TARRASA, CATALONIA

Style: Early Christian Architecture (Romanesque Architecture)
Dates: Circa 453–1100s
Architect: Unknown

The religious building complex composed of the churches of San Miguel, San Pedro, and Santa María, in Tarrasa, is a remarkable ensemble of three medieval buildings that coexist in one single location. The first construction on the site was probably made toward the year 450 when Egara (old Roman name of modern Tarrasa) became a bishopric independent from the diocese of Barcelona. This building, one of the earliest known Christian temples in the Iberian Peninsula, was located on the site now occupied by Santa María, as mosaics and other remnants found on the site demonstrate. According to the liturgical customs of the period, a detached baptistery was usu-

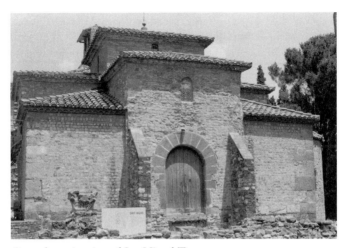

General exterior view of San Miguel Tarrasa.

ally built next to the cathedral; therefore, based on its conceptual similarity with the baptistery of San Giovanni in Fonte (Ravenna, Italy), historians agree that San Miguel, the smallest of the three churches, was Egara's baptistery.

However, after the eighth-century Muslim invasions and their subsequent ravaging raids, the once powerful bishopric declined and never recovered the prestige it had attained in the fifth century. In fact, the modern name of the city—Tarrasa—derives from "terra rasa" (razed land). The absence of reliable written documents and the successive building and rebuilding that took place on the site present serious difficulties in properly dating the construction sequence in which the three buildings were built; in spite of this obstacle, they are an invaluable testimony of *Early Christian* architecture in Spain. All three buildings have features of historical interest, but San Miguel is, architecturally, the most significant.

As the baptistery of Egara's old cathedral, San Miguel was originally dedicated to Saint John the Baptist (Yarza 2000, 67) and located next to the no longer extant fifth-century cathedral. Today, it stands between the two less important but larger churches of Santa María and San Pedro. It has a square plan clearly subdivided into nine squares of approximately equal size; all four interior corners are rounded and it has an abutting *apse* on the east side; outside, the apse is a polygonal volume; inside, the plan is in the form of a *horseshoe*. The rounded corners and vaulted structure of the interior suggest a centralized *Greek-cross* configuration, typical of Early Christian baptisteries; this is emphasized on the exterior where the tallest portion is at the center of the square plan, and then the height progressively decreases generating an incipient cruciform volume.

The harmonious proportions and austerity of San Miguel's exterior are extraordinary, but having suffered decay and numerous restorations, the outside offers few other details of interest. Conversely, the interior is remark-able, a wonderful and vibrant space where one breathes the spirituality of Early Christian architecture. The central space is framed by eight columns—one on each corner of the central square module, and another at the middle of each side—that support eight pronounced stilted arches, two per side of the square, which in turn support the octagonal dome that crowns the space; beginning on the square form of the arcade, the dome makes a quick tran-sition to the octagonal form through very small *trumpet squinches*. Originally, in the center of this space there was an octagonal basin for baptisms by im-mersion, which no longer exists.

The vaulting systems, along with other relevant characteristics of the building—square plan, Greek-cross, stilted arches, *groin-vaulting*—may be a sign of *Byzantine* influences. Framing the central space, the four arms of the Greek-cross are covered with groin vaults supported on two regular arches, while the rounded corners of the square space and the apse are vaulted. The variety of vaulting systems in such a small building is truly marvelous, a demonstration of the high level of skill of Egara's builders, characteristics that can be traced back to the city's Roman origin. This variety of vaulting and the noticeably different size, style, texture, and color of the columns and capitals that support the arcades (surely because they were recuperated from previously existing Roman buildings) generate a somewhat enigmatic and dy-namic space quite unusual for a building of such reduced dimensions.

On the southeastern corner of the building complex, Santa María occu-pies part of the site where the fifth-century cathedral was located. It has a cross plan, with a relatively short nave, a *transept* or *crossing* composed of two similar but asymmetric projecting chapels and a horse-shoe apse within a square envelope. This apse may belong to the ninth or tenth century, but the rest of the building was likely completed in the early 1110s. The interior is entirely vaulted with a stilted *vault* over the short nave, half *barrel vaults* on each of the transept's two abutting arms, and a dome on small squinches marking the crossing. Outside, the crossing is marked by a chamfered square volume that projects above the roof of the nave, topped by a tall lantern-tower likely built much later. The apse has mural paintings from the ninth or tenth centuries. In front of Santa María, mosaics dating from the fifth cen-tury indicate the location of the Early Christian basilica of Egara, while frag-ments found under the floor of the twelfth-century nave seem to have belonged to the basilica's east end.

San Pedro, the newest of the three buildings, is located on the north-western corner of the site. Like its neighbor Santa María, it has a cross-shaped plan with a long nave, a projecting transept, and an apse of unusual characteristics. The existing parts of the apse and transept are probably from the late tenth or early eleventh century, but the nave was built toward the end of the twelfth century. The high vaults of the nave and central portion of the transept—a stilted vault and a regular barrel vault, respectively—are curiously placed at right angles, offering two different spatial directionalities but revealing a clear constructive logic. The transept ends in two shorter rectangular chapels that project beyond the width of the central nave. Yet, the most interesting component of San Pedro is the apse with its three radial semicircular chapels or *apsidioles* opening off the apse's horse-shoe plan.

Considering that all three buildings have fragments that belong to approximately the same time (ninth and tenth centuries), it is conceivable that they were part of an Episcopal center. Thus, despite their small size and diverging state of conservation, the architectural characteristics—variety of vaulting systems, diversity of plan forms, combination of linear and centralized conception—place Tarrasa's ensemble of religious buildings as excellent representatives of Early Christian, pre-*Romanesque*, and early Romanesque architecture at the hinge between the powerful Muslim domains of al-Andalus and the *Carolingian* Empire that emerged from the ruins of the once powerful Roman Empire.

Further Reading

Bevan, Bernard. *History of Spanish Architecture*. London: B. T. Basford, 1938.

Chueca Goitía, Fernando. *Historia de la Arquitectura Española: Edad Antigua y Edad Media*. Vol. 1. Madrid: Editorial Dossat, 1965.

Lampérez y Romea, Vicente. *Historia de la Arquitectura Cristiana Española en la Edad Media*. Vol. 1. Valladolid: Ambito Ediciones, 1999. (Facsimile impression of original 1908 edition.)

Yarza, Joaquín. *Arte y Arquitectura en España, 500–1250*. Madrid: Ediciones Cátedra, 2000.

SAN PEDRO DE LA NAVE, EL CAMPILLO (NEAR ZAMORA), CASTILLA Y LEÓN

Style: Visigothic Architecture
Dates: Circa 680–711
Architect: Unknown

The small church of San Pedro de la Nave, located near Zamora, is one of the two most relevant extant examples of *Early Christian* architecture in Spain. Some of the church's characteristics are so advanced for the period that for a long time scholars dated it in the ninth or tenth century; however, thanks to the thorough and conscientious research undertaken at the beginning of the twentieth century by renowned Spanish historian Manuel Gómez

Moreno, there is no doubt that it was built during the *Visigothic* period that preceded the early eighth-century Muslim invasion. In fact, San Pedro de la Nave—and **San Juan de Baños**, Quintanilla de Viñas, and Santa Comba de Bande—are the only complete remaining testimonies to the architecture of that period; the larger, and surely more relevant, religious monuments that were built in more important Visigothic urban centers (Toledo, Mérida, Evora) were devastated by the centuries-long confrontation between Muslims and Christians.

Originally, San Pedro de la Nave was situated in a different location, serving as the parish church for several small villages in the environs of Zamora. However, the construction of a dam on the Elsa River would have left it under water. Consequently, the church was moved stone by stone to a different location, respecting the general characteristics of remoteness, isolation, and intimacy of the original site. This delicate task was minutely undertaken in 1930–1932 by Alejandro Ferrant, who faithfully reconstructed the original monument. Whereas a few parts demanded the implementation of modern techniques and the use of additional materials, the major components of the existing building are authentic.

San Pedro de la Nave is now located in El Campillo, a small, rather isolated and modest village fifteen miles west of Zamora. Architecturally, it is the best-preserved example of one of the two dominant Visigothic typologies for religious buildings. In effect, San Pedro is regarded as the paradigm of a type that combined a centralized plan—materialized as a *Latin-cross*—and a regular rectangular container; Santa Comba de Bande is another well-

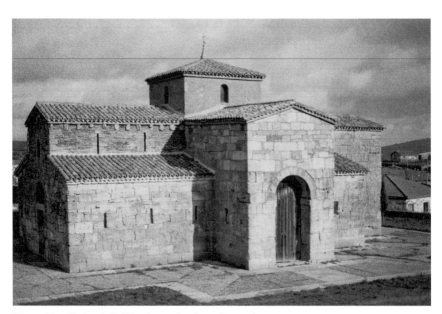

View of San Pedro de la Nave's exterior from the southwest.

known example of this type, while San Juan de Baños is considered the major representative of the other type based on the old basilican model.

The plan configuration of San Pedro de la Nave is the result of a cross shape placed over a rectangle with three of the four arms of the cross projecting beyond the rectangle's perimeter; the edge of the fourth arm—the west end—matches one of the short sides of the rectangular container. However, the cross form is clearly materialized in both the exterior and interior as a volume of larger and uniform height with a tower marking the crossing; conversely, the volumes that define the rectangular perimeter are considerably lower. The two—cross and rectangle—converge on the west front of the building where the cruciform higher volume is flanked by lower portions, unequivocally representing the central and side aisles, respectively. However short, only three bays deep, this west part takes the form of the *basilican* plan, whereas the eastern half—consisting of a *crossing*, a *chancel* flanked by *parabemata*, and a protruding sanctuary—suggests a centralized plan. This differentiation is further emphasized by the ceiling system: the west portion is covered by a timber structure, while the eastern components—crossing, *transept*, and sanctuary—are covered by *horse-shoe vaults*.

The central nave is spatially separated from the side aisles by horse-shoe arcades supported on rectangular pillars, an unusual characteristic for a Visigothic building (usually arcades were supported by cylindrical columns recuperated from other buildings). A small lantern, materialized outside as a short tower that probably did not exist in the original building, provides additional emphasis to the center of the space. However, the most noteworthy aspect of the crossing is the presence of four columns with *capitals* and bases—all carved in one single piece—attached to the *nave's* side of the pillars that indicate the presence of a predominant east-west longitudinal axis. Farther east, two additional little columns guard the entrance to the sanctuary supporting a wonderfully executed horse-shoe triumphal arch.

The building's exterior is rather austere, composed of limpid and straightforward surfaces only animated by the uneven size of the prismatic stone blocks with which it was built, a reddish sandstone quarried near the church's original location. The north and south projecting porches have doorways framed by regular arches; the third projecting porch, the actual sanctuary, has a small horse-shoe arched window that brings in eastern light over the altar in typically Visigothic fashion. The west façade, the only one without a projecting porch, reflects—through its simple silhouette—the different height of the central and lateral naves; yet another beautiful horse-shoe arch marks the opening, horizontally traversed by a single-piece stone lintel that frames the actual doorway. All exterior walls have numerous little vertical slit cuts that, usually generated by a clever displacement of stones, allow some natural light penetration to the church's interior.

If the exterior of San Pedro de la Nave appears as an almost unified composition of added volumes (a Latin-cross, lower aisles, a lantern), the interior is substantially different, comprised of an intricate spatial sequence of small chambers of different heights, roofing systems, and architectural artic-ulation that demonstrate the Visigoths' interest in the compartmentalization and fragmentation of interior space. This spatial conception persisted for centuries, as can be seen in San Miguel de Lillo at **Monte Naranco** and in **Santa Cristina de Lena** (both built in the early ninth century. Yet, the most impressive aspect of San Pedro de la Nave's interior, and perhaps of the en-tire building, is the wonderful decoration, considered as unusually advanced for the period. This is fundamentally composed of carved sculptural relief in columns, capitals, and bases that stand out for their detailed execution and creative display of allegorical and narrative themes, such as the representa-tion of the biblical scenes of Isaac's sacrifice and Daniel in the lion's den, and other typically Visigothic iconography. Other decorations include friezes fea-turing wheels, crosses, stars, and roses carved directly on the stone.

San Pedro de la Nave is one of few monuments that allow us to under-stand the architectural legacy of the Visigothic kingdom before the Muslim occupation of Spain. As such, it is the obligated link between this period and the ninth century's innovative buildings of the *Asturian-Visigothic* kingdom where the first seed of an architecture with distinct national characteristics emerged in Spanish territory.

Further Reading

Bevan, Bernard. *History of Spanish Architecture*. London: B. T. Basford, 1938.

Chueca Goitía, Fernando. *Historia de la Arquitectura Española: Edad Antigua y Edad Media*. Vol. 1. Madrid: Editorial Dossat, 1965.

Lampérez y Romea, Vicente. *Historia de la Arquitectura Cristiana Española en la Edad Media*. Vol. 1. Valladolid: Ambito Ediciones, 1999. (Facsimile impression of orig-inal 1908 edition.)

Yarza, Joaquín. *Arte y Arquitectura en España, 500–1250*. Madrid: Ediciones Cátedra, 2000.

SAN PEDRO TARRASA. *See* San Miguel, San Pedro, and Santa María Tarrasa.

SANTA CRISTINA DE LENA, POLA DE LENA (NEAR OVIEDO), ASTURIAS

Style: Asturian-Visigothic Architecture
Dates: Circa 848–905
Architect: Unknown

The small, charming stone church of Santa Cristina de Lena is, along with the contemporaneous royal building complex at **Monte Naranco** (the Palace of Ramiro I and the church of San Miguel de Lillo) in Oviedo, one of the three major works of architecture of the pre-Romanesque *Asturian-Visigothic* style. Also known as "Ramirense," this style emerged during the brief reign of Ramiro I, king of the Visigothic kingdom of Asturias (842–850). While heavily concentrated in the region of Oviedo, some historians—such as Kenneth Conant—point out the relationship of the Ramirense with contemporaneous Germanic architecture, as well as the potential influence of Oriental sources; these can be explained by the relationship that existed between the Asturian kingdom and Charlemagne (which was intense during the reign of Ramiro's predecessor), and the fluid communication that existed among peoples that populated the Mediterranean basin, respectively. Architecturally, the Ramirense style introduced interesting innovations, some of which anticipated important architectural features typically attributed to buildings of the *Romanesque* and *Gothic* periods.

Santa Cristina de Lena is located on a rugged hillside at Pola de Lena, approximately twenty-five miles south of Oviedo (the kingdom's capital in the ninth century). Little is known of the small church's history, but historians who specialize in this period believe that it may have been part of a royal building complex, similar in concept but smaller in size than the one built by Ramiro I in Monte Naranco. It is generally agreed that the three splendid buildings—the two at Monte Naranco and Santa Cristina de Lena—were very likely designed by the same architect. However, it is impossible to convincingly assert any of these two assumptions because, beyond the astonishingly well-preserved little building, no documents remain about its history.

In addition to the constructive and stylistic innovations that it shares with the buildings in Oviedo, Santa Cristina de Lena presents some remarkable and unusual characteristics that elevate it to a position of individual recognition within the history of Spanish architecture. One of these characteristics is its departure from the typical *basilican* plan of most other Visigothic churches, including Monte Naranco's San Miguel de Lillo. Instead, Santa Cristina de Lena consists of five prismatic volumes—four small, virtually square in plan, attached to the four sides of a larger and rectangular prism

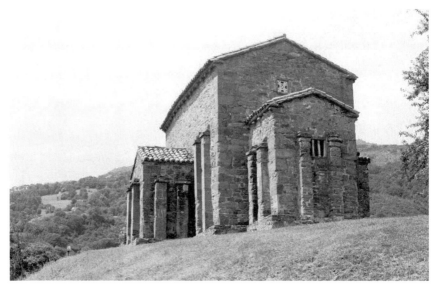

General view of Santa Cristina de Lena's exterior from southeast.

located at the center of the small ensemble; together, the five volumes generate a symmetrical cross-shaped plan with a slightly predominant longitudinal axis, a possible remnant of the old basilican type. Each of the five volumes probably had a different liturgical function: undoubtedly, the central volume was the *nave*, while the front and rear volumes—on the west and east sides—housed the vestibule or *narthex* and the chapel or *apse*, respectively; less is known of the possible function of the two lateral volumes, which may have been used as service chapels for specific liturgical functions, or as shelter for pilgrims.

The whole church is *barrel-vaulted*, a technical innovation also present at the Palace of Ramiro I. But, in Santa Cristina, each of the five distinct volumes is separately vaulted, reinforcing their different spatial identity, and constituting different constructional units. All five *vaults* are reinforced with ribbed arches; those of the higher vault terminate in richly decorated sculptural bands. Yet, the most remarkable aspect of the building's structure is the construction of the exterior walls of the nave, which in effect consist of two separate and independent but linked stone walls, each with a clearly differentiated function: the outer side is made of crudely cut *ashlar* stone that provides a continuous sense of enclosure, while the inner layer consists of a blind arcade supported by attached pairs of columns. In other words, the building's exterior walls have two layers, the outer operates as enclosure, and the inner carries the structural load of the roof and *vault*. This remarkable technical innovation, also present at the Palace of Ramiro I in Oviedo, resulted in a drastic reduction of the walls' thickness, lightening their weight; in turn, it surely determined the need of *buttresses* which, aligned with the ribbed arches of the vaults, counter the lateral thrust of stone vaulting. The vertical buttresses are uninhibitedly expressed on the exterior of the five prismatic volumes, providing a unified vertical rhythm to the otherwise severe and modest stone façades. Moreover, the buttresses modulate the façades and create the perception of an unusual slenderness that recalls the astonishingly balanced proportions of the Palace of Ramiro I.

As Lampérez studied, Santa Cristina's harmonious slenderness is based on its simple, effective, and harmonious proportional system: in plan the nave is composed of a rectangle where the long side is twice its width, while the smaller volumes are square in plan, their typical side measuring one-half of the large volume's shorter side and centered on each of the four sides of the larger prism (Lampérez 1999, 10). As a result, the longer side of the building evidences a rhythmical composition of five virtually identical modules, while the shorter façade is composed of five alternating long and short modules. In both façades the central module projects outside, while the other two progressively recede backward (see plan). Something similar occurs in section: the nave's height is one and one-half its width, while the four smaller volumes are twice as tall as their width or—what is the same—their height is equal to the width of the central nave. The overall result is a rather harmonious sequence of high and low, protruding and receding volumes.

Another unique aspect of Santa Cristina de Lena is the interior partitioning of the nave both in plan and section. In effect, this rectangular space is subdivided into three distinct spatial entities: a central one—of roughly square proportions—preceded by and culminated in a compressed first bay and an elevated altar, respectively. The latter is approximately 3.5 feet higher than the other two, accessible by two narrow stone stairs attached to the two lateral walls. The first bay is spatially compressed in plan and section, as the width is shortened by the two small rooms and the height is lower than the central space because of the presence of a tribune above—likely a royal habitation. Therefore, the telescopic volumetric organization of the exterior is echoed inside with the progressive expansion of the interior space focused on the larger central volume.

The interior spaces are rather dark since there is only one opening of consequential size; located on the eastern end of the whole complex, it illuminates the apse directly from behind. Another opening in the upper part of the central space constitutes the nave's only additional source of light, while a few rather small openings provide limited natural light through the smaller volumes. The *iconostasis* that separates the altar from the nave is another unusual element of this small church. Iconostases, a typically *Byzantine* element that was probably imported through the Mediterranean communication of Iberia with the East, likely existed in other churches of the time, but they are now missing in most of them; they were replaced, eliminated, or vandalized during the Moorish incursions into Christian territories. The small size and remoteness of this little church probably spared it from such actions. Santa Cristina de Lena's iconostasis is beautifully decorated, consisting of an arcade of three stilted arches placed between the nave and the raised altar, and supported on *Corinthian capitals*. The arcade is topped by a stone wall with an elaborated *transennae* between each couple of arches.

Santa Cristina de Lena suffered some unfortunate alterations and additions throughout its history, such as the addition of a small but disproportionate bell tower above the volume of the vestibule or narthex (now demolished). Yet, modest but judicious restorations have returned it to a good present condition in which we can admire its wonderful original conception. In 1985, it was added to UNESCO's World Heritage list of protected monuments.

Further Reading

Bevan, Bernard. *History of Spanish Architecture*. London: B. T. Basford, 1938.

Chueca Goitía, Fernando. *Historia de la Arquitectura Española: Edad Antigua y Edad Media*. Vol. 1. Madrid: Editorial Dossat, 1965.

Conant, Kenneth John. *Carolingian and Romanesque Architecture 800–1200*. 2nd ed. Middlesex: Penguin Books, 1978.

Lampérez y Romea, Vicente. *Historia de la Arquitectura Cristiana Española en la Edad Media*. Vol. 1. Valladolid: Ambito Ediciones, 1999. (Facsimile impression of original 1908 edition.)

SANTA MARÍA DE EUNATE, MURAZÁBAL, NAVARRA

Style: Romanesque Architecture
Date: Circa 1170
Architect: Unknown

The small church of Santa María de Eunate, located in Navarra's Ilzarbe Valley, is one of the most valued standing examples of *Romanesque* architecture in Spain because of its excellent state of preservation, and—above all—because of its unique architectural characteristics. It was built in the second part of the twelfth century, likely in one single construction campaign. The origin of Santa María de Eunate is one of many enigmatic aspects of its history; some historians consider that it was founded by the Order of the *Knight Templars*, while others claim that it was built as part of a hospital complex of the Order of Saint John. The most reliable version is, however, that it was one in a sequence of three burial grounds and chapels in Navarra along the pilgrims' road to the **Cathedral of Santiago de Compostela**—the other two were the Espíritu Santo Chapel in Roncesvalles and the Santo Sepulcro

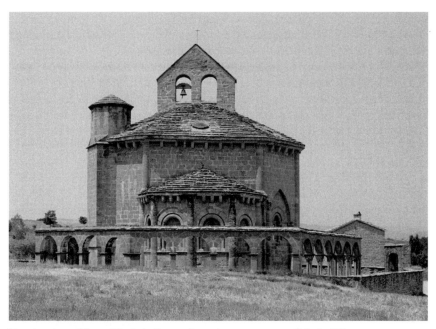

Exterior view of Santa María de Eunate from the east, or rear, of the building.

Chapel in Torres del Río. In all three cases, the construction is unquestionably related to the twelfth century's flourishing and expanding pilgrimage to Santiago de Compostela.

Its relationship to the surrounding landscape is remarkable: isolated in the middle of agricultural fields, it is both a focal point and a place that affords commanding views to the wide and gently sloping valley in which it is located. An imposing austerity and solemnity governs throughout the building both inside and outside; ornamentation, however, is far from absent, appearing in the columns' *capitals*, arches, doors' *architraves*, and roof's stone brackets. Interestingly, despite the few openings and all-stone construction it does not appear as a massive and heavy building thanks to its beautiful and well-balanced proportions and to the walls' carefully cut *ashlar* stone.

The basic architectural features of the building present interesting spatial complexities. The church's exterior volume is entirely surrounded by a freestanding arcade that, separated about 13 feet from the outer side of the wall, echoes and magnifies the irregular geometry of the whole. It has a centralized octagonal *nave*, with a polygonal five-sided *apse* appended to the eastern side. The octagonal plan of the nave was not unusual (the two abovementioned neighboring chapels are also octagonal in plan); its widespread use is interpreted as a symbolical reference to the octagonal Saint Sepulcre in Jerusalem. Both the nave and apse are covered by domed spaces—a segmented and slightly pointed semisphere and a quarter-sphere, respectively—

supported by ribs of rectangular section that converge at the highest point of each space. A series of alternatively octagonal and hexagonal openings punctuate the eight segments of the central dome.

The spatial complexities are more evident in the contrast between exterior and interior. The exterior is geometrically severe and, despite its width-to-height proportions, it has a certain vertical emphasis provoked by the pyramidal form of the roof, the triangular bell tower, the pointed arches, the prismatic volume of the stairs and, especially, by the uninterrupted floor-to-eave columns that mark the octagon's exterior corners. This verticality is only interrupted by the projecting apse and—from the distance—by the horizontal continuous line of the arcade's cornice. Conversely, the interior of the octagonal nave is horizontally stratified, consisting of a sequence of spatially defining constructive layers, rings marked at irregular intervals by thin cornices and eaves; unlike the exterior, the interior corners of the octagonal volume are reinforced by a sequence of two superimposed columns that meet the arching ribs that support the octagonal dome. Interestingly, as if the architects sought to establish a contrasting dialogue between interior and exterior, the perception of verticality reappears in the apse, and in the openings of the western front. Exteriorly, the apse is a five-sided polygonal volume approximately half the height of the nave, but inside it becomes a semicircular space. Additional differences occur in the decoration of the apse's outer wall, particularly at the eave level. This may be an indication that it was built after the nave.

Two arched doors, decorated with vegetal motifs, provide access to the chapel. One is located on the west side, on axis with the apse; the other is on the north side, facing the pilgrim's approach from the road to Santiago. The latter may have carried a more symbolic or ceremonial role, because the portal's stone frame is considerably more sophisticated, consisting of a sequence of receding columns and molded arches; moreover, the decoration of the outermost architrave exhibits an enfilade of figurative images—demons, hybrid animals, dragons, harpies—of undoubted narrative character.

The exterior arcade generates a permeable enclosure within which the chapel stands. Many diverging theories have been posited concerning the origin and function of this unique and uncharacteristic element. One cited often is that it may have supported a covered gallery that surrounded the chapel; another theory is that it was the outdoor gallery of a no longer existing larger complex (probably a pilgrims' hospital or a small convent) to which the chapel belonged. However, in the absence of reliable documents and other remains or traces—built or written—of the existence of additional structures, neither one of these purely speculative theories can be supported. Above and beyond them, considering it in strictly architectural terms, the arcade is a stone-paved gallery, an outdoor porch framed by a permeable screen that contains and separates the chapel from the agricultural fields in which it stands.

The eight-sided arcade, composed of thirty-three arches, exhibits features of interest in its own right. All sides are of dissimilar length, echoing and magnifying the irregularities of the chapel's plan. Consequently, each side of the arcade has an uneven number of arches according to the different length of each side. On five of the eight sides (northeast, east, southeast, south, and southwest) the arches are supported by pillars of square section with unelaborated capitals; on the other three sides, they are supported by elegant and slender pairs of cylindrical columns topped by typically Romanesque capitals. It is unknown if this differentiation corresponds to the original intention of the builders. It is possible that, at one time, all eight sides featured the paired-columns support system, but that in a sixteenth-century restoration, the reduced number of salvaged cylindrical columns were reused on only three sides (those adjacent to the two entrances, which are the most visible), while the supports for the other five sides were rebuilt with undecorated square pillars. In either case, columns and pillars rest on a slightly elevated and continuous podium interrupted only by five narrow openings to access the porch. Not unlike those of the main building, the capitals that crown the cylindrical columns are richly decorated, most of them with vegetal motifs; others feature intriguing masks and faces of unquestionable narrative character the full significance and symbolism of which has been at least partially lost.

Santa María de Eunate has undergone preservation and restoration work in numerous opportunities as far back as the sixteenth century. In the first half of the twentieth century Navarra's Foral government decided to undertake its full restoration. The works concluded in April 1943 with the celebration of solemn festivities. Its octagonal plan, colonnaded outdoor gallery, and the richness of the carved decorative and narrative sculpture are key elements of interest that make Santa María de Eunate a remarkable building, a landmark in the evolution of Spain's Romanesque architecture.

Further Reading

Barrat i Altet, Xavier. *Le Monde Roman: Villes, Cathédrales et Monastères.* Cologne: Taschen, 2001.

Conant, Kenneth John. *Carolingian and Romanesque Architecture 800–1200.* 2nd ed. Middlesex: Penguin Books, 1978.

Lampérez y Romea, Vicente. *Historia de la Arquitectura Cristiana Española en la Edad Media.* Vol. 1. Valladolid: Ambito Ediciones, 1999. (Facsimile impression of original 1908 edition.)

Whitehill, Walter Muir. *Spanish Romanesque Architecture of the Eleventh Century.* Oxford: Oxford University Press, 1941.

SANTA MARÍA DE RIPOLL, RIPOLL, CATALONIA

Style: Catalan Romanesque Architecture
Dates: Circa 1020–1032; restored in 1893
Architects: Abbot Oliva and Lombard stone-masons, with local builders and artisans; restored by Elias Rogent

Toward the middle of the ninth century Christians began to control the Muslim invasion of Iberia on two fronts: the *Asturian-Visigothic* kingdom, protected by the Cantabrian mountains, resisted on the north and northwest of the peninsula, while the Franco-*Carolingian* kingdom, victorious at Poitiers in 732, succeeded in establishing a powerful continental position in the northeast and controlled the *Marca Hispánica*, a region on both sides of the Pyrenees (modern Catalonia) that had social and cultural contacts with other peoples of the Mediterranean (Lombardy, Savoye, Provence, and the Languedoc). Protected by the French kingdom, these regions constituted a cultural conglomerate that shared their knowledge, progress, and religion. It is precisely in this area—particularly in Lombardy—that the first *Romanesque* style emerged, anticipating similar developments in central and northern France. Whereas Castilian Romanesque embraced the influx of ideas from France, Catalan Romanesque evolved as a natural consequence of that active cultural exchange in the Mediterranean basin.

The church of Santa María at the Benedictine Abbey of Ripoll was founded toward the end of the ninth century by Wilfred "el Pilós," count of Barcelona between 874 and 898, a period in which the Marca Hispánica reached a considerable degree of independence from the French kingdom, marking the naissance of national Catalan sentiment. During the reign of Wilfred's successors, Ripoll became Catalonia's religious and intellectual center, one of the most important in western Europe. It had a large library that housed important texts in history, astronomy, poetry, and mathematics and its scriptorium was among the most active book-copying centers in the tenth and eleventh centuries. The first church of Ripoll Abbey was consecrated in 888 and the second in 935, but little is known of their architectural characteristics. A third and greater church was consecrated in 977; according to the consecration act, it had a vaulted *nave* and five *apses*. Yet, a fourth and grander abbey-church was built between 1020 and 1032 by initiative of Ripoll's Abbot Oliva (1008–1046).

Abbot Oliva was the great-grandson of Wilfred 'el Pilós'; he joined the abbey in 1002 when he was thirty-two years old and had already had some government experience. He became abbot of both Ripoll and neighboring San Miguel de Cuixá in 1008 and bishop of Vich in 1018, remaining abbot of the two abbeys until his death in 1046. Oliva is considered one of the great European personalities of the time, a personal friend of the pope and of other influential religious and political figures of the time. He provided a great impulse to Ripoll's development, doubling the library's number of books and building a new church that he considered his greatest achievement, which eventually became the high point of Romanesque architecture in Catalonia.

Ripoll began to decline after Oliva's death but thanks to the support of Count Ramon Berenguer III and his successor Count Ramon Berenguer IV, the abbey enjoyed renewed interest in the mid-1100s. In this period, a magnificent new western sculptured portico was added to the abbey church and important work was undertaken in the cloister. However, with poor financial support, the once powerful and influential abbey declined again in following centuries. In 1428 an earthquake caused severe damage, demanding a thorough rebuilding of the *vault*. Four centuries later, an insensitive full-scale *Neoclassical* restoration completely altered the church's early Romanesque character; to make things worse the whole abbey was sacked and burned in 1835; the church suffered considerable damage, but some parts—fragments of the nave, the *transept*, apses, and one of the towers—were still standing at the end of the nineteenth century when a major restoration undertaken by Elies Rogent brought the church back nearly to its original splendor.

Rogent based his reconstruction project on the dispersed remnants of the church as well as on other Catalan churches and abbeys contemporaneous of Ripoll. The rather faithful restoration was completed in 1893 when Santa María de Ripoll was again consecrated. Therefore, it should be understood that, as Whitehill commented, today Ripoll is "Oliva's church seen through the eyes of a nineteenth century architect" (Whitehill 1941, 39). Nevertheless, its relevance as a religious and cultural center of the eleventh century and, especially, the singular and unique architectural characteristics that make it "one of the grandest works of the first Romanesque style" (Conant 1978, 116) largely substantiate its importance as the paradigmatic example of Catalonia's Romanesque architecture.

Santa María de Ripoll is based in the *basilican* model of Early Christian *Constantinian* churches like St. John Lateran and the Old Saint Peter's basilica (both built in Rome in the second half of the fourth century). Santa María has a T-shaped plan with five naves, a transept with seven parallel apses on the east end, and a west façade composed of a central, slightly abutting, body flanked by two towers. The act of consecration of Oliva's church, dated 1032, stated that the previously existing building had been entirely demolished to make room for a new one; however, scholarly research suggests that most probably Oliva added the transept, the seven apses of the east end, and a new western front to the already existing church. Regardless, the result was surely exceptional: 200 feet long by 130 feet wide at the transept, it was the largest

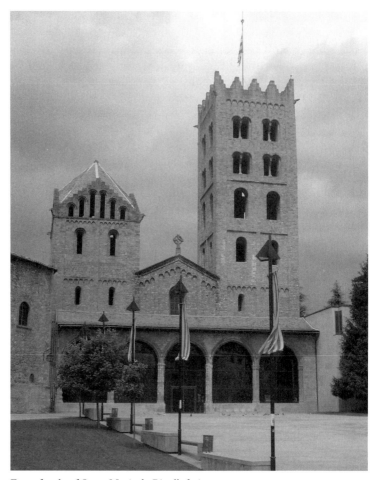

Front façade of Santa María de Ripoll, facing west.

Christian church in Spain, an impressive building and a pioneer of Romanesque architecture not only in Spain but throughout Europe.

Santa María was built by Lombard masons brought by Oliva from Italy, who employed the characteristically Lombard technique of making masonry walls with small pieces of stone bonded together with mortar. This is an important aspect that clearly differentiates Catalonian from Castilian Romanesque, since in the latter it was more customary to use larger blocks of *ashlar* stone. The maneuverability offered by this technique provided the opportunity to explore more plastic effects in the building's exterior such as blind arcades, pilasters, and gable wall passages, all characteristics that derived from Lombard-Italian models (Fletcher 1986, 383).

The interior of Santa María de Ripoll is, despite Rogent's unconvincing reconstruction of the *vaults*, far more interesting than the exterior. It con-

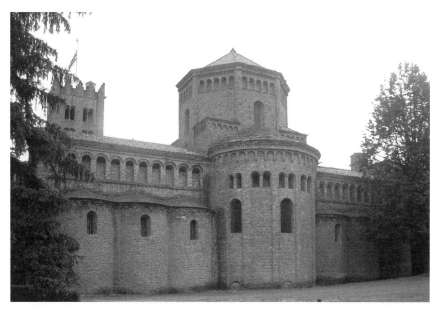

East end of Santa María de Ripoll; notice the masonry construction, blind arcades, and projecting apsidioles.

sists of five naves that presented novel characteristics, all considered authentic based on rather detailed descriptive documents dating from before the church suffered severe damage. The central nave is wider than the aisles; it is defined by seven arches supported by wide and thick masonry pillars that emphasize the nave's directional space. The use of masonry pillars instead of columns was unusual for a building of this size and prestige. The severe and massive unornamented pillars were surely softened by delicate frescoes on the walls, the sophisticated jeweled altar, and the beautiful mosaic pavement at the crossing, as attested by written documents and limited but convincing physical evidence.

Even more innovative was the spatial separation of the four lateral aisles, two on each side of the central nave, divided by an arcade of narrower arches, supported on a system of seven alternating masonry pillars and columns, respectively aligned with the central pillars and the arch opening of the central nave's arcade. On the east end, there is a wide *barrel-vaulted* transept with seven semicircular parallel apses. Immediately attached to the eastern wall, these seven apses—a wider one at the center flanked by three smaller on each side—are covered by half-domes.

The splendid *Gothic* portal added in the twelfth century was conceived as a Roman triumphal arch and organized in seven different sections. While carved one century after Oliva's death, scholars consider it part of his intellectual legacy. Kenneth J. Conant writes that "it may be supposed that some members of Oliva's circle suggested the serious, doctrinal use of figure sculpture on church exteriors—a novelty in Western Christendom. In fact, the use of apocalyptic themes carved in relief on church portals was initiated in early eleventh century Catalonia, and with it one of the most brilliant episodes in the history of sculpture" (Conant 1978, 118). The symbolism of the sacred number seven—repeated in the number of bays, columns, apses, and in the portal's organization—seems to have had a significant role in the spatial organization of the interior space. This is not surprising considering the evolving trend of symbolic and allegoric themes in the design of churches in the Middle Ages, something in which someone of the intellectual caliber and interests of Abbot Oliva surely participated.

The reconstruction undertaken by Elias Rogent in the nineteenth century has some questionable aspects, yet it can be confidently considered a faithful reconstruction through which Santa María de Ripoll recovered its architectural dignity as the most salient example of early Romanesque architecture in Catalonia. Alongside the **Cathedral of Santiago de Compostela**, in Galicia, at the opposite end of Spain's northern edge, it demonstrates the incomparable splendor, variety, and vigorous richness of Spain's eleventh-century's architecture.

Further Reading

Chueca Goitía, Fernando. *Historia de la Arquitectura Española: Edad Antigua y Edad Media*. Vol. 1. Madrid: Editorial Dossat, 1965.

Conant, Kenneth John. *Carolingian and Romanesque Architecture 800–1200*. 2nd ed. Middlesex: Penguin Books, 1978.

Fletcher, Sir Banister. *A History of Architecture*. 20th ed. Oxford: Architectural Press, 1996.

Lampérez y Romea, Vicente. *Historia de la Arquitectura Cristiana Española en la Edad Media*. Vol. 1. Valladolid: Ambito Ediciones, 1999. (Facsimile impression of original 1908 edition.)

Whitehill, Walter Muir. *Spanish Romanesque Architecture of the Eleventh Century*. Oxford: Oxford University Press, 1941.

SANTA MARÍA DEL MAR, BARCELONA, CATALONIA

Style: Catalan Gothic Architecture
Dates: 1328–1383
Architects: Attributed to Guillermo Metge, Berenguer de Montagut, and other unknown architects

Santa María del Mar is the finest example of Catalan *Gothic* architecture, a singular expression of the widely spread style that originated in France in the late twelfth century and expanded throughout western Europe in the thirteenth and fourteenth centuries. In Spain, Castilla was an important center of French-influenced Gothic architecture in the thirteenth century; the **Cathedral of Burgos** and the **Cathedral of León** are the most accomplished Spanish examples directly derived from the classical masterpieces of French Gothic such as the Cathedrals of Chartres, Reims, Bourges, and Amiens. In Catalonia—which in the fourteenth century was part of the increasingly powerful kingdom of Aragon—Gothic architecture evolved parallel to and independently from the evolution of the style in Castilla, eventually developing distinct and singular characteristics.

The salient features of Catalan Gothic are the development of wide, aisle-less and internally buttressed hall churches covered with flat roofs appropriate for public worship without *triforia* and often without *transept*, characteristics that demonstrate the Catalan quest for an ideal of spatial unity, logical, and precise construction, and honest use of compositional and technical means. Gothic techniques were introduced in Catalonia by the *Cistercians* who built the remarkable Monastery of Poblet in the late 1100s. However, it would be thanks to the more modest *Franciscan* and *Dominican* orders that built the single *nave* and internally *buttressed* churches of San Francisco (c. 1247) and Santa Catarina (c. 1228) (both in Barcelona and no longer existing) that Catalan Gothic began to develop singular architectural characteristics related to contemporaneous spatial and technical explorations in southern France, more precisely in the Languedoc region with which the kingdom of Aragon, and Catalonia in particular, had very strong ties. A seven-bay deep single nave hall church was typical of Catalan Gothic. The small church of Santa María del Pino (Barcelona, late 1200s) is the most important standing example of this typically Catalan aisle-less church with internal buttresses lodging side chapels.

Three-nave churches—a higher central nave flanked by narrower and lower galleries—based on of the old *basilican* type continued to exist. The monumental cathedrals of Barcelona (1298–1329) and Manresa (1328–1500s) are among the largest and more important three-nave Catalan Gothic churches; yet, the significantly smaller church of Santa María del Mar is, undoubtedly, the most sophisticated and paradigmatic example of this regional expression of Gothic architecture.

Santa María del Mar is located at the heart of the eastern quadrant of Barcelona's Gothic quarter. Dedicated to Mary, star of the sea and patroness of Jaume I's sailors, its construction began in 1328, a period of prosperity and expansion of Barcelona in which the city's monumental cathedral was completed. In 1383, the vaults of Santa María were completed and the church consecrated. The chronology of leading constructors is uncertain, but it is generally accepted that after the initial participation of Guillermo Metge as

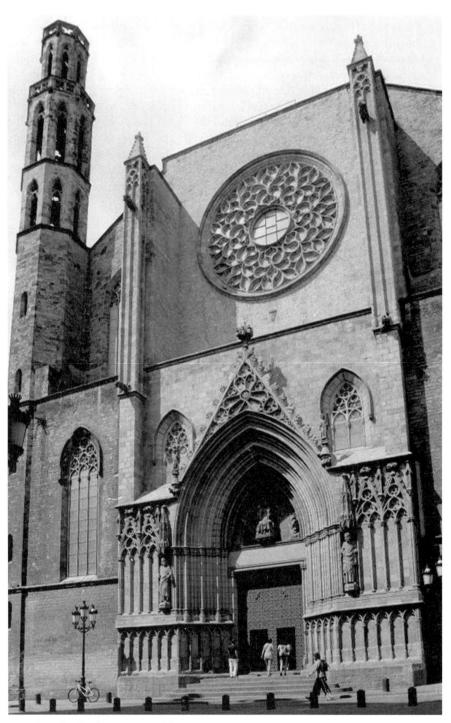

West front façade of Santa María del Mar.

master builder, the church was erected according to the plans and supervision of Berenguer de Montagut.

Santa María del Mar has four entrances: the typical central doorway on the west front, and one on each side, which, located much closer than usual to the west end of the building, do not constitute transepts as in most other contemporaneous churches; instead, these are simple entrances to the parish hall; a fourth entryway was opened in the mid-1500s on the southeastern side of the *apse*, an unusual position for entering a church. The plan of Santa María is a pure example of the typical three-nave Gothic Catalan church: a central nave flanked by lateral naves half the width of the central one and incorporating an internal buttressing system. The east end of Santa María is composed of a half-deep bay and a semicircular apse of seven bays surrounded by an ambulatory with nine radiating chapels in perfect and logical alignment with the lateral naves and the chapels lodged between the internal *buttresses*, respectively, following the arrangement and disposition of the east end of both the Cathedral of Barcelona and the Cathedral of Girona (c. 1313).

The largely undecorated interior of Santa María is a wonderful and diaphanous space, very unusual in previously known Christian architecture. The central nave has four enormous 42-foot-square bays marked by octagonal piers; each bay is covered by a ribbed eight-partite *vault* that rests on the octagonal piers. The flanking naves are half the width of the central bay, generating oblong modules in the longitudinal sense, a reversal of the typical modular partition in classical Gothic architecture. A total of twenty-four side chapels, twelve on each side of the church at a rate of three per bay, are lodged between the bays defined by the internal buttresses that support the vaults. These vaults cover the central and lateral naves at a height of almost 60 feet above the ground. In marked contrast with classical Gothic churches in which the central vault starts springing at a significantly higher point than those of the lateral naves, at Santa María del Mar all vaults spring farther up than the highest point of the piers, generating an ample space that challenges the predominant axiality of classical Gothic space.

The sandstone exterior is as simple, austere, and undecorated as is the interior. The outer walls are pushed to the outer extreme of the building, keeping the simple rectangular buttresses unexpressed at the lower levels of the lateral exterior sides but allowing them to project out above, simply marking the structural rhythm of the interior without any added structural or spatial emphasis. The main façade on the west front is, expectedly, more articulated than the other sides of the building, featuring a *Flamboyant* central gate and a rose window that illuminates the interior space. The whole façade is a pure and honest demonstration of the sectional logic of the interior: the taller central portion of the building culminates in a horizontal edge that corresponds with the taller central nave and the typically Catalan flat roof that covers the vault; this central portion, recessed from the outer edge of the building, is flanked by two protruding buttresses in similar fashion as in the building's sides; likewise, the lower portion is pushed to the outer extremity of the buttressing system, masking their presence behind a continuous surface. Two slender octagonal towers frame the building's west façade; these are more reminiscent of a *Romanesque* turret or a Muslim minaret than of the powerful prismatic volumes crowned by steep-sloped pyramidal roofs more typical of Gothic architecture.

The stern and unarticulated exterior that contrasts with the airy and spatial interior, and the skillful implementation of structural innovations previously tried in other buildings, make Santa María del Mar the most important example of fourteenth-century architecture in Spain, an accomplished synthesis of the singular quest for simplicity, austerity, and logical construction of Catalan Gothic architecture.

Further Reading

Bevan, Bernard. *History of Spanish Architecture*. London: B. T. Basford, 1938.

Chueca Goitía, Fernando. *Historia de la Arquitectura Española: Edad Antigua y Edad Media*. Vol. 1. Madrid: Editorial Dossat, 1965.

Cirici, Alexandre, and Gumí Cardona, Jordi. *L'Art Gòtic Català: l'Arquitectura als Segles XIII i XIV*. Barcelona: Edicions 62 s/a, 1977.

Conant, Kenneth John. *Carolingian and Romanesque Architecture 800–1200*. 2nd ed. Middlesex: Penguin Books, 1978.

Lampérez y Romea, Vicente. *Historia de la Arquitectura Cristiana Española en la Edad Media*. Vol. 1. Valladolid: Ambito Ediciones, 1999. (Facsimile impression of original 1908 edition.)

SANTA MARÍA LA BLANCA, TOLEDO, CASTILLA-LA MANCHA

Styles: Almohad and Mudéjar Architecture
Dates: Circa 1182–1200s
Architect: Unknown

Toledo, a fascinating city located on a rugged promontory surrounded on three sides by the Tagus River at the geographical center of Iberia, was an important urban center and destination for all the peoples that at one time or another dominated or occupied the peninsular territory. The Romans, who conquered the existing village in the year 192 b.c.e., named it Toletum; later, in the sixth century, the *Visigoths*—new rulers of the peninsula—chose it as their capital because of its strategic geographical location. In 712 the city fell to the advancing Muslim tribes that only one year earlier had penetrated Iberia through the Strait of Gibraltar. Expectedly, the recuperation of the old Visigothic capital was an important strategic as well as symbolic objective of the Christian Kings who, after consolidating a resistance to the Muslims in the northern part of the peninsula, in the ninth century launched an inexorable campaign to recover control of the entire peninsula. The recapture of Toledo from Muslim rulers by Christian King Alfonso VI of Castilla in 1085 was a milestone in this eventually centuries-long process of fierce confrontations that culminated in 1492 with the recuperation of Granada, the last Muslim bastion in Iberia.

In the convoluted medieval times, the city's successive rulers—Visigoths,

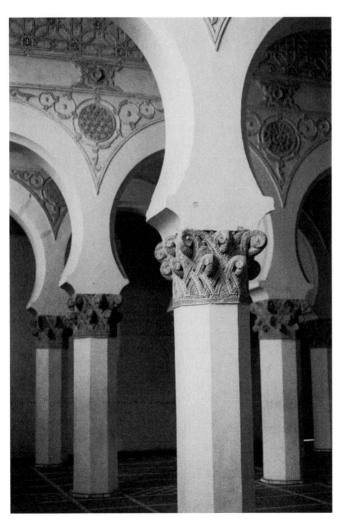

Fragment of the interior of Santa María la Blanca.

Muslims, Christians—were, despite some periods of radical intolerance and rioting, rather permissive regarding issues of culture and religion, allowing the city's inhabitants to profess their faith in exchange for certain imposed limitations (tolls, taxes, limited rights, etc.). Among other things, this religious tolerance permitted the establishment and growth of an important Jewish community. All these aspects, which were not exclusive to Toledo but a general characteristic of central and Mediterranean Spain in the Middle Ages, gave origin to a complex sociocultural phenomena known as "las tres culturas" (the three cultures), in reference to the three clearly different ethnic, social, and religious communities—Muslims, Jews, and Christians—that coexisted in a rather peaceful, mutually tolerant, and integrated way for a considerable period of time. In spite of the limitations imposed on the other two communities by the ruling one, this coexistence resulted in a spontaneous cultural crossbreeding that had remarkable consequences in some areas, such as gastronomy, music, literature, and especially all the arts and crafts related to architecture. Unfortunately, this interesting process of cultural exchange and assimilation that peaked in the thirteenth century was short lived because of the subsequent persecution and expulsion of Jews and Muslims.

Toledo's thirteenth-century synagogue of Ibn Shoshan, better known by its Christian name of Santa María la Blanca, is the most significant standing example of the architectural crossbreeding of the three cultures: a synagogue in Muslim *Almohad* and Muslim-influenced *Mudéjar* styles built during a period of Christian rule in the city. With limited rights and without a developed architectural style of their own, Jews naturally turned to the Mudéjar population (from the Arab "mudayyan," meaning "permitted to remain" and referring to the Muslim population that was allowed to remain in Christian re-conquered territories), which was substantially more skilled and technically advanced than Christians, for the construction of their synagogues.

The building's plan is slightly trapezoidal, almost twice as long as wide, with five *naves* defined by four arcades of *horse-shoe* arches supported on twenty-four octagonal pillars and covered by a wooden structural roof of "par y nudillo" (rafter and dowel) that presents similar technical characteristics to the structure that covers the **Cathedral of Teruel**'s main nave. The typological and stylistic influence of Muslim architecture is obvious; typologically, it is a direct descendant of the typical mosque organization; stylistically, the interior is definitely derived from Almohad examples, while the ceiling-roof is clearly Mudéjar style.

Today, the building's exterior offers few aspects of architectural interest because it underwent numerous modifications. However, the interior is a small masterpiece of the period, a delicate and elegant colonnaded space, both rich and austere, that transmits a suggestive Oriental atmosphere, faithful testimony of the cultural crossbreeding. The lower portion is quite sober; it is a permeable space rhythmically defined by smoothly plastered white octagonal pillars and also a white and plastered band that highlights the arcades of horse-shoe arches; the pristine whiteness and smooth continuity of these two elements is interrupted only by extraordinary *capitals* in carved stucco that are brilliantly adapted to the octagonal shape of the pillars. The capitals are derived from the *Corinthian* order, but the acanthi leaves of the classical original are here replaced by graciously carved pine cones, a frequent motif—according to Chueca Goitía—in *Almoravid* decoration.

The upper part is as elegant as the lower but features much more surface decoration in carved stucco. The central nave is slightly wider than the other four and also more ornamented, including decorative motifs all the way up to ceiling level; the *spandrels* are decorated with medallions and vegetal motifs above which there is a continuous horizontal frieze ornamented with vegetal patterns. Farther above, a blind arcade of *mixtilinear* arches with rich ornamentation in carved stucco closes the plane against the ceiling. As the ceiling's height progressively decreases to the sides, some of these decorative components are suppressed, but a cohesive stylistic integrity and a clear spatial coherence is maintained throughout the building.

In the early years of the fifteenth century, after serious religious riots and the expulsion of Jews from Spain, the building was taken over by Christians who renamed it Santa María la Blanca and adapted it, without much effort, to Christian liturgy. Today, it stands as the most relevant architectural testimony to a unique historical moment in which the three cultures that constituted the base of Spain's medieval society cohabited in the same land, maintaining their own customs and traditions and mutually influencing each other. This fertile crossbreeding generated an architecture of unquestionable elegance, sobriety, and beauty, as represented by Santa María la Blanca.

Further Reading

Bevan, Bernard. *History of Spanish Architecture*. London: B. T. Basford, 1938.
Chueca Goitía, Fernando. *Historia de la Arquitectura Española: Edad Antigua y Edad Media*. Vol. 1. Madrid: Editorial Dossat, 1965.
Yarza, Joaquín. *Arte y Arquitectura en España, 500–1250*. Madrid: Ediciones Cátedra, 2000.

SANTA MARÍA TARRASA. *See* San Miguel, San Pedro, and Santa María Tarrasa.

SPORTS COMPLEX AND TRACK AND FIELD STADIUM OF MADRID, MADRID, COMUNIDAD DE MADRID

Style: Contemporary Architecture
Dates: 1989–1994
Architects: Cruz and Ortiz Arquitectos

The Sports Complex and track-and-field Stadium of the Community of Madrid, popularly known as *"La Peineta,"* is part of an ambitious initiative of the government of the Community of Madrid to create the *Ciudad de los Deportes* (City of Sports) with the intention to host Summer Olympic Games. The project was developed through a closed design competition won, in 1989, by the Seville-based office headed by Antonio Cruz and Antonio Ortiz. The Ciudad de los Deportes is located in Canillejas, a typical metropolitan peripheral neighborhood located on the northeastern edge of Madrid, near the M-40 highway that circumvents the capital of Spain. The track-and-field stadium, completed in 1994, is the central piece of the overall proposal for the Ciudad de los Deportes and, thus far, the only one that has been built.

"La Peineta" is an important building that reflects the city's ambitious pro-

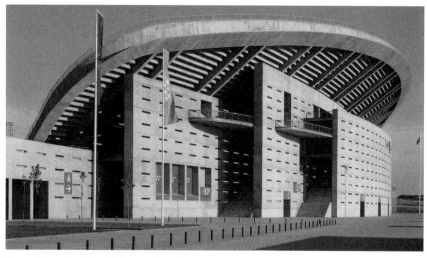

General exterior view of the grandstand for Madrid's Track and Field Stadium. *Photo © Duccio Malagamba.*

gram of architectural renovation at the end of the twentieth century. Its importance lies not only in the quality of its architectural conception, but also in how a facility of these dimensions and characteristics is inserted within the urban fabric of a modern capital as a building complex that intelligently confronts the scale of the metropolis' expanding periphery.

The stadium complex consists of three main elements: an elevated horizontal platform, a large oval space carved off the square platform, and a large, inclined concrete plane. The platform, a precise 360-meter square (approximately 1,200 feet square), appears as the main datum of the facility, the horizontal terrain where the building stands. Considering the absolute lack of other immediate physical references, the decision to create this platform is a design gesture that seems inevitable, the need of a physical element *to position* the entire complex. The oval bowl carved off the platform houses the actual sports field and is placed 9.5 meters (slightly more than 31 feet) below the platform level; it is entirely surrounded by a regular *talus* that could accommodate as many as 25,000 seated spectators in future adaptations; the talus is, for the most part, covered by grass, but one of its two long sides is materialized with built-in tiered concrete stands. Hovering over the entire complex, the inclined concrete plane—the grandstand—provides seating accommodations for 12,500 spectators.

The square platform and its associated elements are inscribed within a much larger, roughly circular, vehicular ring that demarcates the overall stadium grounds. The main parking lots are on the west side, facing the grandstand. On the north, a sequence of green terraces accommodates open-air training facilities for sportsmen. Finally, a three-quarter-crescent-shaped ring with additional parking and sports fields surrounds the stadium's site in the north, east, and south directions. This large area has gardened portions that operate as spatial transitions and filters between the vehicular ring and the platform, on the east and south sides.

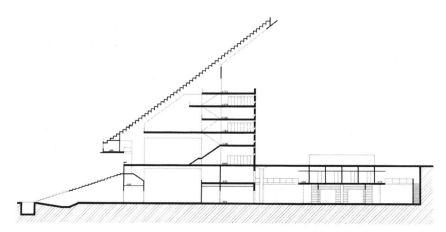

Cross-section through the built areas on the west side of the Sports Complex; the grandstand is the salient element of the section. *Drawing courtesy of Cruz & Ortiz Arquitectos.*

Architecturally and urbanistically, the grandstand is the salient member of the built complex, a high-profile element visible from various points of the city and especially from the M-40 highway. The formal attributes of this architectural element—a large arc that seems to *float* over softly curved walls that emerge from the lower levels cutting through the horizontal platform—has provided the building the nickname "*La Peineta*," because of its similarity with the traditional Spanish ornamental shell-comb. The softly curved concrete walls that support the grandstand act as a counterpoint to its large dimensions and prominent visual presence. These walls have long horizontal incisions that bring soft natural light to the interior as well as provide a horizontal modulation to an otherwise anodyne and austere façade. These horizontal bands—deep black during the day, bright during the night—further emphasize the architectural and formal dialogue between the horizontal platform and the floating grandstand. Whereas the former demarcates the extents of the project as an artificially created landscape, the latter appears as a vertical sign that *situates* the building within a heterogeneous urban landscape.

The built portions of the complex are concentrated on the west side. The congregation of built tiered-seating on one of the four sides of the field—both on the carved bowl and on the inclined grandstand—responds to the initial intention of using this facility as a track-and-field stadium. Moreover, this configuration also allows its utilization for other mass-entertainment events such as musical performances, rock concerts, and festivals, which are necessary to guarantee the financial maintenance of this type of facility.

Public access is provided at the platform level through a system of generously dimensioned stairs that negotiate the little more than 31 feet of difference between the ground level and the platform. Access to the enclosed areas for sportsmen and other stadium users, except the general public attending the events, is provided below the platform. The enclosed areas are located under the platform and the grandstand, housing numerous sport-related facilities such as enclosed track-and-field competition and training facilities, a state-of-the-art gymnasium, an interactive sports museum, sports library, locker rooms for approximately 700 athletes, sports shop, restaurant and cafeteria, and many other leisure and recreation facilities. All these areas are distributed in two stories and receive natural light through elongated rectangular open-air courtyards cut into the platform. An interior vehicular road traverses the entire complex on the west side, servicing the building's needs.

The oval bowl containing the sports field and the tiered seating arrangement that surrounds it brings echoes of the wonderful **Roman Amphitheaters** that still remain in various cities of Spain—such as those in Itálica, Mérida, and Tarragona—while the grandstand resembles a permanent billboard, a sign at the scale of the highway, prominently visible from distant locations, including Madrid's Barajas international airport. Together, these two aspects—the sports facility as both Roman amphitheater and road billboard—may appear as the architects' witty and ironic commentary about sporting and mass-entertainment events for metropolitan populations of the twenty-first century.

"*La Peineta*" is the key sports facility of Madrid's nomination to host the 2012 Summer Olympic Games. However, a major addition will be needed to fulfill the International Olympic Committee's requirements. Cruz and Ortiz have already prepared and submitted the project for the stadium's expansion, which includes the completion of built stands on all sides of the carved bowl, and the provision of a protecting roof to them as well as to the existing grandstand. The objective is to provide seating capacity for 70,000 spectators as required by the games' organizing authority. The addition project also includes updating the stadium's technology and the provision of numerous other related services.

Further Reading

Chueca Goitía, Fernando, Sambricio, Carlos, Capitel, Antón, Ruiz Cabrero, Gabriel, and Hernández de León, Juan M. *Arquitectura de Madrid, Siglo XX*. Madrid: Tanais Ediciones, 1991.

Cruz, Antonio, and Ortiz, Antonio. "Estadio de Atletismo." *El Croquis* 48 (June 1991): 66–75.

Güell, Xavier, ed. *Cruz and Ortiz*. Barcelona: Editorial Gustavo Gili, 1988.

Levene, Richard, and Márquez C., Fernando. "Entrevista." *El Croquis* 48 (June 1991): 5–11.

Saliga, Pauline, and Thorne, Martha. *Building a New Spain: Contemporary Spanish Architecture*. Barcelona: Editorial Gustavo Gili, 1992.

SYNAGOGUE OF IBN SHOSHAN. *See* Santa María la Blanca.

TORRES BLANCAS APARTMENT BUILDING, MADRID

Style: Modern Organic Architecture
Dates: 1962–1969
Architects: Francisco J. Saénz de Oíza, with the collaboration of Rafael Moneo and Juan D. Fullaondo

The establishment of Francisco Franco's dictatorship at the end of the Spanish Civil War (1936–1939) interrupted an incipient and promising process of modernization that was occurring in Spanish architecture. The regime promoted a classical Spanish architecture and suppressed all attempts to develop a modern architecture; in addition to becoming politically isolated from Europe and the rest of the world, Spain was culturally isolated, an aspect that had an obvious impact on the country's architecture. However, in the 1950s, coinciding with the beginning of more stable financial conditions, architects from Barcelona first, and Madrid later, began to challenge the status quo of Spanish architecture in Franco's era. Created in 1952, Barcelona's *Grup R* organized lectures and events that eventually led to a renaissance of modern architecture in Spain. The influential participation of Alvar Aalto and Nikolaus Pevsner—among others—in their lecture series helped to develop a modern architecture with Nordic overtones such as Antoni de Moragas' **Hotel Park** and Xavier Busquets' **COAC Headquarters**.

In Madrid, remarkable modern works were produced even before the 1950s, but mostly as the result of individual efforts. However, in the 1960s, echoing the success of their peers from Barcelona, a group of Madrid architects led by Juan D. Fullaondo created the architectural journal *Nueva Forma* (*New Form*) to promote their vision of modern architecture. The group was composed of architects—such as Antonio Fernandez Alba (author of the marvelous building for the Convent of El Rollo, near Salamanca 1962), Francisco Saénz de Oíza and Ramón Vázquez Molazun—and artists (for example, Eduardo Chillida); their ideas were strongly influenced by Italian critic Bruno Zevi, who promoted an "organic" modern architecture clearly influenced by the work of Frank Lloyd Wright. The Torres Blancas Apartment Building, designed by Francisco Saénz de Oíza, became the group's emblematic work of architecture, the recognized masterpiece of Madrid's organic architecture movement of the 1960s.

The building is located near Madrid's M-30, the city's first circumvallation roadway; more precisely, the building occupies a large portion of a rectangular city block delimited by Calle Corazón de María, Calle Padre Xifré, and the wider and faster Avenida de América. At the time of Torres Blancas' construction the site was at the edge of the city, in what then constituted a major intersection and an important entrance to the urban center. Thus, the design of the building posed several questions related to the image of a residential high-rise on the fringes of the urban fabric as well as regarding the idea of the high-rise as a residential building. The formal and architectural complexities derived from these questions were well understood by Saénz de Oíza, who recognized the importance of this project and its potential as a catalyst to promote modern architecture in Madrid from the beginning of the design process. Consequently, the architect studied alternatives and a wide variety of formal and organizational schemes, before defining the final project.

The first studies revealed an affinity with Le Corbusier's Ville Radieuse

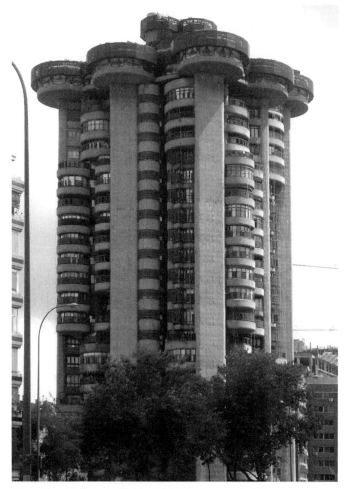

General exterior view of Torres Blancas' apartment building.

(Radiant City), but the first completed scheme demonstrated a radical shift toward an expressionist organic architecture akin to Frank Lloyd Wright's Price Tower at Bartlesville (Oklahoma 1955); in fact, while the general form of the typical floor plan was virtually square, this was subdivided into four triangular quadrants along a central centrifugal axis. The hexagonal forms of the central vertical core and the underlying hexagonal grid that defined the plan's structural members, partitioning, and terraces further emphasized the influence of Wright's work. As the design process evolved, the building's forms changed into a much more radically organic composition of curved volumes and horizontal bands that echoed, however more distantly, the evolution of Wright's own architecture of the 1950s.

The 250-foot-tall building has twenty-eight floors that accommodate two underground levels of parking for 100 cars; 100 apartments distributed in twenty-one stories (some apartments are two-level duplexes); a lounge, cafeteria, restaurant, and a club in the two uppermost levels; and a rooftop with a swimming pool and gardens. The overall subdivision of the typical plan into four quadrants of the earlier scheme remained, but the quadrants' apparent triangular form and underlying hexagonal grid were dissolved in a complex system of clustered curvilinear, circular, and rounded forms. The building is supported by many large hollow concrete columns that accommodate the vertical circulation elements, ducts and pipes, and enclose the apartments' living areas; these open to large circular balconies that cantilever off the main vertical support systems. The visual effect is impressive: enormous windowless concrete columns linked by horizontal bands of concrete, many of which are enclosed spaces (dinning rooms and bedrooms) while others are large exterior terraces intended to accommodate luscious cascading vegetation. The resemblance of Torres Blancas to a tree-like structure—a biological analogy typical of pro-organic architecture theoreticians as well as of Le Corbusier—is quite evident, a manifest demonstration of Saénz de Oíza's syncretic talent. Yet, the building's forms are much closer to the late work of Frank Lloyd Wright and to the intricate structures in exposed concrete of Paul Rudolph than to the work of architects who continued to work in the Rationalist tradition of modern architecture's origins.

The building's design process and construction was closely followed by *Nueva Forma*, which made it an emblem of its organic postulates. However, Torres Blancas became more a singular building than a model for the architects of following generations. As Antón Capitel pointed out, Torres Blancas is "a masterful and unique work of late Spanish organicism" that is important "not only because of its spectacular qualities of its testimony to a particular historical moment. Rather, its importance lies in the peculiar eclecticism and extreme ambiguousness that pervade its form" (see Solà-Morales 1986, 17). Moreover, Torres Blancas Apartment Building is the most significant work of Francisco Saénz de Oíza, an important Spanish architect of the middle of the twentieth century. More importantly, the building marks a singular moment of Spain's twentieth-century architecture that precedes, and probably anticipates, the extraordinary renaissance of the country's architecture and editorial explosion of the last two decades of the century.

Further Reading

Chueca Goitía, Fernando, Sambricio, Carlos, Capitel, Antón, Ruiz Cabrero, Gabriel, and Hernández de León, Juan M. *Arquitectura de Madrid, Siglo XX*. Madrid: Tanais Ediciones, 1991.

"España." Special monographic issue, *Zodiac: A Review of Contemporary Architecture* 15 (Milan), circa 1969.

Ruiz Cabrero, Gabriel. *Espagne Architecture 1965–1988*. Milan and Paris: Electa-Moniteur, 1990.

Saliga, Pauline, and Thorne, Martha. *Building a New Spain: Contemporary Spanish Architecture*. Barcelona: Editorial Gustavo Gili, 1992.

Solà-Morales, Ignasi de, ed. *Contemporary Spanish Architecture: An Eclectic Panorama*. New York: Rizzoli, 1986.

UNIVERSIDAD DE ALCALÁ DE HENARES, ALCALÁ DE HENARES, CASTILLA-LA MANCHA

Style: Plateresque Architecture
Dates: 1541–1553
Architect: Rodrigo Gil de Hontañón

The main façade of the Universidad Complutense de Alcalá de Henares is regarded as one of the highest representatives of the *Plateresque*, a singular Spanish architectural style. It was designed by Rodrigo Gil de Hontañón, the most renowned representative of Castilian Plateresque, who had already completed important works left unfinished by his father, Juan Gil (notably the Cathedral of Salamanca), and constructed a major work, the Palace of Monterrey, which is heavily influenced by other masterpieces of the period such as the *Isabelline* **Palace of El Infantado** (Guadalajara 1480s) or the *Gothic* Plateresque **Las Casa de las Conchas** (Salamanca 1480–1490s). For some critics and historians, such as Fernando Chueca Goitía—an authority on Spain's architecture in that region and period—the Universidad de Alcalá de Henares building is Gil de Hontañón's masterpiece and one of the best compositions of all time in Spain's architecture (Chueca Goitía 1965, 85).

Complutum, the old Roman name of Alcalá de Henares, was already inhabited in *Celtiberic* times; in the twelfth century it became a powerful manor domain of Toledo's archbishops; by the fifteenth century it had become one of the most influential political and religious centers of Castilla. In 1499, Cardinal Cisneros founded in Alcalá de Henares the Universidad Complutense. Cisneros was a Franciscan monk and one of Spain's illustrious representatives of the *Renaissance*, an intellectual who reached to the highest levels of ecclesiastical hierarchy, becoming archbishop of the powerful archdioceses of Toledo by determination of Queen Isabel the Catholic. The university, living testimony of Cisneros' humanistic intellectual legacy, quickly became one of the most prestigious European institutions of the period; some of Spain's most renowned Renaissance thinkers and literary personalities—Tirso de Molina, Francisco de Quevedo, Lope de Vega, Calderón de la Barca, Igna-

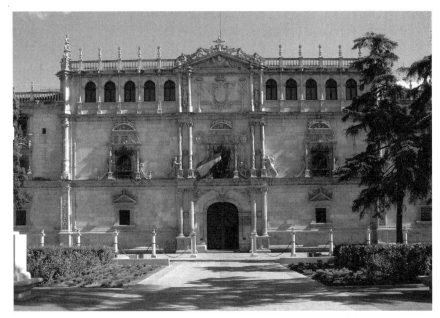

Main façade of the Universidad de Alcalá de Henares designed by Rodrigo Gil de Hontañón.

cio de Loyola, Cervantes—were either students or teachers at this once very influential institution.

The original buildings of the university were begun in 1508 by Pedro Gumiel, Cisneros' favorite architect. They were organized around three square courts organized in a linear sequence. The first of them is the Patio de Santo Tomás, the most important and ceremonial of the whole complex; it is followed by the Patio de los Filósofos (Philosophers' Court) and then by the Patio Trilingüe (Trilingual Court); the Paraninfo or Scholastic Theater (the university's aula magna, the most important classroom) was built in 1517 and is situated on one side of the Patio Trilingüe. The Chapel of San Ildefonso, built in 1510, is the religious center of the university, located off and to the west of the linear sequence of courtyards, next to a smaller court adjacent to the Patio de San Ildefonso. These original buildings constructed under the supervision of Pedro Gumiel were characteristically austere, built with simple and humble materials that—respecting the founder's intention—rejected all visible signs of pomp and monumentality. The walls were unornamented and plastered, while the ceilings and roof structures were magnificent polychrome *artesonados*, synthesis of the Gothic and *Mudéjar* traditions of Spanish architecture. The only remnants of the university buildings erected in Cisneros' time are in the Chapel and in the Paraninfo; the rest were improved, added on, rebuilt, or restored in subsequent years as the prestige of the institution increased, fulfilling Cisneros' famous prediction that "others would build in stone what he had done with mud."

Architecturally, the most relevant of these improvements was the new front façade of the university building commissioned in 1540 to Rodrigo Gil de Hontañón. It consists of a central block flanked by two lower wings that form an equilibrated and well-proportioned composition. Contrary to similar buildings of the same period—the Palace of El Infantado and the Casa de las Conchas, whose façades are markedly asymmetrical—the façade of the Universidad de Alcalá de Henares is perfectly symmetrical, manifesting an architectural resolution that begins to abandon the remnants of Gothic civil architecture (such as in the Gothic Plateresque and Isabelline styles) and an approximation to more purely Renaissance compositional principles. The façade of the university building is an elegantly composed plane of carefully studied proportions that incorporated symbolic references typical of the buildings of this period. The central plane is subdivided into three different portions that respect the strict symmetry of the composition; each of these three portions has openings placed at the center of the plane, thus marking smaller, always symmetrical parts that follow the main composition rules of the whole. In fact, the whole façade seems to be organized by a hidden network of regulating lines that, as in the best examples of classical architecture, govern the composition of the plane, the position of openings, and the basic proportions of the diverse components, even if Rodrigo Gil applied these principles with much more liberty than in known canonical works of classical architecture.

The front façade is composed of a 130-foot-long central block subdivided in three main horizontal bands; the lower one is the building's base which is marked by a relief cornice that extends through the two flanking wings; above, the *piano-nobile* is slightly taller that the base, obviously the most important part of the composition as demonstrated by the more intense relief decoration around the three windows of the central plane; finally, the third level is composed by an open arcaded gallery, a characteristically Plateresque motif conceptually similar to the gallery that crowns the façade of the Palace of El Infantado. However, at Alcalá de Henares, the arcaded gallery is interrupted at the center, emphasizing the central axis of the façade through a windowless plane that features a huge heraldic symbol in stone-relief, a typical feature of Spanish architecture of this period. The central bay of the façade is framed by twin attached columns, while farther to the extremes, a single more robust column marks the limit between the central plane and the two lower wings; windows are notoriously small, but crowned by oversized Renaissance canopies conceived more in relationship with the proportions of the façade than with the actual dimensions of the openings; the central window, which because of location and plastic articulation is the most important, corresponded to the library, the symbolic and practical center of knowledge of the Renaissance university.

The university maintained its political and intellectual prestige until the eighteenth century when it had more than 2,000 students, but in the early years of the nineteenth century it began to decline; in 1836, it had few more than 100 students and had to close. The university buildings were at risk, but the local community succeeded in saving and maintaining them. The Universidad Complutense reopened in 1977, but its buildings, physical remnants of past glorious times, were no longer suitable for instruction and were adapted to become the administrative and symbolic seat of the historically relevant institution, while new facilities were created throughout Castilla. Since 1998, the buildings of the Universidad Complutense and the city of Alcalá de Henares have been protected by UNESCO's World Heritage program. Suitably, every year the building hosts the award ceremony for the Premio Cervantes, the most prestigious award for Spanish-language literature and one of the most important literary distinctions worldwide; the main event is held in the remarkably restored Paraninfo theater, the center of gravity of the university's intellectual activity, a deserved tribute to the historical prestige of the institution, Cisneros' humanistic legacy, and Rodrigo Gil's beautifully composed façade.

Further Reading

Bevan, Bernard. *History of Spanish Architecture*. London: B. T. Basford, 1938.
Chueca Goitía, Fernando. *Historia de la Arquitectura Española: Edad Moderna-Edad Contemporánea*. Vol. 1. Madrid: Editorial Dossat, 1965.

VALDEMINGÓMEZ RECYCLING CENTER, MADRID, COMUNIDAD DE MADRID

Style: Contemporary Architecture
Dates: 1997–2001
Architects: Abalos and Herreros

The new Recycling Plant for urban waste located in Valdemingómez, in the southern periphery of Madrid, and designed by the Madrid-based office of Iñaki Abalos and Juan Herreros, is the most ambitious and important environmental architecture and landscape initiative in contemporary Spanish architecture, and probably one of the most significant worldwide. The Recycling Plant is part of a much larger project for treating and recuperating the existing landfill area and converting it into a future regional park. As the architects commented, "it is one of the city's most attractive projects . . . intended to even-out the social and environmental differences that existed between the north and the south [of Madrid's periphery]" (Abalos and

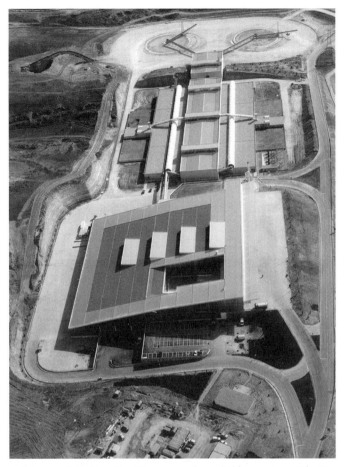

Aerial view of the Recycling Center complex at Valdemingómez. The Recycling Plant is on the center of the image, followed by the Compost Production and Refining Plant. *Photo courtesy of Abalos & Herreros Arquitectos.*

Herreros, project description). Thus, this vast project is relevant not only because of the innovative and high quality of the architecture and landscape
that it proposes, but also because of its role as an agent of social, urban, and
environmental change.

Valdemingómez is located on the southeastern border of the autonomous
community of Madrid; historically an arid land, the area became the dumping ground of Madrid's urban waste; expectedly stigmatized, it was a degraded
area, associated with all the negative aspects of the contemporary
consumption-oriented metropolis. The long-term operation that will recuperate the area with an artificially created topography through the treatment
of the organic waste deposited there will surely reverse its negative image
and transform it into an area for a wide variety of socio-urban uses. The con-

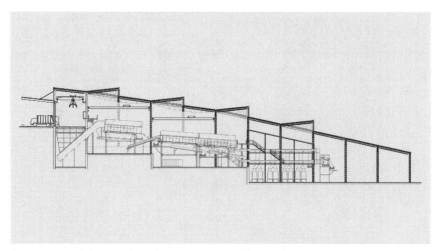

Cross-section of the Recycling Plant. *Photo courtesy of Abalos & Herreros Arquitectos.*

struction of a series of buildings for state-of-the-art treatment and recycling of urban waste was the first step of this ambitious initiative. The commission was given to Abalos and Herreros, an important architectural office based in Madrid that has attracted the attention of many contemporary architectural critics; Ignasi de Solà-Morales, for example, has written that "their built architecture and their projects are attractive because they propose, with a certain amount of modesty, a different path for resolving what are, in may cases, problems that have always existed" (Solà-Morales, in "Abalos & Herreros" 2002, 58).

The series of buildings for the Recycling Plant was a commission that perfectly corresponded with the recent evolution of Abalos and Herreros' architectural proposal as demonstrated in some environmentally conscious projects such as the *Architekturforum* in Bonn (Germany 1997) and the *Casa Verde* (Green House) in Pozuelo (near Madrid 1997). As Ana Yagües commented, "both the program and the materials [of Valdemingómez Recycling Plant] coincide with their interest in exploring creative techniques and processes that are based upon the use and the decontextualization of existing materials" ("Abalos & Herreros" 2002, 214).

The Recycling Center consists of three buildings—the Reception and Weighting Pavilion, the Recycling Plant, and the Compost Production and Refining Plant—inserted in an artificial green site of what used to be an inhospitable land surrounded by vast extensions of dumping grounds. The three buildings are necessarily different in size, organization, and form because of their inherent specific functions. Yet, they are linked by the coherent use of recycled and industrial materials and a rational conception that challenges the traditional reductive understanding of rationalism as a mode of thought and a process of making.

Rather than hiding the building complex, as is often the case in similar circumstances, the transformation of the site has converted the area into a public facility that includes a pedagogical program integrated to the recycling processes, creating an artificial topographic accident in the landscape. The three built structures are organized in a linear sequence placed perpendicular to the main access road that one day, farther to the east, will be one of the main entrances to Madrid's Southeast Regional Park. The first building of the linear sequence is the Reception and Weighting Pavilion; this is the check-in control gate to the site, where the refuse collection trucks are weighted and checked before transporting their load to the Recycling Plant. The pavilion's form resembles a short and wide "T" configured by a small central building that houses the check-in offices covered by a large roof that cantilevers out on the two sides to protect weight equipment, the incoming trucks, and the two small "check-in" booths. Moreover, the "T" form operates as a visual sign that marks the entrance to the protected site. The pavilion's exterior is made in steel and polycarbonate, generating a certain indifferent and cold image; conversely, the interior is much warmer, dominated by the three-ply panels made with recycled wood particles. In fact, the consistent use of recycled materials is one of the salient features of the entire project.

The Recycling Plant, located farther south, is the most important of the three built structures. Under an enormous inclined green roof that echoes the slope of the site in which it sits, this building houses a heterogeneous group of functions such as processing refuse, offices, workshops, and storage; it also includes a small visitors' museum to promote environmental awareness. The large interior is organized as a series of stepped platforms that accommodate the large heavy-duty equipment—machinery for mechanical separation and classification of waste, conveyors for recycling materials, storage—that the facility requires. The museum, offices, and cafeteria are located on the northwest corner of the roughly square building plan around a rectangular courtyard carved off the virtual volume, defined by the large inclined roof; while the double row of trees and a rectangular shallow reflecting fountain suggest more conventionally institutional or domestic images, the uniform use of polycarbonate panels as the courtyard's enclosing material makes no attempt to divert the users' attention from the place. The building's simple bolted structure, with a roof covered with greenery and enclosure made of recycled polycarbonate panels, constitutes a strong architectural manifesto consistent with the environmental nature, function, and purposes of the whole complex.

The third built component is the Compost Production and Refining Plant. This building is dedicated to the production of compost with organic waste not recycled in the Recycling Plant. Eduardo Arroyo has referred to the architecture of this building as "a scale-less powerful machine . . . its design disappears as it is reduced to a mere structural support for the cladding and of those complex non-architectural mechanisms" (Arroyo, in "Abalos &

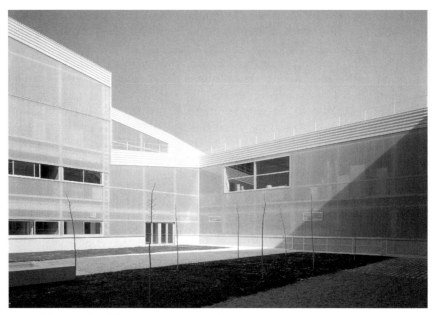

View of the Recycling Plant open-air courtyard. *Photo © Luis Asín.*

Herreros" 2002, 112). In effect, it is a simple building of undoubted industrial character in which the "architecture" may be seen as limited to the design of the system of enclosure, the building's envelope, around the
composting machinery. However, beyond its specific needs as a piece of machinery itself, the composting plant was carefully designed to be part of the
singular landscape in which it is posed, a topographic machine set in an artificial topography.

The Recycling Center complex at Valdemingómez is emblematic of Abalos and Herreros' critical and engaged architectural discourse that avoids the
romanticism of some other environmentally concerned practices in favor of
a process-oriented, discursive environmental architecture. The built complex's relevance is, precisely, related to the critical engagement of its proposal, which makes it a landmark not only of environmentally concerned
architecture but of contemporary architecture as a whole.

Further Reading

"Abalos & Herreros." Monographic issue, *2G* 22 (Barcelona), 2002.
Abalos, Iñaki, and Herreros, Juan. *Areas of Impunity*. Barcelona: Actar, 1998.
Abalos, Iñaki, and Herreros, Juan, with contributing essays by Ignasi de Solà-Morales,
    Eduardo Arroyo, Ana Yagües, et al. *Recycling Madrid*. Barcelona: Actar, 2002.
"In Progress II." Monographic issue, *El Croquis* 106, no. 107 (Madrid), 2001.

WALDEN-7 APARTMENT BUILDING, SANT JUST DESVERN, CATALONIA

Styles: Postmodern Architecture/Modern Revisionism
Dates: 1970–1975
Architects: Ricardo Bofill and Taller de Arquitectura

The Walden-7 building complex is an emblematic building of the 1970s, a period that manifested a reaction against the postulates and results of the architecture proposed by the *Modern Movement*. It was designed by the Barcelona-based "Taller de Arquitectura" ("The Architecture Workshop"), a multidisciplinary collaborative team of architects, writers, mathematicians, sociologists, and poets, founded in 1964 by Ricardo Bofill. Walden-7 is representative of the team's prolific and innovative second phase of work that spanned most of the 1970s; it is also one of its most important realizations in Spain, before engaging in large-scale urban projects, especially in France.

Walden-7 is located in Sant Just Desvern, an industrial suburb of Barcelona approximately six miles south of the city's center. The site for the original project was a nearly thirteen-acre area formerly occupied by the Sanson cement factory, which laid partially in ruins. Bofill's proposal was to create an enceinte that enclosed the old cement factory with a housing scheme that represented a radical departure from the previous prevailing as well as contemporaneous paradigms for buildings of similar characteristics. The two most salient characteristics of Walden-7's innovative proposal are at the scale of both the cell and the city. In effect, the building's rather introspected volumes, the functional organization of spatial units that could be combined in several different forms, taking the individual as the smallest "social cell" (as opposed to the family), and the exploration of an architectural language rich in figurative and historicist associations were part of a novel conception and understanding of the problem of housing in the city. This was also a ferocious reaction—or a "brutal protest," to borrow Bofill's own words as quoted by Christian Norberg-Schulz (Futagawa 1985, 11)—against the long-accepted precepts of postwar architecture, particularly for housing programs. This reaction anticipated the explosion of figurative explorations of the late 1970s and seemed to triumph over the abstraction and proclaimed rationalism of modern architecture. As a collective housing project, Walden-7 was a pioneering scheme because it focused on the individual—and the community of individuals—rather than on the collective, at the same time that it transgressed the boundaries of accepted notions of public and private by creating intimate public spaces, where the individual participates in communal activities, without ever abandoning its individual nature.

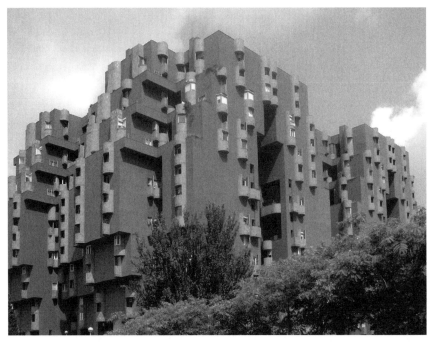

General view of Walden-7's exterior showing the semicircular balconies and the tall vertical slits that communicate with the interior courtyard.

The original project comprised three high-rise housing blocks linked by other multistorey but lower buildings arranged in linear sequences that enclosed the remnants of the existing cement factory, and a central open space of approximately 250,000 square feet. The new portions of the project were primarily devoted to housing, while the cement factory was reserved to accommodate office and working spaces for the "Taller de Arquitectura" as well as other cultural facilities. Together, the housing blocks and the office-cultural components would have constituted a monumental whole of impressive characteristics and scale. However, only a fragment of the original project was eventually completed (the largest of the three high-rise housing blocks and the remodeling and rehabilitation of the factory silos for the Taller's offices); nevertheless, the completed housing portion is a significant and unique example of *Postmodern* architecture.

The built housing block offers the possibility of reading it in different forms: one could see it as a massive high-rise block perforated by large vertical and horizontal voids that create generous spaces for communal activities, or as several sixteen-level paired towers linked together by various types of horizontal and vertical circulation connectors organized around four large shafts—veritable vertical patios—open to the sky. The building's exterior reflects the architects' intentions to create an introspected complex that negates the aggressive and urbanistically chaotic spatial environment in which it is situated, while providing it with a sober monumentality and urban dignity; conversely, the interior is lively, animated by a vibrant color scheme and a complex system of branching corridors, bridges, and passageways that generate dynamic open-air spaces.

The exterior of the building is animated by a staggering silhouette of recessing and projecting levels that challenge its perception as a single massive form. It is fully clad in red tiles and punctuated by tiny semicircular projecting balconies that create an agglomeration of forms that resembles a beehive. The clever manipulation of the building's form allowed the conception of oversized openings in direct relationship with the open shafts defined by the enclosing high-rise volumes; these large openings, veritable "urban windows," bring natural light and air inside the block and reveal the vibrant colorful interior of the vertical patios, providing a sharp contrast with the rather severe exterior of the building.

The communal spaces organized inside of the block consist of four vertical patios arranged around a central elevator core linked to the bridges and hanging corridors that lead to the individual apartments. These communal spaces are fully covered by colorful glazed ceramic tiles; highly protected, they are reserved for the inhabitants of the complex, for whom they become intimate pubic spaces analogous to the city's streets and plazas; expectedly, every single apartment has a view to these patios, partaking of their dynamic communal activity. The ground level is almost entirely dedicated to services and commercial facilities such as a grocery store, pharmacy, bookstore, and other community-oriented activities. The roof houses two swimming pools and other leisure-oriented spaces for the building's community, pinnacle of the proposed communal objective.

The actual living units constitute the most innovative part of Walden-7 because they are not conceived as usual apartments but as individual cells where each cell provides the minimal necessities of comfort for one single individual. Each cell is a 30-square-meter module (320 square feet) equipped with a very small kitchen, a water basin, a toilet, and a bath, all of very limited dimensions. The rest of the space is unspecified, reserved for a wide variety of living activities (eating, sleeping, relaxing); that is, the single individual's cell does not have defined spaces such as "living," "dining," or "bedroom," but a rather generous generic space where each individual is expected to use it as wished. The 30-square-meter modules could be clustered together horizontally or vertically to generate larger units for more than one individual. Interestingly, despite the very limited openings to the outdoors—either to the building's exterior or to the internal patios—the cell's interior spaces are quite luminous, likely thanks to the absence of partitions that would have conditioned the appropriate distribution of natural light throughout the cell.

Taller de Arquitectura proposed a series of possible combinations of the basic module, as well as several ways of equipping the cells with cupboards, closets, and other furnishings, but it was up to the individual to decide whether to take the cell already equipped or as an empty container. For a society firmly rooted in the value of the family as the smallest social entity, Walden-7 was, no doubt, a radical proposal, one where the convergence of ideas of a community based on individuals living in individual spatial cells would lead to the development of a new housing paradigm that would have replaced the largely anonymous and sterile housing blocks of urban peripheral areas. Whereas the construction of the entire original project will not be carried on (the site has been already occupied by other, more traditional, housing blocks), the built block of Walden-7 is an unavoidable reference to the social and architectural critique that in the late 1960s and 1970s questioned the roots of modern architecture's postulates that had prevailed for most of the twentieth century.

Further Reading

Futagawa, Yukio, ed. *GA Architect: Ricardo Bofill and Taller de Arquitectura*. Tokyo: A.D.A. Edita, 1985.

James, Warren A. *Ricardo Bofill-Taller de Arquitectura*. New York: Rizzoli, 1988.

Ruiz Cabrero, Gabriel. *The Modern in Spain: Architecture after 1948*. Cambridge, MA; London: The MIT Press, 2001.

Glossary

al-Andalus: Arabic name given by the Muslims to the entire Iberian Peninsula after they invaded it in 711. The name of Spain's southern region of Andalucía derives from al-Andalus.

Almohad(s): Berber dynasty that replaced the Almoravids and controlled Muslim Spain in the twelfth century until their defeat by Christian armies in 1212.

Almoravid(s): Berber dynasty that controlled a large portion of the Iberian Peninsula and North Africa in the eleventh and twelfth centuries; they were overthrown by the Almohads.

ambulatory: Usually refers to a covered space in which a person walks around a certain place such as a cloister or an apse; in Romanesque and Gothic architecture, it is the space between the central sanctuary and the radiating chapels.

apse: Usually a semicircular or polygonal space at the east end of Christian churches, such as basilicas and cathedrals. Also used to refer to a projecting volume that resembles an apse.

apsidioles: Smaller or subsidiary apses, usually arranged parallel or radially to the center of the main apse of a church; projected part of a building usually oriented from the eastern side of a transept.

architrave: Lower part of the entablature usually formed by a horizontal beam that spans the columns or pillars; later used to generally refer to the molding around an opening, door, or window.

Arian Heresy/Arianism: In early Christianity, a controversy erupted over the person of Christ—whether it was human or divine or whether it manifested both conditions; the followers of the Arian heresy—such as the Visigoths—supported the thesis that the Son of God was a creature and not truly God. This conflict was resolved in 325 at the Council of Nicaea when 300 bishops stated that the person of the Christ is "of one substance" with that of God his Father.

Art Nouveau: Predominant decorative style at the end of the nineteenth century and the beginning of the twentieth century. It is characterized by the use of sinuous, asymmetrical lines based on organic forms; its goal was to be free from any imitation of historical styles. It is conceptually related to Spain's *Modernismo*.

artesonados: Wood coffered ceilings that were very popular in Spanish Muslim-influenced architecture.

Arts and Crafts: Movement of the second half of the nineteenth century predominantly in the United Kingdom that tried to raise the appreciation of craftsmanship in contrast to manufactured industrialized products.

ashlar: Hewn or square-cut stone; it is also used to refer to a masonry wall built with such stones.

Asturian-Visigothic: The Visigoths—a Germanic tribe—established themselves in Spain at the end of Roman rule in the Iberian Peninsula; when Muslims invaded the peninsula in 711, the Visigothic kingdom based in Toledo fell. The Visigoths fled north and established a new kingdom in the northern region of Asturias between 718 and the early tenth century; this kingdom successfully resisted Muslim pressure.

Augustinian: Religious order following the Rule of St. Augustine that developed in western Europe from the mid-eleventh century.

Aurignacian: Refers to the Upper Paleolithic Period in Europe and is characterized by a great diversification and specialization in the use of tools.

baldaquino: Ornamental cover used over a sacred object or an altar; often used to refer to a structure that resembles a baldaquino.

balustrade: A rail supported by balusters or other vertical elements to prevent falls from, for example, balconies, windows, etc; in classical architecture, the rail supported by columns was usually vase-shaped for the same or ornamental purposes.

Baroque: Complex artistic and architectural style that originated in Italy in the early seventeenth century and remained popular well into the eighteenth century.

Baroque-Churrigueresque: *See Churrigueresque.*

barrel vault: The most common form of vault; it consists of a vault in a semicylindrical form.

basilica: In Roman times, a versatile space often situated in or near the forum with a variety of civic functions; it usually consists of a rectangular space with the central axis oriented lengthwise and delimited by columns and illuminated by high windows; later adopted as the basic building type for Christian churches.

belvedere: As used in the texts, an elevated place or built structure with a privileged or commanding vantage point to a landscape or other pleasant scenery.

Benedictine: Congregation of monks, nuns, and lay brothers following the rule of St. Benedict (c. 480–c. 547) that was very influential in the high Middle Ages, especially for the development of Romanesque architecture.

buttress: Generally used in Romanesque and Gothic architecture to refer to a structural element in brick or stone built against or projecting from a wall to lighten its weight while providing structural stability; the term is often used to refer to elements that either resemble a buttress or fulfill a similar function.

Byzantine: Refers to the architectural style originated in Byzantium, center of the Eastern Roman Empire after the division of Rome into the Western and Eastern empires with capitals in Rome and Constantinople, respectively; Byzantine art and architecture was heavily influenced by Eastern cultures; in Western architecture, it encompasses a period between the late fourth century and the 900s. *See also Early Christian.*

capital(s): Upper part of a column that supports the beam or arch above; there are many types of capitals, depending on their shape, proportions, and carved or applied ornamentation. The most common types—Doric, Ionic, Corinthian—derived from classical Greek architecture; other types include Composite, Tuscan, and Visigothic.

cardum (plural cardines): One of the two main intersecting axes usually placed at right angles that characterized the layout of most Roman towns; the plural refers to similar elements of the orthogonal grid of secondary importance parallel to the main cardum.

Carolingian: Term referring to the dynasty—founded by Charlemagne's father—that ruled central-western Europe between 750 and 987; architecturally, the term refers to the style that corresponds with and was heavily supported by the Carolingian Empire. The style is considered to be part of or to have evolved parallel to Romanesque architecture.

catalan vault: Vault typical of Catalonian style that is usually made of bricks and characterized by a flattened arched profile.

cavea: Seating areas of Greek and Roman theaters and amphitheaters; it was generally separated into three parts—the lower portion, or *summa*, was reserved for Roman dignitaries and important citizens; the central section, or *media*, was usually occupied by regular Roman citizens; and the upper level, or *imma*, was reserved for the poor and slaves.

Celtiberic: Refers to the indigenous tribes of Celtic origin that populated the Iberian Peninsula prior to the arrival and occupation of the Romans in the third century b.c.e.

chancel: Eastern end of a church, where the altar is located; it contains the *choir* and is often raised above the level of the nave by steps; in some historical periods, it was separated from the rest of the church by a screen, or *iconostasis.*

choir: Part of a church usually reserved for the singers or the performance of the clergy; also, part of a church between the chancel and the nave.

chorus: In the Roman theater the chorus was the area reserved for seating senators and dignitaries.

Churrigueresque: Uniquely late Baroque Spanish architectural style of the eighteenth century; the term was coined after the work of the Churriguera brothers, who were considered masters of the style.

ciborium: Usually refers to a domed space at the crossing of medieval churches.

Cistercian(s): Monastic order founded in the late eleventh century in Burgundy; it is a stricter, simpler branch of the Benedictines.

Cluniac: Refers to anything or anyone belonging to or following the principles of the order found in the town of Cluny, France, in the ninth century; observing the Benedictine rule, the order had a tremendous influence throughout Europe, especially between the ninth and twelfth centuries.

Composite **(column):** Column composed with the proportions, base, shaft, and entablature of the Corinthian order with a capital including aspects of the Ionic order such as having four identical faces or inserted volutes.

Constantinian: Refers to the period ruled by the Roman Emperor Constantine the Great (285–337), who converted to Christianity and imposed it as the official religion of the Roman Empire.

***conversos*:** From Spanish for "converted people," it refers to people who originally were Jewish or Muslim and had been obliged to convert to Christianity if they wanted to remain in Spain; *conversos* were often segregated from "original" Christians.

corbel: A weight-carrying member that projects from a wall; it is usually stepped upward and outward from a vertical surface made of stone, wood, or iron and may be used to support an object such as an architectural element or a statue; popular in medieval times when they were fancifully decorated.

Corinthian: One of the three classical orders of Greek architecture widely used by Romans who propagated it to their colonies; the capital of the Corinthian column is characterized by acanthus leaves and carved foliage.

crenels: Indentation typical of battlements; also used to refer to elements that resemble it.

crossing: Term that identifies the intersection of the nave and transept of a church; generally, it has a vertical emphasis marked by a tower, dome, or drum.

crypt: A room, usually underground, placed below the main church; it is often low and vaulted, especially in medieval architecture.

curbstone: Stone that constitutes a curb or an edge; also, row of stones that fulfill a similar purpose.

curia: A part of the Roman forum, the curia was the senate house.

decumanum **(plural *decumani*):** One of the two main intersecting axes usually placed perpendicular to the cardum that characterized the layout of most Roman towns; the plural refers to an ensemble of similar elements parallel to the main *decumanum*.

diptych: Composition made of two panels of equal size usually hinged to be folded into one single panel; often used for religious representations, their material, size, and form changed depending on the historical period.

Doric: One of the three classical orders of Greek architecture; characterized by sturdy elements and austere elegance; often referred to as an order representing a masculine character.

Early Christian: Expression used to describe the art and architecture at the beginning of Christianity; it roughly encompasses a period between the third and eighth centuries C.E., especially in the European areas of the western Mediterranean; it is related to Byzantine art and architecture, which refers to the eastern areas of the Mediterranean basin.

Eclecticism: Architectural style of the nineteenth century that is characterized by the free combination of elements from diverse historical styles.

Enlightenment: Intellectual movement originated in France in the eighteenth century that promoted reasoning as a vehicle of progress; it had a great impact on the development of knowledge through systematic studies of nature and science, and the study of the past. Numerous artistic and architectural movements of the nineteenth century—Neoclassicism, Eclecticism, Rationalism, and to some extent Romanticism—emerged as a result of the Enlightenment.

extramuros/extramural: Refers to parts placed or existing beyond the walls or limits of a precinct or delimited area.

Flamboyant: Late Gothic architectural style that originated in France and extended through many European countries; the name derives from the abundance of flame-like stone tracery.

forum: The actual meaning in Latin is "place of public assembly"; in Roman architecture, the forum was the main open public space used for a wide variety of civic as well as religious functions.

fossa arenaia: Long and narrow space located underground—below the arena—in Roman amphitheatres that housed beasts and other elements needed for the arena's games and events.

Jugendstil: Artistic movement of the late nineteenth century in Germany that was contemporary with and exhibited some similarities to France's *Art Nouveau* and Spain's *Modernismo*.

GATCPAC: Acronym made of the initials for *Grupo de Artistas Técnicos Catalanes para el Progreso de la Arquitectura Contemporánea* (Catalonia's Group of Artists and Technicians for the Progress of Contemporary Architecture); it was Catalonia's branch of the GATEPAC.

GATEPAC: Acronym made of the initials for *Grupo de Artistas Técnicos Españoles para el Progreso de la Arquitectura Contemporánea* (Spain's Group of Artists and Technicians for the Progress of Contemporary Architecture); founded by Josep Lluís Sert and other modern architects, it promoted modern architecture and urbanism in Spain.

Gothic: Refers to the art and architecture that dominated across Europe between the eleventh and fourteenth centuries; late forms of Gothic art and architecture extended into the sixteenth century.

Greek-cross: Cross composed of four arms of equal length intersecting at right angles; the form was often used for plans of churches.

Greek theater: Building for outdoor performances in ancient Greece; it was composed of concentric semicircular tiers focusing in a circular stage area where the performance took place.

groin vault: The groin vault is composed of two barrel vaults of equal width intersected at right angles; the weight of the vault is transmitted by the groins (the diagonal intersection of the barrel vault fragments), thus liberating parts of the wall from load-bearing.

Grup R: Group created by Barcelona-based architects in the 1950s that organized lecture series and other architecture-related events and that is credited with reintroducing the debate and discourse of modern architecture in Spain during Francisco Franco's dictatorial regime.

haram: Praying hall of a mosque.

helicoidal: A helix form.

Hellenic: Used to refer to post-classical Greek culture and architecture.

Hieronymite: Important monastic order in Spain; it was favored by the sixteenth-century kings Carlos I (better known as Holy Roman Emperor Carlos V) and Felipe II.

Hispania: Name given to the Iberian Peninsula by the Romans.

horse shoe: Arch that resembles a horse shoe because its lower ends project farther down than the diameter of the circle; they are predominant in Islamic architecture but were already used in early Eastern Christian buildings; the two—Islamic or Early Christian—have some differences based on the construction of the circular figure of origin; the name derived from its resemblance to a horse-shoe.

iconostasis: A screening element that separates the altar from the nave in Eastern churches; it is believed that they were widely used in Early Christian architecture.

Ionic: One of the three main orders of Greek classical art; among the most important details it has are smooth columns and a capital distinguished by rounded volutes.

Isabelline: Uniquely Spanish architectural style of the late fifteenth century that coincided with the reign of the Catholic Queen Isabel I and was characterized by exuberant stone ornamentation; the Isabelline and Plateresque styles predominated in Spain's artistic transition from Gothic to Renaissance.

Knight Templars: Military religious/monastic order created at the time of the Crusades; it spread throughout Europe in the Middle Ages and was suppressed in the early fourteenth century.

lancet/lancet arch: Slender pointed arch or arched opening typical of early Gothic architecture.

Latin-cross: Geometrical cruciform figure in which one of the two arms is much longer than the other; the form is widely used as the typical plan of Christian churches.

lobated arches: Term used to refer to arches composed of numerous lobed figures.

Magdalenian: Period of the late upper Paleolithic (16,000–10,000 B.C.E.) predominantly in southern France and Spain.

Mannerism: Controversial term used by some historians of the Renaissance to refer to the art and architecture of the sixteenth century, especially but not limited to Italy.

maqsura: A screen or barrier that surrounds the mihrab.

Marca Hispánica **(Hispanic Mark):** Region under Frankish or Carolingian rule at the frontier with al-Andalus; it comprised a geographical area that roughly coincides with the modern region of Catalonia on both sides of the Pyrenees.

merlons: Upright or dent of an indented battlement.

mihrab: In a mosque, a niche carved in the quibla, generally at the center; it probably appeared in the eighth century.

minbar: A seat located to the right of the mihrab for the reading of Friday's prayer.

mineral surface: As used in the text, it refers to an area covered with materials of mineral origin or mineral derivates (e.g., stone or concrete).

mixtilinear arches: Refers to arches composed of a multiplicity of curvilinear fragments of different radius.

*mocárabes***:** Three-dimensional ornamental composition made up of geometrical prisms, usually hanging as ceilings; the lower surface ends in a concave surface.

Modern Movement: Refers to the architectural movement that emerged, principally in Europe but also in America, at the beginning of the twentieth century; it marked a radical departure from the architectural styles and practices of the past.

*Modernismo, Modernismo Catalan***:** Artistic and architectural movement originating in Barcelona and related to similar contemporaneous developments in other European countries, such as *Art Nouveau* in France and Belgium, *Jugendstil* in Germany, *Secessionist Movement* in Vienna, Austria, and others.

Mozarab, Mozarabic: Meaning "arabized," it refers to the non-Islamic people, art, and architecture that thrived under Islamic rule or had begun to absorb Islamic culture.

*Mudéjar***:** From Arab language, it means "permitted to remain"; in architectural terms, it refers to a uniquely Spanish style that originated in the late twelfth and thirteenth centuries by the crossbreeding of Christian (Romanesque and Gothic) and Islamic art and architecture.

*municipium***:** Roman town that was subject to Rome but enjoyed a certain degree of autonomy in the sense that it was governed by its own laws; a municipal status was granted to towns after having attained a certain degree of importance.

narthex: Meaning antechamber or porch, it is also used to describe the usually constricted western entrance body or space of a church's interior.

Nasrid(s): The last dynasty that governed a Muslim state in the Iberian Peninsula; Granada was the capital city from 1237 until the Nasrid defeat and expulsion by Spain's Catholic Kings in 1492.

nave: Most commonly used to refer to the central aisle or space of a religious building, such as a church or cathedral; lateral nave(s) refers to the side aisles of a church parallel to the main nave; the term is often used to refer to spaces, for example, in museums or factories, that have characteristics resembling a nave.

Neoclassical, Neoclassicism: Architectural movement or style that emerged in the late eighteenth and early nineteenth centuries and that, in reacting against the extravagances of late Baroque architecture, promoted a return to the ancient classical language of Greece and Rome.

oculus: Circular opening, window, or panel, usually a skylight as in a dome.

ogee: Refers to sinuous and flowing arches with two multiple centers.

Paleolithic: Prehistoric period corresponding to the early part of the Stone Age.

***parabemata*:** Plural of *parabema*, which is a room associated with the *bema* (altar or sanctuary) or a basilica.

***pasarelles(s)*:** A narrow path that connects two different spaces; it is often elevated like a catwalk.

pediment: Triangular portion that usually crowns an opening or portico; it originated in Greek classical architecture.

peristyle: A colonnaded room.

perron: Exterior stepped platform that leads to the main entrance of a building.

Phocean: Originating in the Phocean city of Massilia (modern Marseilles, France).

Phoenician: Member or originary from the ancient culture of Phoenicia in the eastern Mediterranean.

piano-nobile: Main story of a residence or building, usually located one level above the ground floor.

***Plateresque*:** Meaning "silversmith like," it is a uniquely Spanish architectural style of the sixteenth century that operated as a transition between medieval and modern (Renaissance) architectural practices; it was characterized by an exuberant decoration in stone that resembles the intricate work of silversmiths.

***Poitevin*:** Originary from the region of Poitou in central-western France.

Postmodern, Postmodernism: Literary, artistic, and architectural movement that reacted against the general and universal principles of modern postulates.

postscaenium: Rear side of the stage front of Roman theaters.

***programme*:** Used to generally refer to a set of ideas or postulates that work in a coordinated or consistent form.

promenade: As used in the text, it refers to an intentionally created path or sequence of spatial experiences within a building, landscape, or urban setting; also used to refer to a paved public walk or strolling area.

pulpitum: Area corresponding to the stage of a Roman theater.

quadrant vault: A quadrant is a quarter of a circle, plane, or sphere; a quadrant vault is a vaulted space made by, for example, a quarter of a dome.

quibla: One of the most important components of a mosque, it is a wall oriented toward Mecca that indicates the direction of prayer.

rambla: An ample strolling path typical of Catalonian cities such as Barcelona and Tarragona; the term is also used to refer to similar strolling areas in parks or by the ocean, rivers, lakes, or other bodies of water.

Rayonnant: Gothic architectural style that evolved predominantly in France in the thirteenth century; it is characterized by stone tracery in the form of radiating rays.

Reconquista: From Spanish for "reconquest," it describes a seven-centuries-long process launched by the Christian kingdoms of Spain to recover the Iberian territories lost to the Muslims.

Renaissance: Historical period considered as the start of the humanistic era that began in the early decades of the fifteenth century and was characterized by a reaction against medieval art and science and a revival, a renaissance, of Greco-Roman classical culture; it was a tremendously prolific artistic and scientific period.

Renaixença: Conservative cultural and political movement of Catalonia that, in the late nineteenth and early twentieth centuries, promoted a nationalist Catalan sentiment and Catalonian language and culture.

Revivalism: Artistic and architectural trend of the nineteenth century that attempted to revive the styles of the past; thus, buildings were often built in neo-Gothic, neo-Romanesque, and neo-*Mudéjar* architectural "styles."

riwaqs: Porticoes or arcades that surround a mosque or a shrine providing a spatial transition between the *sahn* and the *haram*.

Romanesque: Predominant European architectural style from the tenth to the thirteenth centuries; in most European countries, it was replaced with the advent of Gothic architecture, but in Spain it continued for a longer period, often overlapping with Gothic architecture and also mixing with local architecture of Islamic origin to generate a uniquely Spanish style.

Romanticism: Artistic and architectural style of the late eighteenth and early nineteenth centuries; it reacted against the imposing order of Neoclassicism by favoring intuitive and personal approaches.

sahn: Open-air courtyard enclosed by walls that precedes the *haram* or praying hall of a mosque.

scaenae frons: Stage-front structure of a Roman theatre meant to accommodate a wide variety of stage designs depending on the type of performances presented.

sgraffiti: Decorative engraving made by scratching a surface to create a drawing by revealing a lower layer of highly contrasting color.

spandrel: Refers to the roughly triangular form between the outer curve of an arch (or sequences of arches) and an upper edge, such as a ceiling or cornice line, or a wall.

squinch: Arch or series of widening arches placed in a corner to provide a transition between a square plan form and a dome or drum above.

taifa: Term given to each of the geographical and political entities that resulted from the fragmentation of the Caliphate of Córdoba at the beginning of the eleventh century; there were about twenty-three different taifas dispersed throughout the Iberian Peninsula that were governed by local princes.

talud: Spanish word for a side slope generally made out of soil and often covered with grass that negotiates two areas of different elevation.

talus: *See talud.*

transennae: Lattice windows made of wood, stucco, stone, or even metal.

transept: Usually refers to the arms of a cross-shaped church that are placed perpendicular to the nave.

trencadis: Composition made by irregular fragments of ceramic tiles commonly used by Gaudí in many of his buildings; the technique was often adopted by Gaudí's disciples and other architects.

triforium (plural triforia): Arcaded gallery generally placed above the nave, but also above the choir and transept, of medieval churches.

trumpet squinch: Elongated squinch form that resembles a trumpet.

Tuscan: Refers to one of the Roman orders of architecture as identified in the Renaissance. It is characterized by its simpler details and sometimes by it monumentality.

vault: Roof or ceiling structure of curvilinear section, generally made of stone but also of brick; there are many different kinds of vault forms and construction such as the barrel vault, Catalan vault, groin vault, and quadrant vault.

Visigoth/Visigothic: Germanic tribe that originated in the Baltic region and settled eventually in southern France and Spain; at the fall of the Roman Empire, the Visigoths created a kingdom based in Toledo; their rule of Iberian territories lasted until the Muslim invasion of 711, when they were forced to retreat northward, eventually creating a new Asturian-Visigothic dynasty there.

vizier: High official in Muslim states.

voussoirs(s): Each of the individual wedge-shaped stones that constitute an arch; term is predominantly used to refer to arches in Islamic architecture.

Weimar Republic: Name usually given to Germany's republican period after World War I, which was based on a constitution drawn up by the national assembly (Reichstag) that met in the city of Weimar in 1919; the Weimar Republic ended with the advent of Adolf Hitler and the Third Reich in 1933.

Bibliography

Each entry includes a short list of bibliographic references related to the building or buildings presented; however, these lists are far from exhaustive. The following bibliography includes the texts mentioned in each of the individual entries as well as a small selection of the books consulted for developing the entry texts included in this book.

Books and Articles

Abalos, Iñaki, and Herreros, Juan. *Areas of Impunity*. Barcelona: Actar, 1998.

Abalos, Iñaki, and Herreros, Juan, with contributing essays by Ignasi de Solà-Morales, Eduardo Arroyo, Ana Yagües, et al. *Recycling Madrid*. Barcelona: Actar, 2002.

Allegret, Laurence. *Musées*. Paris: Editions du Moniteur, 1987.

Antequera, Marino. *The Alambra and The Generalife*. Granada: Editorial Padre Suárez, 1953.

Arce, Javier, Ensoli, Serena, and La Rocca, Eugenio, eds. *Hispania Romana*. Milano: Electa Edizioni, 1997. (See especially the article by Xavier Aquilué entitled "Empuries Repubblicana," pages 44–49.)

Barcia Merayo, Luis. *Castillos y Palacios de España*. Barcelona: Editorial Salvat, 1994.

Barrat i Altet, Xavier. *Le Monde Roman: Villes, Cathédrales et Monastères*. Cologne: Taschen, 2001.

Bastlund, Knud. *José Luis Sert: Architecture, City Planning, Urban Design*. New York; Washington, DC: Frederick A. Praeger, 1967.

Bertrand, M. J., and Listowski, H. *Les Places Dans la ville*. Paris: Dunod, 1984.

Bevan, Bernard. *History of Spanish Architecture*. London: B. T. Basford, 1938.

Blunt, Anthony, ed. *Baroque and Rococo: Architecture and Decoration*. New York: Harper & Row, 1978.

Bohigas, Oriol. *Reseña y Catálogo de la Arquitectura Modernista*. Barcelona: Editorial Lumen, 1973.

Borras, Maria Lluïsa. *Lluís Domènech i Montaner*. Barcelona: Ediciones Polígrafa, 1970.

Borrás Gualis, Gonzalo M. *El Arte Mudéjar en Teruel y su Provincia*. Teruel: Instituto de Estudios Turolenses, 1987.

Bottineau, Yves, and Butler, Yvan. *Baroque Ibérique*. Fribourg: Office du Livre, 1969.

Breuil, Henri. *La Cueva de Altamira en Santillana del Mar*. Madrid: Tip. de Archivos, 1935.

Brown, Frank E. *Roman Architecture*. New York: George Brazillier Publishers, 1961.

Bruggen, Coosje van. *Frank O. Gehry: Guggenheim Museum Bilbao*. New York: Guggenheim Museum Publications, 1997.

Buchanan, Peter. "Regenerating Barcelona with Parks and Plazas." *Architectural Review* 175, no. 1048 (June 1984): 32–46.

Buchanan, Peter. "Renewal of Buildings and Culture." *Architecture and Urbanism* 96, no. 12 (Tokyo), 1996.

Buchanan, Peter, ed. *The Architecture of Enric Miralles and Carme Pinòs*. New York: Sites-Lumen, 1990.

Calatrava, Santiago. "Museo de las Ciencias, Valencia." *AV Monografias* 87, 88 (January-April 2000).

Calatrava, Santiago. "Science Museum." *Lotus International* 109 (Milano), 2001.

Choisy, Auguste. *Histoire de l'Architecture*. Paris: Gauthier-Villars, 1899.

Chueca Goitía, Fernando. *Historia de la Arquitectura Española: Edad Antigua y Edad Media* (volume 1), and *Edad Moderna-Edad Contemporánea* (volume 2). Madrid: Editorial Dossat, 1965.

Chueca Goitía, Fernando, Sambricio, Carlos, Capitel, Antón, Ruiz Cabrero, Gabriel, and Hernández de León, Juan M. *Arquitectura de Madrid, Siglo XX*. Madrid: Tanais Ediciones, 1999.

Cirici, Alexandre, and Gumí Cardona, Jordi. *L'Art Gòtic Català: l'Arquitectura als Segles XIII i XIV*. Barcelona: Edicions 62 s/a, 1977.

Conant, Kenneth John. *Carolingian and Romanesque Architecture 800–1200*. 2nd ed. Middlesex: Penguin Books, 1978.

Corea, Mario, Gallardo, Francisco, and Mannino, Edgardo. *Corea-Gallardo-Mannino*. Madrid: Aspan Editores, 1993.

Corral Lafuente, José Luis, and Peña Gonzalvo, Francisco Javier, eds. *La Cultura Islámica en Aragón*. Zaragoza: Diputación Provincial de Zaragoza, 1989.

Cruz, Antonio, and Ortiz, Antonio. "Estadio de Atletismo." *El Croquis* 48 (June 1991): 66–75.

Curtis, William. J. R. "A Patient Search: The Art and Architecture of Juan Navarro Baldeweg." *El Croquis* 54 (1992): 4–22.

Curtis, William J. R. "Lines of Thoughts, Fragments of Meaning." *El Croquis* 61, (1993): 6–26.

Curtis, William J. R. *Modern Architecture since 1900*. 3rd ed. London: Phaidon Press Limited, 1996.

Curtis, William J. R. "Rafael Moneo: Pieces of City, Memories of Ruins." *El Croquis* 64 (1994): 47–66.

Curtis, William. J. R. ("Rafael Moneo: The Structure of Intention." *El Croquis* 98 (2000): 28–41.

Dal Co, Franceso, and Forster, Kurt. *Frank O. Gehry: The Complete Works*. New York: The Monacelli Press, 1998.

Dodds, Jerrilynn D. *Architecture and Ideology in Early Medieval Spain*. University Park, PA; London: Pennsylvania State University Press, 1989.

Drew, Philip. *Real Space: The Architecture of Martorell, Bohigas, Mackay, Puigdomènech.* Tubingen-Berlin: E. Wasmuth, 1993.

Escobar, Jesús. *The Plaza Mayor and the Shaping of Baroque Madrid.* Cambridge: Cambridge University Press, 2003.

Ferguson, Russell, ed. *At the End of the Century: One Hundred Years of Architecture.* Los Angeles and New York: The Museum of Contemporary Art and Harry N. Abrams, 1998.

Fernández Ordóñez, José Antonio, and Navarro Vera, José Ramón. *Eduardo Torroja, Engineer.* Madrid: Ediciones Pronaos, 1999.

Fletcher, Sir Banister. *A History of Architecture.* 20th ed. Oxford: Architectural Press, 1996.

Flores, Carlos. *Arquitectura Española Contemporánea, I 1880–1950.* Madrid: Aguilar, 1988.

Frampton, Kenneth. *Martorell, Bohigas, Mackay: Treinte ans d'Architecture, 1954–1984.* Milan and Paris: Electa-Moniteur, 1985.

Frampton, Kenneth, ed. *Contemporary Spanish Architecture: An Eclectic Panorama.* New York: Rizzoli, 1986.

Futagawa, Yukio, ed. *GA Architect: Ricardo Bofill and Taller de Arquitectura.* Tokyo: A.D.A. Edita, 1985.

García de Cortázar, Fernando. *Historia de España: de Atapuerca el evro.* Barcelona: Planeta, 2002.

Giedion-Welcker, Carola. *Park Güell de A. Gaudí.* New York: George Wittenborn, 1966.

Grodecki, Louis. *Gothic Architecture.* Milan; New York: Electa Editrice and Rizzoli, 1978.

Güell, Xavier, ed. *Cruz and Ortiz.* Barcelona: Editorial Gustavo Gili, 1988.

Güell, Xavier, ed. *M. Lapeña-Torres.* Barcelona: Editorial Gustavo Gili, 1990.

Güell, Xavier, and Flores, Carlos. *Architecture of Spain, Guide.* Barcelona: Fundación Caje de Arquitectos, 1996.

Herrera Casado, Antonio. *El Palacio del Infantado.* Guadalajara: Aache Ediciones, 2001.

Hitchcock, Henry-Russell, and Johnson, Philip. *The International Style: Architecture since 1922.* New York: W.W. Norton, 1932.

Hoag, John D. *Islamic Architecture.* New York: Harry N. Abrams, 1977.

James, Warren A. *Ricardo Bofill-Taller de Arquitectura.* New York: Rizzoli, 1988.

Jodidio, Philip. *Alvaro Siza.* Cologne: Taschen GmbH, 2003.

Jodidio, Philip. *Santiago Calatrava.* Cologne: Benedikt Taschen Verlag, 1998.

Kent, Conrad, and Prindle, Dennis. *Park Güell.* New York: Princeton Architectural Press, 1993.

Lambert, Elie. *L'Art Gothique en Espagne aux XIleme et XIlleme siecles.* Paris: H. Laurens, 1931.

Lampérez y Romea, Vicente. *Historia de la Arquitectura Cristiana Española en la Edad Media.* Vols. 1 and 2. Valladolid: Ambito Ediciones, 1999. (Facsimile impression of original 1908 edition.)

Levene, Richard, and Márquez C., Fernando. "Entrevista." *El Croquis* 48 (June 1991): 5–11.

Ligtelijn, Vincent, and Saariste, Rein. *Josep M. Jujol.* Rotterdam: 010 Publishers, 1996.

Llinàs, Josep. *Josep María Jujol.* Cologne: Benedikt Taschen, 1992.

Llinàs, Josep. *Saques de Esquina.* Girona: Editorial Pre-textos, 2002.

López Cotelo, Víctor, and Puente, Carlos. "Lectura Gótica: Biblioteca en la Casa de las Conchas." *Arquitectura Viva* 33 (November–December 1993) 50–55.

Luz Lamarca, Rodrigo de. *Francisco de Mora y Juan Gómez de Mora: Cuenca, Foco Renacentista.* Cuenca: Diputación de Cuenca, 1997.

Middleton, Robin, and Watkin, David. *Neoclassical and 19th Century Architecture.* Milan and New York: Electa and Rizzoli, 1980.

Moneo, Rafael. "Kursaal Auditorium." *Assemblage* 14, 8–13.

Moneo, Rafael. "Seis Propuestas para San Sebastián." *El Croquis* 43 (June 1990): 7–23.

Montaner, Josep María. *Barcelona: A City and Its Architecture.* Cologne; 1 New York: Taschen, 1997.

Murray, Peter. *Architecture of the Renaissance.* New York: Harry N. Abrams, 1971.

Norberg-Schulz, Christian. *Late Baroque and Rococo Architecture.* Milan; New York: Electa and Rizzoli, 1985.

Norberg-Schulz, Christian. *Meaning in Western Architecture.* New York: Rizzoli, 1980.

Permanyer, Lluís. *Josep Puig i Cadalfach.* Barcelona: Ediciones Polígrafa, 2001.

Piñon, Helia, and Viaplara, Albert. Project Description and Documentation (courtesy of the architects).

Quetglas, Josep. *Imágenes del Pabellón de Alemania.* Montreal: Les Editions Section b, 1991.

Rispa, Raúl-Alonso de los Rios, and César-Aguaza, María José, eds. *Expo '92 Seville: Architecture et Design.* Paris: Gallimard/Electa, 1992.

Rodríguez, Carme, and Torres, Jorge. *Grup R.* Barcelona: Editorial Gustavo Gili, 1994.

Rodríguez Ruiz, Delfín, ed. *Palacios Reales en España: Historia y Arquitectura de la Magnificencia.* Madrid: Fundación Argentaria-Visor Distribuciones, 1996.

Rovira, Josep M. *José Luis Sert: 1901–1983.* Milan: Electa Edizioni, 2000.

Ruiz Cabrero, Gabriel. *Espagne Architecture 1965–1988.* Milan and Paris: Electa-Moniteur, 1990.

Ruiz Cabrero, Gabriel. *The Modern in Spain: Architecture after 1948.* Cambridge, MA; London: MIT Press, 2001.

Russell, Franck. *Art Nouveau Architecture.* London: Academy Editions, 1979.

Sack, Manfred. *Lluís Domènech i Montaner: Palau de la Música Catalana.* Stuttgart: Edition Axel Menges, 1995.

Saliga, Pauline, and Thorne, Martha. *Building a New Spain: Contemporary Spanish Architecture.* Barcelona: Editorial Gustavo Gili, 1992.

Saura Ramos, Pedro A. *The Cave of Altamira.* New York: Harry N. Abrams, 1999.

Schulze, Franz. *Mies van der Rohe: A Critical Biography.* Chicago and London: University of Chicago Press, 1985.

Sear, Frank. *Roman Architecture.* Ithaca, NY: Cornell University Press, 1993.

Solà-Morales, Ignasi de. *Jujol.* New York: Rizzoli, 1991.

Solà-Morales, Ignasi de. *Minimal Architecture in Barcelona: Building on the Built City.* Milan: Electa Edizioni, 1986.

Solà-Morales, Ignasi de, ed. *Contemporary Spanish Architecture: An Eclectic Panorama.* New York: Rizzoli, 1986.

Solà-Morales, Ignasi de, Capitel, Antón, and Buchanan, Peter et al., eds. *Birkhäuser Architectural Guide, Spain 1920–1999.* Basel: Birkhäuser Verlag, 1998.

Sota, Alejandro de la, et al. *Alejandro de la Sota: The Architecture of Imperfection.* London: Architectural Association, 1997.

Stierlin, Henri, and Stierlin, Anne. *Alhambra.* Paris: Imprimerie Nationale, 1991.

Subirana i Torrent, Rosa Maria, ed. *Mies van der Rohe's German Pavilion in Barcelona, 1929–1986*. Barcelona: Public Foundation for the Mies van der Rohe German Pavilion in Barcelona, 1986.

Tafuri, Manfredo, and Dal Co, Francesco. *Contemporary Architecture*. New York: Harry N. Abrams, 1979.

Trigueiros, Luiz, ed. *Alvaro Siza*. Lisboa: Editorial Blau, 1996.

Vázquez Consuegra, Guillermo. *Vázquez Consuergra*. Introduction by Peter Buchanan. Barcelona: Editorial Gustavo Gili, 1992.

Vitruvius. *Ten Books on Architecture*. Translated by Ingrid D. Rowland. Cambridge; New York: Cambridge University Press, 1999.

Ward-Perkins, John B. *Roman Architecture*. New York: Harry N. Abrams, 1977.

Whitehill, Walter Muir. *Spanish Romanesque Architecture of the Eleventh Century*. Oxford: Oxford University Press, 1941.

Wilkinson-Zerner, Catherine. *Juan de Herrera: Architect to Philip II of Spain*. New Haven, CT; London: Yale University Press, 1993.

Yarza, Joaquín. *Arte y Arquitectura en España, 500–1250*. Madrid: Ediciones Cátedra, 2000.

Yeomans, Richard. *The Story of Islamic Architecture*. New York: New York University Press, 2000.

Zerbst, Rainer. *Antoni Gaudí*. Colgne: Taschen, 1992.

Monographic Issues of Journals

"Abalos & Herreros." Special monographic issue, *2G* 22 (Barcelona), 2002.

"Alejandro de la Sota." Special monographic issue, *AV* 68, (Madrid), 1997.

"Alvaro Siza." Special monographic issue, *El Croquis* 68, 69 and 95 (Madrid), 2000.

"Elías Torres & Martínez Lapeña 1988–1993." Special monographic issue, *El Croquis* 61 (Madrid), 1993.

"Enric Miralles & Benedetta Tagliabue: 1996–2000." Special monographic issue, *El Croquis* 100, 101 (Madrid), 2000.

"Enric Mirales-Carme Pinòs." Special monographic issue, *El Croquis* 49, no. 50 (Madrid), 1991.

"España." Special monographic issue, *Zodiac: A Review of Contemporary Architecture* no. 15 (Milan), circa 1969.

"In Progress II." Mongraphic issue, *El Croquis* 106, no. 107 (Madrid), 2001.

"Juan Navarro Baldeweg." Special monographic issue, *El Croquis* 54 (Madrid), 2000.

"Mansilla and Tuñon." Special monographic issue, *2G* 27 (Barcelona), 2003.

"Rafael Moneo." Special feature. *Architecture and Urbanism* 8, no. 89 (Tokyo), 1989.

"Spanish Architecture 1992." Special monographic issue, *El Croquis* 55, 56 (Madrid) 1992.

Index

Pilgrimage churches, 30–32, 214–217, 232–235

Pillars: cruciform, 25, 216, 220; cylindrical, 171; masonry, 239; octagonal, 246–247; square, 34, 99, 235. *See also* Columns

Piñón, Helio (architect), 186–190

Pinòs, Carme (architect), 144–147

Placas, 196

Planes: continuous abstract, 189; dematerialization of, 163, 196; folding and intersecting of, 74; large, inclined concrete, 249

Planetarium and IMAX Theater (Valencia), 46

Plan Maciá, 66

Plateresque architecture, 148; La Casa de las Conchas (Salamanca), 98–101; Universidad Complutense de Alcalá de Henares, 255–258. *See also* Isabelline architecture

Platforms, 75–76; in Kursaal Auditorium and Congress Center (San Sebastián), 95–96; in Madrid Sports Complex, 249–250; in Navigation Pavilion (Sevilla), 143; in Plaza de Tenis (San Sebastián), 184–186; in Valdemingomez Recycling Center (Madrid), 261

Plazas, 60, 64, 87–88; dels Països Catalans (Barcelona), 186–190; del Tenis (San Sebastián), 183–186; Mayor of Madrid, 190–194; Mayor of Salamanca, 194–197; Roman, 70–71

Pola de Lena, Santa Cristina, 229–232

Pórticos, 163, 221, 237; de la Gloria, 35

Postmodern architecture, Walden-7 Apartment Building (Sant Just Desvern), 263–266

Prefabrication, 171

Prehistoric caves, 197–200

Prisms: COAC Headquarters, 57; Kursaal Auditorium and Congress Center (San Sebastián), 95–97; Santa Cristina de Lena, 229–231

Promenades, 48, 63–64, 87, 96, 138; in New Cemetery-Park (Igualada), 145; Plaza del Tenis (San Sebastián) and, 184–186; Ronda (Palma de Majorca), 206–210

Proportion in Islamic architecture, 129, 157

Puente del Diablo. *See* Roman Aqueduct at Segovia

Puente Fernández, Carlos (architect), 101

Puertas: in Ávila City Walls, 10–11; in Cathedral of Santiago de Compostela, 34–35; in La Alhambra, 156

Pugin, Augustus (architect), 168

Puig i Cadalfach, Josep (architect), 15–19, 78, 178

Quibla, 81–83, 129–130

Quiñones, Andrés García de (architect), 105, 196–197

Racetracks, La Zarzuela Grandstand (Madrid), 110–113

Ramblas: in Diagonal Mar Parc (Barcelona), 63–64. *See also* Promenades

"Ramirense" style, 126, 229

Ramiro I, Palace of (Oviedo), 122–127

Rationalism, 65–69, 207

Raymond of Burgundy (architect), 8–11

Rayonnant Gothic architecture, Cathedral of León, 26–29

Recycled materials, 260–262

Recycling Center, Valdemingomez (Madrid), 258–262

Regent, Elias (architect), 237–240

Reich, Lilly, 76

Religious tolerance, 246

Renaissance architecture, 35, 101; Cathedral of Jaén, 22–26; Monastery of El Escorial, 117–122; Palace of Carlos V at Al Hambra (Granada), 148–151

Renaixença, 178

Revival architecture, 16; Palace of Sobrellano (Comillas), 166–169

Ripoll, Santa María, 236–240

Riwaqs, 81, 83

Rodriguez, Ventura (architect), 24

About the Author

ALEJANDRO LAPUNZINA is Director of University of Illinois at Urbana–Champaign Architecture Study Abroad Program in Versailles, France and teaches in the School of Architecture. He has written numerous articles and a book which have been published in Argentina, Brazil, France, Spain, the United Kingdom, and the United States.